Oxford Medical Publi

Oxford Guide to Behavioural
Experiments in Cognitive Therapy

Cognitive behaviour therapy: science and practice series

Edited by

David Clark, *Institute of Psychiatry, London, UK*

Christopher Fairburn, *University of Oxford, UK*

Steven Hollon, *Vanderbilt University, Nashville, USA*

Other titles in the series:

The Treatment of Obsessions

S. Rachman

Oxford Guide to Behavioural Experiments in Cognitive Therapy

Edited by

James Bennett–Levy
Oxford Cognitive Therapy Centre, Warneford Hospital, Oxford, UK

Gillian Butler
Oxford Cognitive Therapy Centre and Department of Clinical Psychology, Warneford Hospital, Oxford, UK

Melanie Fennell
Oxford Cognitive Therapy Centre and University of Oxford Department of Psychiatry, Warneford Hospital, Oxford, UK

Ann Hackmann
Oxford Cognitive Therapy Centre and University of Oxford Department of Psychiatry, Warneford Hospital, Oxford, UK

Martina Mueller
Oxford Cognitive Therapy Centre and Department of Clinical Psychology, Warneford Hospital, Oxford, UK

David Westbrook
Oxford Cognitive Therapy Centre and Department of Clinical Psychology, Warneford Hospital, Oxford, UK

Illustrations by

Khadj Rouf

OXFORD
UNIVERSITY PRESS

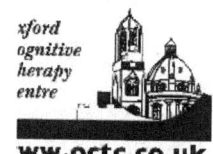

xford
ognitive
herapy
entre

ww.octc.co.uk

OXFORD
UNIVERSITY PRESS

Great Clarendon Street, Oxford, OX2 6DP,
United Kingdom

Oxford University Press is a department of the University of Oxford.
It furthers the University's objective of excellence in research, scholarship,
and education by publishing worldwide. Oxford is a registered trade mark of
Oxford University Press in the UK and in certain other countries

Published in the United States of America by Oxford University Press
198 Madison Avenue, New York, NY 10016, United States of America

British Library Cataloguing in Publication Data

Data available

ISBN 978-0-19-852916-3

Dedication

This book is dedicated to Joan Kirk, founder of the Oxford Cognitive Therapy Centre and previously head of the Oxford NHS adult psychology service, with thanks for the energy, support, wisdom, and warmth without which many of us would have had neither the skills nor the nerve to produce this book.

Acknowledgements

First, and most importantly, we would like to acknowledge those who carried out the experiments and contributed to their design—our patients. This book would not exist without their courage, perseverance, and creativity. Second, we wish to acknowledge colleagues, supervisors, and supervisees, too numerous to name, who have contributed to the thinking of all those involved in this enterprise. Third, we thank our families and friends for their tolerance of the long hours and absences that have inevitably been part of the creation of this book. Fourth, a thank you to those who have generously contributed their stories for *Tales from the Front Line*: David Clark, Helen Close, Ann Gledhill, Lorna Hogg, Claudia Koch, Ali Modaresi, Fiona Kennedy, and Helen Rooney (other *Tales* were contributed by the editors). And lastly, we have been greatly supported by the unfailingly positive and flexible approach of our editor at Oxford University Press, Martin Baum; and the willingness of production editor Kate Smith to adopt late changes with grace and humour.

Foreword

David M. Clark

Oh, do not ask, "What is it?"
Let us go and make our visit

From 'Love Song of J. Alfred Prufrock' (T.S. Eliot 1917)

Cognitive therapy aims to alleviate emotional distress by helping patients to identify and modify distorted patterns of thinking. Beck (1976) likens the enterprise to that of a scientific investigation. Patient and therapist are encouraged to view the patient's beliefs as hypotheses to be evaluated in terms of the extent to which they are consistent with available data about the patient and his or her world. In session, discussions of the evidence for and against a particular belief are common. However, in his first comprehensive treatment manual (Beck *et al.* 1979, p. 56), Beck also pointed out that 'a powerful method with which to investigate the validity of a specific assumption consists of designing an experiment or task to test the assumption empirically'. He went on to discuss how such an experiment could be developed. Patient and therapist first 'specify . . . the assumption they want to test'. A task is then identified that allows an experimental test of the assumption. In particular, the task is set up in such a way that it can be agreed that if the assumption is correct, X will happen, whereas if the assumption is incorrect, some other outcome will occur. Once the experiment has been completed, 'therapist and patient . . . evaluate the results of the experiment . . . consider various interpretations . . . and compare the *actual* results with the patient's *predictions* based on the original assumption'.

Beck's early enthusiasm for experiments was well justified. In the 25 years since the publication of Beck *et al.*'s seminal volume, effective cognitive therapy programmes have been developed for a wide range of disorders (see Hollon and Beck 2003; Nathan and Gorman 2002 for reviews). In most of the programmes 'behavioural experiments' in which patients are encouraged to test their beliefs through action are common. Detailed therapist manuals for many of the disorder-specific programmes are now available. However, currently there is no text that covers multiple disorders and specifically focuses on behavioural experiments. This volume admirably fills the gap.

A number of the empirically validated cognitive therapy programmes that have appeared in the last 25 years, especially those in anxiety disorders and eating disorders, have been developed by researchers working at the Warneford Hospital in Oxford. The distinguished authors of this volume, many of whom contributed to the development of the programmes, are, therefore, particularly well-placed to produce a definitive text. The reader will find here an impressive compendium of commonly used behavioural experiments, along with practical guidance in how to set up the experiments and how to discuss the results with patients. As the authors point out (see Chapters 1 and 2), behavioural experiments are *not* a therapy in themselves. Instead, they are tools to be used in the context of a comprehensive cognitive therapy programme. Such a programme would involve a close working relationship between patient and therapist in which collaborative empiricism and guided discovery are key principles. As Beck *et al.* (1979) clearly stated, a behavioural experiment can only be developed after patient and therapist have identified a particular assumption/belief/process to be investigated. In addition, the experiment is only likely to produce substantial cognitive change if the outcomes that would support different hypotheses are clearly operationalized, the results of the experiment are carefully reviewed, and the extent to which the results proved persuasive, or not, is openly discussed. Patients' doubts about the persuasiveness of particular experiments should be elicited, listened to, and used to develop more fine tuned, and hopefully more persuasive, experiments.

A personal account

Behavioural experiments have played a major role in the cognitive therapy programmes that my colleagues* and I have developed for different anxiety disorders. The Editors of this volume kindly, but perhaps too generously, thought a brief historical account of some of the highlights of the programmes in terms of behavioural experiments might be of general interest.

Whilst a trainee clinical psychologist in the late 1970s, I came across a mimeographed copy of the manual that would eventually become Beck *et al.*'s (1979) classic text. I had my first chance to develop a behavioural experiment when presented with a phobic patient who seemed to obtain very little benefit from a carefully planned exposure therapy programme. Whilst observing the patient's remarkable failure to show habituation during long periods of exposure, I noticed that she had episodes of markedly increased anxiety (panic attacks) during which she breathed quickly and deeply. A medical colleague indicated that the distinctive pattern of breathing constituted hyperventilation and expressed the view that this would generate anxiety by reducing the body's CO_2 level and instigating other biochemical changes. Keen to experience the process for myself, I vigorously hyperventilated and was surprised to discover that although I experi-

*Members of the research group who have been particularly influential in developing behavioural experiments include: Anke Ehlers, Melanie Fennell, Freda McManus, Ann Hackmann, Paul Salkovskis, and Adrian Wells.

enced many body sensations, I did not feel particularly anxious. This observation led to an early, and restricted, version of what was later to be termed the cognitive theory of panic disorder (Clark 1986). In particular, I hypothesized that the patient's anxiety attacks might be caused by interpreting the sensations induced by hyperventilation in a catastrophic fashion. This led to using induced hyperventilation as a way of demonstrating to patients that panic attacks have an innocuous cause. At the time, we often followed the induced hyperventilation behavioural experiment with some simple training in slow, shallow breathing.

Although many panic patients benefited from this combined approach, we noticed that some patients continued to be highly fearful of anxiety-related sensations and seemed driven to control the sensations. This observation, and some perceptive questioning by Martin Seligman (see Seligman 1988), led Paul Salkovskis to hypothesize that controlled breathing was acting as a safety-seeking behaviour that prevented cognitive change in some patients. Salkovskis' (1988, 1991) perceptive analysis proved remarkably fruitful as it transpired that most panic disorder patients engaged in a wide range of in-situation safety behaviours. An effective behavioural experiment followed from the analysis. Patients were encouraged to induce feared sensations and then drop their attempts to control the symptoms as a highly effective way of learning that the sensations were harmless.

A key feature of the cognitive therapy for panic programme (see Clark 1996 for a description) was that it was not simply a set of techniques for discounting specific negative thoughts. Instead, patients were invited to compare two different ways of explaining their problem: on the one hand, the idea that the symptoms they experience are highly dangerous and a sign of a serious physical or mental problem (such as an impending heart attack or insanity); on the other hand, the idea that the problem is their erroneous belief that the symptoms are dangerous and the vicious circle of thoughts, feelings, and sensations that result from this belief.

Developing evidence for an alternative model or way of understanding a problem became even more important when we shifted our attention to hypochondriasis. Like panic disorder, hypochondriasis is characterized by misinterpretation of symptoms. However, the time course of the feared outcomes is typically longer. For example, a panic patient might interpret cardiac symptoms as a sign of a heart attack and imminent death, whereas a patient with hypochondriasis is more likely to interpret the symptoms as a sign of cardiovascular disease that will lead to physical handicap or death in months or years. Clearly, it is impossible to disconfirm the idea that someone may die in months or years in a treatment lasting weeks. In such a case, demonstrating the validity of the alternative, non-disease model is the key aim and the target of most behavioural experiments. For example, a patient who is concerned that he is developing throat cancer may frequently check that his throat is functioning properly by intentionally swallowing. Such checking would produce discomfort and subjective difficulty in swallowing that would be seen by the patient as evidence of throat cancer. Belief in the alternative model, that the problem is his illness belief and the checking that follows from it, could be substantially strengthened by a behavioural experiment in which the patient intentionally swallows several times and observes the effects.

Social phobia has proved a particularly fertile ground for behavioural experiments. Clark and Wells (1995) proposed that the persistence of the disorder could be understood in terms of a faulty processing style in which attention is turned inwards and internal information (anxious feelings, negative images of oneself, and certain types of felt sense) is used to draw excessively negative inferences about how one appears to others. In addition, some safety behaviours contaminate the social interaction by having adverse effects on other people. Each of these points can be elegantly demonstrated by experiments in which focus of attention, safety behaviours, and/or self-imagery are manipulated. With respect to self-imagery, video feedback has proved a particularly powerful way of helping patients see that their view of how they appear to others is excessively negative.

In post-traumatic stress disorder (PTSD), behavioural experiments have proved similarly flexible and powerful. Faulty beliefs such as 'If I allow myself to become anxious when I think about the trauma, I will be unable to cope/will go mad' can be systematically tested. The problematic effects of safety behaviours (for example, attempts to suppress intrusions may increase the frequency of the intrusions) can be convincingly demonstrated. In addition, the potent mixture of inquisitiveness, hypothesis construction, and hypothesis testing that lies at the heart of behavioural experimentation can be used to understand and eventually eliminate highly puzzling symptoms. For example, it is common for patients with PTSD to report moments when they suddenly feel anxious for no apparent reason. Ehlers and Clark (2000) suggest that such episodes often represent activation of a fragment of the trauma memory (the terror) without source identification. Physical stimuli that resemble stimuli that were present at the time of the trauma often seem to trigger such activations. For example, the terror that was experienced in a road traffic accident at night might be triggered by a patch of sunlight on a lawn which resembles a headlight. Once this possible explanation has been advanced, the first experiment involves asking patients to look out for such stimuli in future episodes. If they are identified, the next experiment involves breaking the link between the stimuli and the trauma memory by intentionally using the stimuli to elicit the trauma memory and then focusing on the difference between the trauma and now (for example, 'I thought I would die, but I didn't. The event is in the past and I'm completely safe'). In this way the trauma memory is contextualized and re-experiencing is inhibited (see Ehlers and Clark 2000 for further details).

An invitation

Enough of 'What is it?'. You are now invited to turn the page to the rest of the book where the authors have skilfully laid out the world of behavioural experiments. In the immortal words of T.S. Eliot, 'Let us go and make our visit'.

Preface

This is a book written by clinicians for clinicians. It is intended as a practical, easy-to-read guide, which is relevant for practising clinicians at every level from trainee to cognitive therapy supervisor. Its purpose is to provide a source of ideas which will stimulate the creativity of clinicians wishing to design behavioural experiments tailored to the individual cognitions of their patients.

We have written this book because it is a book that all the contributors wanted on their bookshelves. Despite the fact that behavioural experiments are amongst the most central, and the most powerful, interventions in cognitive therapy, there is a dearth of relevant literature which provides a practical, how-to-do-it focus for their design and implementation. Trainees often ask supervisors for ideas about designing and implementing behavioural experiments for particular patients. Experienced clinicians also may need access to practical ideas when working with their own patients or supervising trainees. In this volume, we have gathered over 200 examples of behavioural experiments across a range of different problems, to fill these gaps.

The fact that this book has emerged from Oxford is no accident, and may be attributed to several factors. In the early 1970s, a Psychological Treatment Research Unit was established in Oxford. This produced a stream of clinically relevant research that refined and tested the principles of behavioural practice. As the cognitive revolution gathered momentum, cognitive methods were gradually intertwined with behavioural ones, until the cognitive perspective assumed predominance. Throughout the remainder of the century, numerous clinicians working in Oxford participated in research projects, applied their ideas to increasingly complex problems, and made their findings widely accessible. Two threads running through more than a quarter of a century of research—rigorous thinking, and its subsequent application in the clinic—have directly influenced their thinking and their work.

During much of this time, two of the British researchers most responsible for the theoretical and practical development of behavioural experiments, David Clark and Paul Salkovskis, were based in Oxford. Salkovskis' concept of safety-seeking behaviours has been particularly important in the development of behavioural experiments. Both Clark and Salkovskis have been highly influential in the development of effective cognitive behavioural treatments for the anxiety disorders and, together with their teams (including some of the present authors), have strongly emphasized the value of behavioural experiments. Clark's 'Foreword' to this book outlines these developments.

Oxford cognitive therapists have also had a particular interest in disseminating cognitive therapy widely, to patients and health professionals. Joan Kirk, one of the present authors, played an important role as head of the local National Health Service adult psychology department, building it up from three people to a far larger department with particular expertise in cognitive therapy. Members of that department have written booklets for patients and therapists and books that have made cognitive therapy methods accessible to the general public; many of them have also contributed to this book.

The diploma training course, 'Cognitive Therapy in Oxford', has been another major influence. This was one of the first specialist cognitive therapy courses in the UK and many of the present authors are teachers and supervisors on the course and/or have been participants. More recently, the Oxford Cognitive Therapy Centre has provided introductory and more specialist courses in cognitive therapy, as well as access to expert supervision, consultation, and therapy.

Hence, we have been able to gather in Oxford a critical mass of people with particular expertise in cognitive therapy, whose orientation places particular emphasis on testing out cognitions in the real world (i.e. behavioural experiments). This has been an important element in the development of this book.

The *Oxford Guide* has been very much a group project. When we started the book, we found that there was still a surprising amount of conceptual development which needed to be done. This has involved a creative oscillation between the first two chapters and the chapters on specific problems; and between the editors and the authors. In this sense, the *Oxford Guide* perhaps extends beyond a 'normal' edited book: the authors are more than simply chapter authors, and the editors more than simply editors.

We anticipate further conceptual and practical developments. The *Oxford Guide to Behavioural Experiments in Cognitive Therapy* represents a step along this path. Christine Padesky's chapter points the way to future directions. One of our predictions is that there will be more chapters in future editions on transdiagnostic issues (e.g. perfectionism, procrastination) and in the area of health psychology.

Finally, it is our hope that the reader will gain as much from reading the book as we have in writing and editing it. For all of us, it has been a fascinating journey. It has significantly affected the way we think about the process of therapy and the clinical work that we do with patients. We hope that it will inspire novel, creative work on the part of cognitive therapy practitioners, as well as further research which investigates the particularly powerful influence of behavioural experiments in achieving therapeutic change.

The Editors
September 2003

Contents

Contributors

James Bennett–Levy
Oxford Cognitive Therapy Centre,
Warneford Hospital, Oxford, UK

Nicky Boughton
Oxford Adult Eating Disorders
Service, Warneford Hospital,
Oxford, UK

Gillian Butler
Oxford Cognitive Therapy Centre and
Department of Clinical Psychology,
Warneford Hospital, Oxford, UK

Helen Close
Department of Clinical Psychology,
Warneford Hospital, Oxford, UK

Myra Cooper
Doctoral Course in Clinical
Psychology, University of Oxford,
Warneford Hospital, Oxford, UK

Carolyn Cowey
Department of Clinical Psychology,
Warneford Hospital, Oxford, UK

Alison Croft
Department of Clinical Psychology,
Warneford Hospital, Oxford, UK

June Dent
Department of Clinical Psychology,
Warneford Hospital, Oxford, UK

Melanie Fennell
Oxford Cognitive Therapy Centre
and University of Oxford Department
of Psychiatry, Warneford Hospital,
Oxford, UK

Paul Flecknoe
Clinical Psychology Services,
St Mary's Hospital, Kettering, UK

Ann Hackmann
Oxford Cognitive Therapy Centre
and University of Oxford Department
of Psychiatry, Warneford Hospital,
Oxford, UK

Allison Harvey
Department of Experimental
Psychology, University of
Oxford, UK

Helen Jenkins
Department of Clinical Psychology,
Warneford Hospital, Oxford, UK

Helen Kennerley
Oxford Cognitive Therapy Centre,
Warneford Hospital, Oxford, UK

Nigel King
Doctoral Course in Clinical
Psychology, University of Oxford,
Warneford Hospital, Oxford, UK

Joan Kirk
Oxford Cognitive Therapy Centre,
Warneford Hospital, Oxford, UK

Joanna McGrath
Oxford Centre for Enablement,
Oxford, UK

Norma Morrison
Oxford Cognitive Therapy Centre,
Warneford Hospital, Oxford, UK

Martina Mueller
Oxford Cognitive Therapy Centre and
Department of Clinical Psychology,
Warneford Hospital, Oxford, UK

Christine Padesky
Center for Cognitive Therapy,
Huntington Beach CA, USA

Melissa Ree
Department of Psychiatry,
Warneford Hospital, Oxford, UK

Khadj Rouf
Department of Clinical Psychology,
Warneford Hospital, Oxford, UK

Joanne Ryder
Department of Clinical Psychology,
Warneford Hospital, Oxford, UK

Diana Sanders
Oxford Cognitive Therapy Centre,
Warneford Hospital, Oxford, UK

Stefan Schuller
Doctoral Course in Clinical
Psychology, University of Oxford,
Warneford Hospital, Oxford, UK

Amy Silver
Doctoral Course in Clinical
Psychology, University of Oxford,
Warneford Hospital, Oxford, UK

Christina Surawy
Department of Psychological
Medicine, John Radcliffe Hospital,
Oxford, UK

David Westbrook
Oxford Cognitive Therapy Centre and
Department of Clinical Psychology,
Warneford Hospital, Oxford, UK

Linette Whitehead
Oxford Adult Eating Disorders Service,
Warneford Hospital, Oxford, UK

How to use this book

The *Oxford Guide* is designed for readers who are learning cognitive therapy and for those who have pre-existing skills. It assumes a basic knowledge of cognitive therapy and a capacity to undertake assessment, cognitive formulation, and basic therapeutic procedures.

A careful cognitive formulation is a prerequisite for designing and implementing effective behavioural experiments. The cognitions to be tested and, importantly, the context in which they are tested, will vary from case to case. Hence, experiments need to be individually designed and tailored to the particular requirements of the patient. The *Oxford Guide* provides plenty of examples of possible behavioural experiments, including some which are prototypical for particular problems. They are a stimulus for readers' own creativity to adapt the experiments to the needs of their patients.

There is a sense in which the *Oxford Guide* has been designed as a 'cookbook'—but *not* one with recipes to be slavishly followed irrespective of the context; rather, its purpose is to help readers understand the principles involved, so that an endless variety of new 'dishes' can be created.

Chapters 1 and 2 provide an introduction to behavioural experiments and a context for the remainder of the book. Chapter 1 discusses the conceptual basis for behavioural experiments: their role in cognitive therapy, their historical derivation, their clinical value, and theoretical explanations, which may account for their apparent impact. Chapter 2 provides a comprehensive practical guide to the design and implementation of behavioural experiments; it should be read prior to the remaining chapters to provide full understanding.

The remaining chapters of the book focus on particular problem areas. These include problems which have been the traditional focus of cognitive therapy (e.g. depression and anxiety disorders), as well as those which have only more recently become a subject of study (bipolar disorder, psychotic symptoms), and some which are still in their relative infancy (physical health problems, brain injury). Also included are several chapters on transdiagnostic problems (avoidance of affect, low self-esteem, interpersonal issues, self-injurious behaviour). All these can be read as stand-alone chapters, but since problems are often interlinked, and useful behavioural experiments may be found in other chapters, a section at the end of each chapter directs the reader to other relevant chapters.

To assist the reader, each chapter has the same basic structure:

1 A basic description of the problem

2 The application of the cognitive model(s) to the particular problem

3 Key cognitions or cognitive constructs

4 Behavioural experiments to test the key cognitions

5 Distinctive difficulties in carrying out behavioural experiments with this population

6 Other relevant chapters

7 Further reading

Readers should note that the book is not intended to provide a comprehensive account of the cognitive models for each disorder; the references and further reading lists at the end of each chapter are for this purpose.

The behavioural experiments themselves are also presented in a standardized format for ease of understanding. Chapter 2 provides an explanation for the categories used. Experiments are set up to test a target cognition or an alternative perspective; a prediction is made, the experiment is carried out, the results are noted, and through a process of reflection, implications for the target belief are evaluated.

Even the best laid plans cannot cover every possibility. Unpredictable events intrude, and experiments do not always turn out the way those who devise them might imagine. Sometimes fortune shines, and there are unexpectedly serendipitous outcomes—and sometimes apparent disaster strikes. Flexibility and a wry sense of humour may be called for. Reflecting these facts, we have gathered together a collection of true—sometimes bizarre—stories of behavioural experiments, and inserted them between chapters under the collective title of *Tales from the Front Line.* These tales are not intended to be taken entirely seriously, and do not always provide a particular therapeutic moral. The message, if any, is simply to be prepared to think on your feet—and if you and the patient can enjoy the humorous aspects of therapy, so much the better!

A note on terminology: we have used the terms 'patients' or 'people' rather than 'clients' throughout the book, and have used the latest version of DSM (DSM-IV-TR, APA 2000) to provide a basic description of many of the problems. There was considerable variation amongst the authors in degree of allegiance to these terms/concepts. The editors decided that, on balance, it was better to retain a standard nomenclature (patients) and to use DSM-IV-TR to provide a descriptive base. However, the shortcomings of both are acknowledged.

When we have referred to patients or therapists in the singular, our rule of thumb has been to alternate between 'he' and 'she'. Although the behavioural experiment examples are based on real cases, identifying features, often including gender, have been changed to minimize any chance of recognition.

Some readers may come to the *Oxford Guide* with little or no knowledge of cognitive therapy. If this is the case, we advise that they study one or more of the basic texts below and/or to attend some introductory workshops in cognitive therapy, prior to starting this book.

Further reading

American Psychiatric Association (2000). *Diagnostic and statistical manual of mental disorders: text revision (DSM-IV-TR)*. American Psychiatric Association, Washington DC.

Beck, J. (1995). *Cognitive therapy: basics and beyond*. Guilford Press, New York.

Beck, A.T., Emery, G. and Greenberg, R.L. (1985). *Anxiety disorders and phobias: a cognitive perspective*. Basic Books, New York.

Beck, A.T., Rush, A.J., Shaw, B.F. and Emery, G. (1979). *Cognitive therapy of depression*. Guilford Press, New York.

Clark, D.M. and Fairburn, C.G. (ed.) (1997). *The science and practice of cognitive behaviour therapy*. Oxford University Press, Oxford.

Greenberger, D. and Padesky, C. (1995). *Mind over mood*. Guilford Press, New York.

Hawton, K., Salkovskis, P., Kirk, J. and Clark, D.M. (1989). *Cognitive behaviour therapy for psychiatric problems*. Oxford University Press, Oxford.

Leahy, R.L. (2003). *Cognitive therapy techniques: a practitioner's guide*. Guilford Press, New York.

Leahy, R.L. and Holland, S.J. (2000). *Treatment plans and interventions for depression and anxiety disorders*. Guilford Press, New York.

Simos, G. (2002). *Cognitive behaviour therapy: a guide for the practising clinician*. Brunner–Routledge, Hove.

Wells, A. (1997). *Cognitive therapy of anxiety disorders: a practical manual and conceptual guide*. Wiley, New York.

Wills, F. and Saunders, D. (1997). *Cognitive therapy: transforming the image*. Sage, London.

CHAPTER 1

Behavioural experiments: historical and conceptual underpinnings

James Bennett–Levy
David Westbrook
Melanie Fennell
Myra Cooper
Khadj Rouf
Ann Hackmann

Behavioural experiments (BEs) are amongst the most powerful methods for bringing about change in cognitive therapy. They are a key component of treatment. They are widely used, and yet, to be successful, they require creativity and sophisticated understanding on the part of the therapist. It is therefore surprising that there is remarkably little written about BEs: about their place in cognitive therapy, their value, or about the practicalities of designing and carrying out BEs. It is this gap that the present book seeks to fill.

The purpose of this first chapter is to provide some underpinnings for conceptualizing the place and role of BEs in cognitive therapy. It is divided into two parts. The first part provides a review of cognitive therapy. It describes the development of the therapy; its standing as a treatment for psychological disorders; its historical roots in behaviour therapy; and its core ideas. The second part focuses on the BE as a key intervention within cognitive therapy. It provides a definition; looks at the historical roots of BEs in the scientific method and in behaviour therapy; examines evidence supporting their effectiveness; and reviews theories which provide some understanding of their impact.

Our aim is to provide a historical and conceptual understanding of the value of BEs, while acknowledging that, in the current state of knowledge, there are large gaps to be filled.

Part 1: an overview of cognitive therapy

Introduction

Cognitive therapy has grown, from the publication of Beck's early work (Beck 1963, 1964, 1967, 1976), to become one of the foremost psychotherapies in the western world (Hollon and Beck 2003). Cognitive models have been developed for a wide range of disorders, and outcome research has repeatedly demonstrated their effectiveness (DeRubeis and Crits–Christoph 1998; Hollon and Beck 2003).

Although it is now commonplace to talk about 'cognitive therapy', in reality there are not one, but many, cognitive therapies (Dobson *et al.* 2000). Leading theorists in the early days of the cognitive therapies included Ellis (1962), Mahoney (1974), Beck (1976), and Meichenbaum (1977). However, the most widely used and validated methods are based on those originally developed by Beck, and in this book, the term 'cognitive therapy' refers to this 'Beckian' version.

Cognitive therapy's emphasis on empirical research, its theoretical base, and its coherence as a therapeutic intervention have meant that, at this stage, it is better validated as an effective treatment for a range of disorders than any other psychological therapy (DeRubeis and Crits–Christoph 1998; Hollon and Beck 2003). For some disorders featured in this book (e.g. panic disorder, social phobia), it is very clearly the treatment of choice. For other disorders (e.g. depression), it appears to be at least as effective as any other treatment (Hollon *et al.* 2002), and has an enduring effect in preventing relapse (Fava *et al.* 1998; Hollon *et al.* 2002). For a number of other disorders in this book, cognitive models have only been developed in the last few years (e.g. bipolar disorder, post-traumatic stress disorder, psychosis), or are still being developed (e.g. brain injury). However, results from some initial outcome trials (e.g. bipolar disorder, post-traumatic stress disorder) appear promising (Gillespie *et al.* 2002; Lam *et al.* 2000). A recent development, reflected to some extent in the present volume, is that clinicians and researchers are now starting to apply cognitive theory transdiagnostically (Fennell 1997; Harvey *et al.* 2004).

A full overview of the theory and therapeutic interventions of cognitive therapy is beyond the scope of this chapter (see Beck *et al.* 1979; Beck 1995; Dobson *et al.* 2000; Hawton *et al.* 1989). However, key elements which provide the necessary context for understanding the role of BEs are described below. First, to provide a background for both the development of cognitive therapy and the role of BEs, cognitive therapy's roots in behaviour therapy are briefly described.

The development of cognitive therapy:
its behavioural heritage

In the first half of the twentieth century, psychoanalysis and its offshoots dominated the field of therapy. However, in the 1950s researchers started to question the theoretical basis and efficacy of psychoanalysis (Eysenck 1952), while at the same time learning theory, and the behavioural approach derived from it, started to influence psychological treatment, practice, and research.

The behavioural approach was based on certain key principles, which fundamentally challenged the prevailing psychoanalytic orthodoxy. For instance, it was asserted that:

◆ 'Mind' was not a legitimate object for enquiry

◆ The problem was the patient's behaviour, rather than invisible (and untestable) processes such as the unconscious

◆ The focus of assessment and therapy should be on what could be observed, operationalized, and measured

◆ In changing behaviour, what was important were the current factors maintaining problems, rather than their assumed origin

◆ Scientific method provided a legitimate framework for developing relevant theory and clinical practice; understanding and application would advance most fruitfully through systematic empirical research

Outcome studies of behaviour therapy in the 1960s and 1970s showed considerable promise, particularly in the treatment of phobias and obsessive-compulsive disorders. However, it also became increasingly apparent that behaviour therapy too was limited, both by its theoretical framework and in the range of problems for which it was effective (Rachman 1997). When Beck (1970, p. 184) declared that 'although self-reports of private experiences are not verifiable by other observers, these introspective data provide a wealth of testable hypotheses', he was articulating the concerns of an increasing number of clinicians frustrated by behaviourists' disregard for a valuable source of data and understanding—cognition.

Although cognitive therapy extended beyond behaviour therapy, and drew on influences from other sources such as psychoanalysis, phenomenology, personal construct theory, and rational emotive therapy (Beck et al. 1979), Beck nevertheless recognized the value of behaviour therapy's emphasis on scientific method, empirical research, and verifiable evidence. He also continued to assert the importance of current maintaining factors, rather than past assumed causes. He retained a number of treatment elements (e.g. session structure, goal setting, short-term treatment, graded task assignment); and perhaps most importantly in the present context, he recognized that behaviour change is a particularly powerful means of achieving cognitive and affective change.

The cognitive model

The theoretical advance made by Beck, and other cognitive theorists, was to assert the centrality of cognition in the psychosocial and emotional functioning of human beings. Thus, the way in which individuals structure their experiences cognitively is held to be a prime influence on their affect, behaviour, and physical reactions. Cognitive theory suggests that psychological disorders do not arise from events *per se* (e.g. a traumatic incident or the loss of a job or relationship). Problems arise from the *meanings* individuals give to events, filtered through the framework of core beliefs and assumptions which they have already developed through life experience. This explains why, for one person, a promotion at work is a cause for celebration and excitement, while, for another person, it represents the potential for failure and may lead to anxiety. Hence, therapists are particularly interested in patients' appraisals of situations, which can be accessed through their thoughts, images, and memories, and may become a prime target for therapeutic change.

Within cognitive theory, cognition is held to exert its influence on emotion, behaviour, and physical reactions in at least two ways: first, through the *content* of cognition and second, through the *process* of cognition. The *content* of cognition affects emotion, behaviour, and physiology through our appraisals of ourselves, others, and the world, and our interpretations of events; for instance, if we think of ourselves as failing, we may feel depressed, and cease to take initiatives. The *process* of cognition influences our experience of the world through the degree of flexibility we have in switching between different *modes* of processing; for instance, the extent to which we are able to shift our attention away from a focus on threat or loss, or the extent to which we get stuck in ruminative styles of thought, or thinking in an all-or-nothing manner (Beck *et al.* 1979; Nolen–Hoeksema 1991).

Beck developed his first cognitive model in the context of depression. *Cognitive therapy of depression* (Beck *et al.* 1979) is a landmark treatment manual which remains as valuable a grounding today for any aspiring cognitive therapist as when it was first written. In the 1980s, cognitive models were developed for some anxiety disorders (Beck *et al.* 1985; Clark 1986; Hawton *et al.* 1989; Salkovskis 1985), and were elaborated and extended over the next decade

(Clark 1999). Since 1990, the range of disorders for which cognitive models have been developed has mushroomed. They include bipolar disorder (Basco 2000), psychosis (Fowler *et al.* 1995), post-traumatic stress disorder (Ehlers and Clark 2000), eating disorders (Cooper 2003; Fairburn *et al.* 1999), and personality disorders (Beck *et al.* 1990; Layden *et al.* 1993; Linehan 1993). The diversity of chapters in the present volume reflects this expansion of cognitive therapy.

Cognitive models typically specify the kinds of cognition implicated in the maintenance of disorders. For instance, catastrophic misinterpretation of physical symptoms (e.g. 'I'll have a heart attack') is central to panic disorder, while an exaggerated sense of personal responsibility (Salkovskis 1999) and catastrophic misinterpretation of intrusive thoughts (Rachman 2003) are held to be central to obsessive-compulsive disorder (e.g. 'If I don't stop thinking this thought, my husband will have a car crash'). The identification of key cognitions for each disorder is a core element of the chapters in this book. They provide the basis for BEs which test the validity of these beliefs.

Cognitive theory recognizes different types of cognition. Automatic thoughts represent the most immediately accessible level. These are the kinds of thoughts that typically run through people's minds automatically and involuntarily. When people are suffering from psychological disorders, automatic thoughts are predominantly negative (e.g. 'What an idiot!', 'I'm useless', 'You can't trust anyone', 'I'll faint!')

At the next level, underlying assumptions are operating principles or rules which generalize across situations ('If I take a challenge of any sort, I'll be bound to fail'), and which may affect both the conclusions individuals derive from situations ('That was lucky, they didn't find me out') and the way in which they behave ('Duck out of challenges if possible').

Underlying assumptions may be fuelled by core beliefs, which take the form of enduring, global beliefs about self, others, and the world. They may be functional (e.g. 'I can usually manage difficulties', 'People generally mean well even if sometimes they get it wrong', 'Most problems have solutions') or dysfunctional (e.g. 'I'm incompetent', 'Others can handle things, I can't', 'The world is an unsafe place'). Underlying assumptions and core beliefs form part of the *schema* system. Schemas are 'deeper' enduring cognitive structures (e.g. 'perfectionist' schema, 'world-as-dangerous-place' schema), with emotional, physiological, sensory, and behavioural components, which characteristically bias the kind of information individuals attend to, store, and retrieve from memory (e.g. focus on past successes, selectively attend only to mistakes, or recall a catalogue of assaults and robberies).

For present purposes, it should be noted that dysfunctional schemas are held to increase vulnerability to emotional disorder, and contribute to its maintenance. Dysfunctional schemas are often the product of troubled developmental histories, though this is not always the case (e.g. they may result from traumatic episodes in adulthood—see Chapter 9).

Another class of belief, whose importance in cognitive therapy has recently been highlighted, is metacognitive belief (Wells 2000). Metacognitive beliefs are beliefs and theories that individuals hold about their own cognitions (e.g. the belief that worrying is uncontrollable and potentially harmful). Wells (2000) has identified different components of the metacognitive system (e.g. metacognitive knowledge, experiences, plans, procedures) which he suggests are implicated in the maintenance of anxiety disorders (see the later section 'Theoretical perspectives on the value of behavioural experiments' in this chapter and Wells (2000) for further details).

In the present volume, in the context of behavioural experiments, the terms 'thought', 'assumption', 'belief', and 'cognition' have been used, rather than schema, since the purpose of BEs is to test *specific* beliefs and ideas. The concept of schema is so generalized that it may not provide the necessary specificity for most BEs.

Cognitive therapy

Cognitive therapy is an active, directive, time-limited, structured therapy, based on the theoretical principles outlined above. Central to the practice of cognitive therapy is the case formulation, which links theory and implementation, and provides the springboard for therapy. A formulation reflects the therapist's hypothesis about the psychological mechanisms underlying the patient's difficulties (Butler 1998; Persons 1993). It specifies the negative automatic thoughts, assumptions, and core beliefs for a given individual, and suggests hypotheses about the processes maintaining them. The formulation provides the rationale and framework for the selection of techniques for intervention; is shared and developed as part of the developing collaborative relationship between therapist and patient; and may assist patients in understanding and normalizing their problems.

The overall strategy in cognitive therapy is:

1 to assist the patient to identify and reality-test unhelpful cognitions which underlie repeated negative patterns of emotion and behaviour; and

2 to develop and test new, more adaptive cognitions that can give rise to a more positive experience of the self, others, and the world.

Cognitive therapists may focus on disrupting the vicious circles of cognition, behaviour, emotions, and physical reactions maintaining the problem, and on reducing vulnerability to the problem's recurrence. For instance, a frequently observed vicious circle in depression starts from the belief that 'Nothing I do will help', leading to social withdrawal and behavioural inactivity, which lowers mood further. The initial focus of therapy is often on increasing the level of activity and testing negative thoughts; later, relapse prevention strategies may focus on reducing vulnerability to future episodes.

As in other forms of therapy, the quality of the therapeutic relationship is central to effectiveness in cognitive therapy (Beck *et al.* 1979; Keijsers *et al.* 2000). From the outset, Beck recognized that warmth, empathy, genuineness, building trust and rapport, and a collaborative relationship were the foundations of effective therapy (Beck *et al.* 1979). The therapeutic relationship is particularly important when working with patients with complex interpersonal issues (Beck *et al.* 1990; Layden *et al.* 1993; Safran and Muran 2000). Sometimes, the therapist and patient may decide to use a therapy session as a 'schema laboratory', and set up BEs to enable the patient's interpersonal schemas (e.g. 'If I say anything critical, I'll be rejected') to be tested within the relative safety of the therapeutic relationship (see Chapter 19).

A variety of therapeutic strategies are used in cognitive therapy—some verbal, some imaginal, some interactive, some behavioural and experiential (see Beck 1995; Hawton *et al.* 1989; Safran and Muran 2000; Wells 1997 for a range of strategies). Guided discovery, a means of helping patients uncover important information which may lie outside of their current awareness, is central to all approaches (Beck *et al.* 1979; Padesky 1993*a*). Some therapeutic strategies have been specifically developed within the context of cognitive therapy, together with a variety of tools and record forms designed to help patients use these methods in their daily lives (e.g. automatic thought records to identify and test negative automatic thoughts, weekly activity schedules to monitor and plan activity, positive data logs to collect evidence which supports the development of new core beliefs; see Greenberger and Padesky 1995). Other methods (e.g. graded assignments, psychodrama techniques, mindfulness) have been borrowed and adapted from other traditions (e.g. behaviour therapy, gestalt therapy, Buddhist meditation)—see, for example, Edwards (1989) and Segal *et al.* (2002).

Amongst the interventions that have been borrowed and then adapted, perhaps the most widely used, and one of the most powerful, is one adapted from behaviour therapy—the behavioural experiment. It is to this that we now turn.

Part II: the behavioural experiment in cognitive therapy

Introduction

According to the *Oxford English Dictionary*, an experiment is: '(1) The action of trying anything, or putting it to proof: a test, trial. (2) A tentative procedure: a method, system of things or course of action adopted in uncertainty whether it will answer the purpose. (3) An action or operation undertaken in order to discover something unknown, to test a hypothesis, or establish or illustrate some known truth.' In a similar vein, experiments in cognitive therapy seek to test hypotheses, try things out, and discover new things, without any guarantee of success.

To our knowledge, there is no generally agreed technical definition of BEs in the literature. In this book, we have operationalized BEs as follows:

Operational definition of behavioural experiments

Behavioural experiments are planned experiential activities, based on experimentation or observation, which are undertaken by patients in or between cognitive therapy sessions. Their design is derived directly from a cognitive formulation of the problem, and their primary purpose is to obtain new information which may help to:

- test the validity of the patients' existing beliefs about themselves, others, and the world
- construct and/or test new, more adaptive beliefs
- contribute to the development and verification of the cognitive formulation

It is easy to lose sight of just how radical a concept the BE is in the context of the history of psychotherapy. First, Beck's formulation of cognitions as hypotheses to be tested—and testing them via BEs—provided a new way for therapists and patients to think about cognition. It enabled the notion of experimentation, derived from scientific principles, to be applied to the patient's experience of the therapeutic process. Second, the BE's focus on behaviour followed behaviour therapy's lead—albeit with a new focus on cognition—in recognizing that *doing things differently* is a powerful means to change both cognition and affect. Again, this represented a significant break from most previous forms of psychotherapy, which mainly or exclusively used in-session dialogue as the method of change.

In the next sections, we examine how the idea of BEs in cognitive therapy has been informed by their relationship to scientific experimentation, and by the focus on behaviour in behaviour therapy.

Behavioural experiments: the scientific context

There is a clear parallel between the role of BEs in cognitive therapy and the role of experiments more generally in testing scientific theories. As in physics or chemistry, experiments in cognitive therapy are designed to help us to build and test a theory by obtaining empirical evidence. In cognitive therapy, the 'theory' to be tested is the patient's belief, rather than a general scientific law, but the philosophical approach is similar.

The acid test of a scientific theory is whether it can predict what happens in the real world, and many BEs follow this logic. The basic procedure for an experiment in science is to derive one or more predictions which follow from the theory to be tested: something along the lines of 'If this theory is true, then in defined circumstances we should find that X happens'. We then look at what actually happens. If the theory's predicted outcome does indeed occur, then we regard that theory as somewhat more likely to be true, and alternative theories as somewhat less likely (the degree of confirmation depending on the rigour and relevance of the experiment). Many BEs adopt a similar approach. Just as in scientific experiments, the impact of the BE may depend on how well we are able to control contaminating variables, which may muddy the waters and make interpretation of the results ambiguous.

Also, as in the wider world of science, there are two broad approaches to gathering the required information. The first approach—and the one which some would consider the only true form of experiment—involves a deliberate manipulation of some aspect of the world: some method of intentionally changing things to produce a particular event or situation. A classic example in physics is Galileo's famous experiment of simultaneously dropping a wooden ball and a cannon ball from the leaning Tower of Pisa to test the hypothesis that an object's weight should affect its speed of descent.*

However, not all branches of science use this type of experiment. In the study of evolution or astronomy, for instance, it is usually not possible to manipulate many of the variables of interest. We cannot re-run evolution to see what happens to the dinosaurs if the Earth does *not* suffer an asteroid impact, or

....

*There is some controversy about whether in fact he ever did this and indeed what the result was: even 'pure' science has its ambiguities!

change the Sun's gravitational field to see what happens to planetary orbits under different conditions. Sciences such as these use an *observational* approach to data gathering, rather than experimental methods in the pure sense. In the social sciences also, researchers frequently rely on *observation* to gather data, as it may not be possible to use experimental methods (e.g. to study the behaviour of football crowds). Under these circumstances, although researchers can carefully choose what observations will be most useful, they do not generally have the power to *manipulate* what happens.

We can also distinguish these two types of experiment within cognitive therapy. The first type is more akin to the 'pure' experimental approach and involves patients deliberately setting out to manipulate the environment from their behaviour. Typically, this necessitates doing something which is different to what they would usually do in a particular situation. For example, the patient may try to answer the question: 'If I go to the supermarket alone and do not take my usual precautions, will I actually faint (as my existing belief would predict) or will I just feel anxious (the prediction of an alternative theory)?'

The second type is akin to observational experiments, in that it is either not possible or not necessary to manipulate key variables. Instead patients set out to observe and gather evidence which is relevant to their specific thoughts or beliefs. For example, a patient may try to answer the question: 'Will people think I'm 'stupid' or 'abnormal' if I sweat in social situations?' In this case, it may be useful to conduct a systematic survey, and enquire what the respondents think about people who sweat. Our use of the term *experiment* will encompass both the experimental manipulation and observational types of experiment.

Another distinction which is useful when thinking about BEs, is that between the hypothesis-testing approach of the traditional sciences (and much of psychological science) and the discovery-oriented approach utilized in some of the social sciences (including, on occasions, psychology). The traditional function of science is to test theories through experimentation or observation. However, sometimes in new fields of research there may be no existing theory to test; data may need to be gathered to build a theory (e.g. Piaget's powers of observation and experimentation provided the data which enabled him to build a new theory of child cognitive development). The development in the social sciences of qualitative methodologies such as grounded theory (Glaser and Strauss 1967) has been a response to the need for a systematic method for building theories from data.

The relevance of this distinction for BEs is that, while many BEs are of the hypothesis-testing type, testing either old or newly developed beliefs, this does not apply to all. Some patients, especially those with deeply held core beliefs (e.g. 'I am worthless'), cannot necessarily identify or find any evidence for a set of new, more adaptive beliefs for themselves. They may not have any 'positive' hypotheses to test. Basic data may need to be collected in order for them to build a new hypothesis. Accordingly, they may need (at least initially) to be guided towards discovery-oriented experiments (e.g. 'What would happen if I acted 'as if' I was valued by others?') or encouraged to try out different ways of behaving in order to collect these data ('How might a valued person act in these circumstances?').

To summarize, the form of BEs in cognitive therapy is mainly derived from, and consistent with, the hypothesis-testing approach to experimentation and observation that has traditionally been utilized in the sciences. On occasions, this is supplemented by a more discovery-oriented approach when patients have little or no idea what will happen when they undertake a BE and need to collect data systematically in order to 'build a theory'.

Behavioural experiments: evolution and revolution

Superficially, the BE in cognitive therapy appears to be strikingly similar to the technique of exposure in behaviour therapy—but there are important, indeed fundamental, differences. As Beck *et al.* (1979) have written: 'For the behaviour therapist, the modification of behaviour is an end in itself; for the cognitive therapist it is a means to an end—namely cognitive change' (p. 119).

In behaviour therapy, a typical strategy for change is graduated, repeated, and prolonged exposure to a feared stimulus (e.g. in anxiety) until such time as anxiety dies down; or, in depression, changing prevailing patterns of reinforcement to increase behavioural activation. In contrast, BEs in cognitive therapy are primarily a means of checking the validity of thoughts, perceptions, and beliefs, and/or constructing new operating principles and beliefs. For the behaviour therapist, emotional change is assumed to occur with the passage of time through the process of habituation, whereas for the cognitive therapist, the aim is to help the patient to conclude that the situation is not really dangerous.

To continue with the example of anxiety, cognitive therapy assumes that anxiety is maintained by thoughts of threat, risk, and danger, the nature of which will vary according to the focus of the anxiety. So, for example, a patient whose panics involved changes in heart rate might predict imminent heart attack, whereas a person with social phobia might predict rejection if their anxiety becomes obvious to others. Patients fail to update these predictions (and the beliefs and assumptions on which they are based) because they understandably take steps to prevent the catastrophes from coming true. The panic patient might avoid exercise because it leads to raised heart rate, while the social phobic might strive to appear perfectly confident in front of other people. These 'safety-seeking behaviours' (Salkovskis 1991) keep the system of beliefs in place, and may indeed make things worse. (More commonly, they are called 'safety behaviours', a term which we shall be using in the remainder of this book.) They may even appear to confirm the predictions, for instance when the patient with panic avoids exercise, becomes increasingly unfit, and then experiences raised heart rate after minimal exertion.

The task in therapy is to identify the particular predictions that patients are making and to discover exactly what precautions they are taking to prevent these from coming true. Only by facing what they fear, without taking unnecessary precautions, will they have an opportunity to discover whether their fears are justified. In the case of long-standing difficulties, substantial and lasting changes in perspective may take time, and BEs may have to be modified or repeated. In many cases, however, provided both predictions and precautions have been accurately captured, the change in perspective can occur with great speed—sometimes after a single key experiment.

This approach may be contrasted with the behaviour therapy approach, in which exposure is seen as the key strategy and prevention of avoidance responses and habituation of fear as the predominant mechanisms.

In summary, cognitive therapy has benefited from behaviour therapy's explicit focus on doing things differently (e.g. in the instance above, ceasing to use safety behaviours), and this has contributed directly to the development of BEs within cognitive therapy. However, the emphasis is different; the target of change in cognitive therapy is cognition, not simply behaviour; and the methods of change are specifically geared towards this end.

The value of behavioural experiments

Clinicians' perspectives

Many clinicians view BEs as a particularly powerful method for producing cognitive change. For instance, Clark (1989, p. 82) noted that BEs 'can be one of the most effective ways of changing beliefs'; and Wells (1997, p. 78) has written that 'behavioural strategies offer the most powerful means to cognitive change in cognitive therapy'. Similarly, in their patient manual, *Mind over mood,* Greenberger and Padesky (1995, p. 113) suggested:

> Developing alternative and balanced thoughts for your Thought Records may be like writing in a new language for you. Like any new language, these new thoughts probably seem awkward and only partly believable . . . *the best way to increase the believability of your alternative or balanced thoughts is to try them out in your day-to-day life.*

Cognitive theory assumes that BEs 'work' because they provide hard evidence relevant to patients' beliefs. As Salkovskis (1991, p. 15) has written in relation to the anxiety disorders:

> According to the cognitive hypothesis, the value of behavioural experiments transcends mere exposure; such experiments allow patient and therapist to collaborate in the gathering of new information assessing the validity of non-threatening explanation of anxiety and associated symptoms.

For example, in panic disorder, BEs may provide evidence about causes of symptoms, their consequences, and the effects of safety behaviours (e.g. see Chapter 3).

In cognitive therapy, evidence to test cognitions may be gathered in a variety of ways. Experiments provide one strategy; verbal strategies, such as the use of automatic thought records and guided discovery, represent another. Although identifying and testing automatic thought records may 'offer a means of loosening belief and presenting a foundation for attitude change', Wells (1997, p. 78) has argued that 'the most significant change in cognitive therapy of anxiety is usually obtained when behavioural reattribution is used'. In the next section, evidence to support this assertion is reviewed.

Empirical evidence

Although BEs are integral to cognitive therapy, there is little research in the literature which focuses specifically on the value of these, or of any other specific therapeutic strategy in isolation. Most outcome research has evaluated cognitive therapy packages, rather than specific strategies.

It might be argued that there are strong *a priori* grounds from the history of the success of behaviour therapy and of cognitive therapy to suggest that BEs are valuable treatment strategies. Experiments are a central feature of many successful cognitive therapy treatments for anxiety disorders such as panic disorder and social phobia (Clark 1997), obsessive-compulsive disorder (Salkovskis *et al.* 1999*b*), and post-traumatic stress disorder (Ehlers and Clark 2000).

The effectiveness of BEs, formulated from a cognitive perspective, is also indicated in research comparing the utility of treatment based on cognitive theory and behavioural theory. As predicted by the cognitive model, BEs where safety behaviours are dropped are more effective in producing cognitive, affective, and behavioural change than exposure where safety behaviours continue to be utilized (Morgan and Raffle 1999; Salkovskis *et al.* 1999*a*; Sloan and Telch 2002).

The only research we know of directly comparing the impact of BEs with another therapeutic strategy—the use of automatic thought records—was conducted with cognitive therapy practitioners, who undertook a training course which involved practising cognitive therapy techniques on themselves (Bennett–Levy 2003*a*). They were asked to compare the utility of automatic thought records and BEs in raising their levels of awareness of internal processes (e.g. thoughts, feelings, physical reactions), and in achieving cognitive and behavioural change. While the two techniques promoted equivalent levels of self-awareness, BEs were rated as producing significantly greater cognitive and behavioural change (see Fig. 1.1).

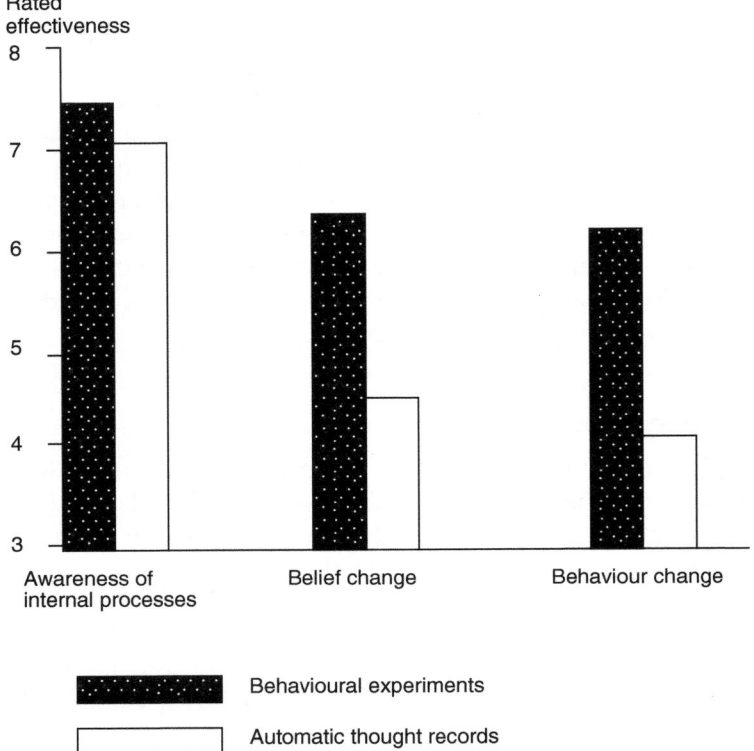

Fig. 1.1 Mean ratings of the effect of behavioural experiments and automatic thought records on awareness, belief change, and behaviour change (from Bennett–Levy 2003*a*).

Interestingly, qualitative feedback indicated that participants ascribed these differences to differences in the quality of evidential experience. New, alternative cognitions derived from automatic thought records tended to be believed 'with the head', but not always 'with the heart' ('I know it rationally but . . . '), while new cognitions derived from experiments were more likely to be believed and accepted ('I experienced it, therefore it must be true'). For instance, one trainee wrote:

> Behavioural experiments give you virtually irrefutable evidence to discredit your maladaptive thoughts and beliefs. Although thought records involve producing evidence against the thought, the evidence provided by the behavioural experiment is much more convincing . . . Everything else was great in terms of understanding, but behavioural experiments were actually the way that I made a couple of changes.

In summary, empirical evidence for the specific effectiveness of BEs is sparse, but is consistent with the perspective of clinicians who have emphasized the importance of BEs in cognitive therapy. Clearly, further research is needed to evaluate the quality of the experience of BEs, and their specific impact, in patient groups.

Theoretical perspectives on the value of behavioural experiments

The cognitive account of BEs specifies that their value lies in disconfirming existing maladaptive cognitions and/or providing evidence for new, more adaptive cognitions. However, our argument goes further. Clinical experience, and the limited empirical evidence available, suggest that BEs are amongst the most powerful therapeutic strategies available to cognitive therapists (Beck *et al.* 1979; Clark 1989; Greenberger and Padesky 1995; Wells 1997). It seems likely that they promote greater cognitive, affective, and behavioural change than purely verbal cognitive techniques lacking an experiential component (Bennett–Levy 2003*a*). This may manifest in greater synchrony (Rachman and Hodgson 1974) across these three systems—cognitive, affective, and behavioural—so that patients do not get into the position of saying 'I can see the alternative, but I still don't feel any different'.

Are there any theoretical grounds to support this assertion? What mechanisms may explain their impact? In this section, we draw on theories from cognitive science, and adult learning theory, in an attempt to provide much needed understanding of how and why change may occur as a consequence of BEs. While it is premature at this stage to attempt a theoretical synthesis, the themes that emerge indicate that the following characteristics of BEs may be particularly relevant:

- ◆ experiential learning
- ◆ emotional arousal
- ◆ the encoding of these experiences in memory in different ways at different levels
- ◆ the practice of new plans and behaviours
- ◆ learning through reflection

In the sections below, we highlight two classes of theory to explain the impact of BEs:

1 *Theories from cognitive science*, which suggest that the multi-sensory, experiential information derived from BEs is processed in a different and 'deeper' way by the information processing system than purely verbally-based information.

2 *Adult learning theories* from education, which assert the centrality of two processes—experiential learning and self-reflection—in creating the most effective learning experiences for humans.

Theories from cognitive science

A number of information processing theories are relevant to the clinical value of BEs. These include:

- The interacting cognitive subsystems (ICS) model of Teasdale (Teasdale 1997; Teasdale and Barnard 1993)
- Brewin's dual representation theory (Brewin 1996; Brewin 2001)
- Power and Dalgleish's SPAARS model (Power and Dalgleish 1997; Power and Dalgleish 1999)
- Epstein's cognitive-experiential self-theory (Epstein 1994; Epstein and Pacini 1999)
- Wells' metacognitive theory (Wells 2000; Wells and Matthews 1994)

The focus in this section is on two of these theories: the ICS model (Teasdale and Barnard 1993), which is broadly representative of a class of multi-level theories that includes Brewin's, Power and Dalgleish's, and Epstein's; and metacognitive theory (Wells 2000), which has a somewhat different emphasis.

While the multi-level theories of Teasdale, Brewin, Power and Dalgleish, and Epstein differ in focus and detail, what they all have in common is that they contrast at least two qualitatively different information processing systems: a more rational, verbal, logical, propositional, information processing system, without links to emotion; and a 'deeper', more holistic, non-linguistic, automatic, and rapid information processing system, with extensive links to emotion. These theories suggest that BEs may provide more powerful subjective evidence for cognitive, affective, and behavioural change than purely verbal strategies, because carrying out experiments means being involved in practical activities with clear emotional and psychological relevance, which are more likely to have an impact at the deeper, non-linguistic level of the 'felt sense'. In contrast, verbal techniques tend only to impact at the rational/logical level. For instance, there is a great difference in the 'felt sense' of safety between reading about the minimal risk of a parachuting accident and carrying out one or more successful parachute jumps.

Focusing here primarily on Teasdale's ICS theory, which has perhaps received the most attention from cognitive therapists, the theory suggests that these differences parallel the difference between what patients describe as 'intellectual' versus 'emotional' belief, or 'believing with the head' versus 'the heart'. Teasdale's argument is that 'intellectual' and 'emotional' belief are products of the different levels of information processing that are accessed, and of the different kinds of experience needed to promote cognitive change in each case. Within the ICS model, for emotional change to occur, patients need to develop 'alternative schematic models' at the implicational (deeper) level, which encompass changes in behavioural, cognitive, emotional, and physical responses. The most direct pathway to create this change is to arrange for 'experiences in which new or modified models are created' (Teasdale 1997, p. 90). BEs are potentially a major source of such experiences, as their emotional qualities increase the likelihood that they will impact at the implicational level. In contrast, it is assumed that purely verbally-based techniques, such as automatic thought records will predominantly have an impact at the propositional (verbal/logical) level, unless completed when emotion is activated. In consequence, they may not be so effective in promoting change.

Although Teasdale contrasts implicational and propositional systems, and seems to imply that the value of BEs lies in their impact on the implicational system, this may be an oversimplification. As will be argued below (see adult learning theory section), BEs may be particularly powerful because they impact on *both* implicational and propositional systems.

Evidence supporting the value of the kind of emotional/experiential encoding which might be experienced during BEs can be derived from experimental research on memory. First, heightened emotion usually facilitates remembering, though accuracy can be compromised (Heuer and Riesberg 1992). Second, the 'enactment effect' indicates that 'memory for . . . actions that one has observed of other people, or that one has only heard about . . . is less good than memory for self-performed actions' (Engelkamp 1998, p. 139). Engelkamp (1998) has suggested that one of the most important reasons for the enactment effect is that information is encoded multi-modally using visual, auditory, kinaesthetic, and/or motor systems. Such results are consistent with multi-level theories suggesting that emotionally/experientially acquired information is likely to have a more widespread impact on cognition, emotion, and behaviour, than purely verbal information.

Another theory which may shed some light on the value of BEs is the metacognitive theory of Wells (2000). Wells draws on the distinction, from the experimental psychology literature, between declarative and procedural memory. Declarative memory contains knowledge and beliefs which are recalled as factual information (e.g. 'Brazil won the World Cup in 2002' or 'My thoughts are uncontrollable'). Procedural memory contains knowledge about plans or procedures which is often automatic and implicit (e.g. 'Aim for the corner of the net when taking a penalty' or 'Take a sleeping pill to get a night without worrying').

The important point made by Wells is that in order for metacognitive processing to change, it is necessary not only to develop a new *declarative* belief

('Worry can be controlled'), but also to develop a different *procedural* memory through the repeated enactment of a new plan or procedure ('Postpone worry until 6.00–6.15 p.m. daily'). The point applies equally to other (non-metacognitive) declarative beliefs. For instance, a challenging situation may elicit, in a person with low self-esteem, declarative beliefs (e.g. 'I am a failure') and characteristic plans which are usually implicit (e.g. gaze aversion, slumped body, automatic thought 'not me!'). Effective therapy will need to change both.

The implication of these ideas for BEs is that it is not enough to focus simply on changing declarative beliefs ('I am a failure', 'Worry can be controlled'), as purely verbal strategies are liable to do. Procedural memory also needs to be changed, and this is best effected through implementation and evaluation. When the new behaviours are enacted ('Volunteer for raffle, act 'as if' I can do it', 'Do worrying at 6.15 p.m.'), BEs will impact directly on procedural memory, and frequently on the declarative beliefs themselves ('I'm quite good at organizing', 'Having dedicated worry time leaves so much more time for everything else!'), in a way that verbal techniques are much less able to do.

Much of the writing in the cognitive therapy literature has focused on identifying and testing *declarative* thoughts and beliefs. Wells' theory reminds us that implicit plans, in the form of procedural memory, are just as much part of cognition as overt or covert declarative beliefs. Such plans may be rather less susceptible to change through verbal-only means. Like the multi-level theories, this theory suggests that the most direct way to change plans, and appraisals, is through interventions which impact *across* information processing systems. Wells argues that the most effective way to do this is through the BE.

Adult learning theory

A second set of theories, suggesting the particular value of BEs, is derived from the field of adult education. Since the time of John Dewey (1938), educationalists have recognized the unique value of personal experience for learning. Later authors have also placed emphasis on the value of reflection (Kemmis and McTaggart 2000; Kolb 1984; Lewin 1946; Schön 1983).

The processes involved in experiential learning and reflection are embodied in the Lewin/Kolb four stage experiential learning model (Kolb 1984; Lewin 1946)—probably the most widely used model in adult education (see Fig. 1.2). Different terms to describe the four stages have been used by different authors; here we shall use the relatively straightforward terms, *Plan, Experience, Observe, Reflect*. According to the model, effective learning proceeds through a series of Plan–Experience–Observe–Reflect cycles.

With regard to BEs, experiential learning and reflection, as well as planning and accurate observation, are clearly key components. Based on the

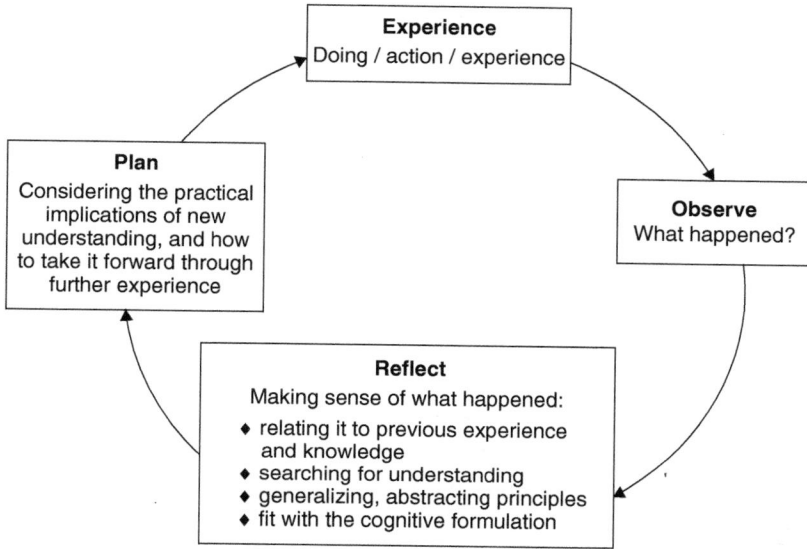

Fig. 1.2 The Lewin/Kolb experiential learning circle.

conceptualization of the problem (*Reflect*), the patient and therapist plan an appropriate experiment to test a declarative belief (*Plan*). The patient carries out the experiment (*Experience*), perhaps changing some aspect of normal perform-ance, observes the results (*Observe*), and, with the therapist, reflects on the implications for the belief (*Reflect*). Further experiments are planned (*Plan*), and the cycle continues. Potentially, the cycle can start at any of these four points.

Essentially, the experiential learning model is a procedural theory, in contrast to the more structural theories outlined above. Although an empirical research base is lacking, the learning circle has high pragmatic value and face validity. Indeed, it provides such a useful structure for describing the steps involved in setting up, carrying out, and learning from BEs that we have adopted it as the organizing framework for Chapter 2.

Although adult learning theory comes from the educational context, while psychological theories of learning (e.g. classical conditioning, instrumental learning, social learning) derive from an experimental tradition, the two approaches can be seen as complementary. The particular contributions of adult learning theory, which make this theory especially useful in the context of personal change, are its emphasis on the uniquely human attribute of reflective learning (Bennett–Levy 2003*b*) and its clarity of procedural description. BEs are not simply about 'carrying out the experiment'. Planning, observation, and reflection are also central components, intrinsic to learning. As Bennett–Levy (2003a) has noted in relation to Teasdale's ICS model, it is likely that BEs work so well because the cognitive (and experiential) components of planning, observing, and reflecting, combined with the experiential component of 'experiencing', mean that, in multi-level theory terms, BEs are more readily processed at *both* the 'deeper' implicational (experiential) level *and* the more conceptual/verbal prepositional level.

Conclusion

The aims of this chapter have been:

1 to site BEs historically and conceptually within the traditions of empirical science, psychotherapy, and cognitive therapy

2 to review clinical and empirical evidence for their effectiveness

3 to reflect on what it is about BEs that leads to change.

The experience of leading clinicians suggests that BEs occupy a particularly important role as a key therapeutic strategy within cognitive therapy. This apparent value may be contrasted with the current dearth of empirical evidence and relevant theory on the subject. There is an obvious need for more research, and more specific theory development.

In this chapter, we have indicated, without going into great detail, that BEs differ along various dimensions—for instance, they may incorporate different methodological approaches (hypothesis testing or discovery) and different types of experiment (experimental or observational). The next chapter, which focuses on the practical application of BEs, expands on these differences and utilizes the adult learning circle to provide a pragmatic framework for clinicians wishing to design effective BEs.

CHAPTER 2

Devising effective behavioural experiments

Khadj Rouf
Melanie Fennell
David Westbrook
Myra Cooper
James Bennett–Levy

Introduction

In this chapter, theory is translated into practice. We move from a broad conceptual and historical context to detailed guidelines for the working clinician. Our aim is to provide a framework within which practising cognitive therapists can approach behavioural experiments with confidence, maximizing patients' chances of cognitive and emotional change.

In Chapter 1, we reminded readers of Beck's cognitive model of emotional disorder, and highlighted the particular value of behavioural experiments as a means of producing cognitive change. We summarized the—as yet limited—empirical evidence that supports their use, speculated on psychological mechanisms that may underpin their effectiveness, and noted theories that might account for their impact.

In this chapter, we identify general principles for devising behavioural experiments. In the remainder of the book, these principles are applied to a range of specific problem areas. This chapter is divided into seven sections. Sections 1 and 2 provide an overview of the nature and purpose of behavioural experiments, and propose the Kolb–Lewin learning circle as a framework for their design and implementation. Sections 3 to 7 describe in practical detail how to carry out each step in the process.

Section 1   A typology of behavioural experiments

Section 2   The learning circle: maximizing opportunities to learn from behavioural experiments

Section 3   Planning: designing the behavioural experiment

Section 4   Experience: the experiment itself

Section 5   Observation: examining what happened

Section 6   Reflection: making sense of the experiment

Section 7   Planning: following up the experiment

The chapter draws on the established canon of good practice in cognitive therapy, and on key texts that have contributed to its development. We also incorporate ideas and methods we have found useful in our own clinical practice. Throughout, we use case examples to illustrate points. In order to include patients' perspectives, we have also interspersed patient quotations from a qualitative study of their thoughts about behavioural experiments (Baxter 2003).*

It is important to emphasize that behavioural experiments should be carried out in the context of a course of competent, formulation-guided cognitive therapy. We do not intend to describe cognitive therapy in detail here, since this information is readily available elsewhere (readers will find relevant texts listed at the end of the section on 'How to use this book'). We shall simply outline some features of the approach that are of special importance in designing effective behavioural experiments.

Thorough *assessment* and the development of an individually tailored cognitive-behavioural *formulation* ensure that experiments are specifically targeted to impact on factors that maintain presenting problems and create vulnerability to psychological difficulties. Such formulations should take due account of factors within the environment (including cultural and social issues), since these will contribute to problem development and maintenance and influence the language patients use to describe and explain distress. It is equally important that patients have a working understanding of the cognitive model and the *treatment rationale* and are willing to accept, at least tentatively, its relevance to themselves. Without this, they may be unwilling to undertake behavioural experiments, which almost inevitably contain an element of perceived risk. Patients' expectations of therapy can usefully be explored, especially where there is a social or cultural mismatch between therapist and patient, as these factors can impact on therapy outcomes (Sue *et al.* 1991; Organista *et al.* 1994; Bernal and Scharron del Rio 2001). Early sessions offer an opportunity for people to experience at first

---

*We are grateful to Hannah Baxter and the patients she interviewed for their permission to use these quotations.

hand the active, collaborative, empirical *style of cognitive therapy*. Cognitive therapists embody this style, treating patients with openness and respect, encouraging teamwork (rather than adopting an expert position), and fostering willingness to approach problems with curiosity and an open mind.

Shared understanding of the cognitive model and treatment rationale, and experience of cognitive therapy's collaborative style, create a basis for establishing a sound *therapeutic relationship*. The relationship provides a safe context for taking risks and trying out new ways of thinking and behaving. Indeed, engaging in the relationship itself sometimes constitutes a sort of extended behavioural experiment, especially for patients with negative beliefs about themselves and others and associated interpersonal difficulties.

1. A typology of behavioural experiments

Once the factors outlined above are in place, behavioural experiments can fruitfully proceed. They take a variety of forms, as summarized in Table 2.1. Some elements of this table are derived from earlier work by Wells (1997) and Padesky and Mooney (1999).

The purposes of behavioural experiments

Behavioural experiments have three main purposes: elaborating the formulation, testing negative cognitions, and constructing and testing new, more adaptive perspectives. The key objective is not to modify thinking *per se* but rather, through cognitive change, to transform emotional state and facilitate problem solving.

Early in therapy, while understanding is evolving, behavioural experiments can play a key role in elaborating the formulation, providing information that may not be accessible purely through memory-based verbal report. Experiments give therapists the opportunity to witness subtle aspects of thinking and behaviour that are invisible to the patient and so not reported in the consulting room. Experiments also encourage patients to make similar observations for themselves. For example, a patient with health anxiety was asked to observe and record the effects of other people's reassurance on his anxious preoccupation with bodily symptoms. He noticed that his preoccupation diminished for a short time following reassurance, but re-emerged (along with his symptoms) within a few hours. For the first time, he acknowledged that psychological processes might contribute to his difficulties.

Behavioural experiments are also a powerful means of reducing the credibility of outdated and unhelpful negative automatic thoughts, dysfunctional assumptions, and core beliefs. Additionally, cognitive therapists emphasize the importance of creating and strengthening new, more realistic and more helpful thoughts, assumptions, and beliefs (Padesky 1994; Greenberger and Padesky

Table 2.1 A framework for behavioural experiments (BEs)

Purpose	Design	Types of BE	Level of cognition	Settings
Elaborating the formulation	**Hypothesis-testing experiments** ♦ Testing hypothesis A ♦ Comparing hypothesis A & hypothesis B ♦ Testing hypothesis B	**Active experiments** ♦ In real situations ♦ Simulated (e.g. role play)	**Automatic thoughts**	**Time & place** ♦ In therapy time ♦ Consulting room ♦ *In vivo* ♦ Homework
Testing negative cognitions			**Dysfunctional assumptions**	
			Core beliefs	**People** ♦ Patient ♦ Therapist ♦ Stooges ♦ Family, friends ♦ Work colleagues ♦ General public
Constructing and testing new perspectives	**Discovery experiments** ♦ Hypothesis vague or absent	**Observational experiments** ♦ Direct observation (modelling) ♦ Surveys ♦ Information gathering from other sources		**Resources** ♦ Tape recorder, video, record sheets, etc.

1995; Mooney and Padesky 2000). Behavioural experiments offer patients an opportunity to assess the validity of fresh perspectives through direct personal experience.

> 'Because you are actually there, you're living the actual experiment and it's not just a paper exercise in front of you, it actually drives it home more that this is a true picture of what is happening . . . ' (Patient)

The first purpose of behavioural experiments (elaborating the formulation) is akin to the 'socialization' function ascribed to them by Wells (1997). The second and third (testing old and new perspectives) echo his 'reattribution' category; as Wells observes, this is the principal function of behavioural experiments in cognitive therapy. Unlike Wells, we have not included a separate 'modification of emotion' category, because in our view these experiments (e.g. the use of distraction in depression) have an important function in addition to temporary relief from distress and interruption of unhelpful cognitive processes that may interfere with engagement in therapy. That is, they provide direct opportunities to test and change cognitions that feed into and thus maintain negative emotional states (e.g. 'My depression is constant and unremitting'; see Chapter 10).

Design of behavioural experiments

As noted in Chapter 1, the two main frameworks used in designing behavioural experiments correspond to two basic research methodologies commonly employed in the social sciences: formal hypothesis testing ('Is it true that . . . ?'), and a more open, investigative, discovery-oriented method ('What would happen if . . . ?').

Hypothesis-testing experiments

> 'I understood them as being ways of checking out things, finding out if certain beliefs I had were true by going into situations . . . Deciding beforehand what I was worried might happen and then trying to see if it did happen . . . ' (Patient)

> 'Experiments to resolve whether what a person thinks is actually going to happen . . . ' (Patient)

Hypothesis-testing experiments can be divided into three subtypes, which may blur into one another.

Testing hypothesis A

The first subtype simply tests the validity of a current unhelpful cognition (hypothesis A). For instance, early in therapy for panic disorder, a patient might have only one explanation for a tight chest—impending disaster (e.g. 'I'm going to have a heart attack'). Before developing an alternative, more benign explanation, this idea could be tested, for example by means of an in-session hyperventilation test (see Chapter 3).

Hypothesis A vs. hypothesis B

The second subtype compares and contrasts an unhelpful cognition with a new, potentially more helpful perspective (hypothesis A vs. hypothesis B). For example, by the middle of therapy for panic disorder, the therapist should have assisted the patient to develop an alternative explanation (hypothesis B) for his tight chest (e.g. 'This could just be anxiety'). A series of *in vivo* experiments could then be designed to see if the 'heart attack' hypothesis or the 'anxiety' hypothesis better accounts for the patient's symptoms.

Testing hypothesis B

The third subtype specifically directs patients' attention towards situations and behaviours that are likely to provide evidence to support a new perspective (hypothesis B). For instance, later in therapy, a patient with panic disorder might wish to test a new understanding of the meaning of physical symptoms: 'Strange physical sensations are quite normal, and nothing to be afraid of'. A series of experiments designed to produce strange physical sensations in a variety of circumstances could be used to accumulate evidence for this new idea.

Discovery experiments

Discovery experiments are undertaken when patients genuinely have little or no idea (no clear hypothesis) about the processes maintaining a problem, or about what may happen if they act in a different way. Discovery experiments can help in the development of the formulation, in designing treatment strategies, and in creating and refining new perspectives. For instance, a therapist might set up an in-session experiment in which a socially anxious patient would hold two conversations: one where (as usual) she focused on how she was feeling and how she thought she was coming across, and a second where she directed her attention away from herself and on to the other person. The patient might never have done this before. Consequently, she might have little or no idea how she would feel or how it would affect the conversation. The purpose of the experiment would be for her to find out, and consider the implications of her discoveries for the formulation and treatment plan. Her observations might also lead towards a new perspective to be tested through future experiments, for example: 'If I forget myself, meeting people can be fun'.

Types of behavioural experiment

There are two main types of behavioural experiment: active experiments and observational experiments.

Active experiments

Active experiments are the most common in practice, and most of the experiments in this book are of this type. In active experiments, patients take the lead role. Once an unhelpful cognition or pattern of behaviour has been identified, they deliberately think or act in a different way in the problem situation. They note what happens, and reflect on its implications for their thinking and behaviour. In this type of experiment, the patient is both 'actor' and 'observer'.

Active experiments use either real situations or simulated situations to test the validity of cognitions. Simulations (including role play) are particularly useful when patients are wary of making changes in real life, when the real situation is rare, or when an opportunity is needed to try out a range of different responses in order to discover which works best. For instance, a patient with interpersonal difficulties believed: 'If I express dissatisfaction, I will be rejected'. Simulation experiments with the therapist role-playing relevant people (e.g. a difficult work colleague) enabled him to try out different ways of expressing dissatisfaction, to obtain feedback, and to formulate a new assumption in draft ('If I express how I feel, there may be a chance to resolve difficulties'). These experiments increased his confidence and skill and he was then ready to attempt expressing dissatisfaction in real situations. First, he practised expressing dissatisfaction to the therapist. Later, he graduated to testing his new policy at work and elsewhere.

Observational experiments

Observational experiments differ from active experiments in that the patient is purely an 'observer' or data gatherer, not an actor. Observational experiments are particularly useful when the thought of direct action is too anxiety-provoking, and when more information is required before planning an experiment in which the patient is the actor. They can be used both for hypothesis testing and for discovery, and new information can be sought from direct observation, surveys, and other sources.

Direct observation (modelling)

A therapist was working with a spider phobic patient. At first, the patient was too frightened to touch even the smallest spider. She thought it would be uncontrollable, that it would jump into her hair and bite her, and that she would be unable to get it out. As a first step, the therapist handled a small spider with the patient watching carefully from a safe distance. Instead of attacking the therapist, the little spider tried to run away. The therapist demonstrated how to handle it in a controlled way, hand over hand. With this new information, the patient was then able to touch the spider herself.

Surveys

Survey experiments can be undertaken by the patient or by the therapist. The aim is to gather a broad sample of factual information or opinion about a question relevant to the patient's concerns. Patients' expectations are often considerably out of line with reality. For example, a vomit phobic believed that he alone felt sick and disgusted if someone nearby vomited. It was helpful to discover that feeling sick and disgusted in the presence of vomit was common.

Before carrying out a survey, it is important to specify how the patient predicts people will respond. This makes the contrast between anticipated and actual results clear. It is also important that the questions used in the survey, and the kind of people to be approached (number, age, gender, etc.), are decided with the patient. The easiest way to find respondents is usually to ask colleagues. However, the patient may view therapists as unusually non-judgemental and thus lacking in credibility. For this reason, it may be as well to include 'real' people (e.g. technicians, secretarial staff, managers, friends) and to make it clear to the patient that this has been done. Additionally, a small number of respondents sometimes do react as the patient fears. This may initially be disconcerting, but in fact is helpful information and facilitates discussion of how far one should allow others' opinions to influence one's own, and what reasons they might have for thinking as they do.

Although it is powerful for patients to conduct surveys themselves, they may feel too uncomfortable to do so. The therapist (who has no particular emotional investment in the issue) may well have less difficulty. A compromise may be possible: for example, the therapist asks 8–10 people what they think, and the patient consults one or two trusted friends. If the therapist conducts the survey, it is helpful to audiotape responses rather than simply writing them down. This increases the credibility of the data as the patient hears not only what people say, but also their tone of voice.

Gathering information from other sources

Evidence to undermine old ideas or support new ones can also be collected from public information sources, including the internet. For instance, a patient who believed that snake-bites in the UK could cause serious injury or death investigated on the internet how many people die or are injured by snake-bites every year.

Levels of cognition

Beck's cognitive model recognizes three levels of cognition: negative automatic thoughts, dysfunctional assumptions, and core beliefs. These have different implications for designing behavioural experiments.

Automatic thoughts

As well as thoughts about external situations and internal events (including body sensations, emotions, and cognitions), negative automatic thoughts can include reservations about the therapist (e.g. 'I'm not sure I can trust him'), about therapy (e.g. 'This isn't going to help'), and about the experiment (e.g. 'That's too scary. I can't do it'). It is particularly important to be sensitive to, and discuss, doubts and fears about experiments.

Situation-specific negative automatic thoughts may require only one (or a few) well-targeted experiments, and so make straightforward targets early in treatment. Working with specific thoughts should not be viewed as superficial or trivial. Highly specific experiments testing particular thoughts can be used to begin undermining broader cognitive structures (assumptions and beliefs), especially if the therapist makes the links explicit (e.g. 'How do the results of this particular experiment relate to your overall belief that others are not to be trusted?', 'How does what we just noticed fit with your general rule that everything you do has to be 100% perfect?').

Dysfunctional assumptions

These cross-situational rules (e.g. 'Unless I do everything perfectly, people will think I'm useless') are usually reflected on a day-to-day basis in unhelpful behaviour (e.g. overworking). Thus they provide a natural focus for experiments. A number of experiments, perhaps over some weeks, may be required to sharpen the formulation of underlying assumptions, and to test and embed new alternatives.

Core beliefs

Core beliefs reflect generalized conclusions about self, others, and the world. Despite this, they can sometimes change substantially within short-term cognitive therapy, especially if experiential learning through behavioural experiments is incorporated. Beliefs are often maintained by habitual, unquestioned, and untested biases in perception, interpretation, and memory, which can prove surprisingly open to updating in the face of new information. Behavioural experiments facilitate this process because they encourage patients to confront situations they have previously avoided, and provide opportunities to acquire evidence inconsistent with their expectations.

However, core beliefs are often longstanding and entrenched, and have been repeatedly rehearsed and reinforced over many years. Consequently, they normally take longer to change than thoughts, and may require extended sequences of interlinked experiments carried out within and between sessions over weeks, or indeed months. Change in degree of belief may be very gradual (Padesky 1994).

Settings and resources

Experiments can be carried out during therapy time, or as between-session self-help assignments. In-session experiments may be carried out in the consulting room (e.g. role plays), or therapist and patient may venture forth from the office to real world environments (e.g. shopping centres, cars, restaurants). Between-session experiments may be conducted in similar public settings, or in settings only accessible to the patient (e.g. work, home, a gathering of friends).

The main person involved in experiments is the patient. However, others may also play a significant role (e.g. the therapist, 'stooges', family, friends, colleagues, members of the public).

Resources needed for the experiment should be identified and prepared in advance (e.g. audio or video equipment). Standard record sheets and diaries may need to be adapted for particular purposes and are crucially important; without them valuable information may be lost.

2. The learning circle: maximizing opportunities to learn from behavioural experiments

The Lewin–Kolb experiential learning circle (Lewin 1946; Kolb 1984), introduced in Chapter 1, provides a practical framework for devising behavioural experiments. The learning circle (see Fig. 1.2, p. 19) suggests that learning and retention are enhanced when learners follow a sequence of steps, each of which builds on its predecessor and forms a foundation for the step that follows.

An alternative framework for thinking about behavioural experiments, the PETS model (prepare–expose–test–summarize), has been described by Wells (1997; 2000). The two models have much in common, and both are useful. However, Wells' model was developed specifically in the context of his S-REF theory, and might be considered to apply best to a narrower range of experiments than is covered here. We have chosen the learning circle as our primary framework because of its breadth of reference and its extensive development as a model of learning within the adult education literature.

According to the learning circle model, enduring change is unlikely to occur unless each step (plan–experience–observe–reflect) is included in the learning process. For example, if direct experience is omitted, new ideas may remain purely hypothetical, emotions may not be engaged, and real-world difficulties can easily be missed. Experience can be wasted, however, if patients do not take the time to consider what they have observed (including their own thoughts, feelings, behaviour, and body sensations). If observation does not then lead on to reflection, patients may fail to relate new experiences to prior predictions, or to appreciate the underlying principles of change. Finally, new understanding may remain theoretical unless its practical implications are thought through and used as a basis for planning further learning experiences—in our context, designing the next experiment.

A patient might enter the circle at any point. For one patient, the entry point might be a distressing and disturbing event (experience), which she had felt too upset to think about, and which the therapist might help her to observe and reflect on. For another patient, the entry point might be the expression of a powerful underlying belief, the implications of which the therapist and patient might then explore together (reflection). Within sessions, the most common entry point is probably the experience of distress, followed by observation: thinking back over the week, or recent events, or specific incidents that need to be understood and tackled. Each entry point is a gateway to an iterative process through which old understandings are brought into focus, questioned, and tested, and new understandings are formulated and their validity tested in everyday life.

The example in Fig. 2.1 may help to clarify how this framework works in practice. The patient was in the middle of cognitive therapy for social phobia. Although much had changed, he was still troubled by self-critical thoughts for two or three hours after awkward social encounters. He could achieve a balanced view once he calmed down, but felt powerless to reduce his embarrassment more quickly. He coped by not thinking about it.

The therapist conducted a small, on-the-spot experiment on thought suppression. She asked the patient *not*, under any circumstances, to think of a green rabbit sitting on her head (experience). The patient's gaze immediately went to the top of her head, and he laughed. When she asked him what he had noticed, he said that as soon as he tried not to think of the green rabbit, it came to mind (observation). The therapist told him about research which shows that attempting to suppress thoughts and feelings in fact keeps them going, and asked him what the green rabbit experiment might tell him (reflection). He decided that trying not to think about awkward encounters was preventing him from letting go of them, as well as depriving him of the

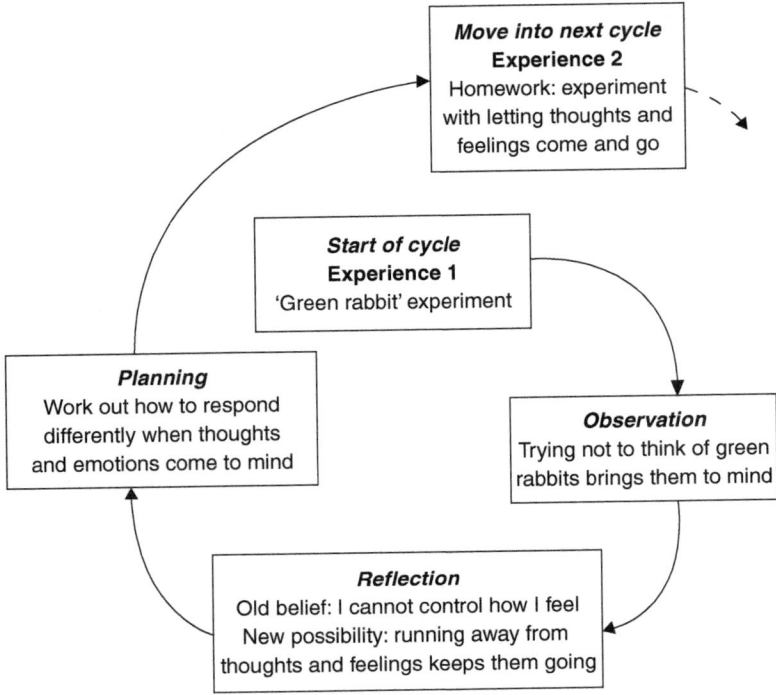

Fig. 2.1 An example of the learning circle.

chance to find a change of perspective right away. They concluded the session by agreeing a homework assignment (planning): the patient would allow thoughts about awkward social encounters to come to mind, rather than trying to suppress them (new experience). He would see what effect this had on his feelings (observation). Thus he could discover whether indeed suppressing his thoughts and feelings was a helpful strategy (reflection). This example illustrates how the circle is not in fact a closed system, but rather an ongoing process in which each complete cycle leads forward into a new phase of learning.

The learning circle provides a framework for understanding the pivotal role of behavioural experiments in cognitive therapy. The contextual factors we identified earlier (assessment, formulation, etc.) set the scene for therapist and patient to embark together on a journey of discovery reflected in the circle as a whole. Specific aspects of behavioural experiments (preparation, the experiment itself, observation, and drawing out implications) shadow the four steps of the circle. We shall now consider each of these in more detail.

3. Planning: designing behavioural experiments

Planning includes both the preparation that precedes an experiment and the thinking ahead that follows it. We shall consider the first here, and return briefly to the second after completing the circle, following the sequence pursued in therapy where each experiment becomes a foundation for the next. Careful planning is a cornerstone of behavioural experiments with vulnerable people whose confidence is readily shaken; for this reason this section has been elaborated most fully.

The box below provides a checklist of relevant questions for therapists and patients to consider in the planning phase. These are addressed in detail in the text that follows. Such questions can be particularly helpful to patients working independently (for example, between treatment sessions and during follow-up).

Checklist for the planning phase

- Is the purpose of the experiment clear? Does the patient understand the rationale for the experiment?
- Have you specified the target cognition(s), and in particular the predicted outcome of the experiment?
- Have you identified an alternative perspective, if appropriate?
- Have you rated degree of belief in the target cognition(s), prediction(s) about the outcome of the experiment, and the alternative perspective (0–100%)?
- Have you taken emotions and physical symptoms into account?
- Have you identified unhelpful behaviour that may be feeding into target cognitions?
- Have you decided what type of experiment will provide the best test of the target cognition(s) (hypothesis-testing, discovery-oriented, active, observational)?
- Have you decided on a time and a place, and worked out what resources you need (including other people)?
- Have you anticipated possible problems and worked out how to overcome them?

(continued)

Checklist for the planning phase *(continued)*

- ◆ Have you made sure that something constructive will be gained from the experiment, no matter what the outcome ('no lose')?
- ◆ Have you decided how to assess the impact of the experiment? Do you have a means of recording the outcome?
- ◆ Have you selected an appropriate level of difficulty—challenging, but manageable?
- ◆ Have you explored and resolved doubts, fears, and reservations?
- ◆ Have necessary medical checks been carried out?

Being clear about the purpose of the experiment

Just as a shared understanding of the rationale for cognitive therapy forms part of the context for successful behavioural experiments, so the purpose of each experiment needs to be clear to therapist and patient, especially if the experiment is to be conducted independently, outside the session. A shared sense of what an experiment is designed to achieve ensures that it is a joint enterprise, rather than something the therapist does to the patient.

'You've got to have a clear goal of what you want to achieve or it is just time wasted . . .' (Patient)

'Discussing the pros and cons of doing it was helpful . . .' (Patient)

Identifying target cognitions and predicted outcomes

Most experiments aim to examine specific thoughts, dysfunctional assumptions, or beliefs. Precise identification of these, and of specific predictions about the outcome of the experiment, is an essential first step: vaguely defined cognitions lead to unfocused and ineffective experiments. This principle applies whatever the level of cognition under consideration. Rating degree of belief in relevant cognitions (0–100%) as soon as they are identified establishes a baseline against which change can subsequently be measured.

Developing alternative perspectives

Sometimes people can readily construct alternatives to unhelpful cognitions, using the kind of question familiar to cognitive therapists (e.g. 'What might be another way of looking at that?', 'What would you say to another person who came to you with this problem?', 'How might a person who cared about you understand this?'(see Beck 1995; Fennell 1989; Greenberger and Padesky 1995 for further examples of helpful questions). Similar questions can help patients to find tentative alternatives to dysfunctional assumptions and core beliefs (Mooney and Padesky 2000; Padesky 1994). Again, degree of belief in alternatives should be rated (0–100%) once they have been identified.

Sometimes patients are unable to access alternatives to old perspectives, especially when these are longstanding, entrenched, and associated with intense emotions and high levels of disability. In this case, tentative alternatives may only emerge when considerable work has been done on undermining the old perspective. This work is likely to involve a variety of verbal, imaginal, and behavioural methods. Initially, alternatives may need to be suggested by the therapist.

An important element in developing alternative perspectives is to help patients to entertain the idea that a belief, even if powerfully convincing, is not necessarily an accurate reflection of reality. Beliefs are opinions, based on experience, not facts. If patients can entertain this idea (which may represent a metacognitive shift), then they may be prepared also to consider the possibility that an alternative perspective might have validity. There is no point initially in expecting patients to welcome these ideas or believe them wholeheartedly: the key point is a tentative acceptance, at least in principle, that there might be more than one way of viewing things, and willingness to explore whether this is indeed the case.

Taking account of emotions and physiological responses

Patients usually come for help because they want to change the way they feel, not because they want to straighten out their thinking. Correspondingly, the purpose of behavioural experiments is not to produce an intellectual appreciation of alternatives to unhelpful cognitions, but to facilitate emotionally grounded change. Inquiring about emotions is therefore essential and ensures that experiments are relevant to patients' concerns. Additionally, change in emotional state is a key indicator of effective cognitive change. For this reason, it is important to assess intensity of emotions (0–100%) as well as degree of belief in relevant cognitions. Emotions, and associated body sensations, are often a focus for experiments in their own right (see, for example, the Chapters 7 and 17).

Tackling unhelpful behaviour

Cognitions influence behaviour, and in turn are maintained by it. People behave as if their thoughts, assumptions, and beliefs were valid; their behaviour makes sense in the light of what they believe to be the case, but prevents them from updating old perspectives. For example, a patient who saw herself as inferior (belief), considered that she would be rejected if she ever put her own needs first (dysfunctional assumption), and predicted in specific situations that people would be angry or dismissive if she refused requests or asked for anything (thoughts): naturally enough, she behaved unassertively. Her unassertive behaviour maintained her sense of inferiority, prevented her from realizing she was entitled to consider her own needs, and stopped her from discovering that most people are in fact responsive to others' wishes. It is important to investigate links between thinking and behaviour, so as to work out how to discover if old ideas are helpful and realistic. The 'inferior' patient, for example, might need to experiment with treating herself with the same consideration she gives to others, and observe the consequences.

In anxiety disorders particular attention needs to be given to identifying the myriad, often subtle, 'safety-seeking behaviours' (Salkovskis 1991) which people use to prevent feared catastrophes from happening (see Chapters 3–9). Safety behaviours often reflect assumptions ('If I do X, Y will happen/it will mean Z'). Unless they are dropped during experiments, patients will be left with the feeling that they have escaped disaster by the skin of their teeth. Many experiments therefore involve:

- Discovering what patients predict will happen if they do *not* engage in safety behaviours
- Testing out what *actually* happens under these circumstances.

It is important to establish in fine detail what patients think will happen, and how they will know if it has. So, for example, in relation to the thought 'If I don't cover my face with my scarf, I will look odd', it would be necessary to inquire how one could tell whether one in fact 'looked odd', and what the likely consequences would be. Otherwise the outcome of the experiment would be hard to evaluate. It is also important to establish whether an action is or is not a safety behaviour. Cultural factors may need to be taken into account: for example, a patient from South-East Asia might avoid direct eye contact not because he feared showing his anxiety (safety behaviour), but as a sign of respect. The therapist may also need to judge whether the behaviour protects the person from a genuine risk. For example, a patient who had been raped avoided going out at night in a lonely part of town. This was a sensible strategy. However, she was also avoiding shopping in the city during the day, when there were plenty of people around. The key question is whether there is any objective evidence that the feared outcome would in fact occur in the absence of safety behaviours.

Selecting the type of experiment

Working out what an experiment is designed to achieve helps therapist and patient to select the type of experience most likely to be helpful. What does the patient need to test or discover? Is the aim hypothesis testing, either to undermine an old pattern of thinking (hypothesis A) or to test a new one (hypothesis B)? Or is open-ended exploration more appropriate (discovery)? Or direct comparison between old and new perspectives? What level of cognition is under investigation—thoughts, assumptions, or beliefs? If thoughts, how can the outcome be linked to the broader issues? If assumptions or beliefs, how do these relate to day-to-day functioning? Would the patient learn most from taking action on this occasion, or would an observational experiment be more valuable? Is the patient ready to operate differently and observe the consequences, or would it be better first for the therapist to model the new pattern? An advantage of the collaborative style of cognitive therapy is that these questions can be answered in consultation with the patient.

Problems can often be approached from several different angles. Understanding what aspect of thinking is most salient can help in deciding which approach might be best for a particular patient at a particular time. For example, a number of experiments could be used to explore the meaning of blushing in public. Each tests a different concern:

- **I look as red as I feel** In session, the therapist could provoke a blush and ask the patient to rate how red she feels and how red she thinks she looks. The patient could then use a mirror or videotape of the session to see if the two are in fact equivalent.

- **If I blush, others will notice** The therapist could encourage the patient to exaggerate the blush by applying blusher and then go into a public place. The patient could look for any signs that people noticed (it would be important to decide in advance how she would know if they had).

- **Others see blushing as a sign of inadequacy** A survey could be used to discover what others think about blushing.

- **If someone did think blushing was a sign of inadequacy, I would be devastated** Finally, the patient could role play responding assertively to someone who did judge them negatively for blushing.

Any, or indeed all, of these possibilities could be helpful to a particular patient, depending on the specific issue currently in the front line. Guided discovery encourages collaborative planning of potentially helpful experiences (e.g. 'How could you check out that idea?', 'What would have to happen/what would you need to do in order to discover the truth of that?', 'How could we find out?').

Selecting a time and a place for the experiment

Should the experiment be carried out in the session, with the therapist's guidance, or should it be done independently by the patient? If in session, should it be conducted in the consulting room, or should therapist and patient make an expedition into the outside world? The answer depends on the stage in treatment, on the purpose and nature of the experiment, and on what the patient wants and is willing to do.

Ultimately, the goal is for patients to have the courage and curiosity to conduct experiments independently in their everyday lives. Initially, however, in-session therapist-guided experiments can help patients to get started on the apparently dangerous business of operating differently and flying in the face of old, negative perspectives. Who has not had the experience of repeatedly agreeing homework with a patient, only to discover in the next session that (for a variety of reasons) nothing has been done? A single, successful in-session experiment (modelling, followed by practice with the therapist's encouragement and support) can cut through fear and procrastination and give patients the confidence to begin flying solo. Additionally, patients can often go further with their therapists than they feel able to go alone and may thus access opportunities for learning that they would otherwise be slow to reach.

'Having somebody to support me was a good thing . . . ' (Patient)

During experiments, patients are often preoccupied with feelings and fears, and processing biases may influence their perceptions, drawing attention to negative information and screening out unfamiliar, positive data. The therapist provides an objective eye, directing attention to information patients might otherwise ignore or discount, noting new predictions for testing as they emerge, spotting subtle safety behaviours that can immediately be tested, checking belief ratings and emotional state, acknowledging patients' courage, and encouraging them to go the extra step that will make the difference. Therapists also help patients to analyse what they have experienced and to consolidate new learning. Sometimes people close to the patient can subsequently be enrolled to perform the same function. The objective, as soon as practicable, is for patients to do this for themselves.

In short, in-session experiments should be viewed as a rich opportunity, rather than a last resort if the patient flatly refuses to engage in experiments at home. Therapists nonetheless sometimes hold back from in-session experiments because they can genuinely be time-consuming (an *in vivo* session might take 1½–2 hours) and difficult to arrange, especially in the high-pressure environment of routine clinical practice. Not everyone has easy access to video equipment or to stooges, and it may be necessary to travel from the office to places such as supermarkets, high buildings, crowded spaces, or wild animal habitats. Nonetheless, a single extended session, though time-consuming and inconvenient in the short term, can have major pay-offs in terms of patient gains in confidence and time saved over treatment as a whole. A two-hour session with an agoraphobic in a shopping centre, for example, can have more impact than 10 hours in the consulting room. Behaviour therapists have always recognized this; cognitive therapists might do well to emulate them.

People and resources

It is important to think through what resources are needed well in advance of carrying out experiments. 'Resources' includes equipment and record sheets, and also people and other living creatures.

Especially when tackling interpersonal difficulties such as lack of assertiveness and social anxiety (see Chapters 7 and 19), it will be necessary to involve other people in behavioural experiments, sometimes with and sometimes without their knowledge. In-session experiments might, for example, involve the therapist's colleagues, secretarial staff, and staff in the hospital canteen, not to mention unsuspecting members of the public. Experiments for homework can involve patients' partners, families, friends, colleagues, and fellow evening class attenders, as well as people unknown to them such as shop assistants, bus drivers, waiters, and the like.

When it is crucial to increase patients' confidence, people who are likely to respond benignly to them should be selected. Later in treatment, when they feel more comfortable with new perspectives, it could be helpful also to set up encounters with a wider range of people (e.g. a famously grumpy shopkeeper). Either way, others' responses can never be predicted 100%, so patients should be prepared for the fact that some people will respond adversely to them. They often assume that this must reflect something wrong with them. Pie charts can be used to generate other reasons for negative reactions (e.g. having a bad day, lack of social skills, the fact that the patient reminds them of their detested Uncle Joe).

When to plan . . . and when not to

Therapists should not assume that an experiment is not worth doing unless it has been planned in painstaking detail. There are important exceptions to the rule, illustrated by the 'green rabbit' experiment described above (p. 31), which was introduced without explanation or preamble. Off-the-cuff experiments, taking advantage of what happens to arise in a session and containing an element of surprise, are often highly effective. Therapists should keep an eye open for opportunities to take swift advantage of the spontaneous and the unpredictable, otherwise they may miss rich sources of information. This readiness is reflected in statements like: 'That's interesting. How could we find out more?', 'While we're at it, let's just see if . . .', 'Well, I wasn't expecting that. Let's work out what happened', and 'Don't stop now, go for it!'. An important message is communicated to the patient: if you keep your eyes open, the world is full of unexpected opportunities for growth. Even familiar, everyday situations can provide openings for new learning.

Giving advance warning

Therapists should think carefully about how much warning of important experiments they give to patients before the session in which these are planned to take place. If, for example, a patient with PTSD knows a week in advance that during the next session he will be expected to return to the site of the trauma, he will almost certainly engage in anticipatory processing leading to unnecessary worry and distress, and may even suddenly discover pressing business elsewhere. The result could be that he is unable to take advantage of an experience with great healing power. On the other hand, brightly announcing that one is expecting a patient to leap into a very frightening situation with no warning could undermine trust and damage the therapeutic relationship. A balance needs to be found.

Explaining the role of behavioural experiments at the outset of treatment when discussing the cognitive therapy rationale provides a general context for specific experiments. Equally, it is important when introducing particular experiments to allow plenty of time to discuss their purpose and exactly what they will involve, and to resolve patients' doubts, fears, and reservations. Patients know best how far they can go; therapists should respect their right to give informed consent, while ensuring that the potential benefits of anxiety-provoking experiences have been understood and accepted.

> 'She'd come up with an experiment but I had to come up with the particulars . . . there were no hidden surprises . . . ' (Patient)

Preparing for problems

Patients often encounter problems when carrying out experiments. In real-life situations, particularly those involving other people, it is rarely possible to eliminate the unexpected—and, after all, part of the point of a genuine experiment is that the outcome is uncertain. As far as possible, both parties should endeavour to anticipate potential problems, using questions such as: 'What problems might come up in carrying this out?', 'What difficulties do you think might arise?', and 'What might stop you doing this task?'. Problem solving can be facilitated by questions like: 'How might you deal with that?', 'What might you do to prevent that happening?', and 'What alternatives might there be?'. Initially, the therapist may take the lead in asking these questions; in the longer term, patients learn to do so for themselves.

> 'Talk it through beforehand to know what you are going to be faced with, what the worst possible scenario is, and knowing some of the strategies to get out of it . . . '
> (Patient)

Planning 'no lose' experiments

Even well-planned experiments can result in unanticipated outcomes. For this reason, it is important not to invest too heavily in a particular result, but to retain genuine open-mindedness about what may happen. Experiments should ideally be set up as 'no lose' experiences; whatever happens will be grist to the mill. If a positive outcome occurs, so much the better. If not, much can be learned about the factors keeping unhelpful ideas in place.

For example, apparently unrealistic negative automatic thoughts can turn out to be true. Discovering this can lead to effective problem solving. A depressed prison officer was considered by his therapist to be paranoid because he believed that he was being watched at work and that people were talking about him behind his back. An experiment (talking to a colleague he still trusted to some degree) revealed that he was absolutely right: his work-mates had noticed that he was not his usual self and were keeping a close eye on him. Bringing this into the open allowed him to begin receiving the support he needed at his place of work.

Assessing the impact of the experiment

What qualitative and quantitative data will allow therapist and patient to judge the impact of the experiment? Qualitatively, judging whether or not the predicted outcome has occurred is an obvious first step. It is also important to operationalize exactly what it would mean to find support for hypothesis A, or for hypothesis B. What would have to happen for a patient to conclude that an old perspective was inaccurate and unhelpful, or that a new one should be developed and explored? Specifying possible outcomes primes the patient to notice relevant aspects of experience. A patient with avoidant personality disorder, for example, was exploring a new idea—'Most people are friendly and helpful'—by repeatedly asking the way to a nearby shopping centre. He worked out with his therapist what behaviour on the part of passers-by would fit this idea (e.g. smiling, making eye-contact, stopping to talk). Initially, the therapist asked him repeatedly which of these behaviours he had observed in each encounter. With increasing confidence, he noticed them himself without prompting, and used new encounters to add to the list. This was the first step towards a sequence of experiments carried out independently in the patient's own environment.

The simplest quantitative way of assessing the impact of an experiment is to repeat 0–100% ratings of belief in target cognitions, predictions, and alternative perspectives, and ratings of intensity of associated emotions and body sensations, immediately after the experiment (and sometimes at intervals during it). These ratings provide a quick and easy way of assessing whether experience has weakened an old idea and/or strengthened a new one, and whether cognitive change is associated with relief of distress. Ratings of emotion may also demonstrate that an experiment was less upsetting in reality than in anticipation.

The extent of belief change is vital information in planning follow-up experiments. In many cases, the aim should eventually be to reduce belief in old cognitions to zero or close to zero. To facilitate this, therapists can ask questions like 'What would have to happen to bring this down to zero?' and 'What does this remaining 10% consist of?' A series of experiments, interwoven with cognitive and imaginal interventions, may be needed to reach this point. Equally, assessing changes in how far patients believe new perspectives is important.

Recording the experiment

An example of a worksheet for behavioural experiments is shown in Fig. 2.2 (other examples can be found in Butler 1999; Fennell 1999; and Greenberger and Padesky 1995). Record sheets of this kind reflect each stage of the learning process and provide a framework for approaching experiments systematically that can be used by patients between sessions and after therapy finishes. They help to highlight gaps at the planning stage, prompt patients to enter experiments alert for relevant information, and ensure that experience is approached thoughtfully and that new learning is remembered. They can become part of the patient's 'blueprint' for future action towards the end of treatment, and so aid relapse prevention.

Considerations and common pitfalls

Ideally, embarking on behavioural experiments will arouse patients' interest and curiosity, stimulating energy and inventiveness. The difficulties outlined below may prevent this from happening. If, however, they are predicted and planned for, they are less likely to disconcert therapist and patient and to stand in the way of new learning.

Date:

Identify the cognition(s) to be tested. Rate degree of belief (0–100%)

Have you identified an alternative? If so, write it down and rate degree of belief (0–100%)

Devise an experiment to test the cognition(s). What exactly will you do? Where and When? What will you watch out for?

Identify likely problems. How will you deal with them?

Outcome: What happened? What did you observe?

What have you learned? How does what happened relate to the target cognition(s) and the alternative(s)? How far do you now believe them (0–100%)?

What next? What further experiments can you do?

Fig. 2.2 Record sheet for behavioural experiments.

Aiming too high or too low

Experiments represent a challenge to prevailing perspectives, and so are likely to appear at least somewhat threatening. Patients may report anticipatory emotions such as: 'Absolutely terrifying', 'Nervous', 'Uneasy', 'Trepidation'.

Aiming too high can provoke intense emotion that prevents learning; aiming too low encourages stasis. In both cases, discouragement and demoralization can ensue. The level of challenge needs to be discussed and selected so that it appears manageable, while extending the patient's range. If necessary, confidence and independence can be fostered by approaching difficult challenges in a graded way through a series of less threatening experiments, with each stage of the process negotiated with the patient. So patients might move from observing modelling by the therapist to taking action, from in-session to between-session experiments, from stooges to strangers, from simulation or role play to real life, and from reliance on the therapist's support and guidance to independence.

'It was not overwhelming, I was not doing everything at once, I think it was the careful staging of it that was most useful . . . ' (Patient)

Predictions that are hard to test

It can be difficult to construct experiments if the predicted outcome is not easy to test. For example, some people with OCD are frightened by predictions of harm that may not occur for many years, or even only after death (e.g. being condemned to damnation for blasphemous thoughts). Some people with psychosis believe that God is punishing them. Other patients may only have problems in specific situations, such as job interviews, that can be simulated in role play but are less easy to arrange *in vivo.*

In such cases, therapists need to identify blocks to constructing an experiment, and find alternative ways of dealing with them. For instance, the patient with OCD could consider theories about causality, make specific, contingent connections rather than spurious links between events, or define an alternative perspective (hypothesis B) and find ways of testing it (see Chapter 5). The patient with psychosis might need to spend extended time in purely cognitive work, considering the evidence for and against such a view, before embarking on related experiments (see Chapter 12). For the patient who has problems with job interviews, the therapist might need to approach organizations that offer interview coaching or set up mock interviews at the local job centre.

Failing to take account of patients' reservations

It is crucial to explore patients' reservations about behavioural experiments at the planning stage. Therapists' failures to note reservations and anxiety-provoking predictions can lead patients to decide against experiments that might have proved helpful. It is important to be alert for concerns expressed non-verbally, hesitantly, or at unexpected points in time, and to ask for reservations even when none are spontaneously put forward. It is particularly important to check whether patients have fully understood the rationale for an experiment, and whether they actually want to do it, otherwise there is a risk that they will feel bullied. This can happen, for example, if therapists are working under time pressure and unintentionally become more didactic. Furthermore, patients' reservations may be justified: behavioural experiments may arouse high levels of emotion and may not work out as hoped. This needs to be acknowledged and prepared for.

Reservations can feel to therapists like inconvenient impediments to the smooth flow of therapy. In fact, they often reflect doubts and concerns that are holding the patient back in a more general sense. If handled sensitively and with respect, they provide valuable opportunities to explore problem maintenance, strengthen the therapeutic alliance, and introduce learning principles that will prove helpful elsewhere (e.g. 'If it is too hard, look for a smaller step', 'Be open minded—it may not be as bad as you think').

Therapists' reservations

Therapists too may have reservations about conducting behavioural experiments (e.g. standing up to an aggressor, or returning to the site of a trauma) and should address these through supervision, or they may hinder the progress of treatment.

'[Not helpful for the therapist to be] pussyfooting around . . . ' (Patient)

Therapists may find themselves doing experiments out of a sense of duty rather than a conviction that they will work. We recommend that they experience the potential of experiments by trying them for themselves, either to work on personal concerns or to test the efficacy of incorporating experiments into their clinical practice (Bennett–Levy 2003a). Finally, it is important to persist with behavioural experiments rather than giving up too soon. It is easy to feel disheartened after a single experiment when little has changed, but once may well not be enough. People often need repeated experiences in order to learn effectively, especially if their difficulties are entrenched.

Legitimate doubts

Therapists may legitimately be wary of embarking prematurely on experiments when establishing trust and engagement is difficult—for example, when working with some people with severe eating disorders, those experiencing psychotic problems, and those with histories of abuse. Particular care should be taken in selecting the methods used for experiments (e.g. videotaping might remind a patient of past abuse). Where legitimate doubts exist, it may be useful to assess with the patient the advantages and disadvantages of doing a particular experiment at a particular stage in treatment. If there is likely to be no net gain, or a substantial risk of destabilizing the therapeutic relationship or making things worse, the experiment should be deferred until circumstances have changed or the possibility of alternative perspectives has been opened up by more extensive cognitive work. The experiment could be dropped completely if this does not happen.

Resolving difficulties in the relationship

Behavioural experiments can be challenging for patients, and embarking on them may therefore highlight difficulties in the therapeutic relationship such as misunderstandings, lack of trust, or unwillingness to take independent action. Some of these difficulties can be pre-empted by openness on the part of the therapist about the nature and function of experiments, and by careful checking for understanding and for the patient's reactions to what is proposed. Sometimes, however, difficulties reflect enduring dysfunctional patterns of relating, which also affect other relationships, and need to be addressed in their own right.

> 'Confidence with the person that you're doing the experiment with has got to be top priority . . . confidence that they know how to react . . . confidence that they're not going to roll around on the floor laughing at you . . . ' (Patient)

Physical health issues

It may be unwise for pregnant women and people with physical health problems (such as asthma and heart conditions) to perform some behavioural experiments (e.g. deliberate over-breathing to induce panic symptoms). Experiments involving strenuous physical exercise may also be inadvisable for some physically ill or unhealthy people. If therapist or patient are concerned that an experiment could be physically risky, a medical opinion should always be sought. Ideally, medical investigation should precede cognitive therapy for panic, health anxiety, chronic fatigue, and other symptoms that might have a genuine physical basis or have serious implications for physical health (e.g. anorexia nervosa): see the relevant chapters for more information.

4. Experience: the experiment itself

If an experiment is to be carried out independently by the patient as a between-session assignment, then once planning is completed the therapist's role is over until they meet again to discuss the outcome. If, however, the experiment is carried out in session, the therapist can help the patient to make the most of the experience in a number of ways. These can be transmitted to patients as sessions progress, so that they become accustomed to being their own therapists when conducting experiments. A checklist of relevant questions for use by therapist and patient is provided in the box below.

Checklist for the experiencing phase

- ◆ (Patient) Do you feel confident enough to embark on the experiment? What further encouragement or support would you find helpful?
- ◆ Are you prepared for full engagement in the experiment, with mindful awareness of what is going on?
- ◆ Have you prepared reminders of what to do and what to look out for during the experiment (e.g. flashcards, worksheets)?

(continued)

Checklist for the experiencing phase *(continued)*

- Are you checking changes in degree of belief in target cognitions, predictions, and alternative perspectives as the experiment proceeds?
- Are you carefully monitoring changes in emotional state?
- Are you alert for cognitions and safety behaviours that might become apparent only once the experiment is under way?
- Are you on the look out for unexpected events and opportunities?
- Have you worked out how to avoid discouragement if all does not go well?
- Have you decided when and how to discuss the experiment (debriefing) so as to protect confidentiality?
- (Therapist) Are you comfortable with accompanying the patient outside the consulting room?

Building morale

Therapists should openly acknowledge the courage it takes to confront old ways of thinking and behaving. Support encourages patients to face difficult situations and to persist when the going gets tough. They may find it hard to give themselves due credit for experiments involving everyday activities (e.g. going on the bus, talking to a sales assistant, cleaning out the cupboard under the stairs). The therapist's genuine praise can help them gradually to see these for the real achievements they are. Where negative beliefs are deeply entrenched, this may be a very slow process. It can be helpful to explore the thinking that blocks change (e.g. 'How come I see this differently from you?', 'What am I paying attention to that you are missing?', 'What biases might be operating here?').

'I found it sort of liberating . . . it gave me encouragement . . . ' (Patient)

'You go through lots of emotions, but coming out of the other side you feel a bit better about yourself . . . ' (Patient)

Encouraging full engagement

For an experiment to work, the patient must be fully immersed in the experience, rather than going through the motions or avoiding it in subtle ways. Prevailing biases in thinking will otherwise distort perception and recall. Therapists can promote mindful awareness through guided discovery (e.g. 'What did you just notice?', 'What's running through your mind right now?', 'What's happening to your anxiety?', 'What do you observe around you?').

> 'Living it, breathing it, seeing it, smelling it, you can't bend it in any other way . . .'
> (Patient)

Providing reminders

During in-session experiments, therapists can help patients to recall the rationale for an experiment when emotion is running high, maintain focus on the target cognitions (especially hypothesis B), and observe what is happening as objectively as possible, in particular searching for evidence that will counter old, unhelpful views. The same function can be fulfilled by flashcards written by the patient when experiments are carried out independently.

> 'My perception of what was going to happen was totally counter to what actually did happen . . .' (Patient)

> 'It seemed like pounding in the blindingly obvious . . . but that was necessary to try and change my habitual ways of thinking . . .' (Patient)

Being sensitive to emotional state

It is crucial to be aware of the emotions felt during experiments, and for therapists to be sensitive to non-verbal signs of emotional state. If the patient becomes extremely anxious or upset, it may be as well for them to withdraw from the situation, at least briefly. If on the other hand a patient is inexplicably calm and cheerful, it is worth investigating whether this is because the experiment is insufficiently challenging, or because disengagement or safety behaviours are preventing them from making full use of the experience.

Emotional state can be an indicator of cognitive change and should follow (for example) the realization that (against expectation) a feared consequence has not occurred and will not occur. Monitoring emotional state will tell therapist and patient whether the experiment has 'bitten'. If patients feel no different, their thinking has probably not changed. Reasons for this will need to be explored and acted on, perhaps by extending the current experiment, or by thinking ahead to another that would have greater emotional impact.

Remaining flexible

Even carefully planned experiments do not always work out as expected. Approaching opportunities for experiential learning with flexibility means that any experience is potentially valuable. Responding flexibly to the unexpected can often be done playfully and with humour, provided the relationship between therapist and patient is sound and there is no danger that the patient will feel belittled or ridiculed. Humour stimulates decentring from the problem, and a lightness of mood is helpful in encouraging curiosity and willingness to have a go.

Therapist and patient should be alert for cognitions that have not previously come to light and emerge only in the real situation. Testing these can then become part of the experiment. Equally, they should watch out for safety behaviours which have not previously been noticed or reported, and ensure that these are dropped. A man who feared that others would attack him carried out an experiment asking people in the street what time it was. After he had successfully approached five people, he told the therapist he thought it was time to go home now. The therapist was surprised, as things seemed to be going so well. It turned out that the patient thought that what had happened so far was a fluke, but that if he 'pushed his luck' he would be attacked for sure. Had he been alone, he would indeed have gone home at this point. With the therapist's support, he was able to ask another 20 people (including young males of whom he was particularly afraid) and his belief that he would be attacked began to crumble.

It is also important to be flexible about altering a planned experiment if it turns out not be helpful, for example because it is too easy or too difficult. A woman who feared ridicule by shop assistants if she asked any questions about what she planned to buy agreed to try the experiment in a particular shop. When it came to the point, she baulked. She was, however, willing to observe the therapist inquire repetitively and at tedious length about a television, while the shop assistant remained unfailingly courteous and friendly. Afterwards, she said the assistant could have been an exception, so they went to another shop—and then another, and another. The patient's comment was: 'Well, of course they'll be polite to *you*, but if it was *me*, things would be different'. To which the therapist's response was: 'I'm not sure. How could we find out?'

Monitoring progress

Finally, it is important to check belief ratings repeatedly, so as to monitor the rate of change. 'What would have to happen?' and 'What would you need to do to take that further?' are useful questions.

Considerations and common pitfalls
Retreat with honour

If things go badly wrong, patients need to be able to back off without losing face or becoming demoralized and giving up altogether. An avoidant patient, in the middle of an extended session at a shopping centre, became very distressed when trying to ask a shop assistant for help, and walked out of the shop, threatening to go home. The therapist put the experiment on hold, and over a coffee they tried to understand what had happened. The patient tried to repeat the experiment, but had to stop again. At a subsequent review, the patient acknowledged that, although it had been an upsetting experience, he could see that it made sense in terms of the formulation. The therapist then realized that further work was needed on the patient's core beliefs. They had been in danger of missing this; before the experiment the patient had glossed over the extent to which his beliefs distressed and disabled him in public places. Thus in the end the experiment was valuable.

When therapists are present, they can help patients to respond constructively to 'failures', whereas patients carrying out experiments on their own may have more difficulty. Therapists would do well to ensure that patients recognize that experiments can go wrong, and that knowing when to back off, rethink, and try another angle is a valuable skill.

Confidentiality

Issues of confidentiality may also arise when carrying out experiments in public places. It is important that what is happening is not obvious to nearby members of the public. This may mean, for example, that detailed discussion of thoughts and feelings should wait until therapist and patient return to a more private place. At the least, they should be careful to keep their voices down—revealing intimate material to the passengers on the bus or the people in the supermarket queue is unlikely to be beneficial. That said, therapists working in the UK have a major advantage: cultural norms are such that they could take all their clothes off, paint themselves pink, and sing the National Anthem without appearing to attract the slightest attention!

In vivo experiments and the therapeutic relationship

Therapists should bear in mind that engaging in in-session *in vivo* experiments may affect the therapeutic relationship. Extended expeditions to real-life situations include time which is not spent 'on task' (e.g. travel time, time taken to walk from one experimental setting to another). This means that the real relationship (the extent to which they like each other or have interests in common) can come into focus, having until then been more or less ignored by both parties.

Within the consulting room, boundaries are relatively clear. Appropriate boundaries for time 'off task' have not to our knowledge been discussed in the literature. What are acceptable topics of conversation, for example, when driving to the site of a road traffic accident some distance away? Should the therapist remain silent unless discussing matters immediately relevant to therapy?

What should she do if she meets a friend or a member of her family when out with a patient? Should they be introduced? If so, how?

Outside the consulting room, the line between clinical and social interaction blurs. The nature of the relationship may also shift when patients observe their therapists, on their behalf, repeatedly entering situations they would fear to approach, or doing things they would find it embarrassing to do. It goes without saying that the therapist retains responsibility for the patient's well-being and safety as a first priority, and must maintain professional objectivity, but in some senses the terms of the therapeutic alliance are renegotiated (if only implicitly) once therapist and patient step out of the consulting room door. It is therefore worth paying careful attention to professional boundaries.

5. Observation: examining what happened

Observation means closely reviewing what happened in the course of an experiment, rather than seeking to establish what it means (reflection). It involves assessing whether an experiment has affected target cognitions and emotional state. Whether or not the experiment was carried out in the therapist's company, the task is for the patient thoughtfully to recall and analyse what happened in as much detail as possible. This careful analysis provides the information necessary for understanding and change. A checklist for the observation phase, for patients and/or therapists, is provided in the box below.

Checklist for the observation phase

- Have you determined what to observe (thoughts, feelings, body sensations, behaviour, others' behaviour, the environment)?
- Do you have a means of recording changes in belief ratings and emotional state and the outcome of the experiment?
- Are you listening with an acute ear for biases in memory and how events are reported?
- Are you watching out for residual safety behaviours?
- Have you investigated the reasons for partial changes and decided what further work is needed?
- Have you examined the reasons for negative outcomes and worked out how to deal with them?
- Have you explored doubts and reservations about what has been observed?

What to observe

Observation covers:

- ◆ Patients' thoughts and feelings before, during, and after the experiment (with particular attention to biases in perception and interpretation)
- ◆ Significant changes in body state or sensations
- ◆ Behaviour, including use of safety behaviours and other self-protective measures that may make it difficult to be open to new experiences
- ◆ What patients noticed about other people involved in the situation, especially in relation to themselves
- ◆ Relevant aspects of the environment (e.g. how big a space was, how crowded a room was, how fierce a dog was, how busy a road was)
- ◆ The outcome of the experiment, including the impact of changes in the patient's thinking or behaviour.

Recording the impact of the experiment

Keeping a written record of experiments, ideally while they are still fresh in the mind, makes the task of observation much easier. Initially, it may be difficult for patients to engage in new ways of thinking and behaving, and at the same time to take careful note of what happens. With practice, action and observation can occur simultaneously. In itself, completing record sheets requires patients to think carefully about what they have observed. Sheets brought to therapy sessions provide the therapist with accurate information on the extent of changes and what has been learned since the last session.

> 'I felt very positive, I was very pleased with myself and came back immediately, opened my little achievement book and wrote that down . . . ' (Patient)

This is the time to re-rate degree of belief in target cognitions and the intensity of emotions triggered by them. In addition, qualitative data are helpful in assessing the impact of experiments: what went well, what did not go so well, what has the patient learned, any other comments they may have. Feedback on outcome from other sources should also be taken into account (e.g. the number or proportion of people who said 'X' in a survey, ratings and comments from stooges).

> 'All the fears that I had didn't sort of materialise and we tried to build on that . . . ' (Patient)

Active listening

The therapist needs to strike a balance between attending empathically to the patient's story and listening for possible biases in attentional focus, perception, interpretation, and memory which might influence their report. It may be important to distinguish between what the patient felt happened (e.g. 'I made a complete fool of myself') and what actually happened (e.g. 'How do you know?', 'What reactions did you notice?', 'How many people laughed at you, or refused to have anything further to do with you?'). At the same time, it is important that such close inquiry is set in a context of acknowledging the patient's perspective and feelings, or damage will be done to the therapeutic alliance.

'She'd maybe ask me stuff so that I say it out loud to reinforce it for me . . . ' (Patient)

Considerations and common pitfalls

Safety behaviours strike again

Therapists should watch out for any sign that the experiment was experienced as a 'near miss', or that the patient would be reluctant to repeat it. Both of these can be signs that safety behaviours are still in use, and that the patient senses that without them disaster might have occurred. This can be checked out with the patient: 'I notice that you have been left with the feeling that it was OK this time, but next time could be different. Is that right? What's happening there? Was there anything you did to stop the worst from happening?' If the answer is 'Yes', the therapist can check that the patient truly understands the unhelpfulness of safety behaviours, and how they operate to keep the problem going and prevent change. Their continuing use is often a marker of the extent to which the patient still finds the old, negative perspective convincing. It may be that more cognitive work needs to be done on creating an alternative, or it could be that a smaller-scale experiment is required to get the ball rolling, or an experiment guided by the therapist who can help the patient to drop remaining safety behaviours.

'Yes, but . . . '

Doubts and reservations about the validity of the outcome of experiments sometimes emerge during the observation phase. Therapists should welcome expression of doubts and view them as an opportunity for further exploration or for testing them in their own right.

Partial change

If an experiment has been successful, both belief in target cognitions and the intensity of painful emotions will have declined, while belief in alternative perspectives will have increased. If not, therapist and patient need to explore the reasons for lack of change and think ahead to further experiments and perhaps a change of tack. Sometimes intellectual appreciation of the outcome of an experiment is not matched by emotional change. This can happen, for example, after an observational experiment that the patient feels has provided useful information, but is not necessarily directly personally relevant. In this case, it makes sense to move immediately to an active experiment, ideally *in vivo*, where the patient will have an opportunity to discover for himself how meaningful the findings are. Sometimes, on the other hand, partial change may simply reflect the operation of a longstanding belief or thought pattern, which has been frequently and repeatedly rehearsed and requires repeated disconfirmation through successive experiments before stable, substantial cognitive or emotional change can occur. One swallow does not always make a summer.

Half full or half empty

Processing biases can result in patients focusing on what did not go well in experiments, to the exclusion of successes. A claustrophobic patient, for example, experimented with driving into a car wash, where she anticipated feeling trapped. She did indeed have a panic attack, and returned to therapy the following week feeling very disappointed. Investigation revealed that, although it was true that she had panicked, she had nonetheless managed to drop all her safety behaviours, and the panic had lasted only 3–4 minutes, instead of going on for ever as she had feared. She then felt more hopeful and willing to try again. So careful inquiry, while not denying genuine difficulties and shortcomings, sets them within the context of the experiment as a whole and helps the patient to see the bigger picture.

Predictions come true

When negative predictions turn out to be true, it is important to return to the formulation to make sense of what has happened. For example, the patient's perspective may have acted as a 'self-fulfilling prophecy', leading her to behave in ways that appeared to demonstrate its truth. For example, a patient with low self-esteem and an impoverished social network joined an aerobics class in order to meet people. She predicted that, if she approached people in the class, they would want nothing to do with her, and this would reflect her lack of worth. As an experiment, she invited someone for a drink after the class but they refused. She became very upset and stopped attending. In her next therapy session, she sifted through the incident with her therapist. She realized that her shyness might have made her seem gruff, that there might have been many reasons why the person could not meet her for a drink, and that, even if this person refused, another person might not. Thus, close observation of what has happened can help to illuminate unhelpful patterns, further clarify the formulation, and develop ideas for new ways of operating in future that can then be tried out in further experiments.

6. Reflection: making sense of the experiment

The purpose of reflection is to understand what the experiment means. This takes review beyond pure observation. It involves making sense of new experience and relating it to pre-existing knowledge, as well as identifying the underlying principles of change that account for its success. The checklist in the box below outlines issues relevant to the reflection phase.

Checklist for the reflection phase

- Have you determined the meaning of the experiment? What questions will help you to do so?
- Have you worked out the implications of the experiment for pre-existing ideas (specific predictions and target cognitions; other thoughts, assumptions, and beliefs; the formulation)?
- Have you made sure that what has been learned in this particular experiment will be carried forward into new situations and across time (generalization)?
- Have you allowed plenty of time for discussion?
- Have you explored reactions to the experiment fully (feedback), including summarizing what has been learned, and reservations?
- Have you made sure that new learning has been consolidated? When will you review?

Determining the meaning of the experiment

Guided discovery helps therapist and patient to explore the significance of what has happened. What does the patient make of it? What does it tell her about the situation in which the experiment was carried out? How might she approach it another time? More broadly, what does it tell her about herself? About other people? About the way the world works? About helpful and unhelpful strategies for managing distress, or relating to others, or achieving her goals? Were there any surprises? Did people react as she anticipated? Did she? What does she make of that? Were there any difficulties, or blocks, or things that went wrong? How can those be understood?

'She'd notice stuff in the things I said and I'd realise it was worth concentrating on . . .'
(Patient)

Relating outcome to previous knowledge and ideas

It is important to make explicit links between new observations and pre-existing ideas, so that the patient has a hook to hang fresh experiences on. How does what happened fit with the patient's original predictions? Have they been borne out, or does new evidence contradict them? How does the outcome relate to old perspectives (hypothesis A) and to new alternatives (hypothesis B)? Which provides a better explanation of what happened? Does the experiment support a new thought, assumption, or belief? If so, what is it? More broadly, how does what happened in the experiment (including difficulties the patient experienced) relate to the current formulation of the patient's problems? Does it suggest any changes in how his difficulties can be understood?

> 'After each one we had a little talk about how did that go . . . and then at the end we came back and said let's see how the reality has compared to your belief beforehand . . . ' (Patient)

Achieving generalization

Relating experiments to existing knowledge structures is one way of ensuring generalization from the specific experiment, particularly if broad cognitive structures (assumptions, beliefs) are taken into account. Explicit identification of the principles of change is also important, as it helps patients to set up future experiments successfully, not only during therapy, but afterwards. Through experiments, patients are learning how to learn. This is why a clear rationale and repeated signposting (clarifying what is being done, and why) are helpful—they clarify the steps which patients need to follow in order to take responsibility for continuing change.

Considerations and common pitfalls

Rushing

It is worth taking plenty of time to reflect on experiments, rather than rushing on to the next thing. Experiments are challenging, and take time and effort. Equal effort in their analysis ensures that every ounce of learning is extracted from each experience.

Failing to ask the patient for feedback

Even after successful experiments, patients may experience doubts or fall back into interpreting what has happened in the light of old ideas. Asking them to summarize what they have learned and new perspectives they have developed, and to describe them to the therapist, can help to identify continuing difficulties in abandoning old perspectives. If the old perspective has been in place for some while, and the patient has consistently acted as if it was true, it will take time for a new perspective to be solidly established.

Assuming once is enough

Reflection may need to be repeated in order to consolidate new ideas. Reflection immediately after an experiment can be reiterated at the end of the session, reviewed by the patient at the end of each day for homework, and returned to in the following session. What may seem initially like a lasting insight can disappear subsequently; for example, if an old belief is activated by subsequent events. Written summaries of key points can help to keep them in the patient's mind and later become part of the therapy 'blueprint'.

> 'Probably the most helpful thing was writing it down actually because it meant if I had a low moment I could think, I could read back what I'd written or think over what I'd done or carry it out again . . . ' (Patient)

Multiple 'Yes, but . . . 's

If at this stage, or any other, it becomes plain that a patient is constantly bombarded by doubts, reservations, and fresh negative thoughts, it may be most helpful to teach him or her to become aware of this process and to practise stepping back from it ('There's another one of those'), rather than attempting to question each one as it arises. A change at the level of metacognition may be more elegant and effective than repeated attempts to alter specific cognitions (Wells 2000).

7. Planning: following up the experiment

Here we return to our starting point: preparing for an experiment. In this case, planning stems directly from what has emerged as the learning process unfolds. Planning is now intended to encourage thinking ahead, as is often

Checklist for the next planning phase

- ♦ What are the practical implications of new understanding? How can it be translated into changes in thinking and behaviour on a day-to-day basis?
- ♦ How can progress be carried forward through new experiments?
- ♦ What else needs to be discovered/investigated/tested?
- ♦ What needs to be done? How exactly will action be taken?
- ♦ What is the next experiment?

illustrated under the heading of 'Further work' in the experiments described in later chapters. Questions like those in the box above may be helpful to therapist and patient.

'It was useful afterwards because you can observe and find out more about it . . . ' (Patient)

Conclusion

In this chapter, we have related the use of behavioural experiments in cognitive therapy to the process of adult learning, and showed how the Lewin–Kolb learning circle provides a practical framework for the step-by-step process of achieving cognitive and emotional change by carrying out behavioural experiments. We have provided detailed guidelines for each element in the process, highlighting key steps and common pitfalls. In the rest of the book, we shall show how these ideas play out in the cognitive therapy of specific problem areas. We end the chapter with some views from patients on the value of behavioural experiments in CBT:

'They [behavioural experiments] are the pinnacle really . . . '

'When you get into the nitty-gritty of it you become a pioneer and you're off . . . '

'It's proper feedback; that's the best you can get . . . '

'I don't think they [behavioural experiments] would work without all the theory behind it but on the whole I'd say they were the most important part [of CBT] . . . '

'I can see that I have moved on, whereas to begin with I didn't think there was any hope for me really . . . '

(Patients)

CHAPTER 3

Panic disorder and agoraphobia*

Ann Hackmann

Introduction

In DSM-IV-TR (APA 2000) a panic attack is defined as a sudden increase in anxiety, accompanied by four or more of a list of symptoms such as palpitations, breathlessness, and dizziness. The term panic disorder is reserved for individuals with recurrent panic attacks, some of which are unexpected. Agoraphobia is not a codeable disorder, but is defined as anxiety about being in places or situations from which escape might be difficult or embarrassing in the event of a panic attack or panic-like symptoms.

Cognitive model

There are several models of panic disorder, the best known being the approach described by Clark (1986). This model suggests that people who suffer from panic attacks do so because they have a relatively enduring tendency to misinterpret bodily sensations (particularly anxiety symptoms) as indicative of an imminent physical or mental catastrophe. Safety behaviours and selective attention maintain the disorder (Clark 1999). Cognitive therapy aims to remove this tendency to misinterpret symptoms (see Clark 1986; Wells 1997). Published studies suggest a high success rate (e.g. Clark *et al.* 1994, 1999; Beck *et al.* 1992; Arntz and Van den Hout 1996; Westling and Ost 1999).

The studies listed above were carried out with patients with only mild to moderate agoraphobia. There are few studies of cognitive interventions in more severe agoraphobia. However, it has been shown that patients receiving 'cognitively delivered exposure treatment' (in which subjects carried out numerous behavioural experiments) achieved higher end-state functioning than those receiving an equivalent amount of exposure delivered in a more traditional manner (Salkovskis *et al.* in preparation). This small treatment trial built on earlier experimental work. (Salkovskis *et al.* 1999) This chapter will be divided into two parts, the first dealing with panic disorder, and the second with agoraphobia.

* With behavioural experiments from Anne Beaton and Martina Mueller.

Panic disorder

Key cognitions in panic disorder

The physical and mental catastrophes feared in panic disorder are numerous, and are usually experienced as imminent. Patients may fear fainting, falling, vomiting, having a stroke, going crazy, having a heart attack, becoming paralysed with fear, not being able to walk properly, suffocating, dying, or being suddenly incapacitated in some other way. There can also be some overlap with hypochondriasis, in which the feared catastrophe is seen as likely to occur at some time further in the future, when the current symptoms of hypothesized disease culminate in severe illness or death. Dizziness or blurred vision may be seen as an early symptom of a brain tumour, and this interpretation may cause an exacerbation of anxiety, and hence of worrying symptoms, leading to a panic attack.

Typical safety behaviours

Safety behaviours are behaviours the patient engages in to ensure that the feared catastrophe does not occur. These include avoidance of certain situations, and a host of other small behaviours designed to abort symptoms and catastrophes. These include holding on to things or people, deliberate changes in breathing pattern, distraction, etc. It has been demonstrated (Salkovskis 1991) that there are logical links between safety behaviours and catastrophic beliefs in panic disorder. Thus, a person who fears that they are about to have a heart attack or a stroke will slow down or stop, whilst someone who fears that they are about to be paralysed by fear will keep moving. People who fear impending insanity may use distraction to control their thoughts, and may also keep tight control over their behaviour.

Triggers for panic attacks

A huge variety of stimuli can trigger a panic attack. People with panic disorder will be acutely attuned to their bodies and prone to notice immediately any physiological changes, which they interpret as signs of impending catastrophe. These might include feeling hot, heart pounding or missing a beat, dizziness, visual disturbance, feeling wobbly, racing thoughts, de-realization, and many other sensations. The causes of these trigger symptoms can also be hugely varied and could include physical exertion, too much coffee, a hot day, a nightmare, or emotions like anger or excitement. The initial symptoms can be spotted so rapidly and the misinterpretation is often made and followed by anxiety symptoms so swiftly that it may seem to the patient that the attack has come out of the blue.

Treatment of panic disorder

Treatment involves generating alternative, less catastrophic, credible explanations for the causes and consequences of the symptoms of which the patient is so fearful, and from which they try to protect themselves by avoiding triggers and carrying out safety behaviours. Detailed accounts of the structure of treatment are given in the references cited above.

Special considerations

The model suggests that people with panic disorder are very afraid of their symptoms and do not understand what is causing them. Therapy may involve asking the patient to do something in order to evoke the frightening symptoms and test their consequences. Understandably, patients will be reluctant to deliberately evoke symptoms which they assume may be lethal or otherwise catastrophic. There are various ways to handle this:

1 If the patient is fairly well engaged, and has a measure of trust, it may be beneficial not to explain in advance that this manoeuvre may evoke the symptoms. This can be helpful in two respects: firstly, the patient is likely to be less reluctant, and secondly, the symptoms evoked are more likely to be unexpected and therefore frightening, and hence seen as more similar to those experienced during a panic attack. The patient may quickly become distressed, and it is important to spend ample time reflecting and debriefing, as described in the example below. Before conducting such an experiment the ground will usually be prepared by verbal discussion. This means that the therapist can then refer back to alternative, non-catastrophic theories about the causes and consequences of their symptoms, and help the patient reflect on which theory is best supported by their experience during the experiment.

2 If it seems that the relationship may be damaged by not being open, explain the rationale. This may mean that the patient holds back, or finds the experience only mildly reminiscent of panic (because the patient knows what is causing the symptoms, and how to stop them). Again, these aspects will need to be addressed, using questions such as 'So those experiences were similar to those in your panic attacks, but not exactly the same—what would the experience have been like if those symptoms had come on out of the blue?'

3 It may help to do the experiment with the patient, so that both of you evoke symptoms that can be compared. The therapist can even start to evoke the symptoms some seconds before indicating to the patient that he should start, so that he can observe how the therapist reacts.

4 If all else fails, it is useful for the therapist alone to bring on the symptoms first, to demonstrate their normal, harmless (though unpleasant) quality.

Caution!

One of the best ways to evoke panic symptoms is to ask the patient to breathe the way they do in a panic attack (i.e. more quickly or deeply than normal). For most people this is unpleasant but harmless. However, hyperventilation is not advisable for people who are pregnant or suffering from conditions such as asthma, epilepsy, or cardiac complaints. There should be no doubts about the health of the patient if embarking on these experiments. However, the treatment can be skilfully adapted to help patients with co-existing physical problems to challenge their catastrophic beliefs without endangering their health.

In a very small minority of people prolonged hyperventilation can give rise to tetany (muscle spasms). If this occurs to a significant extent the patient can be taught slow, controlled breathing to reverse the effect. The symptoms are unpleasant but not dangerous.

Behavioural experiments

- ◆ **Experiments to discover the true causes of frightening symptoms and their triggers**
  Experiment 3.1: to discover a benign cause of rapid heart rate
- ◆ **Experiments to discover the true consequences of not carrying out safety behaviours**
  Experiment 3.2: to determine the consequences of feeling wobbly
- ◆ **Experiments to discover what happens if symptoms are deliberately exaggerated**
  Experiment 3.3: testing the effects of exaggerating dizziness
- ◆ **Experiments to test whether safety behaviours are making things worse**
  Experiment 3.4: testing the effects of exaggerating a safety behaviour (tensing legs)

Other possible behavioural experiments in each category are presented in Tables 3.1, 3.2, 3.3, and 3.4.

Ascertaining the causes of frightening symptoms

Experiment 3.1: to examine a benign cause of rapid heart rate

Problem Ellen had a long history of panic disorder and agoraphobia. Her mother had died a year before treatment started. After that her fears increased significantly—she was unable to venture out unless accompanied by one of her children or her husband, and had become depressed. Her first husband and her mother both died of a heart attack. She was afraid that she would die in the same way, and scanned her body for physical symptoms to support this belief. She also believed that if she felt hot or dizzy during a panic attack she would faint.

Target cognition 'When I get palpitations (i.e. my heart beats more quickly), this is a sign of heart disease, and indicates that I am going to have a heart attack.'

Alternative perspective An increase in heart rate may be the result of lots of benign things, such as an increase in exercise, anxiety, stress, or too much caffeine.

Experiment The patient was asked to run up and down stairs with the therapist for one minute.

Rationale (not explained in advance) An increase in heart rate is the body's way of coping with the extra demands placed on it. In terms of stress or anxiety, it is the body's natural response to an increase in adrenaline, preparing an organism for 'fight or flight'.

Reflection Ellen's heart rate increased and she was out of breath. The therapist described similar sensations. Ellen noted the similarity between these symptoms and those she experienced in a panic attack or when under stress, even though she was less frightened because she understood what was causing them. Ellen was then asked several questions:

- What did she make of the fact that both she and the therapist experienced the same physical sensations?
- What did she make of the fact that symptoms similar to those experienced during a panic attack could be brought on by exercise?
- What did she make of the fact that she didn't have a heart attack despite feeling this way?
- What did she make of the fact that although she kept exercising she did not have a heart attack and her symptoms reached a plateau?

The therapist explained that this experiment was carried out to see whether there might be less frightening explanations for some of her symptoms. It was suggested that Ellen might like to ask a friend to do this experiment and see what happened. She was also asked to reflect on what effect this experiment had on her belief that an increase in heart rate always has a serious cause.

Tip If the symptoms induced had not been seen as similar to those in panic, the therapist would have moved the session on. This format can be used in any experiment where the aim is to help the person discover the true causes of symptoms. Usually it is best to explain the rationale after the test rather than before, as this enhances the likelihood that the patient will be prepared to make the test, and increases the chance that the element of surprise will create a more similar experience to that observed in panic.

A set of similar experiments to discover benign causes for symptoms is laid out in Table 3.1.

Discovering the true consequences of symptoms when safety behaviours are not carried out

People with panic disorder feel they have good reasons for believing that catastrophe may strike, and are therefore motivated to protect themselves by engaging in safety behaviours. Then if no physical or mental catastrophe ensues they are likely to conclude that the precautions they took were necessary and effective, or that they had a lucky escape. The experiments described here are to investigate what happens if the symptoms once evoked are allowed to continue, without the use of safety behaviours. The rationale is explained in advance: as providing an opportunity for the patient to discover if it is worth putting so much effort into preventing a catastrophe that may not occur.

Experiment 3.2: to determine the consequences of feeling wobbly

Problem Sally was 36 years old and suffering from panic disorder with agoraphobia, depression, social anxiety, and an eating disorder. She had been unemployed for two years, following a row at work.

Target cognition 'I feel wobbly when I panic. If I do not hang on to someone or something I will collapse or fall over.'

Alternative perspective 'The wobbliness is just a feeling. I do not need to control it—I will not end up collapsing or falling down.'

Prediction 'If I let go of my shopping trolley (or my husband's arm) when I feel panicky I will fall or collapse.'

Experiment Sally usually went shopping with her husband. She stayed with the trolley and he went to get the food. In this experiment, Sally went into the supermarket where she often felt panicky. She pushed a trolley into the shop and left it in an aisle. She then walked along several aisles alone, which would

Table 3.1 Experiments to determine the benign causes of symptoms

Problematic symptom	Target cognition (theory A)	Alternative view (theory B)	Test theory B	Results of experiment	Reflection and conclusion
Dizzy and light-headed	I must be ill	These are harmless, normal symptoms of over-breathing which could happen to anyone	Patient and therapist breathe rapidly for several minutes, as in patient's panic attacks; observe symptoms	Symptoms similar to those in panic are quickly produced in both therapist and patient	Breathing in excess of requirements produces these harmless symptoms in anyone
Chest pain	Heart trouble	Intercostal muscles (like other muscles) go into harmless spasm if held under tension for too long	Hold air in lungs and breathe rapidly without fully letting go of air	Chest starts to ache; the same thing happens to therapist	Chest pain due to normal spasm in chest muscles
Sudden rush of symptoms	I'm dying or ill	Anxiety symptoms, triggered by frightening thoughts	Asked to read a list of pairs of words (i.e. symptoms and catastrophes)	Patient feels strange and has a rush of unpleasant symptoms	Symptoms are triggered by fears (e.g. thoughts of illness and death)
Disturbance in visual field (sense of movement)	Brain tumour, stroke, etc.	Illusion of movement in response to striped patterns (e.g. floor tiles, blinds, lines of text)	Hold visual grid or other striped pattern in front of eyes and move it gently	Sensation of movement occurs; therapist has the same experience	The visual disturbance does not have a sinister cause

usually make her panic. When she felt wobbly she did not cling onto anything, and remained in the middle of the aisle. The therapist asked if Sally was doing anything else to prevent herself from collapsing. Sally said she was still tensing up her legs, so she was encouraged to loosen them, and try standing on one leg or swaying around.

Result Sally did not collapse or fall over.

Reflection Sally concluded that although she felt very wobbly, this did not mean that she would collapse or fall down. Her belief ratings fell from 90% to 20%. Sally realized that the wobbly feeling is only a symptom of anxiety, and does not lead to weakness or fainting. She saw that she did not need to hang on to anything. In fact, this only made symptoms worse and strengthened her fearful beliefs. This experiment had additional benefits: Sally had not been shopping on her own for two years. Being able to do this experiment greatly increased her confidence and encouraged her to do more.

More experiments that can be used to test the likely consequences of symptoms if not followed by safety behaviours, are presented in Table 3.2.

Discovering what happens if symptoms are deliberately exaggerated

Patients often get to the point where they think that they are reasonably confident that the worst will not happen—but they may have niggling doubts that they have just been lucky and got away with it so far. They may fear that if the symptoms got worse disaster could still strike. The therapist can check this with questions such as 'I wonder if you feel as if you have just managed to get way with it, but there are things you could do which would make it more risky? Is there anything you could do which might tempt the worst to happen?' A sign that lingering worries need to be explored is if belief ratings remain high.

To further enhance the patient's confidence the next step is to see what happens if the symptoms that have been strenuously avoided are exaggerated way beyond the point that they would occur in real life.

Experiment 3.3: to test the effects of exaggerating dizziness

Problem Brian was 40 years old, and had suffered from panic attacks since his father died three years previously. He held down a job and could travel by car, but was afraid of walking alone amongst crowds.

Table 3.2 Experiments to test the consequences of symptoms if not followed by safety behaviours

Prediction	Safety behaviour	Test of prediction	Result	Reflection and conclusion
I will go crazy if I do not control my racing thoughts	Use distraction and try to control mind	Let thoughts race without attempting to check them	Do not go crazy; in fact thoughts seem less out of control	I will not go crazy; if I stop trying to control my thoughts, I may feel calmer
If my throat gets dry with anxiety I could choke or suffocate	Eat sweets and sip water whilst out	Do not use water or sweets	Throat uncomfortable but doesn't close up	Anxiety may make throat dry, but will not choke or suffocate me
If I don't wear dark glasses the neon lights and patterned floors will make me feel ill, and I will collapse	Wear dark glasses and avoid lights patterns	Leave glasses at home and seek out patterns and bright lights	Do not collapse	Feels a bit strange, but I will not collapse
If I do not take deep breaths when I am anxious I will faint/stop breathing	Take lots of deep breaths when feeling nervous	Do not alter breathing pattern when feeling anxious—just leave it as it is	Do not faint or stop breathing; if anything feel a bit better	I will not faint/stop breathing if I stop trying to control my breathing

Target cognition 'If I feel light-headed I will faint. The longer I feel this way the greater the chance that I will collapse.'

Alternative perspective 'Feeling dizzy when anxious is not a sign that I will faint or collapse, even if it persists for a long time. This sensation is caused by breathing more quickly and/or deeply than usual, which is part of the 'fight or flight' reflex when someone is scared.'

Experiment Patient and therapist stood up and breathed deeply, (exactly as Brian would in a panic attack) for five minutes. The therapist ensured that the patient did not use safety behaviours.

Reflection After 30 seconds, Brian felt light-headed, had blurred vision, and was starting to feel panicky. He was willing to continue over-breathing to find out what would happen. By the end of five minutes his fingers were tingling and he believed that he might faint. However, his symptoms had begun to plateau after about 30 seconds. He commented on the similarity between these symptoms and those he experienced in a panic attack. The therapist then disclosed how she felt—she also felt dizzy and light-headed, her vision was blurred, and she felt as if she was swaying to and fro.

Brian realized that he did not come to any harm, and that beyond a certain point symptoms did not get any worse despite being unpleasant. He noted that by not holding onto the chair or wall he allowed himself to find out that he still would not fall down. He realized that he did not need to worry about the symptoms of panic; that he was not going to cross a threshold and collapse—it just didn't get any worse beyond a certain point.

Tip Some therapists are nervous about this experiment, having heard (for example) of people who did collapse after over-breathing at school in an attempt to avoid games lessons or assembly. This is achieved by the Val Salvia manoeuvre, in which deliberate over-breathing is followed by abrupt cessation of breathing and intense pressure in the diaphragm. This is difficult to achieve even with effort, and is different from the increased respiration associated with panic.

This format can be used in any experiment where the aim is to help the person discover the true consequences of symptoms. As before, it is usually best to explain the rationale after the test rather than in preparation for the experiment. Any symptoms the patient fears can be exaggerated in this way. In every case it is helpful for the therapist to model the experiment before the patient tries it. Also, patients sometimes enjoy persuading a friend or relative to test their predictions.

A set of similar experiments is laid out in the Table 3.3.

Table 3.3 Testing the effect of exaggerating symptoms

Feared symptom	Prediction	Experiment in which symptom is exaggerated	Result	Reflection and conclusion
Being hot	If I get hot I will faint	Patient left in a very hot room wearing coat, scarf, etc.; stands by fan heater	Patient does not faint	Fainting not caused by heat alone; people can do hot jobs, etc.; discuss other causes of fainting
Feeling breathless when anxious	I will stop breathing unless I force air in	Patient and therapist practice holding breath for as long as possible	Reflex kicks in and one is forced to breathe.	I do not need to force myself to keep breathing; my body will sort it out
Feeling faint in small or stuffy rooms	I will run out of air in here	Patient in small room, doors and windows shut; therapist sprays air freshener outside door	Patient inside the room almost immediately smells the air freshener	Normal rooms are not air tight; oxygen will get in at all times; I will not run out of air
Feeling wobbly	If I do not walk slowly and carefully I will fall down	Walk quickly, do not think about it; sway and stand on one leg and jump up and down	Do not fall down	This feeling of wobbliness is only a feeling; I am not in danger of falling over

Testing if certain safety behaviours may make symptoms worse

Some things that patients do to try and feel better unfortunately make the symptoms worse. The patient can be encouraged to repeatedly carry out the safety behaviour and observe the results.

Experiment 3.4: to test the effects of exaggerating a safety behaviour (tensing legs)

Problem June had become very anxious about her health, and had lots of panic attacks.

Target cognition When June had a panic attack, she would often feel as though her legs would give way. She tensed her legs as hard as she could, in order to prevent herself from collapsing.

Alternative perspective The other possibility was that focusing on her legs and tensing them as she walked made them feel much worse.

Prediction operationalized June and the therapist both agreed to walk around the shopping centre, first tensing their legs as much as possible, and then focusing away from their legs and letting them relax.

Experiment June and the therapist tried this out.

Reflection June realized that by tensing her legs she was making it harder to walk normally. She and the therapist felt much better when they did not tense up and when they focused away from their legs. June realized that she was inadvertently creating the strange sensations she was trying to control.

Table 3.4. shows some more safety behaviours, their imagined benefits, and likely effects.

Agoraphobia

Key cognitions

It is interesting to speculate why some people with panic disorders are more avoidant than others, and why they avoid particular types of situation (Clum and Knowles 1991). In particular, it is curious that public places are avoided, since help might be more readily available then when alone. It has

Table 3.4 Testing whether safety behaviours can increase symptoms

Safety behaviour	Imagined benefit	Experiment to test effects	Results of experiment	Reflection and conclusion
Trying to control thoughts using distraction and thought suppression (see Chapters 4,5,9, and 14)	Feel calmer	Try deliberately suppressing an image of a pink rabbit	Increase in images of pink rabbit	Thought suppression can have a rebound effect, and could make me feel out of control
Swallowing repeatedly in an attempt to stop throat closing over	Prevent choking or suffocation	Try swallowing lots of times in rapid succession	It becomes difficult, uncomfortable, and almost impossible to swallow	Repeated swallowing actually increases choking feelings

been suggested (Hackmann 1998) that the anxiety equation may throw light on this puzzle. Beck *et al.* (1985) point out that anxiety is a product not only of the perceived probability of a feared event, but also of the perceived cost, and the perceived lack of coping and rescue factors. A recent study of the images of agoraphobics (Day *et al.*, in preparation) suggests that the imagined interpersonal cost of a physical or mental catastrophe is typically inflated, and is combined with doubts about the ability to cope or the likelihood of being rescued.

Agoraphobics are more likely to fear fainting than less avoidant panic patients (Salkovskis, personal communication). This is because they have distorted beliefs about how they imagine others would react (e.g. being totally ignored, attracting a huge embarrassing crowd, being taken to hospital and certified insane). In addition, more avoidant clients may fear that they would not be able to cope on their own if they felt ill, or that they could be separated from loved ones who would not come to rescue them. This is in line with the literature, which suggests that people with agoraphobia are more likely to exhibit features of avoidant or dependent personality, and to suffer from separation anxiety and a perceived lack of self-sufficiency than patients who suffer from panic disorder without agoraphobia. (For a detailed review and fuller discussion see Hackmann 1998.)

In the panic literature more emphasis has been placed on reducing the probability that certain symptoms mean that a physical or mental catastrophe will occur, than on investigating and treating distorted beliefs about coping and rescue factors. It appears that more avoidant clients have catastrophic ideas about how people would react if they vomited, fainted, collapsed, fell, wobbled, lost control, or looked weird. Predictions could include ridicule, being ignored, a crowd gathering, or being forced to go to hospital.

Typical safety behaviours

The most obvious safety behaviour in agoraphobia is clearly avoidance of places from which escape might be embarrassing or help unavailable in the event of a panic attack or panic-like symptoms. In addition, the patient may insist on the presence of a trusted companion, a mobile phone, or to carry a note of their name and address, or refuse to go to unfamiliar places or to travel far from home or from hospitals. They may be unfamiliar with travel, transport arrangements, or the use of maps. They may have had little experience of asking strangers for help or of asserting themselves when appropriate, all of which contributes to their anxieties about coping and rescue.

Behavioural experiments

> ♦ **Experiments to discover how others would react in the event of a physical or mental catastrophe**
>
> *Experiments 3.5 and 3.6: to test how others would react to loss of bladder control*
>
> *Experiment 3.7: to test the reactions of others to fainting*
>
> ♦ **Experiments to see how well the patient could cope in these circumstances**
>
> *Experiment 3.8: to test ability to cope with being lost*
>
> ♦ **Experiments to determine the extent of rescue factors**
>
> *Experiment 3.9: to test the existence of rescue factors in unfamiliar surroundings*
>
> Additional experiments in each category are presented in Tables 3.5 and 3.6.

Determining the reactions of others

In the classic experiment, the therapist accompanies the patient to a public place, then pretends to be going through the feared catastrophe whilst the patient studies passers-by for their reactions. It can be helpful to have two therapists present, so that one can support the patient whilst the other acts out the catastrophe. Therapists are understandably rather reluctant to test such beliefs, but practice helps them test their own predictions, as well as those of the patient. The results are most valuable and encouraging for the patient.

Experiments 3.5 and 3.6: to test the reaction of others to loss of bladder control

Problem Christine was a 50-year-old woman with a 32-year history of agoraphobia with panic and recurring severe depression. Her life had become very restricted by a wide range of difficulties. At a day-to-day level, her pronounced fear that she would lose control of herself and her bodily functions in public was perhaps most disabling, as it prevented her from engaging in many activities which might be beneficial to her self-esteem and mood. Christine had already undertaken a series of behavioural experiments to test the probability of the feared loss of control, and her belief about the likelihood of wetting herself during a panic attack had reduced to 40%. However, the perceived cost had remained unchanged and absolute (belief 100%).

Target cognition 'If I have a panic attack I will lose control of my bladder. This would lead to severe ridicule from others, and I might even end up back in a psychiatric hospital.' (belief 100%)

Alternative perspective 'If I were to wet myself in public, no one would pay any attention to me.'

Experiment 3.5: survey to test the reactions of others to loss of bladder control

Therapist and patient constructed a survey to discover if anyone had ever lost control of their bladder, and what the consequences had been. Therapist undertook a written survey.

Result Around 40% of women had experienced at least some loss of bladder control in the past. All reportedly felt slightly embarrassed about this, but no adverse consequences had followed for any of the respondents.

Reflection 'Perhaps it would not be as disastrous as I fear.'

Experiment 3.6: to directly test the reactions of others to loss of bladder control

Therapist and patient visited the town centre. In a secluded spot, Christine wet the therapist's skirt in a manner consistent with her image of how her own skirt might look if she were indeed to lose control over her bladder. The therapist then strolled through the town. Christine observed the reactions of others from a distance.

Prediction 'People will notice and be shocked by this. I will see them turning their heads or pointing.'

Result No one paid any attention to the therapist or her wet skirt.

Reflection The original belief dropped to 80%. Christine was readily able to acknowledge that no one appeared to care, but expressed doubts that such courtesy would be extended to her.

Follow-on experiment Christine wet her own clothes to appear as though she had lost control of her bladder, and walked around town in the company of her therapist for moral support. No one paid attention to her.

Experiment 3.7: to test the reactions of others to fainting

Problem Susan had panic attacks for several years. She had also been bullied and teased at school, which contributed to her fears that others would ridicule her if she had a panic attack and fainted in a public place.

Table 3.5 Ways to mimic feared catastrophes

Catastrophe	Tips for therapist
Vomiting	Spit out some soup, whilst retching
Wobbly walk	Sway around and stagger whilst walking
Lose control	Wander about talking to oneself and doing odd things
Fall down	Trip oneself up and fall to floor

Target cognition 'If I faint I will be ridiculed—people will laugh and point at me.'

Testing the prediction Two therapists went with Susan to the High Street of her local town. One therapist watched with Susan, whilst the other pretended to have fainted and continued to lie on the floor.

Result One or two people approached the 'patient' to see if she needed help. No one laughed or pointed at her.

Reflection 'People behaved respectfully towards the therapist, but they might jeer or laugh at me.'

Follow-on experiment The experiment was repeated with Susan doing the 'fainting' in a local shop. The results were the same: people were helpful, rather than mocking.

Tips Table 3.5. suggests ways to mimic other feared catastrophes, in order to test the reactions of others. Almost invariably the result is just what the patient would wish. They are not ignored if they would like help, and no one appears to take much notice if embarrassment is feared. Other people seem sensitive and helpful. Most do not appear to conclude that the patient is drunk, mad, seriously ill, abnormal, etc.

Seeing how the patient would cope if there was a catastrophe

Patients often have fears of getting lost, trapped, or separated, not getting home, not being able to explain their problems, or not being able to resist other people taking control in an unwelcome way. Some of these fears sound extreme and childlike, and indeed many of them have been around since childhood and have never been updated. Patients need support and encouragement to do experiments in public places to test their ability to cope if the worst happened.

Table 3.6 Testing ability to cope with feared situations

Prediction	Test	Results	Conclusion
If I do not take this piece of paper I will forget my address	Do not take the paper; go somewhere that makes me anxious	I managed to remember my address	I need not worry that I will forget everthing when I panic
If I faint people will take me to hospital and will not believe that I am OK	Pretend to faint; if unwelcome help is offered be assertive	I was able to assert myself appropriately	People will take me seriously; I am capable of expressing my views

Experiment 3.8: to test ability to cope with being lost

Target cognition 'If I get anxious I will get lost, and I will not be able to ask for directions in a manner that people can understand, and so I will never get home.'

Experiment Pretend to be lost, and ask for directions. If the first person can't help, keep trying others.

Result Patient usually copes as well as any one else in a similar situation. Others seem to react normally.

Reflection 'I was able to ask for directions, even though I was anxious. People were helpful, and I would have been able to get home again. I do not need to worry so much about getting lost. I will be able to cope.'

Tips As these predictions probably reflect longstanding core beliefs it is unlikely that they will change in response to a single experiment. Repeated experiments and other practice will probably be needed, to build confidence. For example, role plays of appropriate assertion can be carried out in session.

Table 3.6 provides more examples of testing ability to cope with feared situations.

Determining the existence of rescue factors

Similar experiments can be carried out with the patient to test beliefs about the lack of rescue factors (e.g. maps, telephones, timetables, taxis, information centres).

Experiment 3.9: to test for the presence of rescue factors in unfamiliar situations

Problem Cheryl was in her forties, with a family. She suffered from panic disorder with agoraphobia, but also met criteria for avoidant personality disorder. As the panic attacks began to subside, Cheryl realized that she was still afraid of travelling to unfamiliar places.

Prediction 'If I go to new places I will not be able to find my way around, or get back home.'

Experiment Cheryl arranged to travel to London by bus, to visit the London Eye.

Result Cheryl managed the trip without any problems. She discovered that everything was clearly marked and signposted, and that she could read the timetable. She also travelled by taxi to a London store, and found that her first ever taxi ride was also easy to cope with—the taxi driver understood her instructions and told her how much she owed him.

Reflection 'I do not need to worry so much about new activities. There are always people around to help, and anyway it is usually made quite clear what one needs to do. However, I am going to have to keep practising, and slowly expand my horizons.'

Conclusion

Panic disorder can usually be treated with a range of experiments encompassing the causes and consequences of symptoms, including attention to any probability, cost, coping, and rescue factors about which the patient is concerned. With more avoidant patients nearly all experiments should be done out of the office, as cognitions are more likely to be accessible, and the full range of predictions can be tested. Behavioural experiments can be used to test negative automatic thoughts and assumptions, and even to weaken core beliefs. Some of the more entrenched beliefs may require more repetition of experiments, verbal discussion, and schema-focused techniques. However, even with very entrenched problems, behavioural experiments can be empowering and effective.

Other related chapters

Co-morbid depression may need treatment in its own right (see Chapter 10). Panic disorder and agoraphobia overlap significantly with health anxiety (see Chapter 4). Underlying issues may include problems with self-esteem (see Chapter 20), social anxiety (see Chapter 7), interpersonal difficulties (see

Chapter 19), and avoidance of affect (see Chapter 17). Thus any of these chapters may be useful. The chapter on physical health problems (Chapter 15) may be of relevance to those with co-existing health problems.

Further reading

Salkovskis, P.M. and Hackmann, A. (1997). Agoraphobia. In: G. Davey (ed), *Phobias: a handbook of theory, research and treatment*. Wiley, Chichester.

Salkovskis, P.M., Clark, D.M. and Gelder, M.G. (1996). Cognition-behaviour links in the persistence of panic. *Behaviour Research and Therapy*, **34**, 453–8.

Tales from the Front Line

An accidental experiment

Arriving at work in the usual post school-run rush, the therapist parked her car and charged upstairs to get ready for the first client of the day.

Half an hour later therapist and patient were considering evidence for and against the belief that the patient was the only person in the world who ever did stupid things, everyone else being mega effective and efficient. The patient would break off every now and then to question why they were wasting their time doing this when it was obviously true that she was indeed the most careless and stupid person ever to occupy a human body.

Just as the therapist began to despair, a loud crashing noise could be heard outside the window that had both therapist and patient out of their seats, peering down into the car park.

The therapist's car had reversed at speed into the side of a brand new vehicle at the opposite side of the car park. In her rush, the therapist had left the hand brake off and her car had made good use of its freedom by rolling backwards down the slight incline, gathering momentum and achieving considerable speed before finally crashing into the other car.

Pausing for consideration, patient and therapist exchanged looks
'You were saying?'

CHAPTER 4

Health anxiety

Amy Silver
Diana Sanders
Norma Morrison
Carolyn Cowey

Introduction

Health anxiety is characterized by fears of having a serious illness either now or in the future. It causes a great deal of distress, both to the patient and to those trying to help. Patients believe that they have serious health problems that are not receiving appropriate diagnosis or treatment. The result is numerous consultations and high use of resources. Medical staff often find it difficult to know how to help, leading them to repeatedly reassure the patient and request further, medically unnecessary investigations. This only serves to intensify the patient's anxiety, reinforcing thoughts such as 'My GP wouldn't have suggested an investigation if she didn't think there was something wrong'.

DSM-IV-TR (APA 2000) uses the term hypochondriasis rather than health anxiety, defined as a preoccupation with the fear of having, or the idea that one has, a serious disease, based on misinterpretation of bodily symptoms. Other criteria are that the problem persists despite medical reassurance, causes significant distress or impaired functioning, and has lasted for at least six months. The person's preoccupations can be focused on bodily functions, physical sensations, or physical abnormalities. Reading medical information, seeing television programmes, or hearing about illness can all trigger fears. The more focused on the target symptom or illness the patient becomes, the more convinced she is that something is wrong, which leads to further monitoring of physical state and in turn, further anxiety.

The cognitive model

The generic cognitive model of emotion (Beck 1976) together with more specific models of anxiety and its maintenance (e.g. Beck et al. 1985; Clark 1999) provide the basis for cognitive models of health anxiety. Salkovskis and

Warwick (1986) and Warwick and Salkovskis (1989) devised a specific model to show how people with health anxiety perceive their bodily reactions and appearance, and medical information, as more dangerous than they actually are. Together with this perception of threat comes the belief that the individual is unable to cope with the threat and its perceived course. Health-anxious patients fear physical or mental catastrophe in a similar way to panic patients. A key difference is in the time-frame, with health-anxious patients fearing catastrophe in the future, and those with panic fearing immediate catastrophe. There is significant co-morbidity between panic disorder and hypochondriasis.

Specific assumptions about illness, symptoms, personal health threats, and health behaviours (such as checking for lumps in breasts or frequent medical consultations) arise from past experiences, including illnesses and medical treatment of friends and family. In addition, sensational media coverage of unusual illnesses, or medical mismanagement, reinforce the individual's assumptions. These assumptions provide both a source of anxiety and a vulnerability to misinterpretation of changes in appearance, of bodily sensations, or of stories in the media. Such distorted information may be used as evidence that the patient has serious organic pathology, so maintaining the anxiety.

A number of different factors maintain health anxiety and the patient's preoccupation with health. These include behaviours such as body checking, increased vigilance to bodily sensations, reassurance seeking and avoidance; cognitive processes including rumination and thinking errors; physiological factors such as increased heart rate and other bodily sensations caused by heightened anxiety; and anxiety and depression (Salkovskis 1996; Warwick *et al.* 1996).

Wells and Hackmann (1993) describe the content of images and associated beliefs in patients with health anxiety, which highlight their exaggerated perceptions of the likely cost of illness and their underestimation of coping and rescue factors. Typical beliefs might be that illness could lead to abandonment by others, and that death could lead to hell or eternal loneliness. Wells and Hackmann (1993) also note that superstitious thinking is common in health anxiety, and is manifest in beliefs such as 'If I think about illness I will get ill' or 'If I picture myself looking well I will tempt fate, and be struck down'. In this way, health-anxious patients are similar to patients who have generalized anxiety disorder (GAD) and obsessive-compulsive disorder (OCD) (see Chapters 5 and 6).

Key aspects of cognition

Exaggerated beliefs, arbitrary inference, and selective attention can result in a confirmatory bias and lead to patients selectively noticing and remembering information that is consistent with their negative beliefs about illness.

Focusing attention can lead the patient to notice aspects of appearance (e.g. skin pigmentation) or function (e.g. bowel movements) that were previously ignored. Patients may perceive such events as novel and therefore abnormal. Symptom focusing can also lead directly to changes in physiological systems: for example, repeated checking for lumps in testicles may lead to soreness which provides further evidence that the content of anxious thoughts is correct. The perception of threat leads to an increase in autonomically mediated sensations that are then interpreted by the patient as further evidence of illness.

Patients with health anxiety use safety-seeking behaviours which they believe enable them to manage their fears. They may avoid doctors, hospitals, or health programmes, to minimize anxiety and prevent feared disasters. The belief that danger has been averted in turn sustains the patient's beliefs. Some employ bodily checking and reassurance seeking, which leads to temporary reductions in anxiety but reinforces health-anxious beliefs in the long term. Such reassurance seeking often involves frequent visits to the doctor, resulting in unnecessary investigations and operations. These behaviours themselves maintain health anxieties: ambiguous medical information can result (e.g. contradictory advice in the face of unclear causes of symptoms, or different advice from different doctors consulted); apparently reassuring information can be misinterpreted (e.g. 'There is nothing wrong now, but come back if the problem persists' being interpreted as 'The doctor believes there is something wrong'); and secondary problems can arise from over-investigation.

Key cognitions

Beliefs about the need to be responsible which maintain preoccupation and worry

◆ Fear of missing something important

Patients may believe that it is vital that they take responsibility for their health, and attend to it very carefully, because: 'Doctors often miss serious illnesses', 'If I don't keep a careful watch on my health something terrible will happen', or 'By going to the doctors and checking out my symptoms I will prevent any serious illnesses'.

◆ Seeking medical information

'I must keep abreast of all the recent health scares', 'I must see what my risk is of contracting X', 'The internet can show me the best way to investigate my symptoms'.

◆ **Seeking medical assessment**

'Detailed tests are the only way to rule out an illness', 'If a doctor sends me for tests, he is convinced that there is something wrong', 'If your symptoms come and go, a test can only be accurate if done when the symptoms are present'.

◆ **Checking behaviour**

'I must check my breasts all the time to see if there are lumps', 'I must check every time I go to the toilet that I haven't been bleeding'.

Beliefs about health, illness, and death

◆ **Normality of symptoms and sensations**

A healthy body does not have symptoms: 'If I experience an unexpected physical symptom I must be ill', 'Bodily changes are always a sign that something is wrong'.

Regularity: 'Both sides of the body should be identical'

Meaning of symptoms: 'Symptoms are always a sign of disease/illness', 'It is possible to know, with absolute certainly, that you are not ill', 'If medication doesn't take away a symptom then I must have a serious illness', 'Symptoms are always explainable', 'I or my doctor must be able to find an explanation for any physical symptom'.

◆ **Increased vulnerability**

'My family is prone to illness', 'I am more likely than most people to get an illness', 'Parts of my body are weak', 'I will die early like my father'.

◆ **The cost of illness or death**

'I must look after my health or I will be a burden to my family', 'If I die my mother's life will be ruined', 'If I am ill no-one will care', 'If I am ill I will suffer terribly', 'If I die or become ill my family will never be able to cope', 'If I die no-one will miss me', 'Death will be lonely' (with an image of self being aware of being dead, buried, and eaten by worms), 'If I die I will go to hell'.

Beliefs about the effects of anxiety and worry

◆ **The deleterious effects of anxiety on health** (see Chapter 3)

'Anxiety can kill', 'There is only so much stress my heart can take', 'There is only so much anxiety that my mind can take', 'If I am not perfectly calm I am in danger of losing control', 'Once anxiety starts to build up you can't stop it getting worse'.

◆ **Metacognitive and superstitious beliefs about thoughts causing or preventing illness** (similar to those in GAD and OCD, see Chapters 5 and 6)

'If I don't control my thoughts I might go mad', 'Thinking I have cancer makes it more likely I will get it', 'If I don't worry about my health, something will go wrong', 'If I let myself think that I am well, I will tempt fate', 'If I imagine myself dead I will die', 'You've got to check or you will get ill'.

Special considerations
Therapeutic relationship

Establishing and maintaining a sound therapeutic relationship with patients with health anxiety can be more difficult than with patients with other problems (Sanders 2000). Often therapists and patients start therapy with different agendas. Whist the therapist's overall aim is to help the patient deal with anxiety, the patient's main aim might be to gain the therapist's support to prove that their problems are physical, and that the doctors may have missed something. Sometimes patients will be resentful about being referred to a psychological therapist rather than a medical consultant or surgeon: occasionally, the patient may not know that they are being offered psychological treatment until the assessment session. Not surprisingly, these differences can lead to difficulties in establishing collaboration. Time needs to be devoted to developing a sound therapeutic alliance; in its absence, the patient is likely to drop out. An emphasis on the collaborative nature of the therapy is helpful.

Practitioners need to remain open-minded and impartial or neutral about what might be causing patients' symptoms, and keep the focus of therapy on what might be maintaining the patient's anxiety. This avoids polarization between physical or psychological explanations, and begins the debate about possible other causes and maintaining factors. It is helpful for the assessment session to focus on the patient's symptoms and explanations, and giving him sufficient time to feel that these have been heard and understood. It is important not to start the process of guided discovery and questioning the patient's beliefs too early in therapy. Those with health anxiety often have many experiences of their beliefs and fears not being taken seriously. Any hint that the therapist is questioning the patient's beliefs during the initial stages of therapy may lead the patient to feel misunderstood, to polarize his views into physical explanations for the symptoms, or to drop out of therapy. It is surprisingly easy to get into an argument with the patient about the cause of symptoms, or to begin to explore alternatives and get into a cycle of 'yes, but . . . ' debates.

The therapist can offer an empathic understanding of how difficult it must be for the patient: 'You have been told that there is nothing wrong, but you have described many things that are causing you problems, and you are feeling very distressed, so it sounds as though there is a great deal wrong at the moment'. Use open, curious questions, to elicit the patient's own understanding as well as exploring psychological factors: 'What do you believe is causing the symptoms?', 'What have other people said?'. It is important for therapy to remain collaborative throughout, and that any problems with collaboration, such as therapy becoming argumentative or the patient feeling defensive, are worked with immediately.

Hypothesis A vs. hypothesis B

Rather than taking a position of persuading patients that their problems are psychological in origin, therapists need to put forward the idea that perhaps the patient is right and that the problem is physical, but perhaps there is another explanation (or a contributory factor), and together they will explore both perspectives. One way of engaging the patient is to offer the therapy as a behavioural experiment in itself, as a chance to identify and test out two hypotheses: hypothesis A is that the patient is indeed ill, and has serious problems so far undetected; hypothesis B is that the patient is worried and concerned about illness, and regardless of whether their symptoms are caused by illness, the worry and concern is a major problem, which can be helped by psychological approaches (Salkovskis and Bass 1997). The patient and therapist can review what the patient has so far done to test each hypothesis: many people realize that they have focused on hypothesis A to the exclusion of hypothesis B, and their search so far has not been useful or helpful. The concept of two testable hypotheses fits well with many behavioural experiments.

Behavioural experiments

> - **Beliefs about the need to be responsible which maintain preoccupation and worry**
>   *Experiment 4.1: fear of missing something important*
>   *Experiment 4.2: delaying visits to the GP*
>   *Experiment 4.3: symptom focusing*
>   *Experiment 4.4: seeking medical information*
>   *Experiment 4.5: testing whether safety behaviour increases symptoms*
>   *Experiment 4.6: over-informing the GP*
> - **Beliefs about health, illness, and death**
>   *Experiment 4.7: normality of symptoms and sensations*
>   *Experiment 4.8: quick, in-session discovery experiments to look at alternative explanations of symptoms*
>   *Experiment 4.9: beliefs about the cost of illness or death*
> - **Beliefs about the effects of anxiety and worry**
>   *Experiment 4.10: controlling worrying thoughts*
>   *Experiment 4.11: if I think about being ill I will become ill*

Some patient beliefs, such as 'I must always be vigilant about symptoms or I may notice too late for treatment to be effective', may get in the way of allowing the patient to risk behavioural experiments, especially those which involve a decrease in self-monitoring. When practitioners experience difficulties in setting up behavioural experiments, they may need to explore the patient's beliefs about doing the experiments, and work with these first.

Experiments for patients with health anxiety can be devised for the three categories of cognitions above: beliefs about the need to be responsible for health; beliefs about health, illness, and death; and beliefs about the effects of anxiety and worry. The majority of the experiments we describe are in the first two categories; experiments concerned with the effects of anxiety and worry and metacognitive beliefs are described more fully in Chapters 3, 5, and 6.

Beliefs about the need to be responsible which maintain preoccupation and worry

Experiment 4.1: fear of missing something important

Problem Heather, a 31-year-old, had a 10-year history of health anxiety. She was aware that she was being irrational about her health fears but could not cope with the distress they were causing her. Most recently, she had become worried by a lump on her neck and frequently touched it to check whether it was still there or getting bigger. Her main fear was of cancer.

Target cognitions If I have any symptom or unusual sensation, it means there may be something seriously wrong with me. I need to be hypervigilant about physical things or I might miss something serious. I have cancer (80% belief rating).

Alternative perspective Focusing attention on a symptom or self-monitoring can blow it out of proportion and make the problem worse.

Prediction If I do not pay attention to the symptom, I will miss something important. I will feel more anxious because I am not keeping a check on it. I won't be able to think about anything else.

Experiment Heather agreed to keep a diary of how often thoughts about the lump or cancer came into her head. On alternate days, she was asked to focus on the problem as much as she wished and to check on the lump whenever she wanted to. She was asked to note how often she was tempted to do this and to make an assessment of her level of anxiety throughout the day on a scale of 0–10. On other days, she was to simply tally the thoughts without responding to them in any way, and just to continue with what she was doing. On that day too, she was to rate how anxious she felt. Each evening she also rated her level of belief in the thought 'I must be seriously ill or have cancer'.

Results Heather brought back diary entries that showed intrusions were higher on the 'think about it and check' days than on the 'resist the urge' days.

Anxiety was also higher on those days. Her level of belief that she had cancer came down from 80% to 30%.

Reflection Heather learned that her safety-seeking behaviours of checking the lump and focusing attention on it were actually making her symptom seem worse and increasing her conviction that there was something seriously wrong.

Tip Troubleshoot in advance to make sure that nothing is going to get in the way of being able to carry this out. For example, weekends may be harder than weekdays because all the family is at home. If any possible obstacles are discussed within the session, it makes it more likely that the experiment will be successfully adhered to by the patient.

Experiment 4.2: delaying visits to the GP

Problem Julian had a three-year history of health anxiety. When he was made redundant, he became a househusband, caring for his two young children. Julian had frequently attended his Practice with a range of symptoms that his doctor tended to investigate further. He had found previous negative results very reassuring until he began to question statements made by the consultants, which he felt introduced an element of doubt. One of his concerns was that something would catch in his throat and he would choke to death, preceded by a great deal of suffering: life was unfair and if anybody was going to be unlucky in this respect it would be him. He wanted a specialist to investigate further to put his mind at rest.

Target cognitions If I do not get the doctor to investigate my symptoms I will undergo a period of suffering due to an underlying illness and die.

Alternative perspective My symptoms will disappear without a visit to my GP and to specialists.

Predictions If I delay a visit to the doctor anxiety will be unbearable and I will be consumed by my health concern.

Operationalize predictions To delay visits to the doctor for two weeks, while measuring levels of anxiety and presence of symptoms once a day.

Experiment Julian agreed not to see his GP for two weeks and thus not request an appointment with a specialist. He documented his level of anxiety once a day on a scale of 0–10, and rated his belief that he had a serious illness.

Results After two weeks, Julian reported that the catching in his throat had gone. His anxiety ratings were high in the days immediately after his last session but decreased over time. As his symptoms disappeared, he started to consider his feelings of low self-esteem, which he had been reluctant to look at before. This became the focus of further cognitive work.

Reflection The patient discovered that visiting the doctor was contributing to a vicious circle, ultimately reinforcing his anxiety. He also discovered that if he waited, his symptoms disappeared by themselves, so reinforcing the idea that symptoms do not automatically mean illness and suffering. He realized that he needed to look at the underlying issues of self-esteem, which made him feel singled out for unfair treatment and suffering.

Experiment 4.3: symptom focusing

Problem Justine, a nurse, was referred with health anxiety. She was very worried about pains in her leg, and frequently visited the doctor. However, her past experience had led her to have little faith in the doctor's opinion. Justine had initially been misdiagnosed with a disease that had a progressive type; it was subsequently discovered that she had a manageable type. As a result, she felt even more responsible for keeping a constant eye on her body and spent a lot of time monitoring her knee for severity of pain and any changes.

Target cognitions If I do not monitor my knee it will get worse and I'll miss the opportunity to report it to my doctor. Anything serious will go undiagnosed unless I catch it early and have very accurate information.

Alternative perspective Paying attention to any part of my body can result in identification of normal sensations that could be reported as 'symptoms'. In this case the symptoms will disappear or reduce if my focus changes.

Prediction If I do not monitor my leg my symptoms will get worse, and my anxiety about getting a serious disease will be worse. I will be consumed by my health concern and will not be able to concentrate on anything else.

Experiment The experiment aimed to test two hypotheses: firstly, the hypothesis that the symptoms were due to a serious condition; secondly, that any part of the body attended to in this way would produce 'symptoms', and her symptoms were a result of the attention that she was paying to her leg. Justine and the therapist chose a part of their body to focus on and, after two minutes, described any sensations. Justine chose her right arm, and after two minutes, described a tingling in her wrist and coolness at her elbow. The therapist reported symptoms in her own thigh. The process was repeated with several different parts of the body, paying attention to these in turn.

Results Justine quickly realized that focusing on her body was a likely source of symptom production and she suggested that she would wait to see if the symptoms developed further over the next week, in the absence of monitoring. She booked a 'monitoring spot' for just before her next appointment, but in fact forgot to monitor at this time and reported an absence of symptoms in her leg.

Reflection This behavioural experiment demonstrated the power of focusing attention on a body part, in contrast to the more general attention we usually use. Redirecting her attentional focus freed Justine to think more about relationship difficulties that she had been trying to ignore.

Tip It is not unusual for a patient's preoccupation with their health to mask other, more painful and difficult problems. It can take time therefore for the patient to begin to let go of the focus on their health and discuss other concerns. This type of experiment may need to be repeated several times, whilst other work is going on in therapy to identify salient issues.

Experiment 4.4: seeking medical information

Problem Ian had a 15 year history of health anxiety, centring on varying problems. He would spend up to four hours a day on the internet and reading medical journal articles, magazines, and newspapers, scanning for medical information. He did this because he felt that he would be better educated about the signs of various conditions and therefore reduce the chance of missing any serious condition. He also felt that this strategy helped him control his anxiety, as he often found information indicating that his risk of having a serious condition was low.

Target cognitions Seeking out medical information helps me reduce my anxiety because being informed is the only way of making sure I do not miss anything and get appropriate treatment (100% belief rating).

Alternative perspective Seeking out medical information contributes to my anxiety by keeping me focused on my health all the time.

Prediction If I stop looking on the internet or reading medical information my anxiety will increase.

Operationalize predictions To cease information seeking, thereby testing the prediction.

Experiment Although Ian understood the rationale for complete cessation of seeking medical information, he felt unable to do this. Instead, he planned a three-week graded programme of reductions in seeking medical information. He kept a diary of level of activity and health anxiety, rated 0–100. Hypothesis A was re-rated weekly during this three-week period at therapy sessions.

Results Ian's diary sheets showed an initial increase in health anxiety and then an overall decrease. His activity levels had increased over the two-week period, including socializing, playing sports, and creative writing. His agreement with the belief 'seeking out medical information helps me reduce my worry' reduced from 100% to 60%.

Reflection Ian noticed that some of his health anxiety was related to information that he was discovering on the internet and in magazines. He reflected that it might be the case that the less he read about illness, the less he fed his health anxieties. He also reflected that he was able to distract himself from his health worries by doing engaging activities such as creative writing.

Tip The patient needs to be committed to stopping the safety behaviour. Ensure that more subtle forms of medical information seeking are ceased, such as websites with automatic emails or watching popular medical TV programmes. People can have covert ways of seeking reassurance, such as casually mentioning symptoms during conversations with friends and watching their reaction, or asking friends who are unwell to describe all their symptoms in detail. Similar experiments can be conducted with different types of reassurance seeking.

Experiment 4.5: testing whether safety behaviour increases symptoms

Problem Barbara was convinced she had throat cancer because she was experiencing difficulty swallowing. Her difficulty occurred both when eating and when she was doing nothing, but was less in evidence when she was busy. She was having difficulty concentrating at work because of her anxieties. In session, it was obvious that she was swallowing much more often than was normal, which she explained was her way of keeping her throat open, and was intended to stop herself choking.

Target cognitions The difficulty I have in swallowing and eating means I have throat cancer (90% belief rating).

Alternative perspective My difficulty in swallowing is related to my anxiety and the fact that I am constantly checking up on how my throat is feeling by swallowing repeatedly (30% belief rating).

Prediction I need to keep monitoring the symptom to make sure it is not getting any worse. It would be foolish to ignore it, as it is important to have things diagnosed as soon as possible.

Experiment Barbara monitored her symptoms by frequent swallowing. It was suggested in session that both the therapist and the patient should exaggerate her safety behaviour, and swallow eight times in succession, and then report to each other what the experience had been like.

Results This was extremely hard to do. Long before the count approached eight, both Barbara and the therapist were having difficulty in continuing: their mouths were so dry that it was very uncomfortable to swallow. They were very aware of their throats, which felt different from normal, and they experienced the same types of sensations.

Reflection Barbara was surprised that the therapist was experiencing the same sensations as her. In general, she learned that performing an action more frequently than normal will make the area feel different, and in particular that her safety behaviour of continually swallowing to check how her throat was feeling was actually producing the symptom. Her belief in the target cognition reduced to 70% and her belief in the alternative perspective increased to 40%.

Tip Be sure to do the experiment with the patient. Then it is less likely that the individual will give up as soon as it becomes uncomfortable—and it does.

Experiment 4.6: over-informing the GP

Problem Ahmed was referred for cognitive therapy after two years of anxiety about his health. He visited his GP very frequently to report a range of physical symptoms and problems, sometimes making appointments twice a week. He had had numerous negative investigations, but was never reassured for very long. We identified part of the problem as him having a poor relationship with his GP. Ahmed started each consultation with a huge list of symptoms and problems which he wanted to discuss at length, but felt the GP never listened fully: 'He doesn't know the full story so he might have missed something'. He felt he was being labelled as a problem patient, which made him feel more desperate about not getting proper help.

Target cognitions I need to tell the GP every minute detail of all my symptoms otherwise he will not understand and I will not get the proper diagnosis and treatment.

Alternative perspective GPs are trained to find out what is important in making a diagnosis. Each appointment is only 10 minutes. I get frustrated when he interrupts me and seems not to listen, but he also gets frustrated by me telling him lots of irrelevant details. This makes for a bad consultation, which maintains my anxiety.

Prediction If I don't tell my GP everything on my mind, he might miss what is important. If he misses it, I'll never get proper treatment.

Experiment Ahmed made an appointment to see the GP to discuss his concerns about his frequent headaches. He started by saying that he wanted to discuss his headaches and find out whether he needed any further tests or treatment. Before the consultation, he role played the consultation with his therapist, focusing on mentioning only the most important details and answering questions.

Results To his surprise, the consultation went well. The GP listened to his concerns and then asked a lot of questions which he was able to answer briefly—when he got the headaches, what made them worse, what helped and so on. He then discussed possible causes and treatments, including trying relaxation, pain control, or taking regular medication to prevent them. Ahmed was asked to keep a diary of the headaches and come back in three weeks.

Reflection Ahmed felt that his concerns had been taken seriously, and that he was able to listen to the GP, learning that there were a number of options for treatment. An improved relationship with his GP meant that he could obtain suitable help, rather than continuing to use his GP in an inappropriate way.

Tips It is very important not simply to teach patients to become more efficient and effective in gaining reassurance. The aim is to help patients to use medical services more appropriately and in a way which does not maintain their problems. This kind of experiment is most useful later on in therapy, when patients are able to believe alternative hypotheses about the causes of symptoms and live with a level of anxiety about their health.

Beliefs about health, illness, and death

Experiment 4.7: normality of symptoms and sensations

Problem Nathaniel believed that he was ill with an undiagnosed disorder, due to symptoms of headaches, tiredness, pins and needles, and a 'slow adjustment' to temperature change.

Target cognition Symptoms are signs of illness.

Alternative perspective Symptoms are normal for most healthy people.

Prediction Other people will not experience symptoms like mine, because I am ill and they are not.

Experiment Nathaniel was asked to rate the target belief (60% belief rating). Both the therapist and Nathaniel conducted a survey. Friends were asked to recall the frequency of headaches, tiredness, pins and needles, and a 'slow adjustment' to changes in temperature in the last month. Those who had such experiences were asked to explain how they understood these symptoms.

Results Most of the respondents had experienced all of the symptoms they were asked about. Their explanations included stress, not eating properly, early signs of a cold, weather, sitting in a funny position, working too hard, late nights, and drinking. Nathaniel's belief rating reduced from 60% to 40%.

Reflection Nathaniel reflected that many people experienced symptoms frequently. He also reflected that other people had different interpretations of their symptoms, and that his were much more catastrophic.

Further work It is worth noting the small change in belief that is typical for this patient group. Although Nathaniel's belief shifted, more work was done in this area using guided discovery and verbal reattribution techniques in sessions.

Tip Some patients dismiss information from small surveys because they feel that they are different from 'normal' people in some way. The patient can be asked how many others would have to be surveyed in order to get convincing information: this can highlight how extreme the patient's views can be. For example, one patient realized that he would need to ask everyone in the world for him to be convinced that his symptoms were normal, which helped him to see that his beliefs had set him apart from the rest of the human race.

Experiment 4.8: quick in-session discovery experiments to look at alternative explanations of symptoms

'My body is not functioning properly'

The patient and therapist hold up their arms at right angles to the body for two minutes. Depending on how strong they are, they will start to notice pain in the arm muscles. This demonstrates that physical sensations and pain can result from simply using muscles in an unusual way. Discuss the different interpretations that can be given—'I have MS' versus 'I am unfit'. This can be extended to a survey, by asking 20 people to hold up their arms and monitor the effects.

'Dizziness is evidence of a brain tumour'

Therapist and patient get up and down from their chairs very fast, turning their heads in order to induce dizziness. They both feel giddy, indicating that dizziness can easily be induced in normal people, but is often not noticed. They can discuss how the balance system quickly adapts to changes in posture, but the slight feelings of dizziness are normally ignored unless the person is anxious about them.

Experiment 4.9: beliefs about the cost of illness or death

Problem Sophie worried that if she died her husband would not be able to cope with caring for their two children.

Target cognition When I die my husband would not be able to cope with the children and they would end up in social services care.

Alternative perspective If I died my children would be looked after in the family.

Prediction If I asked my husband about what would happen if I died, he would say that he wouldn't give up work and that therefore he would not be able to care for the children at home.

Experiment Sophie developed a questionnaire with the therapist which included questions such as 'How do you think your life would change in a practical way if I died—for example, with what you did during the day?', 'Who do you think would look after the children during the day?', 'In what way do you think the children's life would change?', 'Do you think the children would ever end up being in a home?'. She then gave this questionnaire to her husband, sister, and parents.

Result The questionnaire data showed that none of the people completing it perceived themselves as not being able to cope with increased demands of child care. Her husband did not anticipate stopping his job but felt that he would employ an au pair or ask the grandparents for help during the day. All the family members thought it a ridiculous question about the children going into a home. After handing back the questionnaires, Sophie had conversations with her family members that confirmed their responses and they talked about her concerns and worries in more depth.

Reflection Sophie learned that her family felt they would cope with her death in so far as to prevent too much change to the children's life. She learned that they would miss her and that the children's life would be worse but manageable. She learned that her husband believed his life would be harder without her, not only for emotional reasons but for practical ones too. However, he felt that he would cope. He stated that there is no way that their children would live in a home.

Tip This experiment was hard for Sophie as she had to admit her fears to her family. She did it in stages, asking her parents first, as she felt this was easiest. Then, when she had the results, she went to her sister and husband. Care has to be taken that this information doesn't get discounted as it is hypothetical and cannot be tested in reality.

Beliefs about the effects of anxiety and worry, and thought–action fusion

For examples of other experiments in this category, see Chapters 3, 5, and 6.

Experiment 4.10: controlling worrying thoughts

Problem Abigail had longstanding fears of illness, predominantly cancer and HIV and AIDS. She spent a lot of time worrying and self-monitoring, which caused a great deal of distress. She believed that if she could not bring her thoughts under control, she would go mad. Abigail felt that she was increasingly unable to exert any control over her thoughts.

Target cognition If I don't control my thoughts, I'll go mad.

Alternative perspective Abigail had no idea about an alternative. The experiment aimed to help her discover an alternative.

Prediction If I let the thoughts go and do not control them, they will spiral out of control and I will go mad.

Experiment Abigail and the therapist aimed to try and lose control of their thoughts and discover what would happen. Abigail reported that going mad would feel like thoughts whirring round her head to such an extent that rational, directed thought would be impossible. There was a discussion about how loss of control could be achieved. She thought that filling her head as much as possible with catastrophic thoughts about illness might cause her to lose control. The therapist thought that the equivalent for her would be to imagine being in a plane that was in danger of crashing. It was agreed that both would sit with their eyes closed and try to have these terrifying thoughts to the exclusion of all else and report what happened.

Results Neither therapist nor patient went mad—in fact, Abigail reported that it had actually been difficult to keep her mind on the thoughts, which was not what she had expected. By the end of the five minutes, she only felt a little more anxious than at the start. She found it useful to know that the therapist's experience was similar. She did not believe that by doing it for longer she would have lost control. She realized that it must be harder to lose control of one's thoughts than she had imagined. In the discussion that followed, she was able to see that perhaps she was trying to control something that did not need to be controlled, and her belief rating in the target cognition came down to 20%.

Reflection This experiment enabled Abigail to collaborate in further experiments that, initially, she found too risky because of the danger of relinquishing control (e.g. allowing the thoughts to 'flow over' her instead of trying either to suppress them or find a definite answer to them).

Tip It is important to elicit from the patient something that is a perceived credible threat to their control.

Experiment 4.11: if I think about being ill, I will become ill

Many people with health anxiety believe that thinking about illness will, in some way, contribute to illness. It is difficult to test this belief with any degree of certainty, since we are all unable to predict whether we will get a particular condition in future, and cognitive processes in anxiety may lead the patient to draw conclusions about events that are in fact unrelated. However, behavioural experiments that test the impact that thoughts can have on one's physical state in the immediate future are possible: for example, one could make time once every hour for a week to think about having a cold and then see whether one does, in fact, get a cold. This can then be used in a guided discovery way to illustrate that the link between thoughts and physical state is not direct.

Distinctive difficulties in working with health anxiety

Cost of changing beliefs

For people with health anxiety, the cost of changing their beliefs and behaviour is perceived to be very high: in many cases, their very lives are felt to depend on continuing to be preoccupied with health. Therefore, these patients are likely to hold on to their beliefs strongly. In therapy, we need to spend time exploring these beliefs and using guided discovery to find alternative ways of thinking. For example, a patient who was extremely terrified of motor neurone disease saw that the likelihood of his getting the disease was extremely small, but believed that the cost would be unthinkable. Using guided discovery and experiments collecting information about the disease, he discovered that it was indeed a terrible disease, but from reading information from patient associations, found that people did, somehow, find ways to live with it and that they gained support and love from others despite the disease. Guided discovery enabled the patient to see that his health anxiety was already causing him significant distress and disability, and it was possible to tackle this in the present, rather than put his energy into focusing on something improbable in the future.

Providing certainty about the future

It is important not to set up experiments designed to demonstrate the absence of present illness, or certainty about the future: clearly, it is impossible to prove that the patient is not suffering from any disease processes and will never do so in the future. Rather, practitioners are attempting to help patients discover that their current behaviours, such as checking and seeking reassurance, whilst aimed at reducing their fears of illness, actually make them more likely to experience unpleasant symptoms and to feel more anxious, in turn reinforcing the unhelpful beliefs. Therefore, the focus of therapy and behavioural experiments has to be kept on maintaining factors, rather than on disease explanations.

Other relevant chapters

Problems with health anxiety can be similar to general anxiety and worry: thoughts about health can resemble ruminations, and experiments from Chapter 6 are relevant. Health worries and maintaining factors (including a type of thought–action fusion) can overlap with obsessive-compulsive disorder (see Chapter 5). Underlying issues may include problems with self-esteem (see Chapter 20), interpersonal issues (see Chapter 19), and avoidance of affect (see Chapter 17). The chapter on physical health problems (Chapter 15) is relevant to patients with co-existing health anxiety and physical problems. Many patients also need help with panic attacks (see Chapter 3), and it is often best to tackle these first.

Further reading

Bouman, T.K. and Visser, S. (1998). Cognitive and behavioural treatment of hypochondriasis. *Psychotherapy and Psychosomatics,* **67**, 214–21.

Papageorgiou, C. and Wells, A. (1998). Effects of attention training on hypochondriasis: a brief case series. *Psychological Medicine,* **28**, 193–200.

Salkovskis, P.M. and Bass, C. (1997). Hypochondriasis. In: D.M. Clark and C.G. Fairburn (ed.), *Science and practice of cognitive behaviour therapy.* Oxford University Press, Oxford, pp. 313–39.

Sanders, D. (2000). Psychosomatic problems. In: C. Feltham and I. Horton (ed.), *Handbook of counselling and psychotherapy.* Sage, London, pp. 515–25.

Sanders, D. and Wills, F. (2003). *Counselling for anxiety problems.* Sage, London.

Tales from the Front Line

Just when you thought that therapy had made a difference . . .

Joe, a man in his mid-fifties, had been referred for cognitive behaviour therapy for pain management and depression. He had not been out of his house for over a year. He had recurrent negative automatic thoughts like: "I can't go out. I can't do anything. The pain's too bad." He lived one hour's drive away from the hospital, and in order to attend sessions he was picked up by ambulance and brought to therapy. The round trip to the hospital took 4 hours: one hour for the journey in, one hour's therapy, an hour for coffee and a meal at the hospital, and an hour to go home.

Therapy had focused on getting him active again. A series of behavioural experiments was undertaken at home to test the thought that going outside would prove too much. Gradually, Joe found that he was able to walk down the street, and round to the local shop. He gained confidence in using his wheelchair for longer distances, started to take a taxi to the shopping centre, and went for drives with his daughter. After such a long time housebound, he was now engaging much more fully with life in the outside world.

At the end of therapy, when his mood and activity level were much improved, the therapist, who'd been delighted by the apparent success of the behavioural experiments, asked him: "Was there anything in particular that stood out in making the difference for you?"

"Oh yes", Joe said, "coming by ambulance here and back again has made the biggest difference in the world. It showed me I can get out and about."

CHAPTER 5

Obsessive-compulsive disorder*

Norma Morrison
David Westbrook

What is obsessive-compulsive disorder?

Obsessive-compulsive disorder (OCD) is characterized by recurrent obsessions and/or compulsions. Obsessions are persistent thoughts, images, or impulses which have, at least at some time, been experienced by the sufferer as intrusive and inappropriate, and which cause marked anxiety or distress. Compulsions are repetitive behaviours or mental acts which the person feels driven to perform as a response to obsessions or in relation to rigid rules, and which are intended to reduce distress or the risk of some feared event.

For a DSM-IV diagnosis of OCD, a person must have obsessions or compulsions which at some point during the course of the disorder they have recognized as excessive or unreasonable, and which cause marked distress, last more than one hour a day, or significantly interfere with the person's normal functioning (DSM-IV-TR, APA 2000).

In clinical practice, the most common forms of OCD are:

♦ Contamination fears and associated cleaning rituals (e.g. the fear that touching certain objects will cause someone to become ill, leading to washing of hands, clothes, etc. to avoid contamination).

♦ Doubt and uncertainty, in which people fear that something bad will happen if they do not carefully check their actions or do something the 'right' number of times or in the 'right' way (e.g. checking doors are locked or appliances are unplugged, repeating actions, etc.).

* Thanks to Rebecca Mitchell and Khadj Rouf for contributing behavioural experiments to this chapter.

◆ Thoughts which the person sees as strongly inappropriate or immoral, often associated with the fear that these thoughts imply that they might carry out some objectionable action (e.g. sexual, blasphemous, or aggressive thoughts).

Cognitive models of OCD

There are several cognitive models of OCD. Salkovskis (1985) first proposed that obsessional problems begin with normal intrusive thoughts, and that the difference between these and obsessions lies not in their occurrence or controllability, but in the way in which OCD patients *interpret* the intrusions: in Salkovskis' model, as an indication that they may be responsible for harm or for its prevention (Salkovskis 1994). This negative interpretation leads to anxiety and discomfort, and neutralizing behaviour results as an attempt to reduce this (e.g. compulsions, avoidance, sharing or passing on responsibility, seeking reassurance, and striving for absolute certainty). Since neutralizing prevents disconfirmation of the beliefs about responsibility, the patient continues to try to exert control over both mental activity and potentially harmful events, thus maintaining the problem.

Other cognitive models emphasize other aspects of the problem. Wells (1997) stresses the metacognitive aspect (i.e. beliefs about the significance of the intrusions) and suggests that while some neutralizing may be intended to prevent negative outcomes, other neutralizing is intended to relieve distress. He also emphasizes the importance of attentional strategies in the maintenance of OCD. Freeston *et al.* (1996) acknowledge the importance of responsibility but also highlight the importance of overestimation of threat, intolerance of uncertainty, and perfectionism.

Key cognitions in OCD

The Obsessive-Compulsive Cognitions Working Group (1997) reached a consensus about which were the important belief domains in OCD :

Thought–action fusion This can take two forms. First, where the person believes that merely having a 'bad' thought can produce a bad consequence (e.g. believing that thoughts about my partner having a car crash can make that more likely to happen and, consequently, that some action must be taken to prevent its happening). The second form is where having thoughts about some bad action is regarded as morally equivalent to actually performing that action (often because it is taken as indicating a hidden *desire* to perform that action).

Inflated responsibility An exaggerated belief that one has the power to produce or prevent negative outcomes. This results in the person feeling obliged to take every possible action to prevent the feared consequence, or to constantly monitor to make sure that nothing they have done or left undone could have had a negative result.

Beliefs about the controllability of thoughts The belief that it is both possible to control one's thoughts and images, and desirable or necessary to do so (for example, because of potential harmful effects of thoughts, as outlined above).

Perfectionism The belief that there is a right way to do everything and that it is one's duty to do it that way (e.g. 'Making any small mistake is as bad as failing completely').

Overestimation of threat An exaggerated estimation of the probability or severity of harm (e.g. 'Bad things are likely to happen unless I constantly act to prevent them').

Intolerance of uncertainty The belief that it is absolutely necessary to be certain, and that if one cannot be certain, then one will find it impossible to cope; often related to overestimation of threat and fears about responsibility.

Behavioural experiments

In general, behavioural experiments in OCD are designed to help patients explore two different perspectives on their problems. The typical starting view of most patients is that there is a real and substantial risk that harm may come to them or others, and therefore their obsessional behaviours are essential to prevent that harm. The cognitive formulation proposes that the problem is due to an exaggerated *fear* of such harm, and that although the obsessional behaviours are aimed at reducing risk, their main effect is to maintain the fear. There are therefore two classes of behavioural experiment: those designed to test out the reality of the predicted feared harm and those aimed at testing out or demonstrating the processes which may serve to maintain the fears.

Both types are illustrated in the examples that follow, classified under the key cognitive themes as follows:

- ◆ **Thought–action fusion**
    Experiment 5.1: thoughts leading to action
    Experiment 5.2: thoughts causing events to happen
    Experiment 5.3: fear of harming due to loss of control (internal cause)
    Experiment 5.4: fear of harming due to loss of control (external cause)
- ◆ **Inflated responsibility**
    Experiment 5.5: testing the role of responsibility
    Experiment 5.6: responsibility for 'bad' actions of others
- ◆ **Controllability of thoughts**
    Experiment 5.7: control of thoughts
- ◆ **Perfectionism**
    Experiment 5.8: perfectionism
- ◆ **Overestimation of threat**
    Experiment 5.9: overestimation of threat (contamination)
    Experiment 5.10: overestimation of threat (harming)
- ◆ **Intolerance of uncertainty**
    Experiment 5.11: intolerance of uncertainty
    Experiment 5.12: inappropriate criteria—waiting till it 'feels right'
    Experiment 5.13: establishing what is normal

Thought–action fusion

Experiment 5.1: thoughts leading to action

Problem Eva avoided sharp implements because she had frequent intrusions about sticking them into her husband, members of her family, or acquaintances. She hated helping her husband with the washing up because she was plagued with thoughts about the kitchen knives.

Target cognition If I have these thoughts, I must want to do it (belief rating 100%). If I have these thoughts, I am likely to do it (belief rating 100%).

Alternative perspective I am only having these thoughts because the idea is so repugnant to me. Thoughts cannot make me do anything.

Prediction If I stay close to sharp objects, I will not be able to resist the urge to use them.

Experiment Eva was given an appointment when there were no other staff in the building. A large bread knife from the department kitchen was placed on the table between her and the therapist, handle towards her. Her anxiety was rated during the session, together with her beliefs in the target cognitions.

Results At first she was highly anxious and visibly sweating but as the session wore on, she gradually became calmer. By the end of the session she rated her belief in the target cognitions as 20%, and the alternative perspective as 80%. Her anxiety dropped from 100% at the start to 20% at the end. She did not attack the therapist.

Reflection Eva could not dispel all anxiety as there was still a slight belief in the thought. However, this experiment laid the foundation for belief in the alternative perspective, and eventually she came to believe it 100%. She learned that having this sort of intrusive thought did not mean that she was likely to give in to the thought and do it.

Tips The fact that the therapist was confident enough to do this when there were no other staff in the building had already introduced doubts in Eva that her theory was correct, so that she was able to contemplate trying it. A previous history of severe mental illness or of causing harm to self or others would obviously be a cue to get a second opinion before such an experiment.

Experiment 5.2: thoughts causing events to happen

Problem Gwen had obsessional thoughts about harm coming to her family. Any thought of anything bad happening to one of them had to be cancelled out by rituals.

Target cognitions If I think something bad, it might happen (belief rating 70%). If I have not done anything to prevent it, then it will be my fault (belief rating 80%).

Alternative perspective A thought is just a thought, and cannot make things happen.

Prediction If I think a bad thought, it will happen. My anxiety will get so high, I will be unable to resist neutralizing.

Operationalizing the prediction See what happens as a result of gradually increasing 'bad' thoughts, first about the therapist (being less important to the patient than family members) and then about her family. Does the thought result in actual harm, or just anxiety?

Experiment Gwen first tested thoughts in session by thinking that the therapist would have a heart attack in the next 10 minutes, then that the secretary of the department would have one during the treatment hour (an excuse was found to go and see her to make sure she was still alive). Eva then agreed to spend 10–15 minutes every evening for the next few weeks thinking increasingly 'bad' thoughts as follows:

1 My therapist is going to sprain her ankle before the next session.
2 My therapist is going to have a heart attack before the next session.
3 My husband is going to come downstairs this morning and twist his ankle falling down the last few stairs.
4 My daughter is going to fall in the playground and hurt her knee.
5 My husband will fall seriously ill this week.
6 My daughter will fall seriously ill this week.

She rated her anxiety level and how much she believed that anything bad would happen, before and after doing her homework.

Results Belief ratings were never higher than 70–80% as she 'knew' her bad thoughts were illogical. Anxiety ratings started at 90%. Both ratings steadily came down to zero. As each time period passed and her prediction failed to come true, she gained confidence. She also found that although her anxiety was high initially, it gradually came down.

Reflection Gwen learned that thoughts are just thoughts and do not automatically make things happen, and that she could cope with the anxiety of testing this out.

Tips It helped to start these thought experiments by using absurd examples such as winning the lottery by thinking the right numbers; then moving on to neutral examples; and finally tackling bad thoughts.

Experiment 5.3: fear of harming due to loss of control (internal cause)

Problem Debbie was referred with intrusive thoughts of harming her baby son. She knew she did not want to, but believed that the thoughts were a sign that she was going mad, and might therefore lose control and do it in spite of herself. She showed extensive avoidance, both of being alone with the children and of 'dangerous' objects. She was greatly distressed by this, and fearful that social services would come and take her baby away.

Target cognitions If I have these thoughts, I could lose control and do it (belief rating 100%). These thoughts are a sign that I am going mad (belief rating 90%).

Alternative perspective These thoughts only keep coming because they are so appalling to me; they are only thoughts and cannot make me do anything.

Prediction These thoughts might make me harm my baby. I need to continue to avoid being alone with him in case I lose control and do something bad to him.

Experiment Debbie would spend 15 minutes each evening with the baby when he was at his most defenceless (asleep in a darkened room). She would repeat to herself 'I am going to strangle Jamie' and imagine herself doing it. She agreed to rate her anxiety at the beginning and end of each 15 minutes, and to rate her belief in the target cognition. She would come back a week later with the results.

Results Each evening her anxiety would start off high but rapidly decrease, and as each day passed, the initial level of anxiety decreased. She had no urge to cause actual harm to the baby. Her rating of her belief in the target cognition reduced to 10% by the end of the week, and her belief in the alternative increased to 85%.

Reflection Debbie learned that even when the opportunity was there, she did not harm the baby. She could see that she had become so distressed because the thought was so horrible to her, and that even by encouraging the thought she did not go mad.

Tips Be sure to differentiate between a diagnosis of post-natal depression and OCD before carrying out this sort of experiment. If in doubt, one could get a second opinion. One needs to be sure that the thought is ego-dystonic (i.e. not in keeping with the patient's other beliefs and values) and that the patient is neutralizing in some way to prevent the catastrophe happening. If the patient has a high level of anxiety or revulsion when she has the thought, this may strengthen the therapist's confidence that the thoughts are obsessional and therefore not dangerous.

Experiment 5.4: fear of harming due to loss of control (external cause)

Problem Tessa feared that she might lose control of her behaviour and carry out some harmful act such as attacking someone. She believed she could easily be hypnotized and that, in a trance state, she was very likely to commit some aggressive act, either by losing control or by suggestion. She believed that almost any repetitive visual stimulus might be hypnotic, and she therefore feared and avoided looking at a line of trees from a moving car, anything swinging back and forth, flashing lights, etc.

Target cognition Any repetitive visual stimulus will result in my becoming hypnotized against my will and, if this happens, I will be very likely to commit an aggressive act (belief rating100%).

Alternative perspective I am very frightened of losing control, but not likely to be hypnotized against my will (belief rating 5%).

Prediction Original belief: if I see a repetitive stimulus I will be hypnotized and I could be made to do anything against my will. Alternative belief: if I see a repetitive stimulus I will become anxious but not hypnotized, and will retain normal control over my actions.

Operationalizing the predictions Tessa agreed to allow the therapist to display a repetitive stimulus whilst she monitored whether this resulted in her being hypnotized and whether she experienced any loss of control over her behaviour.

Experiment The therapist waved a pendant necklace in front of Tessa's eyes (Tessa's only experience of hypnosis was from watching movies). She agreed to monitor her level of consciousness by checking whether she was capable of answering questions normally and performing actions which she chose, regardless of whether the therapist told her to do them. Before the experiment, there was a discussion of what signs and symptoms of anxiety she might expect and how these differed from a true hypnotic trance state. During the experiment, she also agreed to test whether she was 'under the therapist's power' by seeing whether she could ignore orders to do trivial actions (e.g. scratching her ear).

Results She became very anxious at first, but soon discovered that she was able to control her behaviour in a normal way, and was easily able to ignore the therapist's suggestions for specific actions.

Reflection Tessa found this experiment useful, and it had some effect in lowering her belief in the target cognition to 50% and increasing her belief in the alternative to 25%. However, as these ratings suggest, she still had some anxiety about hypnosis and further work was required to tackle her reservations (e.g. that it still might happen if she was caught unexpectedly by one of the feared stimuli).

Tips It may be important to clarify with patients before any experiment that the alternative prediction does not usually imply 'Try this and everything will be fine' but often predicts that they *will* become anxious or uncomfortable. It may also be helpful to clarify beforehand what sensations may be associated with such emotional states. Otherwise there is a danger that the patient will interpret any emotional reaction as evidence confirming their beliefs (e.g. these sensations mean that I *am* hypnotized), and subsequent attempts to attribute the sensations to anxiety will be less convincing.

Inflated responsibility

Experiment 5.5: testing the role of responsibility

Problem Susan was unable to resist checking a number of domestic appliances before leaving the house, but was unconvinced that responsibility played a role in maintaining her OCD.

Target cognition I cannot risk leaving without checking these things.

Alternative perspective The risk is not high, but my sensitivity to responsibility is making me feel this way.

Prediction I will not be able to resist checking even if someone else takes over the responsibility. If I do resist checking and leave the house, my anxiety will be so overwhelming that I will have to go back.

Experiment The aim was to test whether manipulating responsibility would make any difference to Susan's ability to resist carrying out the checking rituals. The therapist wrote a letter declaring that for one week she would take over all responsibility for any consequence resulting from Susan resisting checking. This was typed on official-looking notepaper and signed by both the therapist and Susan. The patient took it away with her, with instructions to bring it back the following week.

Results Susan returned for the next session having had much more success in resisting checking. Most mornings she had been able to leave home with only one check on some objects and none on others.

Reflection Susan could see that when the therapist took on the responsibility, her task became much easier, and therefore that responsibility did play a part in her problems. Also, she had found that her anxiety had not been overwhelming when she had resisted. This enabled her to try again without the assurance of the 'responsibility guarantee'.

Tips Remember to reclaim the letter after the agreed period, so that it does not become a persisting source of reassurance to the patient and hence a safety behaviour.

Experiment 5.6: responsibility for 'bad' comments from others

Problem Karen felt an overwhelming sense of anxiety and responsibility if someone around her said something 'bad'. Comments such as 'I could strangle him' or 'I hope they get their comeuppance' would lead to Karen feeling compelled to ask the speaker to 'take it back'.

Target cognition If someone says something bad and I do not get them to take it back, then I will be responsible for something dreadful happening.

Alternative perspective If someone says something bad it is possible that nothing bad will happen as a result of what was said, and I will not be responsible for any consequences.

Prediction If someone says something bad and I do not ask them to take it back, something awful will happen; my sense of anxiety will be unbearable and I might go mad (belief rating 100%).

Experiment Karen agreed for a period of half a day to resist the urge to ask someone to 'take it back' by telling herself to take the risk and treat it as an experiment to see how anxious she became and whether anything bad happened.

Results Karen experienced an enormous amount of anxiety at first, but it decreased throughout the afternoon. Nothing 'bad' happened as a result of her not asking people to take back things they had said.

Reflection Karen's belief diminished to 50% but she realized that she would need to engage in the experiment repeatedly for the belief to diminish further. She was pleasantly surprised that her anxiety levels were manageable and that she did not go mad.

Tips Karen was aware that she might associate distant bad events with her not having asked people to take it back. This was discussed before engaging in the experiment. She agreed that she could not extend her 'magical' thinking to such an extent, and would only take notice of bad events directly related to what the person had said.

Controllability of thoughts

Experiment 5.7: control of thoughts

Problem James had obsessional thoughts about behaving inappropriately towards children. He was very distressed by these thoughts, and felt that the only way he could be sure of not acting on them was to keep tight control of them. He took the fact that he could not control them as evidence that he was going mad.

Target cognition I need to, and should be able to, control my thoughts.

Alternative perspective Nothing will happen if I do not control my thoughts.

Prediction If I do not control my thoughts, I will be overwhelmingly anxious and I will do something bad.

Operationalize the prediction It was decided to compare attempting to control his thoughts as much as possible with allowing them to come and making no attempt to stop them (cf. experiment 5.12).

Preparation for the experiment Discussion took place as to whether James had ever actually lost control, and what would it be like if he did. He also wanted guidance on how to allow thoughts to come, after he had spent so long striving to do the opposite. A long time was spent in motivating him to take this risk.

Experiment Compare anxiety and control between (a) a day of attempting to control his thoughts as firmly as possible and (b) a day when he allowed the intrusive thoughts to come, just counting them instead of reacting emotionally, and trying not to suppress or argue with the thoughts.

Results James reported that on the 'thought control' day, he became as anxious as usual because he was unable to keep the thoughts at bay. Much to his surprise, on the day he was just making a tally of them, his anxiety was lower. By turning the intrusions into a cue for a task, he avoided the immediate rise in anxiety experienced on the first day. He also found that allowing them to come did not make him act upon them or feel out of control: on the contrary, he felt more in control.

Reflection James realized that when he relaxed control he did not do bad things, nor did the frequency of the thoughts increase. He could see that he was trying to control something that neither needed to be nor could be controlled. His belief that if he reduced control he would go mad and do bad things reduced considerably.

Perfectionism

Experiment 5.8: perfectionism

Problem Moyra washed her hands between 50 and 100 times per day and had severe dermatitis as a result. She was concerned about being dirty and 'a mess' and thought that others would think badly of her if her appearance was not perfect. She only wore clothes for a day, and was overly concerned about household cleanliness.

Target cognition If I don't wash, then I'll be dirty and others will reject me.

Alternative perspective If I reduce my washing, others will not notice.

Prediction Moyra anticipated feeling anxious if she was dirty, and was concerned that others would notice that she looked or smelt dirty.

Preparation for the experiment Moyra identified a tendency towards black and white thinking and perfectionism, which made her reluctant to let her standards drop. She was asked to consider how often colleagues wore the same outfit on consecutive days, how often they washed their hands, and how often they had marks on their clothes. Moyra was then asked whether they appeared extremely dirty, and whether she had rejected them. This helped generate evidence which made her feel less anxious about trying the experiment.

Experiment Moyra deliberately stained her top with brown sauce, then went to work wearing it. She made sure she looked at others carefully to see whether they rejected her by moving away, showing disgust, or commenting on her appearance. Moyra also wore the same outfit for at least three days running.

Results and reflection Moyra discovered that no-one noticed the mark on her top. She managed to comment to a colleague, 'Oh dear, I've spilt sauce on myself' but the colleague did not seem at all concerned. Her anxiety reduced considerably during the course of the experiment, and she managed to forget that she was wearing the same outfit over the next three days. She said she had learned that there were many steps before she became dishevelled and smelly, and that she could afford to be less perfectionist.

Further work Moyra was encouraged to push the boundaries of cleanliness by wearing clothes for more than three days. She also decided to reduce hand washing, agreeing to wash only after going to the toilet, when preparing or eating food, or if she had visible soiling of her hands.

Tips Grading the behavioural experiments allowed Moyra to move through a manageable sequence of challenges to her perfectionist beliefs. Preparatory cognitive work was essential to help her engage in doing behavioural experiments. Once she had thought about the range of views of what is clean, she was more willing to let her high standards go.

Overestimation of threat

Experiment 5.9: overestimation of threat (contamination)

Problem Sarah had been referred for treatment of washing rituals and checking. She was having difficulty resisting washing, although intellectually she had accepted the cognitive model.

Target cognition If I touch anything that I judge to be contaminated, I must wash immediately or (a) I will get sick (belief rating 70%); and (b) I will not be able to cope with the anxiety (belief rating 90%).

Alternative perspective If I do not wash, nothing dreadful will happen and the anxiety will gradually diminish.

Prediction If I do not wash, I will have a stomach upset or something similar, and the anxiety will be overwhelming.

Operationalizing the predictions It was decided to find something anxiety-provoking for Sarah to touch in session, as she was having trouble resisting ritualizing at home. She would then have a long drive home, thus also 'contaminating' her car, which would give her the opportunity to find out whether the anxiety did go down.

Experiment Sarah was asked to identify something that she would find extremely difficult to touch. She spotted a half-eaten apple left over from the therapist's hurried lunch. She agreed to touch the apple, and then touch her face and clothes. She was obviously distressed and rated her anxiety as 12 out of 10. She then agreed that she would not wash her hands before going to her car, and she would drive home, cut herself a sandwich, and eat it before washing her hands. She rated her anxiety after 10 minutes as 6 out of 10, and by the end of the session as 4 out of 10.

Results Sarah reported that her anxiety had decreased somewhat on the drive home, but increased at the prospect of preparing and eating the sandwich without washing her hands. However, she was able to do it and felt very pleased with herself. Neither she nor her husband suffered any ill effects, and belief ratings came down to 20% and 10% respectively.

Reflection Sarah learned that she was overestimating the threat of contamination and that the anxiety was not as high as she anticipated, nor as difficult to cope with. She said at the end of therapy that this had been a turning point and that it made it possible for her to start to eliminate her rituals. It marked the beginning of changes in her beliefs about contamination and about her ability to cope with anxiety.

Tips This experiment is easily adapted to use anxiety-provoking objects in any therapy room. Most OCD patients with contamination fears will have difficulty in touching their shoes or door handles; the department toilets will also provide a fertile source of experiments.

Experiment 5.10: overestimation of threat (harming)

Problem Martin worried that he was exposing himself to women, or touching them inappropriately, as he walked past them in the street. He became obsessed with the thought that he was a sexual predator and a menace to women.

Target cognitions I touch women or expose myself at every opportunity. I am a menace to women.

Alternative perspective I do not actually touch women or expose myself to them. It is my worry that makes me believe I do these things.

Prediction I will not be able to walk past women in the street without behaving inappropriately towards them. The anxiety will be so bad that I will have to cross over to avoid walking near women.

Operationalizing the prediction It was agreed that Martin would walk past women in the presence of the therapist, without crossing over or circumventing them.

Experiment Martin walked up and down a street with the therapist. Initially, the therapist walked next to Martin, then she walked in front of him so as not to reassure him that she was monitoring him.

Results Martin did not expose himself to women, or touch them inappropriately, and he was able to 'brush past' a woman standing in a bus queue without believing that he had assaulted her. By recording his anxiety levels Martin was able to see that he could manage high anxiety and that it decreased with practice. He was also gradually able to reduce checking behaviours (e.g. checking that his trousers were done up).

Reflection Martin became more confident that he was not a menace to women and that his avoidance, checking, and ruminating had maintained his fear.

Intolerance of uncertainty

Experiment 5.11: intolerance of uncertainty

Problem Frank thought he had a defective memory and therefore had to keep checking doors, switches, etc. He reasoned that even slight uncertainty meant that there was a risk that the action had been left undone and that the consequences could be catastrophic. He believed everyone else would always be 100% sure of having done such actions.

Target cognition I must be able to remember with absolute certainty that I have locked the door; if I cannot remember it, I probably have not done it (belief rating 100%).

Alternative perspective It is normal to be unable to remember doing such everyday actions.

Prediction Everyone else will be able to remember actions such as locking the door or turning off taps.

Operationalizing the prediction Carry out a survey to find out whether other people do remember this sort of thing.

Experiment Frank agreed to survey 12 people, asking if they could remember locking their door when they left home that morning and, if not, how certain they were that their door was locked. The therapist did the same survey with 12 colleagues.

Reflection Frank was surprised to find that it was common for people to be unable to remember carrying out this task. This made him realize that his memory was no different from the other people surveyed. The only difference was that he inferred from his uncertainty that he had left his door unlocked, whereas others assumed their doors *were* locked. His belief rating dropped to 20%.

Experiment 5.12: inappropriate criteria — waiting till it 'feels right'

Problem Robert was referred for treatment of compulsive checking of his home, his car, and his work. Each time he checked something, his criteria for stopping was that it 'felt right'.

Target cognition I need to check until it feels right; if I leave before it feels right, I will be overwhelmingly anxious all day (belief rating 100%).

Alternative perspective Feeling right is not an appropriate way to judge if something has been done or not. If I turn away after one look, I will feel anxious but that will subside.

Prediction If I turn away before it feels right, the anxiety will last all day and I won't be able to cope.

Operationalizing the prediction It was decided to compare the amount of checking and his distress between (a) checking as much as possible, and (b) looking just once and turning away.

Experiment Robert agreed to spend one day checking as long as was necessary to feel absolutely sure that the door was locked, the tap off, etc. He was asked to note how much time he spent checking and the level of his anxiety. The following day, he would only check once and then make himself turn away, again recording checking and anxiety. He was asked to repeat this for a further two days.

Results Robert complied with the plan most of the time. He returned with a diary sheet which showed considerably more time spent checking and a higher level of anxiety on the 'until it feels right' days. On the 'only once' days, less time was spent checking but also, contrary to his expectations, there were less intrusive thoughts and a lower level of anxiety. His level of belief in the target cognition came down to 10% and his belief in the alternative perspective rose to 90%.

Reflection Robert realized that the more he tried to be sure by doing things till they felt right, the more he introduced doubts. He came to see that by trying too hard, he was making his goal of certainty more elusive and his level of distress higher.

Experiment 5.13: establishing what is normal

An area that does not fit into the major OCD belief themes is that of helping the patient establish what is 'normal'. Frequently, OCD patients have been carrying out their rituals for so long that they no longer know what other people do in the same situations and cannot remember how they used to act before they developed the problem.

Problem Harriet was referred for help with obsessional cleaning and washing. She also had considerable difficulty preparing raw food, especially chicken. A sticking point in therapy was that she said that after having the problem for 20 years, she no longer knew what was normal and what was not. She pointed out that the media bombard us with advertising about the need to use the newest cleaning substances and get rid of all germs. She was also married to a food scientist who had described the effects of *E. coli* and salmonella to her in detail.

Experiment It was suggested to Harriet that a way of finding out what was 'normal' would be to observe what other people did. As she was going to spend a long weekend with her sister-in-law, she was asked to observe closely what her sister-in-law did about cooking, cleaning, and washing over the weekend and compare that with what she did. She was to note how long her sister-in-law took to do things such as clean surfaces and prepare food, and how often she washed her hands, then compare that with what she was doing.

Results Harriet came back with a description of normal domestic life. She was aware that this differed considerably from her own habits, but at first was undecided whether this might be because her sister-in-law was an irresponsible housewife. After discussion, she was ready to admit that this was probably a fair representation of normal life and that a reasonable target would be to approximate to this.

Reflection Harriet was surprised to find out how little store others set by the warnings about germs in the media. This provided a chink in her belief that what she was doing was essential, which paved the way for further behavioural experiments and reduction in rituals.

Distinctive difficulties in OCD

For any behavioural experiment to be devised and implemented effectively, it is obviously crucial to have a clear conception of the thoughts or beliefs to be tested. A common difficulty in OCD is that for various reasons patients may be reluctant to, or unable to, divulge the exact contents of their cognitions.

Reluctance to report

OCD sufferers are often ashamed or embarrassed about their thinking (which by definition they recognize to some extent as irrational). Some patients may fear that if they divulge the true extent of their thinking they will be thought 'mad' and 'locked up in a mental hospital'. It may be helpful to offer such patients examples of common obsessions and compulsions, so that they are reassured that the therapist is familiar with these kinds of thoughts. Asking patients if they can describe the worries that are blocking disclosure may also enable the blocks to be dealt with through verbal challenging, before addressing the actual content of the obsessional thoughts.

If patients suffer from obsessional thoughts about aggressive or illegal acts, they may fear that some kind of legal action will be taken against them, or that their children will be taken into care. Gentle, careful questioning and a focus on building trust can usually overcome these worries, together with simple education about OCD and how it differs from severe mental illnesses such as psychosis. Careful assessment is obviously also necessary in order to be confident that the thoughts are indeed obsessional in nature and not true expressions of dangerous impulses.

Unclear feared consequences

Some OCD patients find it difficult to describe their fears because they have become so adept at avoiding provoking situations and/or rapidly neutralizing upsetting thoughts that the fears never become conscious. In such cases, small exposure experiments, in which they deliberately confront some anxiety-provoking situation without neutralizing, may be sufficient to bring the fears to consciousness.

For other patients, the fear may simply be that their anxiety will become completely intolerable or will go on forever. This group may find it helpful to do exposure experiments like those described in experiments 5.9 and 5.10 above, to test out their fears about the processing of anxiety.

Finally, there is another group who believe that *something* bad will happen to them or loved ones, but who cannot specify what it might be. For such patients, it may be more useful to do experiments aimed at building up the alternative perspective rather than trying to test out specific feared consequences.

'Far future' catastrophes

It is quite common in OCD that the patient's feared catastrophe lies far in the future: 'If I touch this contaminated doorknob today, I might develop cancer 10 years from now' or 'If I have this blasphemous image now, I will be condemned to suffer in hell when I eventually die'. Clearly, in such cases, it is not possible to obtain definitive evidence that the disaster will not occur. It may be more useful to do experiments aimed at building up the credibility of the alternative benign perspective, rather than directly challenging the target cognition.

Other related chapters

Obsessional fears often have some overlap with health anxiety (see Chapter 4). Depression (Chapter 10), social anxiety (Chapter 7), and low self-esteem (Chapter 20) are also common. Occasionally, obsessional beliefs may verge on the delusional in their intensity, when Chapter 12 on psychosis may be helpful.

Further reading

Freeston, M. and Ladouceur, R. (1999). Exposure and response prevention for obsessive thoughts. *Cognitive and Behavioral Practice*, **6**, 362–82.

Salkovskis, P. (1999). Understanding and treating obsessive-compulsive disorder. *Behaviour Research and Therapy*, **37**, S29–S52.

Salkovskis, P., Forrester, E., Richards, H. and Morrison, N. (1998). The devil is in the detail: conceptualising and treating obsessional problems. In: N. Tarrier (ed.), *Cognitive behaviour therapy for complex cases*. Wiley, Chichester.

Salkovskis, P. and Kirk, J. (1989). Obsessional disorders. In: K. Hawton, P. M. Salkovskis, J. Kirk *et al.* (ed.), *Cognitive behaviour therapy for psychiatric problems*. Oxford Medical Publications, Oxford.

Whittal, M. and McLean, P. (1999). CBT for OCD: the rationale, protocol and challenges. *Cognitive and Behavioral Practice*, **6**, 383–96.

Tales from the Front Line

Seeing red

Brian was an ex-alcoholic, and afraid that his slightly florid complexion might give him away. He was really self-conscious in public places, where he believed he would blush so badly that people would not be able to restrain themselves from pointing, laughing, and speculating about his drinking. He was very resistant to testing this out, but reluctantly agreed that if the therapist would make her face as red as he imagined his would be in the worst case scenario he would accompany her on an expedition to see how others would respond.

The therapist brought some scarlet blusher to the session, and the patient supervised its application. They then set off for a local shopping centre, where the patient sat comfortably in an open-air café whilst the therapist approached the counter and ordered drinks. The patient watched like a hawk to see whether as she turned away the counter staff might giggle, comment, or point at her. Luckily this did not happen. Flushed with success the therapist approached the patient and sat down with the drinks.

However the patient was not reassured: "You know, watching you I decided that you were not nearly as red as I might be, so it was not a fair test. Would you mind making yourself redder across your forehead and nose, and down your neck?" he said. The therapist willingly agreed to take the next step, and hurried off to the Ladies. Imagine her consternation when she got there and discovered half a dozen others touching up their make up in front of the mirror. Applying large amounts of scarlet blusher to her neck and forehead in such an intimate setting was enough to make the therapist horribly self-conscious, but surreptitious monitoring of the reaction of the other women provided excellent material to challenge her own negative beliefs, as no-one appeared to bat an eye-lid.

A further benefit was that the patient's beliefs were significantly reduced when her second order from the café counter produced no negative reactions despite her most unusual appearance.

CHAPTER 6

Generalized anxiety disorder

Gillian Butler

Khadj Rouf

Introduction

Generalized anxiety disorder (GAD) is defined as 'excessive anxiety and worry (apprehensive expectation), occurring more days than not for a period of at least 6 months, about a number of events or activities' (DSM-IV-TR, APA). So the disorder is defined in terms of a cognitive process: worry, of a minimum severity level, to distinguish it from normal worry. This worry is perceived as difficult to control, leads to significant distress or impairment, and must be associated with at least three of six anxiety symptoms. It should not be due to another psychological, physiological, or medical condition.

Over two-thirds of GAD patients report that they 'have always been worriers', suggesting that the tendency to worry reflects a trait, and features of dependent and/or avoidant personality disorder occur in over 50% of cases (Brown and Barlow 1992). The typical worrier with GAD worries about the possibility that something 'bad' could happen ('What if . . . ?'), and the worry spreads from one thing to another, especially at night or when distractions are few. Worrying about an aspect of another anxiety disorder (a threatened panic attack or serious illness) does not count as GAD.

Comorbidity with other disorders, especially social anxiety and depression is common (Wittchen *et al.* 1994; Kessler *et al.*, in press). Worriers often feel inferior, think that they are judged negatively, and feel hopeless about being able to change. The problem potentially interferes with all aspects of life and reduces confidence and self-esteem. Many people with GAD deal with their sense of vulnerability by seeking reassurance, depending on others for support, and by attempting to keep themselves safe from perceived risks. The main symptoms include high levels of tension, finding it hard to relax, inability to concentrate, and insomnia.

Cognitive models

The generic cognitive model (e.g. Beck *et al.* 1985) suggests that anxiety and worry arise when the number of perceived threats outweighs perceived resources (internal and external) for dealing with them. More specific theories have recently been developed and are still being evaluated. Three are outlined here.

First, the metacognitive model of GAD (Wells 1997, 2000) distinguishes two types of worry. The first type, about possible threats (e.g. worrying about whether to change jobs), is triggered by (mistaken) beliefs about the benefits of worrying (e.g. 'worrying helps me decide what to do'). The second type, or meta-worry, is about potential negative or catastrophic effects of worrying (e.g. 'worrying will drive me crazy'). It increases distress and leads to counterproductive attempts to control it. In general, worry ceases when worriers achieve a sense of safety or a reduced sense of risk. So, it is reinforced by the non-occurrence of feared events, and partially reinforced by the occasional occurrence of negative events. When metaworry predominates, the sense of safety becomes increasingly elusive.

Borkovec's model (e.g. Borkovec and Newman 1999; Borkovec et al., in press) suggests that worry is the product of attempts to avoid more acute distress. Confrontation with threats (e.g. vivid imagery) is reduced by the reiterative, cognitive process of worrying. Although worrying feels bad, the impact of disturbing imagery is worse. Worry may become increasingly elaborated, generating numerous thoughts and images of a future that exists only in imagination (Borkovec et al. 2002). This accounts for the rapid spread of worry from one thing to another. Worrying has been shown to interfere with emotional processing, to reduce flexibility in responsiveness, and to be associated with rigidity in cognitive, physiological, affective, and behavioural systems.

The third model, developed in Quebec (Dugas et al. 1998; Ladouceur et al. 2000), suggests that people with GAD are intolerant of uncertainty. They are reluctant to give threatening material their full attention and, therefore, despite having the appropriate skills, are slow to initiate the process of problem solving. Instead they appear to catastrophize at length, and to anticipate the consequences of something going wrong. They focus on feared outcomes rather than on seeking solutions, and find it especially hard to accept uncertainties that cannot be resolved. Worrying may feel like thinking things through so as, for example, to anticipate problems or to avoid acting impulsively. However, worrying makes it harder to focus on problems, to concentrate, and to make decisions, and so it increases rather than reduces feelings of uncertainty.

All three theories contribute to our present understanding of worry and how to treat it, and the theme of finding it difficult to tolerate uncertainty is consistent with all of them. However, worry can also be understood as a normal process that, within limits, provides a useful alarm mechanism, prompting one to prepare for action (Davey and Tallis 1994). For example, hearing a child's persistent cough triggers the alarm system, worrying about it prompts action, and continuing to do so when the cough does not respond to treatment prepares the way for further action. Worry prompts anticipatory coping: worrying about future difficult times (retirement, children leaving home, a parent's death) may initiate emotional processing or prompt support seeking. Some of the superstitious statements worriers make ('Unless I worry something is bound to go wrong') may reflect a 'sneaking suspicion' that worry is useful without a clear understanding of why or to what extent.

Development of relevant beliefs

Relatively large numbers of people with GAD report experiences of being, at an early age, in positions that threatened to overwhelm their coping abilities, such as dealing with a sick or alcoholic relative, or running a home for absent or overworked parents (Roemer *et al.* 1991). Belief systems developed at this stage may contribute to the sense that something catastrophic or unmanageable could happen at any time (Borkovec 1994; Davey and Tallis 1994) and to the overlap with features of dependent and avoidant personality disorder. The thoughts and beliefs of worriers could also be partially determined by the stage of cognitive development reached at the time of the relevant childhood experiences. Immature thinking may lead children to overestimate their responsibility for finding solutions to parental problems; or non-contingent events may be linked in (supposedly) causal chains.

Key cognitions

Two central aspects of cognition provide useful starting points for behavioural experiments in GAD. The first of these is metacognitive beliefs about worry, both positive and negative (Wells 2000); and the second is a set of thoughts grouped here under the heading of 'intolerance of uncertainty'. The typical beliefs expressed by people with persistent GAD who may have overlapping diagnoses of avoidant or dependent personality disorder will be included in this second category.

Metacognitive beliefs

Metaworries concern the perceived, dire consequences of worry, and are of two kinds: thoughts about loss of control and thoughts about harm or danger. Examples of the first are: 'There's nothing I can do to stop worrying', 'Worrying just gets a grip on me', 'I can't let myself think anything problematic in case I start worrying', 'Once a worry starts it just has to burn itself out'. Examples concerning harm or danger are: 'This worrying is going to drive me mad', 'If I go on worrying, I'll make myself ill', 'Something terrible will happen if I can't get to grips with this worrying', 'I'll be so tired out by worry that I'll never get through tomorrow', 'Worrying will prevent me thinking straight'.

Positive beliefs about worry focus on its supposed benefits, for example: 'If I keep on worrying about this I'll discover what's best to do', 'Worrying things through allows me to lay them to rest', 'Worrying is the best way I know to work things out', 'I need to worry; it helps me to keep things under control'. Dysfunctional worry, whether positive or negative, interferes with decision making, problem solving, and concentration.

Intolerance of uncertainty

Uncertainty reflects a general attitude ('It's terrible not to know what lies ahead') and also concerns about risk or rescue factors. These are apparent in statements like: 'Something is bound to go wrong', 'You never know what might happen next', 'I can't handle it when things go wrong', 'Others are never there when you need them'. Underlying beliefs tend to cluster round the themes of inadequacy or incompetence, and variations reflect a personal sense of vulnerability. Uncertainty may also trigger a 'felt sense' that is more like a feeling than a thought, and that is perceived as confirming beliefs about the inevitability of worry: 'Even though I know there's nothing wrong, I still feel worried', 'I'm just a worrier. That's just me', 'I wake up worrying. It's even in my dreams'. Worries about some of the terrible things that might happen, such as serious illness to a child or the consequences of climate change, are not amenable to solutions, or even resolvable in a lifetime, so they are inevitably associated with uncertainty.

Worriers find it difficult to live with remaining doubts, and their efforts to remove them are reflected in assumptions and operating principles that predominantly increase hypervigilance and rigidity: 'If I keep on the look out, then I'll know what to do', 'You've got to be prepared', 'If you don't watch out, something terrible will happen', 'Not to have a routine is to lay yourself open to chaos'. Some of these assumptions are also likely to be endorsed by society ('forewarned is forearmed'), with numerous culturally determined variants. Many messages we give our children when they are worried may inadvertently encourage the rigidity that is associated with GAD: 'Steel yourself and have a go', 'Keep trying', 'Grit your teeth and hang in there'. Behaviours determined by such rules are likely to interfere with the flexibility needed for accepting uncertainty, indicating that experiments to increase flexibility should be beneficial.

Two subsets of cognitions are associated with the avoidant and the dependent aspects of GAD: 'Wouldn't it be terrible if . . . ' and 'I couldn't handle it if . . . '. When dangers lie ahead, worriers protect themselves, which may create a link with avoidant personality disorder, or they seek support and reassurance within dependent relationships. Similar themes concerning inadequacy and incompetence are apparent in their beliefs.

Typical cognitions of more avoidant worriers include: 'That's too dreadful to think about', 'Don't even mention it . . . It'll only make me worry', 'If I don't . . . watch the news/read the paper/talk about it . . . I'll be OK'. Avoidance is more common in GAD than was originally thought and can take subtle forms (prevarication, use of medication or alcohol, etc.). People may avoid thinking about anything worrying, as if it were true that 'what the eye doesn't see, the heart doesn't grieve about'. Avoidance may be inconsistent and determined by current feelings, by a perceived need for protection, or by a wish to withdraw. Left unchallenged, cognitions linked to avoidance will contribute to the maintenance of worry and may prevent emotional processing.

Typical cognitions of more dependent worriers include: 'What if something goes wrong? I won't know what to do', 'I can't manage without help', 'Other people are stronger than me/know best/would know what to do/don't get things out of proportion'. Reassurance seeking commonly follows such thoughts.

Behavioural experiments

◆ **Testing metacognitive beliefs**
  Experiment 6.1: a series of metaworries
  Experiment 6.2: metaworry about harm
  Experiment 6.3: positive metaworry

Table 6.1: outline experiments for changing metacognitive beliefs

◆ **Increasing tolerance of uncertainty**
  Experiment 6.4: increasing flexibility
  Experiment 6.5: living with uncertainty
  Experiment 6.6: facing underlying fears
  Experiment 6.7: building self-reliance

Table 6.2: outline experiments for increasing tolerance of uncertainty

The main purpose of experiments is to work with the appraisals that maintain the process of dysfunctional worry rather than with its content. It may be necessary to focus temporarily on the content of specific worries, for example when helping people to face their fears or encouraging them to use problem-solving skills. However, the ultimate purpose of experiments is to re-examine beliefs that lead to worrying and beliefs about the process of worry.

Testing metacognitive beliefs

These experiments are designed to test unhelpful beliefs about worrying. Wells has developed attention training (ATT) specifically for interrupting repetitive, self-focused processes, and reports that preliminary results support the value of this method as a way of reducing worry. It can be combined with behavioural experiments and used to assist in the re-evaluation of metaworries concerning both control and danger (Wells 2000, pp. 139–47).

Experiment 6.1: a series of metaworries

Problem Samira was a 21-year-old student approaching final exams, whose intrusive worries were interfering with her ability to concentrate, relax, and sleep. She described herself as 'a worrier'. She had witnessed domestic violence as a child, felt responsible for ensuring a subdued atmosphere at home and for upholding the family name. She cared for her depressed mother without support from others.

Samira felt tense most of the time, her self-care routines had deteriorated, and she had withdrawn from social contact in order to study. Her main worry was that she would fail her exams and not fulfil her ambition to become a GP. The worry had spread to concerns about being attacked when walking from college to town, worry that she had not locked her door properly, and concerns about her home situation.

Target cognition I have no control over my worry (belief rating 90%).

Predictions Not suppressing worry means that it will run out of control.

Experiments

1 Demonstration of the impact of thought suppression. Samira was asked not to think about pink elephants in the session.

2 Postponing worry. Samira wrote down key words about her worries during the day, and planned to delay thinking about these until her 'worry time' at 8.00 p.m. Then she would let herself worry as much as she wanted. This experiment had two purposes: to find out whether she could delay her worry, and to find out whether she could control her worry once it had started.

Result and reflection

1 Samira understood the paradoxical impact of trying not to worry. This encouraged her to consider adopting a passive stance to her worries, letting them wash over her without engaging with them.

2 She found it difficult to remember to write down her worries. When she did, it was easier to delay thinking about them, as she was less concerned about forgetting something important. She also found that setting a 'worry time' had a paradoxical effect. She felt silly when focusing on the worries, leading her to be more objective about the importance of worrying. Both findings helped her to realize that she had more control over her worry than she had expected, and her rating of the original belief was reduced to 20%.

Experiment 6.2: metaworry about harm

Samira also held unhelpful beliefs about the dangers of extensive worry.

Target cognition and prediction Worrying will drive me insane (belief rating 90%).

Alternative perspective Worry feeds my anxiety levels. I will not go mad from worry.

Experiment In session, Samira deliberately tried to drive herself mad by focusing on the content of specific worries such as 'I will fail my degree', 'I will never be a GP', and 'Everyone will be ashamed of me'. Although she understood that worrying would not drive her mad, she remained unconvinced when she was worrying. Preparatory work focused on understanding the function of safety mechanisms, such as thought suppression, in maintaining the problem, and clarified the rationale for testing her prediction about going mad.

Result and reflection Samira's anxiety increased initially when focusing on this material, particularly as she was still uncertain about the outcome of her exams. She became tearful. However, her anxiety reduced over approximately 20 minutes, and her belief in the original thought was reduced to 30%. She remained concerned that long-term worrying could make her unwell, reinforced by frequent colds and minor illnesses during periods of high stress.

Further work Continuing such experiments allowed Samira to make important distinctions between unhelpful worry and useful concern. She learned to test out a more passive approach to worrying thoughts, which helped her to stop ruminating.

Experiment 6.3: positive metaworry

Samira was surprised to discover she held positive beliefs about worry. The formulation helped her to understand how these could maintain and reinforce the worrying.

Target cognition If I worry about things, then I will prevent something bad happening (belief rating 100%).

Alternative perspective There are events that are beyond my control. Worrying cannot keep me safe.

Predictions Samira predicted that she would feel highly anxious about something going wrong if she did not worry. She was concerned about 'not covering all the angles' regarding potential disasters.

Preparation for experiment Cognitive work, followed by homework, was designed to question the likelihood that worrying prevents disasters. Samira gathered information about instances when she had worried about possible disasters and something unexpected had gone wrong. She also collected information about times when she had worried and something bad had happened anyway. Samira was able to generate both kinds of disconfirming evidence, once she started to look for it.

Experiment She practised dropping the worry, and 'switching off' instead. If worries came into her mind, she was encouraged to adopt a passive attitude towards them, and let them pass rather than attaching to them. This process was facilitated using the image of dandelion seeds floating past her, without her trying to catch them.

Results Samira learned to adopt a process-based approach to tackling worry, rather than dealing with the content of worry. The experiment showed her that worrying did not affect the outcome of events.

Reflection Samira started to view her worry as a safety mechanism, which put a check on her anxiety, preventing it reaching its peak. She realized that worrying meant that she was never really facing up to and processing her underlying fears.

Further work Further experimental work tackled the avoidant aspects of her worry, and involved imaginal exposure to feared catastrophes. This helped her to recognize that when her anxiety was high, she tended to catastrophize. She needed persistence to break the habit of anticipating problems in advance.

Table 6.1 Outline experiments for changing metacognitive beliefs

Thought to be tested	Suggested experiments	Potential value
I can't stop worrying	On and off time; deciding what else to do	It is possible to choose not to worry
Worry is helpful	Survey; observe self	Distinguish helpful from unhelpful worry
I feel so worried; I'll never get back to sleep	Keep pencil and paper by the bed and write down what the worries are; deal with them in the morning if necessary	'Out of the head, onto the paper' can help someone to leave the worry aside and go back to sleep
This is unstoppable	In imagination: write the worries on paper and throw them in the fire or a river; put them in a box and close the lid; etc.	Leave the worry behind

Increasing tolerance of uncertainty

Experiments should focus on changing thoughts that reflect the intolerance, not the identification of uncertainty. The aim is to help people live more comfortably with uncertainty, and to reduce unproductive attempts to remove it or to keep control; and to help them to be less rigid in thinking and more flexible.

Experiment 6.4: increasing flexibility

Problem Nicola had two young children, and her husband was working long hours, when her chronic worrying increased. She developed increasingly rigid routines in an effort to keep uncertainty at bay, until they expanded to fill every waking hour.

Target cognition 'I have to keep to my routine, or all hell will break loose.' Without it she would worry about all the terrible things that could happen, and she could elaborate on potential catastrophes at length. The experiment aimed to help her to tolerate the uncertainty that came from relaxing her habit of overplanning.

Experiment Break the routine in small ways. Make specific decisions about what to change, and predict what will happen. Starting point: the children's clothes—leave them till they 'need' washing; stop folding and tidying them each evening.

Examples of predictions 'It will feel strange and scary', 'I will worry more', 'I will hear my mother's voice calling me a slut', 'I will feel overwhelmed and out of control when I see things lying around', 'I will get angry with the children, and it's my fault not theirs'.

Results Nicola did it with difficulty, and felt 'odd'. She did not worry more, but felt lost having 'time on her hands' and was haunted by her mother's attitudes. She was pleased to be taking constructive steps that she believed were right.

Evaluation Nicola realized how negative her predictions had been and how many of them were produced by worrying, and that making plans about how to change felt different from worrying. Her anxiety increased before making a change, but she was relieved to have started, and dismayed by how much in her life there was to change.

Further work She worked to become more flexible, taking care not (inadvertently) to add rigidity by overplanning the changes. She developed and clarified her own values in contrast to those of her mother. She was encouraged to think about the adaptive value of flexibility versus rigidity, and she surveyed others, to help with setting new standards. Further experiments were used to broaden her activities in social and occupational ways.

Experiment 6.5: living with uncertainty

Problem Maureen worried 'about all the things that could go wrong'. She had a tense relationship with her husband, who abused alcohol; her adult children had numerous problems for which Maureen provided support; and she was especially stressed by the uncertainties surrounding attempts to sell her house. Worries constantly crowded into her mind: 'I end up worrying about everything'.

Target cognitions I don't know what's going to happen. What if no one wants to buy the house? I'll be trapped here for ever. There's nothing I can do (belief rating 88%).

Alternative perspective Worrying only makes me feel worse.

Preparation for experiment Maureen monitored her worrying with the aim of learning to 'catch it early'. She learned to use the worry decision tree (Butler and Hope 1995, p. 181) as a way of specifying particular worries and turning worrying into problem solving. This asks a series of questions—Is there any action to be taken? If so, what action? When should it be done?—before switching attention to something other than worry. Maureen listed ways of occupying herself and her mind to turn to when each 'branch' of problem solving came to an end.

Prediction Maureen was sceptical. She doubted if this would help.

Experiment As soon as Maureen started to worry she would focus first on deciding what (if anything) she could do to solve the current problem, then turn her attention to one of the other things on her list.

Results After one week, Maureen discovered that she could carry this plan through, and that she could sometimes settle her mind by 'going on with daily life', using the ideas on her list for occupying herself. Belief change: Maureen preferred to re-state her original belief—'There is something I can do about worrying even when there's nothing more I can do about what I'm worrying about' (belief rating 60%). She planned to keep practising the method.

Reflection 'I can accept the uncertainty more easily if I know that I've done what I can.' Maureen found it helped to describe exactly what she was worrying about. This reduced the vague sense of uncertainty that triggered her worry, and demonstrated that she needed to deal with 'feeling worried' first. This was easier if she caught it early, before the worries had spread from one thing to another.

Tip Check that distracting activities are not used as a type of avoidance.

Experiment 6.6: facing underlying fears

Problem Jen's husband, Tom, had recently been diagnosed with heart disease. His blood pressure was dangerously high, and his father and brother had both died from heart disease. Jen had always been a worrier, and she sought help as her worry, distress, and exhaustion were interfering with her concentration and preventing her from supporting Tom.

Target cognitions Jen's cognitions were numerous and quickly spread from one thing to another: 'Everything's going to change and I can't handle it', 'I can't manage without Tom', 'It's selfish to be thinking about me rather than him', 'I'll never get over it if he dies', 'How can I cope with the mortgage?', 'What shall I tell the children', and so on. As Jen's thoughts skated rapidly over a shifting range of worries, the first experiment was intended to find out more about her fears. The key cognition was 'I don't dare think about it. I can't face up to what might happen'. She agreed to do the experiment described below in order to find out what would happen if she made an effort to face her fears.

Alternative perspective Facing the worries might point the way towards dealing with them.

Experiment In the session, Jen focused on a single worry at a time, allowing her mind to dwell on it, expand on it, and to try to accept her feelings as they arose. She asked to do this in silence, with her therapist reminding her to refocus roughly every 15 seconds. As a starting point she chose the worry that felt to her most 'important'—'It's selfish to be thinking of me rather than him'.

Result An image came to Jen's mind of Tom, in great pain, in the middle of the night. She saw herself in a panic, not daring to turn away from him to telephone for help, with tears streaming down her face, and not a single coherent thought in her head. Her main fear was that her incompetence would put his life at risk, and she was ashamed of needing help when he was in pain.

Further work Focus on the content of her worries prompted problem solving. Jen decided to talk to her GP about what she should do if Tom became seriously ill in the night. She also spoke to a neighbour, who offered to help in an emergency. She made a list of what to take if she had suddenly to go to hospital. She concluded that facing her fears had helped her to make plans, and she felt calmer, though still 'living on a cliff-edge'.

Second set of cognitions Nothing's certain any more. Something terrible could happen at any time.

Experiments Two sets of experiments were planned to help Jen to accept, and live with, the uncertainty that she faced.

1 Creating as much certainty as possible around the practical aspects of her life (e.g. shopping, washing, cooking, and household chores). Her mind felt less chaotic when daily life felt organized. She also found regular contact with her children helpful.

2 Scheduling opportunities for relaxation and pleasure. For example, she and Tom planned something to look forward to each week (e.g. a special meal, a visit to their daughter, a video) With Tom's support she also planned independent expeditions and meetings with friends. Finally, she found the courage to talk to him about their finances.

Results Jen was relieved to have confronted the uncertainties in her life. Her worry and sense of dread diminished (slowly), as each day passed uneventfully. She accepted the uncertainty with less fear.

Experiment 6.7: building self-reliance

Problem Ben worked as a trainee manager at a sports centre, and had become so worried about his performance that he constantly sought reassurance from others. His manager and co-workers had started to ignore his requests and to show their irritation with him.

Target cognition I can't rely on myself to get things right.

Experiment As soon as he felt uncertain about something, Ben would make a small (even arbitrary) decision about what to do, and stick to it. If tempted to seek reassurance he would glance at his flashcard, which summarized its agreed disadvantages. Examples of work situations that had previously provoked reassurance seeking were used to predict relevant situations (e.g. when to advertise the next exercise classes, how to supervise part-time evening-class leaders, how to allocate weekend work fairly, etc.).

Prediction Ben predicted that he would make serious mistakes, and that his manager would criticize him at their weekly meeting.

Results At first Ben dithered, and felt extremely uncomfortable as he tried not to seek (overt) reassurance. He watched others to see whether they noticed, and eventually made a decision (to ask someone to move some bicycles that had been dumped in the parking lot). His request was met with a grumble, but appreciated by car users. Continued practice taught Ben that the quicker he made decisions, the better he felt. He made few mistakes, and began to appreciate when to seek advice from others appropriately. The experiment improved both his confidence and his work performance (as judged by his manager). However, he readily discounted his successes as trivial, and found it harder to operate in a similar way when making 'important' decisions.

Further work This work felt repetitive, and slow, both to Ben and his therapist, but persistence was rewarded, as Ben learned to tolerate the anxiety he felt when relying on himself to make decisions, and gradually his confidence grew.

Tip The aim of this series of experiments was to change Ben's reassurance seeking directly. As would be expected, related dysfunctional assumptions ('I have to check things with others, or I'll mess things up', 'I mustn't do anything wrong or I'll lose the job') and underlying beliefs ('I'm no good at this', 'Others don't make stupid mistakes') were also relevant. Encouraging Ben to make decisions provided information that prompted re-examination of these cognitions also, and led to further experimental work to help him establish more functional operating principles.

Table 6.2 Outline experiments for increasing tolerance of uncertainty

Thought to be tested	Suggested experiments	Potential value
Something terrible might happen	Notice how this thought triggers ideas about terrible things that might happen; generate positive and neutral outcomes instead; think about these when worrying; brainstorm in session first	Recognize the negative bias and start to replace it with more realistic, more helpful ways of thinking
It's dreadful not to know	Try applying relaxation or mindfulness skills to provide a present focus and to reduce emotional arousal	Accept the uncertainty as inevitable; focus on the present without anticipating future threats
I don't know how to live with uncertainty	Survey others to find out how they cope with uncertainty; think of uncertainties you (or others) can live with	Discover that trying to remove uncertainty is impossible; that pleasures can coexist with uncertainty; that recreation and relaxation contribute to accepting it as inevitable, even if uncomfortable, etc.
The only way to cope is to keep control	Practise letting go of worries, or disengaging from them; do what you can and then distract	Trying to control the future is like trying to control the weather; build strategies for dealing with bad times instead

Distinctive difficulties

Content versus process

Patients often concentrate on content and find it hard to think about the process instead. Metaphors may help (e.g. fighting individual worries is like trying to put out a forest fire at ground level; it may be more effective to use a helicopter to get an overview, and to try to quench the flames from a height).

'What if . . . ?'

Worries are often phrased as questions: 'What if . . . ?', 'Whatever shall I do when . . . ?'. Ask the patient to answer the question to identify underlying beliefs and testable predictions.

Ambivalence

Patients may report feeling compelled to worry even though it causes distress. Subtle distinctions between productive and non-productive worry are more easily made if they are given different names (e.g. the functional process could be called a 'preoccupation' or 'concern', and the word 'worry' kept for the dysfunctional activity).

Process issues

Dependent worriers, or those who are concerned about disapproval, may feel embarrassed to disclose the full extent of their worries, or wish to please the therapist and hide their reservations about therapy. They may also engage in subtle reassurance seeking, or continually question the therapist, diverting therapy away from process-based solutions. It is useful to anticipate explicitly these difficulties (e.g. by including them in the formulation and discussing how to handle them in advance). Therapists should meet scepticism about change with understanding, eliciting doubts and reservations and encouraging an experimental approach.

Comorbidity

GAD often coexists with other (Axis I and Axis II) disorders; severe depression or hopelessness may have to take priority in therapy. The patient may not even recognize worry as problematic, but see it as a natural response to problems or as an integral part of their personality. Clinical judgement is needed in selecting priorities, though theoretically it is useful to search for and work on beliefs through which the problems are linked. Aim to change one thing if the patient has multi-layered problems, and emphasize the positive impact of small changes as part of a process (as the Japanese poem says, 'Slowly, slowly little snail, Up Mount Fuji').

Concentration and memory

Concentration may wander when people are tired or when they start worrying. Feedback, summaries, written notes, and tapes of sessions can help; material may have to be revised and repeated. Writing things down can provide some instant objectivity, and making a blueprint at the end of therapy is important as the insidious nature of worrying means that relapses are to be expected. Sleep problems which (subjectively) interfere with memory and concentration may warrant attention in their own right (see Chapter 14).

Invisible experiments

When experiments cannot be operationalized into observable phenomena (e.g. switching attention, or using imagery to disengage from worry), the purpose and method need to be especially clear.

Vague worries

These are often described as feelings, rather than thoughts. Patients may be able to identify behavioural markers such as nail biting, staring into space, or pacing to help them to recognize that they are worried, and then tune in to what is running through their mind. Some people who report no thoughts, although they continue to feel worried, benefit from relaxation and mindfulness-based techniques that help them to attend exclusively to present experience.

Subtle avoidance and reassurance seeking

These make it hard to plan behavioural experiments in advance. The rationale should be explained, and patients encouraged to notice relevant internal signals (e.g. the wish to withdraw, the need to question others) and to experiment with facing the fear or relying on their own judgement instead. Therapists may forget to ask about the outcome of self-set, spontaneous experiments, without a reminder.

Worry about insoluble problems

Analogies can help to loosen the idea that worry has an influence over consequences (e.g. hoping to win the lottery will not make it happen). Weighing up the pros and cons of worrying may also help patients consider whether it is worth spoiling life now by worrying about future eventualities. The aim is to foster a more accepting attitude, and behavioural work to build confidence (and supportive relationships) may supplement more specific worry-focused work. Estimating the actual probability of catastrophic negative events sometimes helps, as worrying increases subjective estimates of risk, but often worrying re-emerges, and for more obsessional worriers it will not help, as any degree of uncertainty is too much to tolerate.

Medication and substance misuse

Using alcohol, prescribed medication, or non-prescribed drugs can be safety behaviours, and experiments may reveal their counterproductive, longer-term effects. If the medications are prescribed, and so endorsed as a general way of coping, it is important to collaborate with the prescriber. Motivational interviewing techniques may help patients to see the long-term disadvantages of using self-medication.

Emotional processing

Worry interferes with emotional processing, and concerns about the implications of past events may persist for long periods. Working on the themes that arise during worrying may resolve 'unfinished business'. However, working on these may also bring up traumatic memories (see Chapter 9).

Expectations for the future

It is important not to raise false hopes. Worries will recur in people's lives. A flexible attitude, that fosters curiosity about the future rather than the effort to control it and to hide from risks and dangers, is likely to provide a more lasting basis for change.

Other related chapters

Social anxiety (Chapter 7), depression (Chapter 10), and low self-esteem (Chapter 20) are common secondary consequences of GAD, and these chapters may provide additional ideas. Obsessive-compulsive disorder (Chapter 5) and health anxiety (Chapter 4) may be relevant to those worriers whose ruminations tend to the obsessional, or whose worries specifically focus on their health. One model of worry suggests that it is a way of avoiding triggering painful feelings, so Chapter 17 on avoidance of affect is also relevant.

Further reading

Borkovec, T.D. and Ruscio, A. (2000). Psychotherapy for generalized anxiety disorder. *Journal of Clinical Psychiatry*, **62**, 37–45.

Butler, G. and Hope, T. (1995). *Manage your mind*. Oxford University Press, Oxford, pp. 173–191.

Ladouceur, R., Dugas, M.J., Freeston, M.H., Leger, E., Gagnon, F. and Thibodeau, N. (2000). Efficacy of cognitive behavioural treatment for generalized anxiety disorder: evaluation in a controlled clinical trial. *Journal of Consulting and Clinical Psychology*, **68**, 957–64.

Persons, J.B., Mennin, D.S. and Tucker, D.E. (2001). Common misconceptions about the nature and treatment of generalized anxiety disorder. *Psychiatric Annals*, **31**, 501–7.

Wells, A. (2000). *Emotional disorders and cognition*. Wiley, Chichester.

Tales from the Front Line
The healing power of insults

Joe, a fireman, feared that ex-colleagues would view him negatively because he had been medically retired from the service with PTSD. Verbal testing had only been partially effective in reducing his concern.

During a carefully planned return to one of the trauma sites, fire engines happened to drive by. The firemen rolled down the windows, heads poking out, hollering, "How are you doing you f****** w*****". A few minutes later, a second fire engine passed by, again windows were swiftly lowered, helmeted heads poked out, "Joe, you b***** t*****, good to see you mate". The patient returned the greetings (albeit using fewer expletives). "Well", Joe said turning to his therapist, "now I know I'm still one of them!"

CHAPTER 7

Social anxiety*

Gillian Butler

Ann Hackmann

Introduction

Social phobia is defined as 'a marked and persistent fear of one or more social or performance situations in which the person is exposed to unfamiliar people or to possible scrutiny by others. The individual fears that he or she will act in a way (or show anxiety symptoms) that will be humiliating or embarrassing.' (DSM-IV-TR, APA 2000). Note that people with social phobia may not actually do anything humiliating or embarrassing; they only have to fear that they will (or think that they have). Their symptoms do not even have to show (though the sweating, blushing, and trembling that plague people who are socially anxious, sometimes do show); they only have to think that they might. Social phobia is thus defined in terms of what happens in the mind, and behavioural experiments designed to help people think again about social situations form a central part of its treatment.

Shyness in those who do not meet diagnostic criteria for social phobia can be understood and treated in similar ways, and in this chapter they will be addressed together, using the term 'social anxiety'. Social anxiety can lead to isolation and loneliness, reduced opportunities for developing intimacy, and the frustration that comes from working below potential abilities. For example, promotion at work often requires increasingly varied, demanding, and public social interactions. Being socially anxious is not the same as being introverted. Socially anxious introverts often continue to enjoy solitary activities, and may therefore retain some satisfaction in a life that otherwise remains more isolated and lonely than they would prefer. Socially anxious extroverts suffer greatly, as they are naturally happiest in company but the phobia interferes with their ability to access this source of pleasure.

*We are grateful to Melanie Fennell for providing experiments for this chapter.

Social anxiety has many variations. Some people find it difficult to make intimate relationships, and feel most anxious when interacting with someone they find attractive. Others are relatively comfortable within the confines of their close family and become fearful when meeting new people or entering larger groups. Social phobia can be specific (active in situations such as eating or writing in public) or generalized. The latter appears to be more common in clinical practice.

In clinical populations, social phobia is equally prevalent in men and women (Wells and Clark 1997). It often begins in late adolescence, and can lead to low self-esteem, depression, and substance abuse. Comorbidity with generalized anxiety disorder is especially common, and in more severe cases of generalized social phobia, shades into avoidant personality disorder. The problem appears to occur the world over, with cultural variations: everyone is susceptible to embarrassment and humiliation, but the circumstances that cause these feelings differ. However, the principles upon which treatment is based apply generally, and they can be employed sensitively and flexibly.

Cognitive models

Cognitive models of social phobia, in particular that of Clark and Wells (1995), have been well supported by findings from recent research (Clark 2002). Clark and Wells' 1995 model provides an especially clear basis for understanding the mechanics of the problem and for cognitive-behavioural treatment (Wells 1997, 2000), whose effectiveness is well supported by research (e.g. Clark *et al.*, in press; Harvey *et al.* 2000; Heimberg 2002). The main elements of this model as they relate to the use of behavioural experiments are described below.

Self-focused attention

Self-focused attention has been informally described as 'the engine that drives social phobia'. When feeling anxious, social phobics become literally *self-conscious*, and being supremely aware of their internal sensations and emotions has counterproductive effects. First, on the basis of their feelings, people draw (frequently erroneous) conclusions, for instance about what others can see and about the judgements they then make. Second, self-focus dominates attention, occupying centre stage at the expense of information about external events (e.g. what people are saying, their facial expressions). Consequently, socially phobic people often lack accurate information about others and their interactions with them, and describe imagery consistent with this: in their images they tend to see themselves as they guess others see them, on the basis of the contents of their self-consciousness and memories of past experiences (Hackmann *et al.* 1998, 2000).

Safety behaviours

Social phobics adopt numerous safety behaviours in an attempt to reduce the perceived risk of being judged negatively, and these function as an important maintenance factor. They can be relatively obvious (e.g. avoiding eye contact) or more subtle (e.g. only talking to 'safe' people), and patients are the best judge of when they are 'in self-protective mode'. Using safety behaviours heightens self-awareness: trying not to attract attention, for example, increases the sense of being potentially noticeable or at risk. Safety behaviours can also attract unwelcome attention: for example, speaking quietly may encourage people to draw near so as to hear better. In addition, they 'contaminate' social interactions: saying little or avoiding eye contact may discourage others, or make them feel they are not liked. Even when safety behaviours are only partially successful, they are reinforced by the thought that things might have been worse without them—by the sense of having just had a lucky escape.

Perceived social danger

Self-awareness and safety behaviours are understood as responses to feeling at risk, and are reflected in all levels of cognition—thoughts, assumptions, and beliefs. Perceived social danger can often be clarified by finding out what people think might happen if they stopped trying to protect themselves. Assumptions such as 'You've got to do things right if you're going to be acceptable' or 'Other people are always judging you' can play a central role, as they influence social behaviour. For example, thinking 'If I say what I think others will reject me' links with not expressing opinions. So, assumptions are an especially fruitful source of hypotheses about which behavioural experiments may be useful.

Aetiology

Although little research has been done on the origins of social phobia, theoretical and clinical considerations suggest a number of contributory factors are relevant, and attention to these can help when devising behavioural experiments.

Core beliefs and schema influence what is perceived as socially dangerous, and patients describe experiences consistent with their underlying cognitive frameworks. They may have been criticized, rejected, or bullied, or treated as if they were different or odd or weird. Their current behaviour is likely to have been shaped by these experiences and by the beliefs derived from them, and often produces interactions with others that appear to confirm these beliefs. In addition, recurrent images of the self in social phobia can be linked to upsetting memories of being teased or bullied (Hackmann et al. 2000).

Schema-focused techniques may be needed to help those with the most severe problems, including work on transforming the meaning of early memories. However, carefully selected behavioural experiments, repeated over a period of time, are also helpful.

Key cognitive processes and key cognitions

Three cognitive processes and two aspects of cognition, corresponding to the different aspects of the model outlined above, are described next. The processes (self-focused attention, safety seeking, and biases in self-image) have far-reaching cognitive, emotional, and behavioural consequences that link them to the theme of perceived social danger. This theme has two key aspects: concerns about being evaluated negatively by others, or being judged and found wanting, and concerns about not being able to cope with rejection or criticism.

Links between the cognitive processes and key cognitions mean that experiments focused primarily on one aspect of social anxiety provide information that is relevant to the others, and may have wide implications. So two broad categories of experiments will be described: those designed initially to explore cognitive processes, and those designed to explore the theme of perceived social danger.

Key cognitive processes

Self-focused attention

In social anxiety, self-focus dominates attention; the symptoms feel so dangerous that monitoring them (and attempting to hide them) takes priority, and these cognitive activities interfere with concentration and performance and thus contaminate social interactions. Less attention is focused on other people—the supposed source of threat—and on their behaviours (verbal and non-verbal). This biases the perception, interpretation, and recall of socially relevant information, and gives rise to a wide variety of thoughts such as: 'I'm starting to blush', 'I look completely inept', 'I sound stupid', 'No-one is interested in me'. However, it is the deployment of attention that is at issue here, and experiments that change the focus of attention are an important source of new information to set against the limited and biased information that otherwise dominates socially anxious thinking.

Safety seeking

Thoughts that prompt safety seeking reflect fears of being observed or found out (e.g. 'I must hide my nervousness', 'I can't let them see') and also ideas about the value of safety behaviours. People often believe that, without them, they would feel more anxious, their symptoms would be more obvious, or their performance would be worse, and even provoke rejection. They then make corresponding predictions: 'If I speak up I will make myself ridiculous', 'People will think I'm odd, and dislike me'.

Biases in self-image

The cognitive context provided by focusing on oneself, using safety behaviours, and thinking that the situation is socially dangerous contribute to a commonly held assumption: 'How I feel is how I look'. Such ideas appear to be central in social anxiety, and arise when people base their appraisal on biased information, as reflected, for example, in the images they have of themselves (Wells *et al.* 1998).

Perceived social danger

Negative evaluation by others

This is reflected in the layers of thoughts, assumptions, and beliefs that make social situations seem so threatening: for example, 'People will notice', 'People will judge me', and 'Then they will reject me'. The main beliefs predominantly concern acceptability, belonging, and its opposite, being rejected. Patients may believe that their actions should fall within a narrow range to be acceptable to others. When beliefs about social danger are activated, self-focused attention and the desire to seek safety are likely also to be present, and failure to recognize this may prevent people gaining the maximum benefit from experiments. For example, deciding to invite someone out may produce inner turmoil which dominates attention and triggers efforts to hide symptoms of nervousness, preventing full engagement in the experiment. In addition, socially anxious people often misinterpret the reactions of others to their anxiety. Although most of the time their attention is self-focused, they readily notice what they believe to be judgements or signs of disapproval, and redouble attempts to control their behaviour.

Not coping

The final key aspect of cognition concerns the damaging and destructive effects of harsh criticism, which people suppose they would not be able to handle. A useful strategy for dealing with them—the assertive defence of the self—has been developed by Padesky (1997). This involves learning to respond assertively to a critical voice, with coaching from the therapist, and is fully described in Chapter 20.

Behavioural experiments

◆ **Exploring cognitive processes**
Experiment 7.1: a sequence of experiments
Experiment 7.2: focusing externally
Experiment 7.3: dropping safety behaviours
Experiment 7.4: comparing image and reality
Experiment 7.5: selective attention
Experiment 7.6: contrasting feelings and reality
◆ **Re-evaluating social danger**
Experiment 7.7: observing the extent of danger
Experiment 7.8: building confidence gradually
Experiment 7.9: a survey concerning social danger

As indicated earlier, experiments in social anxiety can have multiple implications: reducing self-focused attention (paying closer attention to others) can help people to interact with fewer safety behaviours and, for example, to express an opinion when normally they would keep quiet. If this elicits interest they may think 'I'm not as stupid as I feel', potentially changing their self-image (or self-opinion). The interaction could then provide information to contrast with current assumptions and beliefs. Changing one cognitive process can thus provide opportunities to change other maintaining processes and to re-evaluate key cognitions. However, changes are often transitory, not fully processed, or interpreted in less than constructive ways. So plenty of time should be allowed for exploring the implications of experiments.

Exploring cognitive processes

The impact of confronting, in early sessions, the effects of self-focused attention, safety seeking, and uncritically accepting a biased self-image is considerable, especially when people receive accurate information about their performance and when a combination of in-session and between-session tasks is used. In some of the examples, information is gathered through video recording and use of stooges. If these are not available, therapists may need to make creative use of role play, audiotapes, rehearsal, repeated practice, and so on, instead.

Experiment 7.1: a sequence of experiments

Problem Sue had always been shy. At 17, she had a prolonged period of illness, but felt under pressure to socialize despite feeling unwell. Her friends noticed that she was under par and teased her. She became anxious that if she was not 100% confident she would be a target for ridicule. She imagined herself looking blank-faced and twitchy, and developed ways of concealing her anxieties (avoiding social situations, not drawing attention to herself, avoiding eye contact, and ending conversations quickly). She believed that, if she did not do these things, people would notice her nervousness and make fun of her.

Target cognition and prediction People will notice my anxiety unless I take steps to conceal it. If they do, they will think I'm a weakling.

Experiment (a): the impact of self-focused attention In order to find out how Sue really came over to others, she had two short, videotaped conversations with a stooge. Both of them rated her performance immediately after each conversation. First, she focused her attention on how she was coming across and on using safety behaviours to ensure that her nervousness did not show (avoiding eye contact and saying as little as possible). Second, she focused on the other person and attempted to absorb herself in the conversation, making eye contact (to gain more accurate information about the stooge's reactions) and aiming to say more in response to questions.

Results Sue was 80% successful in obeying the two opposing sets of instructions, providing a clear contrast between them. The results are summarized in Table 7.1, and show clearly that impression management was unhelpful. Using safety behaviours, Sue felt more nervous and less confident. She also appeared more nervous and less confident to the stooge. Her ratings of how she came across were more negative than the stooge's in both conversations. The stooge noticed Sue's anxiety in both conversations, especially the first, but did not conclude that she was a weakling.

Table 7.1 Ratings of Sue's conversation (0–100)

Questions	With safety behaviours			Without safety behaviours		
	Sue[1]	Stooge[2]	Video[3]	Sue	Stooge	Video
How nervous did Sue feel?	50			30		
How nervous did Sue look?	80	50	50	0	5	0
How confident did Sue feel?	40			80		
How confident did Sue look?	20	30	60	60	90	80
How well did Sue come over?	20	40	50	70	90	80
How much of a weakling did Sue appear?	20	0	0	20	0	0

[1] Sue's rating of the conversation

[2] The stooge's rating of the conversation

[3] Sue's 'objective' rating, after watching the video

Reflection 'Putting someone else's point of view alongside mine was really useful. Some of my impressions are way off! The safety behaviours aren't helping at all. They make my nerves more obvious, and make things worse.'

Experiment (b): homework Sue experimented with switching self-focused attention and safety behaviours on and off in social situations, and observed the impact on how she felt and on her sense of how she was coming across. This confirmed the in-session results. When she was focusing on the conversation things flowed better, she felt more confident, and noticed that others seemed more relaxed with her. Two people commented on how cheerful she seemed.

Experiment (c): watching the videotape Next, Sue predicted what she would see on the videotape, based on her impression of how she had come across at the time (the original ratings). She watched the tape as if it was of someone towards whom she felt well disposed. This was to reduce possible contamination of her immediate perceptions by her impression of herself at the time. To retain this detached perspective, the therapist referred to the person on the videotape in the third person (e.g. 'How nervous does she look?', 'How well is she coming over?'). The results (see Table 7.1) show that, when viewing herself impartially, Sue's perspective was closer to the stooge's than to her original ratings.

Reflection 'My own thoughts are way off what others can see. I'm not a very good judge of how I come over, am I? Now I have a sense of what I really look like, it's not nearly as bad as I thought. I can use the image of myself as I looked on the tape when I catch myself thinking I look bad.' Working on these processes thus helped Sue to start re-thinking her beliefs about being a weakling and her assumptions about needing to hide her symptoms.

Experiment 7.2: focusing externally

Problem Ricky had been socially anxious since his mid teens. To compensate, he made huge efforts to be the life and soul of the party, and to behave as he thought confident people would. He was intensely preoccupied with how he came across and with which strategies to use in order to come over well. After social interactions he conducted detailed post-mortems, trying to remember everything he had done and how others had reacted.

Target cognitions and prediction If I keep focusing on myself and on how I come across, I'll find a way out of this. If I stop, I've had it.

Preparation for the experiment Ricky played with his focus of attention in session with the therapist and also on his own, to practice flexibility of focus.

Experiment Ricky conducted a specific attention-switching experiment at the till in the shop where he worked, which he found particularly anxiety-provoking because of the possibility of making mistakes in public.

Results Ricky succeeded in absorbing himself completely in what he was doing. He thoroughly enjoyed himself and hardly had a moment's anxiety.

Reflection Instead of having to struggle not to think about himself, Ricky realized that all he had to do was 'be there and stop wandering off in my head to all the horrors'. He understood that his preoccupations were just ideas, not real, and not worth the attention he was giving them. He said: 'I feel completely free for the first time since the problem started'.

Further work Ricky's social anxiety virtually disappeared. He did well at his job, was promoted, and was able to face new, challenging situations with the same fresh stance.

Tip At first Ricky seemed to be using externally focused attention as another safety behaviour ('So long as I can do this . . . '). He was reluctant to let go of self-focus because it seemed to him to be the only way of solving the problem.

Experiment 7.3: dropping safety behaviours

Problem Tracy suffered from frequent, unpredictable blushing for which she had often been teased, and she had developed the safety behaviour of hiding behind her hair. She worked in an open-plan office where she usually sat with one hand hiding her face, reducing her ability to work. People repeatedly asked her what was wrong, and had started to treat her with 'velvet gloves', which made her more self-conscious.

Target cognitions I can't let people see me blush. It shows up my weaknesses. They all think I'm feeble enough as it is.

Alternative perspective Blushing is not the most important thing about me. Everyone does it sometimes, and doing it more than most is something about me that I can't help, just like being red-haired. (These alternatives were the product of much work on the significance of blushing.)

Experiment Tracy decided to 'go for it'. She tied her hair back, worked using both hands all day without hiding her face, and sat up straight so everyone could see her. If she started to blush she planned either to ignore it (if she could) or to say something light-hearted about it like 'Here I go again'.

Results Tracy managed to do everything she planned, and she blushed quite frequently. People noticed her blushes, and even mentioned them. However, she discovered that they took their cue from her. They either ignored the blushing or treated it as 'just one of the things about her'. If she mentioned it humorously, the whole event had far less significance, and her desire to hide rapidly diminished. It became obvious that her attempts to hide had never succeeded, but had instead tended to attract attention while indicating that she was embarrassed.

Tips Achieving substantial, lasting change with one crucial experiment is relatively rare, and the groundwork needs to be well-prepared. Many patients find it too difficult to give up their safety behaviours all at once, and can be helped by using observation experiments first, as described below.

Experiment 7.4: comparing image and reality

Problem Steve was an insurance salesman, who often had to go on courses. He particularly dreaded coffee breaks, when he thought others would notice his hands shaking.

Target cognition If I take a cup of coffee my hands will shake visibly, and I may spill the drink. I can disguise the shaking by holding the cup in two hands, turning away as I drink, and holding the cup really tightly.

Alternative perspective I may be making things worse by holding the cup so tightly. If I just let the shaking happen, it may not be very obvious. It may be that the most noticeable thing is holding the cup with two hands, and turning away to drink.

Preparation for the experiment Steve experimented with tightening and loosening his grip on the cup, and discovered that more tension made his hands shake more, not less.

Experiment Steve collected a cup of coffee, carried it to his chair, drank the coffee without extra tension in his hands, then mimed with an empty cup the extent to which he thought he had been shaking. All this was videotaped.

Results From the videotape, Steve rated the degree of shaking when carrying and drinking coffee without safety behaviours, and compared this with the mime of shaking. He found a big discrepancy between his image and reality, and conceded that the shaking was in fact invisible.

Further work Steve made another video, in which he collected and drank some coffee, used two hands to drink it, and turned to the side with each sip. Viewing this video demonstrated to Steve that the only visible oddity in his performance was the safety behaviour. As homework, he exaggerated the shaking and spilling, and watched people around him to check whether they noticed. He did this in a supermarket café where he was not known to anyone, and no-one even glanced at him.

Tips Doing several experiments successively, tackling different aspects of the problem in detail, helps to keep the focus sharp. In-session experiments are usually followed by between-session experiments, recorded on worksheets (see Chapter 2). Therapists should ensure that patients make clear, specific predictions.

Experiment 7.5: selective attention

Problem Peter, a university lecturer, who had become increasingly anxious about giving lectures, had been mildly socially anxious all his life. He remained shy when meeting new people, and requested help after he had refused an invitation to lecture abroad. Fear of speaking to large (potentially critical) audiences had become a dominant preoccupation, and much of his waking life was spent worrying about how he could prevent his discomfort from showing and others discovering his weakness. He thought that his speech had become distorted due to anxiety, and was convinced that when lecturing he could no longer speak fluently.

Target cognitions 'I'm speaking oddly. It sounds so strange that everyone will notice.' The experiment described below was designed as a preliminary exploration, to discover more about how his speech sounded while lecturing.

Experiment Peter taped his next lecture and brought the tape to the next session. He said he had become anxious within the first few minutes, and knew exactly what he was saying when his speech became odd. Together, the therapist and Peter decided to find out first whether the speech oddity was noticeable and, and if so, to what degree. They listened to the tape together, and the therapist agreed to indicate when she noticed something 'odd' about his speech.

Results The therapist could not detect anything unusual despite listening repeatedly to the tape, even after Peter disclosed exactly when the problem occurred.

Reflection Peter realized that others would be unlikely to notice something odd in his speech. Further discussion revealed that he was aware of feeling breathless as he started to speak (self-focused attention), and reacted to this by attempting to control his breathing, only taking an in-breath when he reached the end of a sentence (a safety behaviour). When he discovered speech oddities were not noticeable, even when symptoms were present, he gave up the safety behaviour and was able once more to focus on the topic of his lecture rather than on his speech production.

Tip Selective attention can reduce the threshold for observing a particular phenomenon. Peter had become conscious of his in-breath when lecturing, and noticed its effect on his speech. This was not observed by the therapist, even when her attention was drawn to it.

Experiment 7.6: contrasting feelings and reality

Problem Jane was an accountant, and had to deal with clients face to face. She was afraid that people would find her stupid or boring, and would notice signs of anxiety and lack of confidence.

Target cognition If I do not plan what to say and monitor everything as I say it, I will say stupid things and leave gaps in the conversation.

Alternative perspective Trying to plan and monitor everything at the same time as talking would be difficult for anyone. It is only necessary to plan a few points, and focus on the other person rather than on myself. This will feel easier, and may even come across better.

Experiment During a role-play interaction with a client, using a stooge, Jane planned only a few bullet points, and neither monitored her speech nor planned what to say next. The stooge and the therapist rated Jane's performance, using 0–100 ratings of how intelligent and how interesting she seemed and how many gaps there were in the conversation. Jane rated her performance on the basis of how she felt, and the three sets of ratings were compared. She watched the video to rate how she actually came across and counted the gaps in the conversation.

Results Jane felt better not monitoring or planning what she said. To her surprise, she was rated as 70% intelligent and 80% interesting, in contrast with her predictions (based on how she felt) of 25% and 10%. The stooge did not notice any gaps, whilst Jane estimated that there were about thirty. When rating the video, as if she were impartially rating someone else, Jane surprised herself by giving ratings of 55% for intelligence and 60% for being interesting. She only noticed five gaps, and these seemed quite natural.

Reflection Jane realized that her feelings did not reflect her performance. She received high ratings and felt more comfortable, despite putting in less effort. The planning and monitoring had significantly increased her level of stress, and possibly interfered with her performance.

Tips It is more effective to rate degrees of a positive rather than a negative quality: being 60% interesting is more encouraging than being 40% boring. When asking people to rate their performance from a video it is important first to operationalize predictions (e.g. exact shade of redness, precise number of gaps), and then to watch in a detached manner, as if rating another person. Similarly, when using an audience, patients should first decide what they want to find out (e.g. 'How anxious did this person seem?' or 'Would you like to spend time with them?')

Re-evaluating social danger

Experiment 7.7: observing the extent of social danger

This experiment was designed to test whether symptoms are noticeable, and whether people react harshly to them when they are exaggerated. It was not designed to change beliefs about what it would mean if people did notice the symptoms, but it clearly could lead on to such work.

Problem Bill had been worried about blushing ever since his friends teased him for going red when chastised by a teacher as a teenager. He avoided getting hot, speaking in a group, and making requests in shops.

Target cognition If people notice that someone's cheeks are red they will laugh or point or make remarks about it.

Alternative perspective When out in public most people are engrossed in their own thoughts and activities, and may notice little else. If they do notice red cheeks, people are unlikely to react obviously to them.

Prediction People will notice and show negative, judgemental reactions. They will stop, stare, point, or whisper.

Experiment The therapist made her cheeks extremely red using blusher make-up, and went shopping with Bill. He observed the reactions of others when she asked for advice or made purchases.

Results No one took any notice of the therapist's blushing cheeks. Nobody laughed, pointed, or made comments behind her back. This inspired Bill to add blusher to his own cheeks and to go shopping, while the therapist observed reactions. The results were the same.

Reflection Most people ignore others when they are out in public and seem pretty unobservant. Adults are unlikely to react in an obvious way even if they do notice someone with red cheeks.

Tips Predetermined criteria of relevance to the patient should be defined, and subsequently it is helpful for patients to engage in similar activities without artificially exaggerating symptoms.

Similar experiments that could be done first by the therapist, if the patient was not ready:

- Exaggerate shaking in a public place (e.g. a café) or spill a drink
- Ask stupid questions (e.g. 'Where is the library?' when standing by the sign, or 'Where do you put the cassette in?' when looking at a video recorder)
- Test thoughts about others being rejecting or critical by raising controversial issues or expressing strong likes and dislikes
- Make complaints
- Leave deliberate gaps in conversation or try stuttering; use 'ums', 'ahs', and silly remarks
- Simulate sweating with water on the face or under arms, and test reactions in busy places

Experiment 7.8: building confidence gradually

Problem Carole had developed numerous ways of ensuring that she could pass without notice, yet she was desperate to make friends. She dressed in dull colours, never wore high heels, avoided walking across the hallway of the health centre where she worked as a receptionist, had lunch alone tucked away in a corner, and tried to hide if she thought a colleague was likely to start up a conversation. She managed her work by standing behind the counter (half hidden) and 'behaving as' a receptionist.

Target cognitions Carole predicted that if she hid away less she would feel more anxious and self-conscious, and would not be able to concentrate. She would make mistakes in her work, and when colleagues spoke there would be a long pause before she could reply.

Preparation for the experiment Because of the chronicity of the problem, careful preparation, and a high degree of mutual trust, was needed before Carole attempted experiments on her own. She tended to dismiss small changes as irrelevant, and readily lost sight of the rationale for specific experiments.

Experiment Carole decided to stop hiding by wearing a pink T-shirt to work.

Results Carole's initial anxiety and self-consciousness were high, but decreased steadily during the day. Otherwise nothing remarkable happened, except that she felt 'a bit more like everyone else'.

Reflection Carole realized that unless she persisted, and explored other ways of not hiding, she would continue to think that on this day she had just been lucky.

Further work Over the next six months Carole stopped hiding away and began to interact on an informal level with her colleagues. As her social confidence grew she made fewer mistakes in her work and was better able to concentrate. Progress was not smooth, but for the first time she felt safe at work and realized that by trying to hide she had invited a special kind of attention. People had tried to draw her out. When she came out of her own accord they just accepted her as part of the work team.

Tip At this stage, Carole's improvement was limited to the workplace; she was still lonely and self-conscious elsewhere. The principles she learned were then applied more generally, so as to meet more people, and to initiate interactions with strangers and with acquaintances.

Experiment 7.9: a survey concerning social danger

Problem Paul, a bank clerk, had feared that he might blush or look obviously nervous since his early teens. He believed that his anxiety was a sign of inadequacy, and that others would share this view if they knew about it. His social life was restricted, and he requested help when a promotion demanded more face-to-face contact with customers.

Target cognition If people notice me blushing or looking nervous they will consider me inadequate.

Experiment Paul's therapist suggested a survey to find out what people think about people who blush or look nervous. The therapist conducted the survey, as Paul was too embarrassed. They defined its content together, and decided to sample 10 people, including both genders and a range of ages, not all of them clinicians. The questions agreed in advance are listed in Table 7.2.

Predictions The interviews were audiotaped and, before listening to the tape, Paul predicted how many respondents would react as he feared. As his thinking had already changed substantially, he also rated how many he would have expected to react in that way before treatment, and compared these two ratings with the results of the survey.

Results See Table 7.2. People responded favorably to the questions. Every respondent but one assumed that blushing was a sign of heat or embarrassment, not inadequacy.

Reflection Paul was surprised to find that most people said they would assume they had done something wrong if someone they were talking to became visibly nervous. He thought it was reasonable to find visibly nervous people hard work and to tend to avoid them, as he felt the same way himself. He commented: 'My thinking has changed a lot, though I can see that I still tend to overestimate negative reactions. People don't think what I thought they would as much as I expected—and if they do, I don't mind as much. That's just how it is.'

Table 7.2 Paul's survey results

Target cognitions	Pre-therapy	Now	Survey results
If someone saw me blush, they would assume it was a visible sign of feeling anxious or being shy	8	4	1
People think it's strange for a man to blush	8	4	3
People think someone should have grown out of blushing by the age of 30	8	5	1
People see blushing as a sign of inadequacy	9	1	0
If someone appeared very nervous while talking to them, people:			
(i) would assume they were socially anxious	7	3	0
(ii) would think badly of them	7	1	0
(iii) would think they were too much like hard work and avoid them in the future	8	2	0

Further work Paul entered increasingly difficult social situations to check out others' responses. He produced a pie chart showing all the possible reasons, apart from his inadequacy, why people might respond negatively (as he realized they sometimes did). He kept a record of situations that he had previously ignored in which people reacted positively or neutrally to him, and of 'golden moments' when he felt particularly anxious and had an opportunity to check out his worst fears.

Distinctive difficulties

Wandering attention

Attention is always shifting, and will often need redirecting. The process of attention shifting involves two steps: first, deciding not to focus internally, and second, deciding what else to focus on instead. Otherwise, the instructions operate like thought suppression ('Don't think about yourself') and increase preoccupation. Attention training (see Wells 2000, pp. 139–47) may be useful when patients find it hard to focus externally. It is also likely that a degree of self-focus is helpful in social interactions. Refocusing outwards should be balanced and not exaggerated.

Contamination

Social anxiety can contaminate interactions, within therapy as well as elsewhere. If patients appear withdrawn, hostile, or unfriendly, therapists should adapt their own (verbal and non-verbal) behaviour to set them at ease, and process issues may need to be explicitly addressed. Fear of negative evaluation may also interfere with homework reports and feedback.

Rejection

When fears are confirmed, and others are rejecting, rude, or unfriendly, it is important to work with the meaning of the behaviour, rather than with the probability of its occurrence.

Acceptability

Not washing, or listening, saying nothing or disclosing inappropriately personal information to strangers can lessen the chances of meeting goals such as making friends, and may need addressing. However, it is a mistake to suppose that skills training is necessary. The use of skills is inhibited by anxiety, and as confidence increases so does the fluency of social behaviour.

Goals

It is important to agree appropriate goals early in treatment. People may feel disappointed unless their expectations (e.g. of developing friendships or intimate relationships) are first modified.

Mind reading

Socially anxious people often make predictions about what other people think (e.g. 'They thought I was stupid') or about their attitudes (e.g. 'Nobody takes me seriously'). Clear criteria for judging whether such predictions are true should be agreed (e.g. sighing and casting the eyes up, walking away, mockery), or the prediction could be phrased in terms of longer-term, observable consequences (e.g. recorded on a data log), or in terms of feelings, which can be contrasted with some measure of external reality.

Curiosity

An attitude of curiosity about others is enormously helpful. Curiosity focuses attention outwards, producing a more spontaneous interaction, with less safety seeking. However, when social anxiety overlaps with avoidant personality disorder, the experience of feeling socially at ease is rare, and social lives are impoverished, so people may not know what to be curious about. With prompting, interest can build gradually. Loss of interest in others may also be a product of coexisting depression which, if secondary, is likely to respond to work on the social anxiety.

Solitude

The benefits of solitary activities should not be underestimated as a source of pleasure, self-respect, and self-esteem (Storr 1989). When these begin to change, patients may have more energy for the behavioural experiments that can be so beneficial.

Other related chapters

Further ideas will be found in the chapters on generalized anxiety disorder (Chapter 6), with which social anxiety commonly overlaps, self-esteem (Chapter 20), avoidance of affect (Chapter 17), and interpersonal problems (Chapter 19). It is worth remembering that when people have been suffering from a problem for some time, they can feel inadequate and at risk of negative evaluation by others.

Further reading

Butler, G. (1999). *Overcoming social anxiety and shyness.* Robinson, London.

Clark, D.M. and Wells, A. (1995). A cognitive model of social phobia. In: R.G. Heimberg, M.R. Liebowitz, D.A. Hope, and I. Schneier (ed.), *Social phobia: diagnosis, assessment, and treatment.* Guilford Press, New York.

Wells, A. (2000). *Emotional disorders and cognition.* Wiley, Chichester.

Tales from the Front Line
The wise never presume

After 20 years of accident-free driving, Claire had had a head-on collision with another car, and subsequently presented with an extensive range of driving-related safety behaviours, including repeated checking at junctions, driving well below any given speed limit, and avoiding busy or unfamiliar roads. Attempts to test the utility of her safety behaviours as part of homework assignments had been largely unsuccessful, because Claire found it too frightening. To overcome this therapeutic hurdle, it was agreed that the therapist would be a passenger in Claire's car.

Things did not go well from the start. Whilst struggling to back out of her drive, Claire confessed that she had always had trouble manoeuvring her car in restricted spaces. At a roundabout she put on the handbrake and took the car out of gear, checking at length for oncoming traffic. Other drivers were evidently growing impatient and gave vent to their frustrations by extensive use of car horns, expressive gesticulations, and rapid overtaking. This upset Claire, who struggled to put her car back into gear, acknowledging conspiratorially that she had never managed to do this without the use of both hands. Once in gear, Claire failed to check that the roundabout was still clear of traffic, and drove on, narrowly missing another car. After they entered the dual carriageway, Claire proceeded to drive at 15 miles per hour. Following the therapist's gentle suggestion that a somewhat higher speed might be safer, Claire bravely attempted to increase her speed but was unable to change into 5th gear, because she did not know where it was. Things deteriorated further, when after taking a wrong turn Claire had to reverse around a bend. This completely defeated her skill, and after several hair-raising attempts the therapist agreed to take over.

Twenty years of accident-free driving turned out to be a testimony to other people's driving skills.

CHAPTER 8

Specific phobias*

Joan Kirk
Khadj Rouf

Introduction

Specific phobia is defined as a persistent fear of an object or situation, exposure to which leads to immediate anxiety and even panic (DSM-IV-TR 2000). Anticipatory anxiety is a central feature. Levels of fear are often related to the proximity of the frightening object/situation and appraisals about the ability to escape it. Although sufferers recognize the fear as excessive or unreasonable, they either avoid the object/situation (overtly or covertly) or endure it with dread. These symptoms must be present for at least six months, and must significantly disrupt everyday functioning.

Specific phobias are often categorized into five subtypes:

1 Of animals

2 Of the natural environment (e.g. wind, lightning)

3 Of blood injury/injections

4 Situational (e.g. lifts)

5 Other uncommon or atypical phobias (e.g. noise). These may share elements of agoraphobia and panic, health anxiety, and social phobia (see Chapters 3, 4, and 7 respectively).

A further general category is fear of fear (Rachman and Bichard 1988), which crosses the boundaries of the other five. This means that two layers of fear should be considered—the first associated with the phobic stimulus, the second concerning the meaning or consequences of anxiety. The latter, triggered by the arousal that results from encountering the phobic stimulus, may be as important in maintaining anxiety as fear of the stimulus itself.

*With behavioural experiments from Ann Hackmann, Melanie Fennell, Philippa Saul and acknowledgment to Ian Gilders for preparation of diagrams.

Mild phobias are common in the general population (up to 11.3% lifetime prevalence). Most people (up to 90%) do not seek help, and phobias may only reach clinical significance if the stimulus is frequently encountered or unavoidable. Specific phobias may coexist with other conditions including obsessive-compulsive disorder, post-traumatic stress disorder, and health anxiety. Depression, hopelessness, and low self-esteem may be secondary to longstanding phobias, associated with cognitions such as 'I am a hopeless case and will never recover'.

Cognitive model

The radical conceptual and methodological shift represented by the use of behavioural experiments (see Chapter 1) is particularly evident in work with specific phobias. For the last forty years an effective evidence-based treatment has been available: exposure therapy, originally based on a theoretical rationale emphasizing repeated, prolonged exposure to feared objects/situations and suggesting that fear is reduced through habituation and extinction.

The underlying mechanisms of exposure therapy are unclear, and behaviour therapists have incorporated a range of cognitive variables into their understanding of specific phobias—for example, 'emotional processing' (Rachman 1980; Foa and Kozak 1986), 'perceived control' (Rachman et al. 1986), and 'self-efficacy' (Barlow 1988). There is promising evidence for the role of cognition in the maintenance of specific phobias. For example, Shafran et al. (1993) found that reducing belief in key cognitions in claustrophobics led to fear reduction, and Thorpe and Salkovskis (1995) showed that the content of harm cognitions correlates with phobic anxiety levels and patterns of avoidance. Cognitive factors may also be central to effective treatments for specific phobias. It has been argued, for example, that exposure is only effective if cognitive change occurs (Foa and Kozak 1986; Salkovskis 1991).

Cognitive therapy acknowledges the role of behaviour in maintaining anxiety disorders, but its prime focus is on thinking: phobic anxiety is construed as a rational response to situations seen as dangerous as a result of biases in perception, interpretation, and memory. It proposes that careful identification of fear cognitions will allow precisely targeted, efficient interventions. These are designed to facilitate new understanding that feared stimuli are not (or are unlikely to be) dangerous, so that escape, avoidance, and other safety-seeking behaviours are unnecessary.

There is as yet no agreed cognitive model of specific phobias. The preliminary model illustrated in Fig. 8.1 integrates relevant theories.

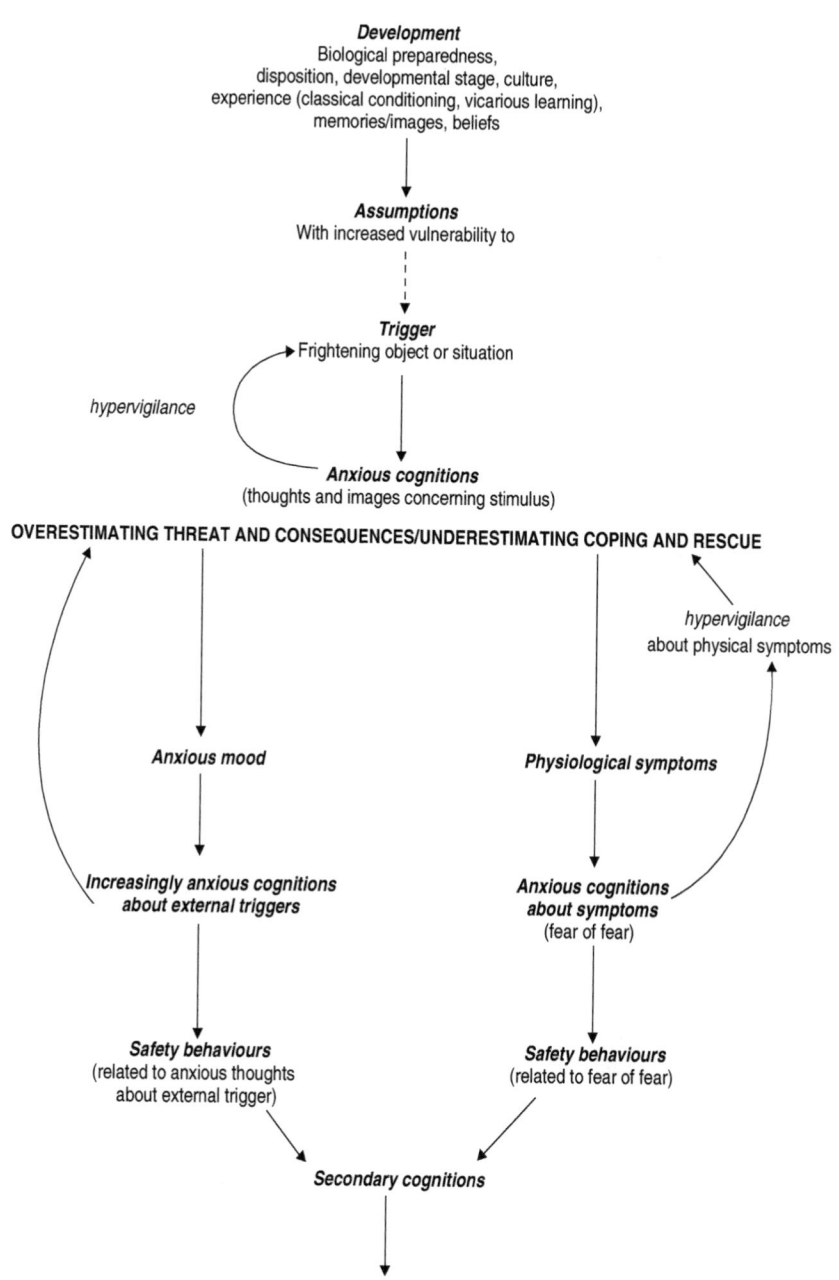

Fig. 8.1 A model of the development and maintenance of specific phobias.

Development

Classical conditioning/learning models (Davey 1997)—including vicarious learning (Cook and Mineka 1989)—can account for the development of many specific phobias. Frightening experiences may result in enduring images and memories. More broadly, biological (evolutionary) preparedness (Seligman 1971; Rachman 2002), dispositional factors, and developmental stages may also be relevant, as may cultural beliefs and expectations (Davey 1994). Phobias can also reflect broader beliefs about the self and the world—for example, sense of incompetence or vulnerability to harm, intolerance of uncertainty, etc.

Triggers

External objects/situations are interpreted as threatening, leading to symptoms of anxiety. These may in themselves become a focus for fears similar to those found in agoraphobia and panic disorder, social phobia, and health anxiety (e.g. fears about losing control, or illness).

Maintenance

Important maintenance processes include:

- **Anxious predictions,** based on exaggerated estimates of harm/danger (discussed more fully below).
- **Physiological arousal**—a potential focus for further anxious predictions.
- **Hypervigilance** for cues related to phobic objects. Cameron (1997), for example, noted changes in information processing in fearful situations (e.g. spider phobics scanning the environment for evidence of spiders' webs). Excessive attention may also be paid to physiological symptoms of anxiety, with minor changes interpreted as signs of imminent danger.
- **Safety behaviours** that unintentionally prevent anxious predictions from being disconfirmed. Beliefs about phobic objects/situations are highly varied and often idiosyncratic (e.g. 'Wasps will harm me by flying into my ears'), as are associated safety behaviours (e.g. covering the ears when a wasp appears). Table 8.1 gives a flavour of this variety.

Key cognitions

Cognitive processes contributing to specific phobias (including fear of fear) comprise overestimates of the probability and extent of harm and underestimates of personal coping resources and external rescue factors (Beck *et al.* 1985). These processes bias the perception and understanding of both external objects/situations and anxiety symptoms in highly idiosyncratic ways. In addition, the meanings patients attach to having a phobia (secondary cognitions) are important.

Table 8.1 Common predictions and safety behaviours associated with specific phobias

Phobic stimulus	Examples of predictions (related to harm, coping, and rescue)	Examples of safety behaviours
Animals	'If I see a dog, it will run over and bite me'; 'Wasps are vicious and attack for the sake of it'	Avoidance, including places (e.g. parks), saying words (e.g. 'dog'); checking (e.g. for animal's presence)
Natural environment		
Heights	'If I stand too close to the edge, I'll lose control and fall'; 'I'll be killed'	Leaning against walls, holding onto handrails, sitting down
Water	'I'll be fighting for air, and panicking'; 'No-one will save me'	Avoidance, including travelling by/over water, swimming, water sports
Lightning	'I'll be burnt to death'; 'I'll definitely be hit'	Staying inside during storms, wearing special footwear/clothes
Blood injury/injection/pain		
Dental/medical procedures	'The pain of the procedure will be unbearable'; 'The dentist won't stop if I want him/her to'; 'There is nothing I can do'	Avoidance
Needles	'The pain will be unbearable'; 'The needle will snap off in my arm'	Avoidance
Blood injury	'I will faint and make a fool of myself'; 'I'll faint and lose control of my bowels'	Avoidance; carrying smelling salts
Situational		
Claustrophobia	'I won't be able to get out of here'; 'I will lose control'	Avoidance; sitting near exits, keeping windows open, taking deep breaths
Transport	'I will be trapped in a burning car'; 'I will die and leave my family behind'	Avoiding busy roads, roads with no immediate exits; carrying travel pills to reduce physical symptoms; distracting while flying
Being alone	'I'll be murdered by an intruder'; 'I can't cope with the loneliness'	Having continual company, leaving television/radio on, taking unnecessary security precautions
Atypical		
Noise	'I'll go deaf'; 'I won't be able to cope with the sudden noise'	Avoidance, carrying medication to calm nerves, tissue in ears
Vomit/vomiting	'I can't cope with the smell/taste/sound of vomiting'; 'I won't be able to breathe'; 'If others vomit, I'll get ill'	Eating small amounts, avoidance of public places, checking whether others look/feel ill

Overestimation of the probability of damage, harm, pain, or injury

Patients believe that catastrophic events (such as suffering horrendous wounds) are highly likely. For example, a dog phobic may believe that any dog he encounters will inevitably savage him. Patients also overestimate the amount of fear they will experience when encountering a phobic stimulus (e.g. 'My heart will pound out of my chest'). Some people overestimate the predictability of the phobic stimulus (e.g. 'Lightning strikes houses every time there is a storm'), while others view the stimulus as highly unpredictable (e.g. 'You never know where a spider will run'). Some ascribe underlying motives to the phobic stimulus (e.g. malevolence, aggressiveness).

Such overestimates are based on biases in perception and memory. For example, a person phobic of horses notices the horse running towards her, but not the farmer carrying hay behind her. She selectively recalls one incident when she was chased by a stallion, and forgets many other times when horses showed no response to her presence.

Overestimates of the consequences of damage, harm, pain, or injury

Phobic patients also make catastrophic predictions about the consequences of harm. For instance, the dog phobic might predict lasting facial disfigurement, as well as overestimating the consequences of his anxiety (e.g. 'I will die of fright').

Underestimates of coping

Patients have heightened perceptions of personal vulnerability when they encounter phobic stimuli (e.g. 'If this rat turns on me, there is nothing I can do to stop it biting me'). Equally, they may believe they will be unable to cope with the symptoms of anxiety (e.g. 'I won't be able to control myself').

Underestimates of rescue factors

Patients discount or minimize the presence of external rescue factors, such as the willingness of others to help. For instance, the dog phobic may think that, if a dog attacks him, witnesses will ignore his screams. He may imagine others ridiculing his fear (see Chapter 3 on agoraphobia and Chapter 7 on social anxiety). Other misperceptions include the inaccessibility of medical help, medication, and emergency services, and the fragility of physical structures.

Secondary cognitions

Secondary cognitions include negative self-judgements ('I am weak', 'My life is wasted') and thoughts about what it means to have a phobia ('I am mad'), about others' opinions ('They think I'm weak and ridiculous'), and about the future ('I will never get over this'). These can lead to depression, hopelessness, loss of confidence, and low self-esteem.

Behavioural experiments

- **Animal phobias**
  Experiment 8.1: moth phobia—fear of anxiety symptoms
  Experiment 8.2: moth phobia—overestimate of harm
  Experiment 8.3: bird phobia—intensive two-day treatment
- **Natural environment phobias**
  Experiment 8.4: wind phobia—effect of safety behaviours on overestimate of harm
  Experiment 8.5: wind phobia—overestimated consequences of anxiety
- **Blood injury/injection phobias**
  Experiment 8.6: needle phobia—using modelling to test predictions of harm
- **Situational phobias**
  Experiment 8.7: claustrophobia—overestimated consequences of anxiety
  Experiment 8.8: height phobia—investigating fearful cognitions
  Experiment 8.9: height phobia—overestimated consequences of anxiety
  Experiment 8.10: height phobia—investigating the role of safety behaviours
  Experiment 8.11: driving phobia—overestimate of danger
- **Atypical phobias**
  Experiment 8.12: noise phobia—secondary cognitions
  Experiment 8.13: noise phobia—overestimated consequences of anxiety
  Experiment 8.14: vomit phobia—secondary cognitions about coping

Animal phobias

Experiment 8.1: moth phobia—fear of anxiety symptoms

Problem Leon had a longstanding fear of moths and flying insects. He experienced severe anxiety when faced with moths, including physical symptoms such as headaches and vomiting.

Target cognition If I see a moth, I will pass out (belief: 100%).

Alternative perspective If I see a moth, I may experience anxiety symptoms, but I will not pass out (belief: 10%).

Prediction Leon believed that if he looked at a picture of a large hairy moth, watched the therapist handling a small moth, or touched a small moth, he would pass out (belief: 75–100%).

Experiments Leon embarked on a series of experiments, beginning with situations he felt able to tackle. He looked at pictures of moths of increasing size, and gradually moved on to touching them. The therapist modelled each step before Leon tried it. He described his physical symptoms, and rated his anxiety every few minutes. He was encouraged to drop safety behaviours such as looking away, and to focus on features he found disgusting, such as the insect's hairy thorax.

Results Leon did not pass out. His anxiety reduced after about 20 minutes. His belief in the target cognition gradually fell to 15%, while his belief in the alternative increased to 80%.

Reflection In early experiments, Leon still believed he might pass out, and his anxiety remained high. As the experiments continued, he gradually accepted that he would not faint and his anxiety reduced.

Experiment 8.2: moth phobia—overestimate of harm

Leon's experiments were also used to test his belief that moths would harm him.

Target cognition The moth will harm me physically (belief: 100%).

Alternative perspective The moth cannot harm me physically (belief: 15%).

Prediction If I touch this moth, it will hurt me (belief: 95%).

Results The moth did not hurt him; indeed, sadly, it died in his hand. His belief that it would harm him gradually fell to 15% over the series of experiments. Belief in the alternative perspective increased to 75%.

Reflection Leon realized that it was the moths that were fragile, not him.

Further work Leon visited a local butterfly house for homework. After this experience, his belief in the alternative perspective increased to 95% and his belief in the target cognition reduced to 5%.

Tips Animals used during behavioural experiments should be treated humanely and with respect. They should, if possible, be set free when they are no longer needed.

Experiment 8.3: bird phobia—intensive two-day treatment

Problem Rosa had a severe bird phobia. When she was four, a strange noise had scared her while she was with a babysitter who was watching a horror film about birds. Both became frightened, and Rosa remained terrified of birds. She found it difficult to go out alone, and would hide behind strangers, using them as 'human shields'.

Target cognitions Rosa believed her fear could kill her if she encountered birds: her heart would 'give way' (belief: 95%). If she looked at a bird, it would see the fear in her eyes and would fly towards her and try to scare her to death (belief: 100%).

Alternative perspective Rosa's fears were natural in the light of her childhood experience. On prolonged contact with birds, her anxiety would rise, but it would soon fall again if nothing untoward occurred. Her heart would not give way (belief: 5%).

Prediction Despite her intense conviction that her predictions were true, Rosa was willing to test them out. She completely agreed that her current behaviour could be maintaining her fear.

Experiments Rosa undertook a series of experiments with birds. At each stage, her therapist modelled approach behaviour and eye contact, so that Rosa could observe the reactions of the birds. Then she repeated the experiments herself. First, she stood in the corridor while her therapist entered a room in semi-darkness, where two tiny birds were sitting quietly in a small cage. Rosa observed what happened to her fear ratings, entered the room when she was ready, approached the cage, and observed the effect of eye contact on the birds. She repeated these experiments in the hospital grounds with wild birds, then in town amongst pigeons, and then in a park with water birds. On the second (final) day she visited a bird reserve, where she observed the reactions of bigger and more excitable birds, including parrots and ostriches. Finally, she entered a large cage with the park-keeper and let birds fly around her.

Reflection Rosa observed that her heart rate settled down quickly, with no sign of her heart giving way. She noted that birds tended to protect themselves, and flew away rather than attacking her. Even with prolonged eye contact, no bird appeared to notice her fear or make any attempt to scare her. Her confidence grew quickly, and she was astonished to discover that many birds were beautiful.

Further work As a final experiment, Rosa watched the original film about birds. She had always believed it would kill her. In fact she was able to laugh about it with friends.

Tips Rosa conquered her phobia in two extended sessions. Through such sessions, confidence gained from relatively easy tasks can rapidly carry patients into highly feared situations.

Natural environment phobias

Experiment 8.4: wind phobia—effect of safety behaviours on overestimate of harm

Problem Michael developed a severe phobia of wind following storms that caused countrywide structural damage. His safety behaviours included listening repeatedly to weather forecasts, and he became anxious at any evidence of windy weather, actual or imminent.

Target cognitions If the wind builds up, the house will be damaged, and I shall be financially ruined. I need to keep my property safe (belief: 75%).

Alternative perspective The more I keep making sure the house is safe, the more convinced I am that the wind is dangerous. If I reduce my safety behaviours, I will worry less about the wind (belief: 20%).

Prediction Michael predicted that if he reduced checking his roof from daily to monthly, he would worry more about damage by wind (belief: 100%).

Experiment Three times daily, Michael rated his worry about wind, from 0 ('not at all worried') to 100 ('as worried as I could be; continually on my mind'). He reduced checking the roof, and removed a concrete block from his dustbin lid.

Result For the first week there was little change, but as Michael persisted, his worry ratings came down. His belief in the target cognition decreased to 35%, and his belief in the alternative perspective increased to 80%.

Reflection Michael was surprised that reducing checking made him feel less concerned. He reduced another safety behaviour (listening to weather forecasts) and obtained a similar result. However, he thought it would be difficult not to take precautions if the weather became windy.

Experiment 8.5: wind phobia—overestimated consequences of anxiety

Target cognition Unless I block out all sounds if it gets very windy, I shall lose control and go screaming down the road like a madman (belief: 95%).

Alternative perspective If it gets windy, I shall get scared, but I know those feelings and would not go off my head, even if I could hear the sounds. I would have to sit it out until it stopped, but I could manage that (belief: 20%).

Prediction Michael predicted that if it became very windy he would lose control, unless he blocked out the sound.

Experiment Should it become very windy, Michael would drop as many safety behaviours as possible. He would stay in his living room with his ears uncovered so as to hear the wind.

Results On the first windy day, Michael did not stay in the living room, but managed not to climb into bed and cover his ears. He became very anxious (90), but did not lose control as he had feared. His belief in the target cognition decreased to 75%, and his belief in the alternative increased to 40%.

Reflection Michael was pleased that he did not 'lose it', and felt more confident about staying in the living room next time.

Further work It was less windy on succeeding days, and Michael stayed in the living room for increasing lengths of time, listening to the wind. His belief ratings gradually changed to 30% and 65%, and his anxiety level dropped to 40. He persisted in dropping safety behaviours, when it was windy and when it was not.

Blood injury/injection phobias

Experiment 8.6: needle phobia—using modelling to test predictions of harm

Blood injury phobia is different from other specific phobias, because negative predictions about fainting are often accurate. Training patients to use applied tension in order to avoid fainting is a recognized treatment component (Öst and Sterner 1987).

Problem Caroline avoided medical procedures and had a history of fainting when she saw blood or witnessed injections. She now needed medical treatment, including giving blood samples.

Target cognitions The pain of an injection will be unbearable (belief: 90%). The needle will snap off in my arm, and it will be impossible to remove it (belief: 85%). I will pass out (belief: 100%).

Alternative perspectives It is possible to withstand the pain (belief: 10%). The needle is unlikely to break (belief: 25%). I can take precautions against fainting (belief: 35%).

Preparation for experiment Caroline was taught to use applied tension.

Experiment While Caroline observed carefully, a nurse gave the therapist a saline injection in the arm. The therapist modelled coping, including looking away during the injection. She explained to Caroline that she did not like injections, but could tolerate them.

Result Caroline did not faint, and the needle did not break in the therapist's arm.

Reflection Caroline found it helpful to discover that the therapist disliked injections and found them painful, but coped. This inspired her to have an injection herself.

Tips Therapist modelling is a powerful way of reducing concerns about danger and feared consequences for those initially too fearful to confront the feared object/situation. Finding a sympathetic nurse to administer the injections was helpful.

Situational phobias

Experiment 8.7: claustrophobia — exaggerated consequences of anxiety

Problem Maria had lifelong claustrophobia. She understood how anxious thoughts and safety behaviours maintained her anxiety, and most of the time had a low belief in the target cognition. Consequently, she was willing to do a behavioural experiment in a very difficult situation.

Target cognition If I am in a small enclosed space that I cannot get out of, I will lose control and go mad. I'll scream and shout, be admitted to a psychiatric hospital, and never recover (belief outside phobic situation: 5%; belief when approaching phobic situation: 85%).

Alternative perspective Although I will feel very scared, and get unpleasant symptoms, and may even bang on the door, that's all that will happen. High anxiety does not lead to madness. I will not end my days in a psychiatric hospital (belief outside phobic situation: 60%; belief when approaching phobic situation: 10%).

Experiment Maria was locked in a cleaning cupboard, with no light and no handle on the inside. She agreed to stay there for 5–10 minutes.

Result Maria became very anxious, but did not become panicky or scream, partly because she thought the therapist would rescue her if she became upset. The therapist went out of hearing for 20 minutes, and the experiment was repeated. Maria became very anxious, but did not go mad.

Reflection Maria thought that she retained control because she was observing what was happening to her. She was more persuaded that high anxiety does not lead to madness (belief outside phobic situation: 85%; belief in phobic situation: 45%).

Further work Maria began to reduce avoidance in everyday situations, and her anxiety continued to diminish.

Experiment 8.8: height phobia—investigating fearful cognitions

Problem Julie had a height phobia, and in phobic situations became acutely anxious with physiological symptoms (e.g. freezing, weak and trembly legs) that she perceived as dangerous in 'exposed' settings. Following the thought 'I can't stay here', her anxiety would increase and she would rapidly leave the situation. She was unaware of thoughts, images, or impulses associated with the initial surge in anxiety.

Question What are the thoughts, images, or impulses that occur when I am in an exposed setting?

Experiment Julie and her therapist visited a bridge with a broad balustrade and a steep drop on one side. Julie walked slowly across the balustrade for 15 minutes. She rated her anxiety out of 10 every three minutes.

Result Julie became aware of an image of floating through the air, head first, arms outstretched, 'like a stuffed doll from a children's book'. Her anxiety ratings remained high, although they decreased from 9 to 6 as the experiment proceeded.

Reflection Julie was previously unaware of the image because she left situations immediately anxiety symptoms appeared. She was reassured that she had not fallen from the bridge's balustrade and commented, 'I have not tripped over for 20 years, so why should I do it when I am taking extra care?' She also found relief in doing the ratings: 'It took me out of the fear, even if it was only for 10 seconds'. She wondered whether this distraction might be helpful in other situations.

Tips Although Julie was highly anxious, the therapist encouraged her to stay in the situation and, when she froze, advised her that she could take a break at any time by climbing down: the aim was to find out more about her cognitions, not to remove her anxiety.

Doing ratings *in situ* can provide temporary distancing from anxiety.

Experiment 8.9: height phobia—overestimated consequences of anxiety

A further experiment investigated what might happen if Julie could transform the image into one where she had wings on her back and could float down through the air.

Target cognition I'll get so panicky that I'll lose my balance, and fall through the air like the stuffed doll; I will die (belief: 85%).

Alternative perspective I've never tripped, and I'll come to no harm. I will feel grim, but will manage better if I give wings to the doll in the image (belief: 20%).

Experiment Julie attempted to walk across a suspension bridge, holding the transformed image in her mind.

Result Julie found it difficult to cross the bridge and could not focus on the transformed image. Her anxiety (8 out of 10) and belief in the target cognition (80%) hardly changed.

Reflection Trying to transform the image kept Julie's attention focused on her anxious cognitions. She wondered about the role of safety behaviours: 'When I hang onto the ropes at the sides, I walk unsteadily and it makes me aware of how inadequate the ropes are. I may be better walking unaided.'

Experiment 8.10: height phobia—investigating the role of safety behaviours

A further experiment allowed Julie to investigate the impact of her safety behaviours.

Target cognition Unless I hold on or use my stick, I'll get panicky, lose my balance, fall through the air like the stuffed doll, and die (belief: 100%).

Alternative perspective If I drop my safety behaviours, I'll feel very anxious but I won't trip—I never have (belief: 20%).

Experiment Julie planned to walk across the bridge without her safety behaviours. Before the experiment, she practised transforming the image of the doll.

Result Without holding on, Julie became so anxious that she froze. She was too anxious to transform the image. She distracted herself (a temporary safety behaviour) by counting and marching in time across the bridge. She walked more steadily and quickly, and did not fall. Her anxiety rating reduced from 9 to 5. Her belief in the target cognition decreased to 40%, and her belief in the alternative increased to 80%.

Reflection Julie knew that distracting herself was not ideal, but it allowed her to find out that she walked more easily if she omitted her safety behaviours.

Further work Julie continued to test her predictions about tripping and falling, without using safety behaviours. Gradually, she was able to walk without counting. After three more experiments over five days, her belief ratings were 0% (tripping) and 100% (not tripping); her anxiety rating reduced to 2.

Experiment 8.11: driving phobia — overestimate of danger

Problem Jackie and her family were involved in a car accident where no-one was seriously hurt, but the whole family were shocked and terrified. Afterwards, Jackie became extremely frightened of travelling by car. She was terrified for her children and surrounded them with pillows on even the shortest journey.

Target cognition Unless I take all possible precautions, there will be another accident, and we will all be killed (belief: 100%).

Alternative perspective In fact, the roads are no more dangerous than they were before the accident; it's my thinking that has changed (belief: 30%).

Experiment Jackie and her therapist used a ride in the therapist's car to observe Jackie's safety behaviours and to check out her belief that, without these, another accident was sure to occur.

Results Jackie held on tight, braced her legs against the floor as if braking, and was extremely vigilant for other cars. She felt certain that, unless she did these things, another accident was inevitable.

   With the therapist's encouragement, Jackie gradually released her grip and relaxed her legs. Nothing happened. However, she still felt that only her vigilance was keeping them safe. After some discussion, she agreed to close her eyes for a short distance. This was very scary, but again nothing happened. Gradually, Jackie increased the time she kept her eyes closed until she was able to do so for about five miles on a busy dual carriageway. She experienced recurrent frightening images of impending accidents while her eyes were shut. To investigate whether these images reflected reality, the therapist asked her to open her eyes briefly when they occurred in order to check whether what she could actually see matched what she saw in her mind's eye. This was never the case. By the end of the outing, Jackie felt much more comfortable about travelling without her safety behaviours, and her conviction that another accident was constantly about to happen had diminished (belief: 35%).

Reflection Jackie saw how her safety behaviours had maintained her fear. However, she was not fully convinced that there was no need to be afraid.

Further work It was necessary for Jackie to test out her fearful predictions repeatedly before she felt confident that it was safe to travel by car. Her husband and a trusted friend (both drivers) became allies in helping her to regain her confidence. Her biggest achievement (during follow-up) was to begin driving lessons.

Tips Therapists should clarify the insurance implications of taking patients out in their own cars or of travelling in patients' cars. It may be advisable to enlist the help of a professional instructor, especially if the patient needs to regain confidence as a driver.

Atypical phobias

Experiment 8.12: noise phobia — secondary cognitions

Problem Lydia had a chronic fear of noises, particularly balloons bursting. She thought that she was alone in having a startle response when balloons popped, and that this showed she was abnormal.

Target cognition I'm abnormal because I have a bad reaction to balloons (belief: 100%).

Alternative perspective It is normal to be startled when a balloon pops (belief: 20%).

Prediction 40% of people will say that they like loud bangs, by rating them 6 or above on a 10-point scale.

Experiment The therapist conducted a survey of psychologists, rating how much they liked loud bangs on a scale from 0 ('not at all') to 10 ('very much'), how much they liked single as opposed to repeated bangs, and how they would feel if they saw someone playing with a balloon and squeezing it tightly.

Result Only 25% of people rated loud bangs at 6 or above on the scale. This reduced to 16% if the source of the noise was unidentifiable.

Reflection Lydia was encouraged and felt less abnormal. It was useful to know that even well-balanced people like therapists disliked loud bangs.

Tips Qualitative data from surveys can be particularly useful (e.g. one person saying that she hated loud bangs).

Experiment 8.13: noise phobia—overestimated consequences of anxiety

Problem Lydia believed that, if a balloon might pop, she could not cope with the anxiety. Her only option was to leave the situation.

Target cognition I cannot cope with anxiety; I have to run away (belief: 100%).

Alternative perspective Anxiety is unpleasant, but it won't harm me and I can tolerate it (belief: 10%).

Prediction If I sit with my anxiety, I will feel uncomfortable but nothing awful will happen.

Experiment With her therapist, Lydia watched a video that contained loud noises (e.g. a drum being banged, bubble-wrap being popped, and a balloon bursting). It included several minutes of balloons being squeezed and poked (without bursting). Lydia rated her anxiety at five-minute intervals.

Result Lydia did not leave the room or put her hands over ears, although she became very anxious. Her anxiety reduced relatively quickly and her belief in the target cognition reduced to 40%, and in the alternative cognition, increased to 65%.

Further work Lydia took the video home and watched it twice daily for two weeks, to increase her belief that she could cope with anticipatory anxiety and weaken thoughts like, 'I cannot cope, I am a burden, I can never change'. She actively sought opportunities to be near balloons and hear loud noises, particularly bursting balloons.

Experiment 8.14: vomit phobia—secondary cognitions about coping

Problem Jenny had a phobia of other people vomiting, and believed that if she saw somebody vomit she would be unable to cope and overwhelming chaos would ensue. Jenny was unsure how other people react in such situations. The therapist suggested conducting a brief survey to find out how others feel.

Target cognition I will not be able to cope if I see someone vomit. Other people can cope, and this means I am a freak (belief: 95%).

Preparation for the experiment Jenny and the therapist prepared a one-page questionnaire. This described witnessing an adult stranger vomiting in public, and asked respondents what they would think, how they would feel, and what they would do. They rated how much the situation would bother them, from 0% ('not at all') to 100% ('so much that I would be unable to cope').

Responses would help Jenny to judge what was a 'normal' reaction, and how this differed from her prediction about her own reaction.

Experiment Jenny was reluctant to involve her friends in the experiment, so the therapist distributed the questionnaire to 50 colleagues and acquaintances.

Results 21 questionnaires were returned, containing a huge variety of responses (2% 'bothered' to 80% 'bothered'; average rating 33%). The qualitative data suggested that although feelings of sympathy were common, most respondents would experience some degree of revulsion or feel sick themselves. Most would offer help only if necessary, and a significant minority would walk away. Jenny's belief that she was a freak was reduced to 15%.

Reflection Jenny was surprised to learn that most people would not 'cope' with this situation and that there was nothing unusual in wanting to walk away. She decided that she was not 'a freak', and that the goal of therapy should be to drop her safety behaviours (including avoidance), rather than aiming to feel entirely relaxed about people vomiting.

Distinctive difficulties

Acknowledging courage

By definition, people are terrified of phobic stimuli, and need great courage to test out their fears. People may have trouble accessing frightening predictions, so it may be necessary to go into feared situations to help elicit worrying thoughts. The general principles of establishing a trusting, respectful, and collaborative relationship with the patient and deriving a shared formulation are therefore particularly important (see Chapter 2).

Multiple sessions versus single-session therapy

Öst's (1997) review of treatment for specific phobias concluded that one extended session is as effective as longer treatments, and is particularly helpful in promoting out-of-session coping. It may be important, however, not to agree detailed goals in advance of the session, or patients may be too afraid to participate.

Grading

It is useful to test predictions at the highest anxiety point that the patient can tolerate. However, it is often necessary to adopt a step-by-step approach, initially using predictable, static stimuli (e.g. with animals) so that trust in the therapist can develop. Experiments are designed to test idiosyncratic beliefs, not to facilitate habituation, so this process can be much less gradual (and thus more efficient) than traditional graded exposure.

If tasks are graded, the patient should identify negative thoughts and residual safety behaviours that may undermine the impact of experiments (e.g. 'I managed to stand by the first floor window, but if I had gone higher, I would probably have jumped out'). These can then be used as the basis for further experiments.

Secondary cognitions

Beliefs about the meaning of the phobia may need tackling. They may include embarrassment, loss of confidence and low self-esteem, incompetence, and vulnerability to harm. Patients' fears may be embarrassing and shameful to them, and the opportunity to discuss them may be important in normalizing phobic anxiety.

Dealing with very high anxiety

If patients become highly anxious, therapists should remain calm and encouraging, and not buy into their catastrophic predictions (e.g. 'I am going to lose control'). Patients can take breaks if tasks are very difficult—bearing in mind that the aim is to test predictions and not to habituate to anxiety. In the short term, it may be helpful to use coping techniques (e.g. distraction, relaxation), but these should be dropped as soon as possible to avoid perpetuating unhelpful predictions.

Patients too scared to do experiments

Therapist-guided experiments can allow patients to progress when it would be too frightening for them to carry out experiments alone. Modelling and careful titration of level of difficulty are also helpful. Flashcards can be used to spell out the alternative perspective being tested, and to remind patients how the experiment fits with the formulation. It is important that they are aware of the long-term benefits of facing their fears, and a cost–benefit analysis may be helpful. See Chapter 3 on panic and agoraphobia for further ideas.

Avoidance of affect

Patients who habitually avoid affect may attempt to do so during behavioural experiments, and thus have no opportunity for emotional processing or to learn that anxiety symptoms have no dire consequences. Therapists should avoid colluding with patients for fear of upsetting them, but instead explore the perceived risks of experiencing emotion, possibly by setting up relevant behavioural experiments (see Chapter 17).

Subtle safety behaviours

Persistent anxiety may indicate the continued use of subtle safety behaviours (e.g. keeping an eye on the stimulus (monitoring), reassurance seeking, distraction, rushing through the experiment, and shifting attention so the patient has the sense of 'being there and not there'). These may be automatic and habitual and so difficult to identify. The creative use of metaphors and stories can be useful in eliminating residual safety behaviours.

Interpersonal maintaining factors

Blocks in therapy occasionally indicate that the phobia performs some function (e.g. eliciting care and concern from others). Relatives may unwittingly reinforce avoidance in order to contain the patient's distress. Such issues need to be formulated sensitively, and it may be necessary to educate relatives. Behavioural experiments may be relevant; for example, if patients worry that without the phobias their relatives would no longer show concern for them, they could test out more adaptive ways of obtaining affection and support.

Comorbidity

If a phobia is comorbid with other disorders, it is important to determine whether it is the primary problem. If not, it should usually be tackled only if it remains once the primary disorder has improved. Even if another disorder is secondary (particularly depression), it is sometimes necessary to deal promptly with it because of its global effects on functioning. Supervision can help therapists to disentangle complexities of this kind.

Generalization

Care should be taken to plan generalization from in-session to out-of-session experiments, and from therapist-guided experiments to working alone. Generalization can be particularly difficult where intermittent natural phenomena are concerned. For example, fears of lightning may have to be tackled in artificial conditions, with the real test many months later, when a storm breaks.

Other relevant chapters

Specific phobias commonly include fear of fear, and experiments testing panic-related cognitions can be relevant. Patients may also report concerns involving the reactions of others; Chapter 7 on social anxiety may be helpful here. Associated problems include depression (see Chapter 10) and low self-esteem (see Chapter 20).

Further reading

Beck, A.T., Emery, G. and Greenberg, R. (1985). *Anxiety disorders and phobias: a cognitive perspective*. Basic Books, New York.

Davey, G.C.L. (ed.) (1997). *Phobias: a handbook of theory, research and treatment*. Wiley, Chichester.

Tales from the Front Line
An unsolicited testimonial

Jordan worried about everything - his health, whether people liked him, whether his work was good enough, whether the books on his shelves were in the right order. One of his main concerns was whether his ability to communicate information and ideas to a group was good enough for him to pursue the academic career that was his goal. He was convinced that he came across as incoherent and inept and, since a panic some months ago, had completely avoided teaching assignments. The therapist set up an experiment at her place of work. Jordan would give two short presentations to a group, and they would be asked to provide feedback on how he had done. In the first presentation, Jordan would use his usual safety behaviours (e.g. avoiding eye contact, reading from a script, sitting very still, discouraging questions). In the second he would take the risk of engaging with his audience, speaking from brief notes, getting up to use the whiteboard, and inviting comments and questions.

Both presentations seemed to go well, especially the second. Afterwards, Jordan and the therapist carefully reviewed the audience feedback. Suddenly the door burst open and a member of the audience came in. She was sorry to interrupt, but everyone was out in the hallway talking about the presentations and how interesting they had found them, and discussing points that had been raised. She was a member of a group of graduate students who regularly got together to debate thorny ideological issues, and she wanted to invite Jordan to join.

This was a turning point for Jordan. He could have interpreted bland written feedback in many ways, especially given time to worry about his performance in retrospect. But there was no discounting this spontaneous invitation and the obvious interest and excitement of the speaker.

When last heard from, Jordan was delivering lectures to 400 students at a time.

CHAPTER 9

Post-traumatic stress disorder

Martina Mueller
Ann Hackmann
Alison Croft

Introduction

DSM–IV-TR (APA 2000) defines post-traumatic stress disorder (PTSD) as a response to a profoundly distressing event, involving re-experiencing, avoidance, numbing, and symptoms of hyper-arousal. To be deemed traumatic, the event must involve threatened or actual death, or serious injury to the self or others. The response must involve intense fear, helplessness, or horror.

Cognitive model

The most comprehensive cognitive-behavioural model of PTSD to date was developed by Ehlers and Clark (2000). The model integrates psychological facets of the disorder described by earlier authors (e.g. Brewin *et al.* 1996; Foa and Rothbaum 1998; Conway 1997; Horowitz 1997; Janoff–Bulman 1992). It suggests that PTSD arises if a person processes a traumatic event and/or its consequences so as to generate a sense of current, serious threat.

Two processes are postulated to create the perception of threat: negative appraisals of the trauma and/or its consequences; and a disturbance of autobiographical memory characterized by strong perceptual memories (such as intrusive images and emotions) which are disconnected from their context and from intellectual understanding of the trauma. Ehlers and Clark (2000) suggest that these processes are compounded by unhelpful cognitive and behavioural coping strategies (e.g. thought suppression, avoidance). These maintain symptoms, inhibit the processing of trauma memories, and prevent adaptive change in the negative appraisal of the trauma and/or its consequences.

The goals of treatment, therefore, are to help patients to:

- Process trauma memories fully and thus reduce re-experiencing
- Identify and amend unhelpful appraisals which maintain the sense of ongoing threat
- Drop safety behaviours.

Treatment is multifaceted and includes education, reliving the trauma, and helping patients to re-engage in activities previously of importance to them. Cognitive components of treatment are predominantly used to test unhelpful appraisals and to aid the processing of trauma memories into the autobiographical memory base. Reliving and cognitive work are interwoven to integrate new perspectives into the trauma memory.

Key cognitions

Ehlers and Clark's (2000) model distinguishes two main subgroups of cognitions that can lead to a persistent sense of threat. These commonly interrelate, and may maintain each other.

1 **Appraisal of trauma consequences**

- Unhelpful appraisals of PTSD symptoms (e.g. 'I'm weak').
- Unhelpful appraisals of trauma consequences (e.g. altered relationships and circumstances, losses). These may lead to an overgeneralized sense of permanent change, and in turn to unhelpful emotional and behavioural reactions.

2 **Appraisals of the traumatic event**

- Pre-existing negative beliefs may be intensified (e.g. 'Bad things happen because there is something wrong with me') or positive beliefs may be shattered (e.g. 'I'm in control of my destiny'). Pre-existing cognitions can act as a mental filter or, if shattered, lead to new, extreme, negative, and overgeneralized beliefs.
- Distorted appraisals made at the time of the trauma may become fixed in memory as if they were real events. For example, a patient who thought that her small children had been decapitated in a car crash, continued to believe at an emotional level that her children were actually dead, even months after they had escaped the car unharmed.

Whilst the nature and complexity of appraisals vary widely, almost everyone develops safety behaviours, logically related to their particular concerns. Safety behaviours prevent disconfirmation of unhelpful appraisals, and behavioural experiments are an excellent way to examine their utility. Unhelpful appraisals and associated safety behaviours can sometimes change after only one experiment, but usually (particularly in complex presentations) more are required, and they may need to be conducted in more than one area. For example, a patient believed her flashbacks to be evidence of 'going mad'. She also felt guilty about actions taken during a sexual assault ('I should have been able to fight him off'), and came to see all men as potential rapists. This led to a host of safety behaviours.

Detailed formulation of maintaining factors and their interactions provides a sound basis for deciding what to tackle first in treatment.

Behavioural experiments

The experiments described in the following section reflect the main cognitive and behavioural maintaining factors described above.

- **Testing unhelpful appraisals of symptoms**
  Experiment 9.1: fear of loss of control
  Experiment 9.2: fear of flashbacks

- **Re-evaluating altered appraisals of the self and the world**
  Experiment 9.3: altered perception of appearance
  Experiment 9.4: adapting to disability
  Experiment 9.5: altered appraisal of the world

- **Re-evaluating distorted appraisals at the time of the trauma**
  Experiment 9.6: shame-based appraisal
  Experiment 9.7: fear-based appraisal
  Experiment 9.8: guilt-based appraisal
  Experiment 9.9: integrating new information
  Experiment 9.10: return to the trauma site

- **Examining the helpfulness of safety behaviours**
  Experiment 9.11: overgeneralization of danger following rape
  Experiment 9.12: overgeneralization of danger following a road traffic accident
  Experiment 9.13: overgeneralization of danger following military trauma

Testing unhelpful appraisals of PTSD symptoms

A common unhelpful belief about symptoms of PTSD is fear of loss of control (e.g. 'Intrusions mean I'm going mad'). Such ideas represent a major obstacle because they lead to thought suppression and avoidance, and prevent processing of trauma memories. Safety behaviours designed to avert loss of control

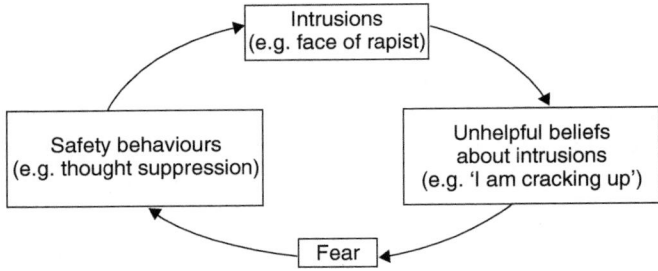

Fig. 9.1 Common vicious circle maintenance of unhelpful appraisals.

over internal events (e.g. intrusions, emotions, physiological arousal) maintain unhelpful appraisals (see Fig. 9.1).

Experiment 9.1: fear of loss of control

Problem Eva had severe PTSD and comorbid depression following a road traffic accident. She firmly believed that she would lose control over her mind and body if she engaged fully in treatment.

Target cognition 'If I allow myself to think about the accident, I will turn into a demented wreck' (belief rating: 90%). This would involve 'becoming like some of the patients I see walking down the hospital corridor'. Eva most feared losing touch with reality permanently, or becoming so upset that she would be swallowed up by misery and unable to function.

Alternative perspective After discussion, Eva arrived at a tentative alternative perspective: 'I will be able to contain my distress when I talk about the crash, and not turn into a demented wreck'.

Prediction 'If I talk about the accident with my therapist I will become upset and frightened. With support, my distress will reduce to manageable levels by the end of the session, and I will be able to cope with the rest of my day.'

Experiment Eva was warned that her intrusions might increase in frequency for a time, and strategies for coping with this were discussed. She then described the accident to the therapist.

Result Eva's distress ratings reached 95% whilst talking about her worst memories. She was tearful and visibly frightened, but remained coherent and in control. After the session, she walked in a nearby park before returning home. Her intrusions did indeed increase in frequency and intensity during the following days, but then decreased again.

Reflection Eva learned that, although she became very distressed, her emotions did not run away with her. She felt confident enough to relive the crash in the next session, and her belief in the target cognition reduced to 30%.

Tips Many patients experience an initial increase in intrusions when they no longer use thought suppression. This might reflect increased awareness of images or thoughts, or suggest that suppression can indeed work in the short term. For patients who believe that exposure to trauma memories may lead to catastrophic consequences such as going mad or having a heart attack, it may be useful to conduct preliminary experiments akin to those used in the treatment of panic disorder (see Chapter 3 on panic disorder).

Experiment 9.2: fear of flashbacks

Problem Chris had been in a severe road traffic accident. Afterwards, exposure to the smell or sight of blood caused distressing flashbacks, which were difficult to manage. His wife was due to give birth imminently. Although he wanted to be present at the birth, Chris feared he might 'fall apart if there is any hint of blood'.

Target cognition If I see or smell blood, I will have uncontrollable flashbacks and be unable to cope. I must avoid the birth.

Alternative perspective If I prepare for the birth by learning to manage blood-induced flashbacks, I will cope constructively.

Experiment Chris smelt and looked at warmed animal blood. He tried out a range of competing smells and tastes to see if this would help him to discriminate between the past (the accident) and the present moment, and observed changes in the frequency and intensity of flashbacks. Chris chose strongly contrasting tastes and smells such as lemon, cough sweets, and aftershave, and brought these, together with a container of animal blood (obtained from a helpful butcher), to the session. He looked at and smelt the blood whilst testing various tastes and smells as anchors to the here and now.

Results Flashbacks initially occurred as predicted. Chris managed these using well-rehearsed coping strategies (letting the flashbacks run through his mind without suppressing them, discriminating between 'now' and 'then', and focusing on stimuli not present during the traumatic event). He found that strong menthol cough sweets were the most useful taste/smell to help him discriminate between blood in the trauma and blood now. The flashbacks stopped and his intrusions became much more manageable. Chris and his therapist also discussed naturally occurring discriminators that he might use during the birth (such as his surroundings).

Reflection Chris now felt 70% confident that he would be able to cope during the birth of his baby.

Sequel Chris attended the birth. Using strong cough sweets and other anchors to the here and now, he had few intrusions and no flashbacks.

Tips Poor discrimination between trauma stimuli and those present in the here and now is a central feature of PTSD. This can be helped by teaching people to make overt discriminations. Introducing contextually meaningful aids to discrimination (such as smells and sounds not present in the trauma memory) can make this easier.

Re-evaluating altered appraisals of the self and the world

Altered appraisals fall into three main categories:

- Altered perceptions of the self (e.g. 'I used to be able to cope with things but now I'm weak')
- Difficulties in adapting to (sometimes radically) altered circumstances (e.g. chronic pain; loss of status, job, or relationships; and bereavement).
- Altered perceptions of the world (e.g. 'The world is a malign, hostile place')

Experiment 9.3: altered perception of appearance

Problem In a car crash in an open-topped car, Steve was partially scalped. Reconstructive surgery was painful and protracted. Nonetheless, his objective post-operative appearance was unequivocally normal, although he had been told that in later years he would probably lose his hair in an atypical way. Steve believed that his injury had permanently altered the appearance of his head and hair, and this was very noticeable to others. To avoid anticipated ridicule he always wore a hat and did not visit a hairdresser.

Target cognition I used to be attractive, but now I look ridiculous (belief rating: 80%). Other people, even those close to me, will be put off by my appearance (belief rating: 90%).

Alternative perspective My perception of my appearance is stuck in a time warp, and does not reflect what I look like now. Whilst there may be subtle differences from my pre-accident appearance, I look as attractive as before. If I allow others to see my head, they will not ridicule me.

Experiments Steve used photographs of himself before the accident and photographs taken very recently to compare his current appearance with his appearance before the accident. This allowed him to investigate just how different he looked. He also took his hat off when out to dinner with friends, and carefully observed their reactions.

Results Steve could not identify any differences in his hairline between the photographs, although he did note that he clearly looked younger before the accident. This confirmed that the pictures were detailed enough to pick up subtle changes. When he took his hat off during dinner, people remarked on this saying 'I've never seen you without your hat; don't you look different'.

Reflection The first experiment allowed Steve to update his self-image by looking at photographs taken very recently, rather than relying on a 'felt sense' that he had changed. The images provided an opportunity for more detached observation, and Steve's original belief reduced from 80% to 35%. The outcome of the second experiment could have been interpreted as evidence that his appearance had indeed altered. However, Steve observed that 'they seemed to find the absence of the hat a bit odd, but then I've been wearing one even in the strangest places for a long time'. His belief that people would be put off and ridicule him reduced from 90% to 10%.

Experiment 9.4: adaptation to disability

Problem Sarah suffered a whiplash injury during a road traffic accident. The injury caused ongoing pain, despite physiotherapy. Sarah had been advised not to undertake activities that might strain her neck. Before her accident, Sarah had viewed fitness as an essential part of a successful life.

Target cognition Since the accident my body is fragile and I must protect myself from injury (belief rating: 90%).

Alternative perspective My body remains strong and healthy. There are some things I can no longer do safely, but other things are fine. If I continue to protect myself by avoiding activities I love, I will become more depressed.

Prediction If I go running again for 15 minutes each day, I will feel better, not worse.

Experiment Sarah went running in the early morning with no safety behaviours (e.g. guarding her body in case somebody bumped into her).

Result Sarah felt better physically and mentally. Nothing happened to hurt her.

Reflection Sarah realized that her body was much stronger than she thought.

Further work In accordance with medical advice, she increased her engagement in other activities she had previously enjoyed.

Example 9.5: altered appraisal of the world

Problem Michael had been a bomb disposal expert in Northern Ireland. He developed PTSD after exposure to multiple traumas. He had responded to call-outs to bomb alerts, shootings, and booby traps, and was involved in several explosions. He had encountered violent deaths, human remains, and injury to fellow soldiers. These experiences confirmed a pre-existing assumption that 'to survive I must protect myself from others'.

Target cognitions 'All Irish people pose an immediate threat to my safety, and must be avoided at all costs.' Michael believed that he would *always* remain a target, even on the mainland as a civilian, and adopted extensive avoidances and safety behaviours. His original belief rating was 100%. This reduced to 80% following a search for evidence.

Alternative perspective Michael discovered that no veteran had been targeted outside Ireland since the beginning of available records. There had also been changes in the political climate since his time in Northern Ireland. Very gradually, his belief became less certain. An alternative possibility was tentatively proposed, focused on discriminating between now (being a civilian in England) and then (a uniformed soldier working in conflict zones). This was: 'Even if Irish people hear my English accent they will not show animosity'.

Prediction If I visit pubs frequented by Irish people and speak with an English accent no one will pay particular attention to me, or make hostile comments. They will be as polite to me as anyone else. In testing this hypothesis, I will become very frightened and experience a strong desire to escape. If I stay I will not lose control, and my fear will lessen.

Experiment The most powerful test would be to visit pubs with various political affiliations in an Irish community in England. The experiment would be therapist-guided, to ensure Michael's safety, to provide support and encouragement, and to observe and eliminate emerging safety behaviours so as to offer a real test of the new alternative. Michael and his therapist visited three Irish pubs, beginning with an apolitical pub, and ending with a pub known for its affiliation to a paramilitary group. Michael ordered the drinks. They chose seats within earshot of others. Michael sat with his back towards people he assessed as potential threats, to reduce scanning. Their conversation was predominantly neutral and quite loud.

Results Michael and the therapist were treated with courtesy everywhere. The owner of one pub asked for 'money for the cause' and was (as per prior agreement) duly given the small amount he requested. Michael's level of fear was initially very high, but dropped sharply as it became increasingly clear that no one meant him any harm. He did not experience any loss of control, even when required to make a donation to a paramilitary organization. He was not treated differently from anyone else, and commented that everyone had been really friendly.

Reflection Michael's original belief that all Irish people pose an immediate threat reduced to 20%. The experiment enabled him to undertake a trip to Northern Ireland to visit several trauma sites.

Tips Therapist-guided experiments are on occasion the most effective way to help patients to confront their sometimes overwhelming fears. Trust, collaboration, preparation, and clear boundaries are crucial to the success of these therapy outings in the real world. They can in fact be interesting and enjoyable for both the patient and the therapist.

Re-evaluating distorted appraisals at the time of the trauma

Reliving the trauma is generally used early in treatment to aid the processing of traumatic memories and to identify unhelpful appraisals, made both at the time of the trauma and afterwards, and stored in the trauma memory. Cognitive methods are used to examine appraisals and to search for alternative perspectives. In later reliving sessions, this new information is integrated into the trauma memory, either verbally or using image transformation (for a more detailed account see Grey *et al.* 2002). To increase conviction in their validity, new perspectives are tested using behavioural experiments.

Experiment 9.6: shame-based appraisal

Problem Kate is a survivor of a serious train crash in which many people died. Following her escape, Kate tried to help a man who was badly burned. She could do little to alleviate his suffering, but thought she might provide some comfort if she made a telephone call on his behalf. After dialling the number Kate could think of nothing to say, and another passenger completed the call. This event shattered Kate's previously held belief that she was competent and in control. Subsequently, she began to feel deeply ashamed, and had become very withdrawn.

Target cognition Being struck dumb means that I am inadequate, useless. People will ridicule me if they discover this (belief rating: 85%).

Alternative perspective Through exploration Kate found two possible reasons for her reaction: 'I was so perplexed by everything that had happened, and was seeing dreadful things' and 'I always like to think things through carefully before I say anything. But then I had no time to think'. An alternative explanation might be: 'My reactions were reasonable in the circumstances; I remain the competent, articulate person I have always been'.

Predictions If I try to explain something I will generally be understood. If someone doesn't understand, they will usually ask for clarification rather then making derogatory remarks.

Experiment Kate thought that the best way to test her predictions would be to ask for something unusual (insoles) in several shops. She thought this would be a fair test of both parts of the prediction, anticipating that young sales assistants would be unlikely to know what insoles were. She agreed to visit three stores in the following week.

Results Kate visited two stores. In the first, an older sales assistant said they no longer stocked insoles. In the second, Kate encountered a young French assistant whose command of English was 'not up to insoles'. Kate briefly tried to explain her requirements but gave up, concluding: 'This girl feels bad because she can't understand me'.

Reflection Kate was heartened by the results. She did not interpret the younger assistant's failure to understand insoles as evidence of her own incompetence. Rather, she empathized with the employee, and felt protective. Rating of her original belief fell to 45%.

Further work Detailed discussion revealed that Kate had selected assistants on the basis that she would not be overheard by other shoppers—she feared they would deride her explanatory efforts. This further safety behaviour needed to be dropped. Later, she tested her belief in other, more personally meaningful situations, such as explaining a work problem to her boss and discussing her opinions with her husband. After three further experiments rating of her original belief dropped to 10%.

Tip Whilst conducting behavioural experiments, watch out for residual or emerging safety behaviours. These will dilute the efficacy of the experiment.

Experiment 9.7: fear-based appraisal

Problem Barry sustained a serious head injury during an explosion. During initial examination of his wounds, the trauma surgeon said 'No'. Barry thought this meant he was dying.

Target cognition When the surgeon said 'No' during the examination, this meant he was giving up on me, and I would die (belief rating: 70%).

Alternative perspective I was immediately transferred to a bigger hospital. The surgeon said 'No' to indicate that I couldn't be treated there, not that I was as good as dead.

Experiment Talking to staff in the Accident and Emergency Department would allow Barry to discover if what he thought was true. The therapist arranged a visit to find out how severe head injuries were managed there. The Ward Sister gave a clear description of the procedures performed and the reasons for them. Barry discovered that the hospital did not have a neurosurgery department, and could only stabilize him.

Result Barry's belief that people had given up on him because he was dying dropped to 0%.

Reflection Barry realized that the surgeon's comment reflected the resources available at the hospital, not the severity of his injuries.

Tip If the patient had been correct in his original assumption, further work would have been needed during reliving to help him update the trauma memory, incorporating the knowledge that he was in fact alive and well. This could be done verbally or through imagery.

Experiment 9.8: guilt-based appraisal

Problem Mary was involved in a road traffic accident, which was not her fault. The other car caught fire, and Mary's first action was to free the driver (who was responsible for the accident), rather than attending to her own children.

Target cognition I am a bad mother.

Alternative perspective I acted on instinct, because I thought the car would explode. I knew my children were safe and not badly injured. I am a caring mother and have good relationships with my children.

Prediction If I tell people close to me, they will not criticize my actions.

Experiment Mary talked to her husband, children, and friends about how they viewed her actions during the trauma.

Result No one thought her actions indicated that she was uncaring or a bad mother. In fact, everyone commented that she had acted with great courage and they were proud of her.

Reflection Mary appreciated that she had acted in the best possible way under the circumstances.

Further work This experiment was followed up using an anonymous survey of a larger, more widely representative group of people.

Re-evaluating distorted appraisals at the time of the trauma

Trauma memories can be quite inaccurate. Sometimes this becomes apparent as the therapist and patient discuss the events. At other times it is far from clear. Whenever possible, it is advisable to obtain original information (e.g. photographs, emergency services' reports, newspaper articles, television footage) and to return to the site of the trauma. Information gained is used to test the accuracy of the trauma memory and appraisals made during the event. This aids processing of trauma memories. Outlined below are two examples illustrating the impact of this sort of discovery experiment on appraisals.

Experiment 9.9: integrating new information

Problem Joe had dealt with many potentially traumatizing events in his 20-year career as a fire-fighter. The incident which caused him the most distressing intrusions happened 16 years ago, when he was called to photograph the wreckage of a crashed helicopter. The crash was reported in the local and national press. Following his attendance at the scene, Joe had avoided any further contact with the event. In preparation for reliving, Joe described the incident in detail, including several drawings. He was certain that his memory was correct. He believed that the helicopter was a single-engine 'Squirrel', and crashed because of engine failure. If it had had twin engines the accident would not have happened. His most distressing recollection was that a very small child had been killed.

Experiment Joe and his therapist sought details from newspaper reports of the crash and from the inquest. These told a different story. No infant was killed; neither was a young girl whom Joe had thought dead under a shroud. The helicopter was a twin-engine 'Squirrel' and crashed, not because of engine failure, but because it encountered freezing fog. Integrating this new information with the trauma memory needed to be done very cautiously. Joe had been troubled by his vivid recollections for a very long time. To discover that some of this was a trick of the memory, rather than based in fact, was potentially very painful. Joe read the reports in session. The photographs contained in the original articles caused most distress, but were also most valuable. The pictures had been taken some time after he left the scene, and showed that by this time the remains of the victims had been covered up.

Result Joe was initially puzzled by the absence of a dead baby, but eventually realized that this was a memory from a different crash scene which had merged with the memory of the helicopter crash. Identifying other errors helped him realize that his memory was not completely accurate.

Reflection Joe saw that at an *emotional* level, the event had still been ongoing. He learned that avoidance of thinking or learning about the event had prevented him from making sense of and coming to terms with it, and began to discriminate between this and other traumatic scenes from his working life.

Tips Exposure to multiple traumas in adulthood can lead to a merging of memories and their associated meanings. As in this case, sometimes this takes the form of 'superimposing' images from one trauma on another. In other cases, trauma memories merge to form a representational memory of the worst aspects of a number of traumas (e.g. a generic dead body rather than a specific one). Whilst it is helpful to work with the overall meaning of these memories, it is desirable to try to disentangle interwoven images and memories wherever possible.

Experiment 9.10: return to the trauma site

Problem Laura was driving her family home when they were involved in a head-on collision with another car. Her husband was trapped in their car, but he and the children only sustained minor injuries. Laura was immobilized by the ambulance staff, who laid her down on the grass verge. She was unable to do anything to help her children or even to see what was happening to them. All she could remember of the scene was looking at the blue sky, hearing the clamour of sirens and cutting gear, smelling smoke from the burning vehicle, and the terror and guilt she was experiencing. Laura made good progress in therapy through reliving, behavioural experiments, and cognitive reappraisal. She also started driving again; however, she still took long detours to avoid returning to the scene of the accident.

Target cognitions Laura believed that returning to the scene of the accident would overwhelm her. She would re-experience the horrific sights and sounds of that day, and might discover that she had deceived herself in thinking there was nothing she could have done to prevent the accident.

Experiment Laura returned to the trauma scene with her therapist. She was encouraged to talk about the accident (indicating the positions of the vehicles involved, and where she had lain on the grass verge), and to describe the differences between the time of the accident and the visit to the trauma site in detail.

Result Rather than being overwhelmed by the visit, Laura found that she was only mildly anxious. She was especially struck by how remarkably ordinary the scene was. She commented that, far from looking horrific, this was a beautiful spot, and the sounds were not those of sirens, but of birds singing. By retracing her route before the accident, this time in the therapist's car, she obtained concrete evidence that there was no way that she could have seen the other car coming. The traffic coming the other way was not visible until it was right on the brow of the hill.

Reflection This experiment was a major turning point. Laura was able to dismiss her thought that she was responsible for the accident, and no longer viewed the trauma scene as a place of horror.

Examining the helpfulness of safety behaviours

Safety behaviours are perceived to reduce threat. They can be restricted to situations reminiscent of the original trauma (e.g. driving very cautiously to avoid another accident), or become widespread to encompass many areas of life (e.g. a rape survivor checking the central heating boiler in case it might explode). A degree of overgeneralization of danger ('It happened before so it will happen again') is almost universal in PTSD.

Whilst some safety behaviours are common, others are more idiosyncratic. Detailed assessment (including associated cognitions) is a prerequisite to setting up any behavioural experiment. Education to normalize symptoms and aid the development of helpful coping strategies is also a crucial part of treatment, as is a detailed, shared conceptualization of the way in which safety behaviours may lead to a failure to disconfirm beliefs (see Fig. 9.2).

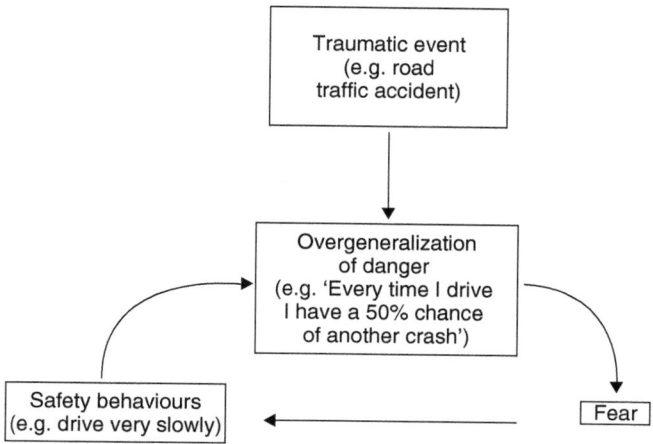

Fig. 9.2 Vicious circle maintaining overgeneralization of danger.

Experiment 9.11: overgeneralization of danger following rape

Problem Caroline had chronic PTSD after being raped at gunpoint several years earlier. Her attacker had since been caught and had received a long prison sentence. She lived alone and felt very vulnerable when returning to her flat in the early hours of the morning after working as a barmaid. She checked repeatedly that her door and windows were locked on leaving and on entering the flat, slept with a knife under her pillow, and often avoided going to sleep until it became light.

Target cognition Unless I take these precautions I am putting myself at risk of further attacks (belief rating: 90%). I will become so fearful that I will be unable to continue living in my own home (belief rating: 95%).

Alternative perspective I was not raped because of my lack of care. It's OK to take reasonable precautions, but I don't have to check my flat repeatedly. If I try to reduce my checking, I will probably become more anxious at first, but this should decrease over time.

Experiment Caroline would try to check her doors and windows only once, and record her anxiety levels each night on going to bed. She would also try going to bed and engaging in basic sleep hygiene strategies, so as to enhance her chances of getting a better night's sleep.

Result Caroline's anxiety initially increased but, over a week or so, it gradually began to diminish. She noticed that, over a longer period, she began to feel more relaxed in her flat and her sleep improved. She was eventually able to remove the knife from under her pillow.

Reflection Caroline's belief in the target cognitions reduced, as she accumulated evidence that her safety was not dependent upon repeated checking.

Experiment 9.12: overgeneralization of danger following a road traffic accident

Problem After a major road traffic accident, Andrea became very concerned that everyday situations were a likely hazard to her children (aged 6–16), and imposed restrictive rules on them. They were not allowed in the kitchen, the playground, the garden, or to go swimming.

Target cognition I must protect my children from every conceivable risk, or they will be harmed and die (belief rating: 90%).

Alternative perspective If I allow my children more freedom, I will become very frightened initially. This will subside when I come to realize that they are safe. With sensible precautions, they are unlikely to get badly hurt in everyday environments. If they do not learn to deal with them now, they will be at greater risk later.

Experiment Andrea allowed the children into the kitchen when she was preparing supper, keeping safety instructions to a minimum. She watched what they did.

Result The children were much less irritable with each other when they were allowed to drift in and out of the kitchen. They did not cut or burn themselves.

Reflection Andrea realized that, in keeping them out of the kitchen, she was forgetting how sensible they were. She concluded, 'I keep seeing danger where there is none'.

Further work Andrea allowed the children greater freedom in other areas of their lives. Her belief in the target cognition dropped to 25% after three weeks.

Experiment 9.13: overgeneralization of danger following military trauma

Problem On the basis of his experience as a bomb disposal expert, Michael (the soldier described in Experiment 9.5) feared public waste bins because they might contain bombs. He avoided public areas containing bins, checked their contents, and scanned the environment for suspicious characters.

Target cognition All public bins are very dangerous because they can contain bombs. If I venture near one it is likely to explode (belief rating: 80%).

Alternative perspective On mainland Britain bins are very unlikely to contain bombs; I can therefore safely walk around. If I walk near bins I will become very frightened, and want to escape. If I stay my anxiety will gradually subside.

Experiment Michael agreed to walk slowly and linger in public areas containing bins, perhaps even leaning against some without checking their content.

Result Michael experienced very high levels of anxiety and had a flashback when doing this alone, and left the area. In the next session, his therapist guided him through the same experiment, modelling leaning against bins and anchoring him in the present. His anxiety increased, then dropped sharply. Michael then repeated similar experiments alone. His belief in the target cognitions dropped to 30%.

Reflection Michael saw that escape and avoidance had kept him from learning that bins are OK. He realized that facing things helps.

Distinctive difficulties

Comorbity

Around 60% of patients with a primary diagnosis of PTSD meet criteria for at least one other disorder, most commonly depression (Kessler *et al.* 1995). Disorders such as panic and generalized anxiety disorder are also frequent. In addition, patients may present with an increased use of alcohol and/or street drugs, and are more likely to suffer from physical complaints independent of trauma injury (Broscarino 1997). For a subgroup of injured patients, chronic pain and disability present real challenges in achieving healthy adaptation. Grief over losses, and sometimes profound bereavements, further complicate the picture. Detailed case conceptualizations are therefore crucial in developing appropriate treatment plans.

Treatment of more complex presentations may require careful unpicking of several, often knotted, strands. To avoid getting lost or muddled, therapists should have a sound knowledge of CT techniques used in the treatment of associated disorders, sufficient time to plan interventions, and regular supervision.

Pre-existing problems

Not everyone who has experienced a traumatic event has previously been problem free. Some people have prior disorders, whilst others have longstanding beliefs about themselves and others, which make healthy adaptation to a traumatic event difficult. A small subgroup of people will have chosen lifestyles or professions likely to lead to encounters with potentially traumatic events, as a way of compensating for perceived character weaknesses. It is vital to understand how pre-existing difficulties, beliefs, and coping styles interact with, and maintain, appraisals subsequent to a traumatic event. Assessment of premorbid functioning will allow therapists to make a realistic assessment of what/how progress can be achieved.

Avoidance

In PTSD, attendance rates for treatment are lower than for other disorders. It is unclear why this is so, but clinical impressions suggest that it reflects fear of being destabilized or overwhelmed. Two main strategies can be used to increase attendance rates. First, it is helpful to provide patients with detailed information about treatment options, the challenges these pose, and what can be done to support them adequately. This enables patients to make well-informed choices. Second, early and clear identification and testing of fears surrounding treatment (such as fear of loss of control) helps to reassure patients and builds trust.

Avoidance of memories, associated appraisals, and affect may also present a significant barrier to full engagement in therapy. More or less subtle avoidances in treatment sessions (e.g. distancing from the trauma memory during reliving) can dilute treatment efficacy, and must therefore be addressed proactively. (Readers may wish to consult Chapter 17 on avoidance of affect.)

Fears about reliving

Some therapists and almost all patients are reluctant to use reliving as part of treatment for PTSD, at least initially. Therapists are understandably reluctant to do anything that may (however temporarily) appear to inflict further pain and distress. However, once they have experienced the power of reliving, they develop confidence in its use. Almost all patients dread reliving for obvious reasons. Therapists can do much to reduce this dread by transmitting confidence, showing obvious empathy, and systematically addressing concerns. It is important, particularly in very complex presentations, to assess a patient's readiness for reliving and any other direct work on trauma memories. It is essential to be aware of possible contraindications (e.g. high risk to self or others, being a perpetrator) and strategies to overcome them.

Building trust

For many people, building a trusting relationship is a key component of therapy. This is especially true for those who feel ashamed or guilty, because they often find it difficult to disclose crucial facts about the trauma and their responses until they have learned that it safe to do so. People traumatizsed by the actions of others may simply not trust anyone for fear of being hurt again. Yet without a measure of trust, therapy is unlikely to progress far. Explicit discussion of possible areas of difficulty, keeping a careful eye open during sessions for breaks in trust, and unfailingly doing as promised, are useful strategies. For patients with profound lack of trust, more focused and extended work can sometimes be necessary (see Chapter 19 on interpersonal difficulties).

Other relevant chapters

Many patients with PTSD suffer from comorbid disorders, most commonly depression (see Chapter 10) and panic disorder (see Chapter 3). Low self-esteem (Chapter 20) is also a common consequence following exposure to a traumatic event. More details on ways to tackle fears about facing distressing thoughts, images, and emotions may be found in Chapter 17 on avoidance of affect. Chapter 19 on interpersonal difficulties is particularly relevant for patients who have become detached from or grown to distrust those close to them after trauma.

Further reading

Brewin, C. (2001). A cognitive neuroscience account of PTSD and its treatment. *Behaviour Research and Therapy*, 39, 373–93.

Ehlers, A. and Clark, D.M. (2000). A cognitive model of PTSD. *Behaviour Research and Therapy*, 38, 1–27.

Grey, N., Young, K., and Holmes, E. (2002). Cognitive restructuring within reliving: a treatment for peritraumatic emotional 'hotspots' in post-traumatic stress disorder. *Behavioural and Cognitive Psychotherapy*, 30, 37–56.

Tales from the Front Line

One man's meat . . .

A patient feared that her head and her hands would shake, and that other people would stare, point, and laugh at her. To test this out, the therapist and patient went out to a supermarket. The therapist modelled her best head- and hand-shaking movements, throwing items off the shelves, and dropping coins at the till whilst the patient observed at a distance. She concluded that nobody had taken any notice, apart from the person at the till, whom she felt looked concerned rather than judgemental. The patient subsequently agreed to go to another shop, choose an item, and pay for it whilst being observed by the therapist. She did this without any observable difficulties, or any reactions from others.

As they left the shop together, the patient promptly vomited on the pavement. The therapist thought this must be mortifying for the patient, and that this had blown the whole experiment. However, the patient just walked on, and when asked how she felt, said she was very pleased that she managed to buy something herself. When asked about the vomiting she said that she did not mind that at all, that she threw up a lot and was used to it.

CHAPTER 10

Depression

Melanie Fennell
James Bennett–Levy
David Westbrook

Introduction

Depression is so frequent that it has been called 'the common cold of psychiatry' (Seligman 1975). The World Health Organisation estimates that by 2020 it will be second only to cardiovascular disease in terms of worldwide burden of ill health (Murray and Lopez 1998). In mild or short-lived forms, depression is an almost universal experience; in more severe forms it can become a crippling disorder.

For a diagnosis of major depression DSM-IV-TR (APA 2000) requires five or more of the following symptoms: depressed mood; pervasive loss of interest or pleasure; significant weight change or change in appetite; sleep disturbance; observable agitation or retardation; loss of energy; feeling worthless or unnecessarily guilty (not just about being depressed); poor concentration or decision making; and recurrent thoughts of death or suicide. At least one of the first two symptoms (mood, anhedonia) must be present. This pattern must be present most of the day, nearly every day, during a continuous period of at least two weeks, and must cause significant distress or impairment of functioning.

DSM-IV-TR also recognizes a chronic low mood state, dysthymia, in which there may be fewer symptoms than in major depression, but which persists for at least two years. Finally, depression often does not present in the 'pure' form described above; for example, 50% of depressed patients also have an anxiety disorder. This chapter focuses on unipolar depression (see Chapter 11 for bipolar disorder).

Cognitive model

The cognitive model of depression was A.T. Beck's (1967) first well-articulated model of a specific disorder, and remains influential. It proposes that early loss leads to the formation of enduring cognitive structures, which render the person vulnerable to depression in the event of future losses. Thus, core beliefs derived from early experience (e.g. 'I am stupid'), together with related conditional assumptions (e.g. 'If I can maintain a very high standard, people may not notice my stupidity'), predispose a person to depression. Events that evoke core beliefs and contravene underlying assumptions (e.g. a challenging new job) then trigger depression. Once activated, the system colours the process and content of thinking in such a way as to perpetuate low mood and other symptoms of depression.

Cognitive therapy first tackles negative thinking (undermining cognitive and behavioural maintenance factors), and then re-evaluates underlying assumptions and beliefs so as to reduce future vulnerability (Beck *et al.* 1979). Classically, patients are offered up to 20 sessions (moderately to severely depressed outpatients on average recover within 15). The treatment has a well-established evidence base (Hollon *et al.* 2002).

Key cognitions

Three facets of cognition are important in understanding the development and persistence of depression: the *content* and *process* of negative thinking, and *cognitive vulnerability.*

Content

Themes of loss, self-devaluation, and hopelessness pervade the thinking of depressed people. Beck's 'cognitive triad' is a central feature: distorted, negative views of the self (e.g. 'I am useless'), the world (e.g. 'Nothing ever goes right for me'), and the future (e.g. 'It will always be like this'). Depression about depression (e.g. 'This just proves how useless I am') may also be prominent. Suicide may seem to be the only solution (e.g. 'There's no other way out').

These thoughts play a critical role in the maintenance of depression. A system of reciprocal feedback develops, where negative thinking intensifies low mood and physical depletion, undermines motivation and energy, and reduces engagement in satisfying activities. These changes in turn appear to confirm negative thinking. Thus the system feeds upon itself.

Process

Thinking in depression is characterized by pervasive biases, which incline the person to notice and recall information congruent with depressed mood, and to screen out and forget information inconsistent with it. The result is an apparent absence of positive experiences, past and present. This perceptual bias is complemented by biases in interpretation (Abramson *et al.* 2002). Negative events are explained in terms of factors that are internal (me, rather than external circumstances or other people) and stable across time and place. Such events are seen as having implications for the future, and for self-worth. In contrast, positive events are attributed to factors that are external (not me) and specific to the time and the place, and are not seen as having implications for the future or for self-worth. A similar attributional style has also been found to characterize people at risk of future depression.

Other cognitive processes contributing to the persistence of depression include:

- Errors in logic such as overgeneralization (drawing general conclusions from specific events), selective attention (paying attention only to negative aspects of experience), and all-or-nothing thinking (Beck *et al.* 1979)
- 'Ruminative response style' (Nolen–Hoeksema 1991)
- 'Overgeneral memory' (inability to access specific memories, especially of positive events) (Williams *et al.* 2000)
- Reduced 'meta-cognitive awareness' (inability to see thoughts as thoughts, rather than as reality) (Teasdale *et al.* 2002)
- Cognitive aspects of depression itself, such as problem-solving deficits, concentration problems, and mental slowness.

Cognitive vulnerability

As outlined above, Beck's model suggests that vulnerability to depression can be understood in terms of the environmental activation of negative core beliefs about the self, the world, and the future, together with unhelpful assumptions which guide day-to-day thinking and behaviour (Ingram *et al.* 1998).

More recently, an alternative way of explaining cognitive vulnerability to future depressions in people who have already experienced an episode has been put forward—the 'differential activation hypothesis' (Segal *et al.* 2002). This suggests that recurrent depression occurs when normal depressed mood, by a process of association, triggers a constellation of negatively toned thoughts, feelings, body sensations, and behaviours. These are perpetuated by ruminative thinking (Nolen–Hoeksema 1991), creating a 'depressive interlock', which becomes increasingly independent of environmental triggers and difficult to interrupt. This perspective suggests that low mood of the kind that anyone might experience is toxic for people with previous experience of depression.

Behavioural experiments

Behavioural experiments are used to test negative automatic thoughts and to re-evaluate underlying beliefs and assumptions, and so reduce future vulnerability. In addition, they counter the cognitive processes outlined above. That is, they encourage conscious processing and enhance memory of positive experiences, they interrupt rumination, and they promote decentring from negative thoughts, so that these come to be viewed as something the depressed person does, rather than a reflection of objective truth.

The experiments that follow are organized in the order in which they are usually carried out in treatment. They reflect the step-by-step acquisition of cognitive-behavioural skills. Starting with the specific and concrete, they only subsequently move to more generalized and abstract themes. There are a number of reasons for this:

♦ Negative statements about the self, the world, and the future are plentiful in depression, and can tempt therapists to assume a need for schema-focused interventions. In fact, many will turn out to be a reflection of depressed mood, and disappear once the patient has recovered (see Chapter 20).

♦ Even genuinely unhelpful assumptions and core beliefs are not usually appropriate early treatment targets. Low mood and cognitive deficits characteristic of depression make analysis at high levels of generality painfully hard, whereas being able to make small changes in thinking and behaviour fosters hope (e.g. 'There *is* something I can do') and enhances the credibility of the cognitive model.

♦ Research shows that positive outcome in cognitive therapy for depression is predicted by the extent to which early sessions focus on specific, concrete interventions (Feeley *et al.* 1999). For many people, these are the sessions in which most change occurs.

Throughout the experiments listed below, the pervasive themes (self, world, future) identified above will be evident, as will the cognitive processes that maintain depression:

♦ **Engagement**
   Experiment 10.1: introducing the cognitive model
♦ **Activity scheduling**
   Experiment 10.2: checking out perceptions of activity
   Experiment 10.3: checking out perceptions of pleasure and mastery
   Experiment 10.4: changing patterns of activity
♦ **Testing negative automatic thoughts (the cognitive triad)**
   Experiment 10.5: negative thoughts about the self
   Experiment 10.6: negative thoughts about the world
   Experiment 10.7: negative thoughts about the future
♦ **Reducing vulnerability to depression: testing assumptions and beliefs**
   Experiment 10.8: perfectionism
   Experiment 10.9: belief about poor judgement
   Experiment 10.10: sense of failure
♦ **Relapse and recurrence: planning for the future**
   Experiment 10.11: short circuiting depression and hopelessness

Engagement

The first step, once assessment is completed and cognitive therapy appears to be the treatment of choice, is to introduce the cognitive model of depression. Depressed patients are not likely initially to absorb a full longitudinal case conceptualisation, but a simple vicious circle illustrating the links between negative thinking and mood is relatively easily communicated.

Experiment 10.1: introducing the cognitive model

Problem Mike believed his depression was an illness. He doubted that psychological treatment would have anything to offer him.

Target cognition Talking therapy won't help.

Alternative perspective It may be worth a try.

Experiment The therapist had already developed a problem list with Mike. She asked him to rate how depressed he felt 'right now' on a scale of 0–100 (0 = not at all depressed; 100 = as depressed as he possibly could be). She asked him to focus for a few moments on the problems he had described, and then to re-rate how depressed he felt. She then asked him to focus on what he could see out of the consulting room window. She asked detailed questions to help him to become absorbed in what he saw. After a couple of minutes, she asked him to rate his mood again.

Results Mike's depression intensified when he focused on his problems. In contrast, when he was able successfully to absorb himself in the view from the window, his mood lifted somewhat.

Reflection Mike could see that the results of the experiment fitted with a vicious circle linking mood and thinking. That is, when he pondered on his difficulties, he felt worse; when he distracted himself from them, he felt a little better.

Further work Mike remained doubtful, but agreed to give cognitive therapy a try. The therapist did not attempt to convince him that it would work, but suggested trying it as an extended experiment. Approaching the methods with an open mind and carefully tracking progress would provide a chance to discover if it suited him.

Tips Distraction experiments can be useful in demonstrating the mood–thinking link. Distraction (attentional redeployment) also interrupts depressive rumination, and is a helpful tool in the depressed person's mood management kit. However, it does not resolve the issues underlying depression. Therapists should be careful to ensure that it is not used to avoid issues that should be faced.

Activity scheduling

Activity scheduling (monitoring and modifying patients' activity levels) is a vital component of cognitive therapy for depression. Therapists sometimes view it as boring, trivial, or simplistic and move swiftly on to more obviously cognitive territory. This deprives patients of a powerful intervention.

Used within a cognitive framework, activity scheduling becomes a rich source of behavioural experiments. It offers an incomparable opportunity for identifying and testing a wide range of negative thoughts, as well as counteracting unhelpful cognitive processes (rumination, overgeneral memory, selective attention to the negative, etc.). The following sequence of experiments with a single patient illustrates this. It uses a key tool from cognitive therapy for depression, the weekly activity schedule (WAS) (Fig. 10.1)—an hour-by-hour diary on which activities are recorded and planned (Beck *et al.*, 1979; Fennell, in press). It shows how the WAS can be used flexibly to test a series of negative automatic thoughts.

Time	Monday	Tuesday	Wednesday	Thursday	Friday	Saturday	Sunday
6–7 a.m.							
7–8 a.m.							
8–9 a.m.							
9–10 a.m.							
10–11 a.m.							
11 a.m.–12 p.m.							
12–1 p.m.							
1–2 p.m.							
2–3 p.m.							
3–4 p.m.							
4–5 p.m.							
5–6 p.m.							
6–7 p.m.							
7–8 p.m.							
8–9 p.m.							
9–10 p.m.							
10–11 p.m.							
11–12 p.m.							

Fig. 10.1 Weekly activity schedule (WAS) (see text).

Experiment 10.2: checking out perceptions of activity

Problem Doreen had been depressed for 18 months. She was low in mood, energy, and motivation. Right from the beginning of therapy, she was critical of herself for being so lazy.

Target cognition I'm not doing anything.

Experiment The therapist explained that inactivity is a normal symptom of depression. She introduced Doreen to the WAS and explained how it could be used to get a clearer idea of how she was spending her time. If Doreen recorded what she did on the sheet over the next three days, they would look at the results together when they met again. Doreen said she thought the sheet would be empty. The therapist suggested that, in order to get started, they work through today together, writing down what Doreen had done, hour by hour.

Results Prompted by the therapist to recall the day in detail, Doreen was surprised to see that in fact she had been quite busy. She had done a little cleaning at home, been shopping for the day's food, made a phone call to the town council about the family home, and arrived on time for her session on the other side of town.

Reflection When the therapist asked how this fitted with her idea that she was 'not doing anything', Doreen said, 'It doesn't look that way, does it?'

Further work Feeling encouraged, Doreen agreed to check out her original thought by keeping a record of what she did until the next session. She discovered that her prediction that the WAS would be empty was incorrect: she was more active than she had thought.

Tips It is particularly important in depression to prepare for and rehearse homework assignments, identifying negative thoughts that might stop the person from carrying them out successfully, and finding ways of tackling them. These can be written on a flashcard for the patient to consult; at this stage, patients are unlikely to be able to work out alternatives to negative thoughts by themselves.

Experiment 10.3: checking out perceptions of pleasure and mastery

Problem Doreen was doing more than she thought, but she still felt that she was not getting satisfaction from what she did.

Target cognition Everything's a bore.

Alternative perspective I could be mistaken about that too.

Experiment The therapist suggested that it might be useful to find out whether this thought accurately reflected what was really happening. She suggested continuing the written record, with an addition—each activity was to be rated for pleasure ('How much did you enjoy it, out of 10?') and mastery ('How much of an achievement was it, out of 10, *given how you felt at the time?*'). Doreen predicted ratings of 1 or 2 out of 10. Again, the therapist suggested working through today so as to be sure that the task was clear. Doreen would then complete the record and the ratings for herself over the few days until their next session.

Results Reviewing the day so far once again illuminated Doreen's biased perceptions. Although some of her activities were neither pleasurable nor satisfying, she had enjoyed a conversation with her husband, had noticed the blossom in the park on her way to the session, and conceded that arriving on time again, given how tired and slow she felt, could count as an achievement.

Reflection Doreen realized that she was getting more out of what she did than she thought.

Experiment Doreen agreed to keep an open mind about how much pleasure and mastery there was in her day, and to continue with the record. She discovered that, before starting to observe her life more closely, she had either not noticed or forgotten things she enjoyed. As they came into focus, she began to feel less depressed and better about herself.

Tips People usually readily understand the concept of pleasure, but have more trouble with mastery. They tend to assume that only major achievements can be given ratings for mastery. In fact, when a person is depressed, the simplest activities are real achievements. Failing to recognize this helps to maintain depression.

Experiment 10.4: changing patterns of activity

Problem Monitoring her activities showed Doreen that she was doing more than she thought, and deriving some satisfaction from what she did. It was also clear though that she was spending a lot of time in bed or just sitting doing nothing. Her ratings of pleasure and mastery showed that these were not rewarding activities. Indeed, they provided space for rumination and tended to make her more depressed. However, Doreen did not feel she had the energy to do more.

Target cognitions I'm too tired. It would be better to wait until I feel better.

Alternative perspective This policy hasn't got me very far up until now.

Experiment Doreen would compare two strategies when she felt tired. On one occasion, she would retreat to bed for as long as she wanted. She would record how she felt after doing this, and rate it for pleasure and mastery. On a second occasion, she would engage in an activity that might be pleasurable or give her a sense of achievement. Again, she would record her feelings after-wards, and rate the activity for pleasure and mastery. To make sure that Doreen had a range of possible activities available (nothing might come to mind at the time), she made a list in session.

Results Doreen did not carry out the experiment as planned. She realized, when she came to do it deliberately, that going to bed would only make her feel worse. So she did something pleasurable instead (made a cake for her little granddaughter's birthday).

Reflection Doreen felt really pleased with herself. She enjoyed making the cake—and her granddaughter enjoyed eating it.

Further work Doreen began planning each day in advance, drawing on an extended list of activities that might provide pleasure and mastery. She contin-ued over several weeks, until she felt that her pattern of activities suited her, and that she was enjoying what she did and giving herself credit for it without needing the record sheet.

Tips In some cases, patients' activity levels at the beginning of treatment are extremely low. If they have been depressed for some time, it may be difficult to think of things to do to fill the day. The therapist will have to be ingenious, creative, and persistent in helping the patient gradually to build up a reper-toire of satisfying activities. Ideally, a combination of pleasure and mastery is the goal. It may be necessary along the way to work repeatedly with a wide range of negative thoughts, and the therapist must guard against being con-taminated by pessimism and lack of confidence.

Testing negative thoughts (the cognitive triad)

Experiment 10.5: negative thoughts about the self

Problem Rosie had got depressed shortly before college exams and dropped out of college. She had gone back to live at her parents' home and felt too depressed to see her friends. She had not seen them for five months.

Target cognition My friends will think I'm thoughtless and selfish and won't want to know me. Belief rating 90%.

Alternative perspective One or two of my friends may be missing me. Some have tried to contact me and I've made excuses. Maybe they'll understand. Belief rating 20%.

Predictions Tamsin, my best friend, will be really angry. She'll think I'm pathetic, and won't want to know me anymore. If we do meet, I'll probably cry all night and feel really foolish.

Experiment The experiment was for Rosie to phone Tamsin and suggest meeting up for coffee or dinner.

Results It took several weeks before Rosie felt ready to pick up the phone. She needed two further preparatory sessions with her therapist during which she recognised that although she *felt* like Tamsin would think she is pathetic, it was actually rather more likely that Tamsin would be relieved and happy to see her. When she did ring, Tamsin expressed surprise and delight. They made a date to go out and the evening went really well. Far from feeling foolish and crying all night, Rosie had the best evening she had had in a long time.

Reflection Rosie realised that Tamsin did still want to know her and had felt greatly relieved that she had got back in touch. At their next meeting, Rosie checked with Tamsin whether she thought other friends would react in a similar way. After further experiments with other friends, Tamsin belief that her friends wouldn't want to know her dropped to 10%, and that they would be understanding climbed from 20% to 80%,

Tip Making a clear distinction between what depressed patients *feel* might happen, and what they think is objectively most likely to happen can be important in building confidence to take the first step.

Experiment 10.6: negative thoughts about the world

Problem John had become increasingly depressed since the death of his wife Georgina, three years ago, from breast cancer. He was now off work, and his low mood and irritability were affecting his teenage children. Despite being popular with his colleagues and friends, he had become more and more socially withdrawn, even though he knew that Georgina would have wanted him to enjoy himself, as she always had done when she was alive.

Target cognitions Life is wretched. Without Georgina, there's no point in trying to go out and enjoy myself.

Alternative perspective Time moves on. She would say: 'Go out and enjoy yourself'. She would want this for me, and for the children.

Prediction Two Christmas functions were coming up—an office party and a dinner with colleagues, some of whom were also good friends. John predicted that there was only a 50% chance that he would attend these functions (going seemed pointless) and that his enjoyment would not be rated as more than 3 out of 10.

Results John attended both the party and the dinner. He rated his enjoyment of the party 8 out of 10, the dinner 6 out of 10. He noted how warm and pleased to see him his colleagues were, and was surprised by how much he had laughed. At the office party he was even able to talk about how low he had been when he left work. The dinner with colleagues was more awkward: several junior colleagues were sitting near him, which inhibited him from talking about recent experiences.

Reflection John felt 'liberated'. Finding out how much his friends cared for him, and hearing from his children how delighted they were to find 'the person we used to enjoy' again, convinced him of the value of his new perspective. He reflected that Georgina would never go away and would always occupy a special place in his heart.

Further work This was such a breakthrough that John invited 12 friends to lunch shortly after Christmas. In the New Year, he initiated an evening out with a group of friends from university who met intermittently every few years. His mood improved dramatically, and he was ready to return to work six weeks after Christmas.

Tips If bereavement is seen as having enduring implications for the self, the world, or the future, grief can shade into depression over time. Therapists need to be sure, however, that depression is the problem, and not pure grief.

Experiment 10.7: negative thoughts about the future

Problem Jenny suffered chronic, severe depression associated with emotional and physical abuse during childhood. She had had several admissions to psychiatric hospital and had been unable to work for over a year. She had, however, done some voluntary work as a teacher's assistant at a local primary school. This went well for a while, but when her mood dipped again she felt unable to continue. The school was aware of her problems and willing for her to work when she felt able to.

Target cognition There's no point in my going to the school; it's better for me and them if I don't go.

Alternative perspective Discussion revealed considerable evidence that Jenny had been successful in her role in the school; in fact there was often a queue of children wanting to work with her. However, she had had no formal feedback from the teacher with whom she worked. On the basis of this discussion, Jenny formulated an alternative possibility: 'It is worth continuing because (a) I am probably reasonably good at it, (b) I might still enjoy it, and (c) I could ask the teacher how she thinks I am doing'.

Predictions If my thoughts are right, then if I go back to school, I will not enjoy it at all. No one will have missed me or want to talk to me. The teacher will be unenthusiastic or negative if I ask for feedback. On the other hand, I may not enjoy it as much as I used to (because I'm more depressed), but it may be all right. The teacher's feedback might be positive. If it is negative, I can consider whether I need to make any changes.

Experiment Jenny decided to try at least one more school session. She would rate how much she enjoyed the session, and note what kind of response she got from the children. If a suitable opportunity arose, she would ask the teacher for feedback on her performance.

Results As soon as Jenny arrived, several children immediately asked where she had been, saying they had missed her. She felt very anxious at first, but settled down to some degree, and rated her enjoyment as 4 out of 10. She had no opportunity to ask for feedback but, buoyed by what had happened, returned for another session. She talked to the teacher, who said that she valued Jenny's help, and that she had been missed.

Reflection Jenny had been very sure that going back to school would be a negative experience. She realized how easy it would have been never to discover how much she was appreciated.

Tips Expectation of negative outcomes is central to depression. It leads to hopelessness, and if sufficiently generalized, to suicidality. Behavioural experiments are a powerful means of discovering that even very convincing predictions can be wrong. Sometimes, however, they are correct. In this case, therapy turns to helping the patient to cope constructively with whatever has happened.

Reducing vulnerability to depression: testing assumptions and beliefs

Experiment 10.8: perfectionism

Problem Lisa had a history of falling into 'holes'. Suicidal thoughts had been prevalent for about 10 years, and she made one serious attempt five years ago. She was highly competent, but felt unable to get on top of her job. She recognized that she had perfectionist standards and, if they were not met, could sink precipitously, feeling that she had let everyone down.

Target cognition Irrespective of how much gets thrown at me, I should be able to cope. If I can't do everything perfectly by myself, I'll feel a complete failure. I'll be letting everyone down.

Alternative perspective It's perfectly OK to ask for help if there's too much work. That's what I'd tell another person to do. It's nothing to feel ashamed or guilty about. The boss will probably agree with anything constructive I suggest—he has a lot of respect for me. (This was worked out with the therapist; Lisa found it difficult to find an alternative on her own.)

Prediction If I hand over any tasks, my boss will think less of me.

Operationalize prediction Lisa predicted that, if she continued to believe that she should be able to cope with anything, she would feel 80% disappointed and 90% deflated after seeing the boss. He would show clearly that he was disappointed in her (frowning, sighing, avoiding eye contact). However, if she could accept that asking for help was reasonable, she would only feel 20–30% disappointed and 20% deflated. Her boss would be helpful.

Experiment Lisa went to see the boss to negotiate handing over some tasks and prioritizing others.

Results Her boss questioned why she needed to hand over parts of the job in rather more detail than Lisa had expected, but he accepted her reasons. She did not feel as bad about this as she had expected: 60% relieved, and only 20% disappointed and 10% deflated. When she told some colleagues, they were sympathetic. One even said: 'Why not give other things up?'

Reflection Lisa felt pleased that she had made this breakthrough without any adverse consequences. It helped her begin to entertain the idea that she did not have to do everything perfectly all the time, and that others did not expect it.

Further work Lisa had been a perfectionist for a long time. She needed to practise applying her new standards over time in a range of different situations (e.g. no longer having to make the family holiday 'perfect').

Tips See Chapter 20 for further ideas on perfectionism and low self-esteem.

Experiment 10.9: sense of failure

Problem Alan, a family doctor, was depressed for the second time in five years. His depression was partly maintained by occasional mistakes he made at work. Alan distinguished between 'mistakes' (such as forgetting to return a phone call) and 'clinical errors of judgement' (misdiagnosing a patient in circumstances where the accurate diagnosis would be apparent to any competent doctor). He viewed both as unacceptable. Minor mistakes were evidence of incompetence, which would inexorably lead to serious clinical errors.

Target cognitions Alan's distress reflected a disabling core belief ('I'm a failure') which derived from his sense that he had never lived up to the advantages his upbringing had bestowed on him. This was supported by an associated assumption: 'To be worthy of this privilege, I must be successful at everything I do, at all times'. Making mistakes, to his mind, confirmed the core belief and contravened the assumption.

Alternative perspective Following detailed discussion, Alan tentatively concluded: 'Everybody makes mistakes. They are not evidence of incompetence which will lead to significant clinical errors. Nor do they mean that I am a failure.'

Prediction Alan thought that the most meaningful test for him would be to ask other family doctors if they ever made mistakes. He predicted that no one else would make the kind of errors that he made, and that they would share his view that small mistakes could easily lead to clinical errors of judgement.

Experiment Alan and his therapist agreed to test this prediction with a survey. Alan thought the survey might be biased if he did it himself with his own colleagues. The therapist therefore agreed to conduct audiotaped interviews with eight family doctors Alan did not know. She briefed them about the nature and format of the interview, and then asked the following questions:

- How long have you been practicing as a family doctor?
- What do you consider to be the most difficult aspects of your job?
- Do you ever worry about relatively minor errors such as forgetting to return a telephone call?
- Have you ever made minor errors? If yes, how frequently?
- Do you ever worry about making significant clinical errors of judgement, which may lead to misdiagnosis?
- Have you ever made such an error? If yes, how did you cope with it?
- Why do you think mistakes happen?
- What strategies have you found helpful in managing worry about making mistakes?

Results After identifying possible negative biases in how he might respond to what he heard, Alan listened to the audiotape in the session. The answers were very clear. All the doctors worried about making significant errors to some degree. Only one worried about minor mistakes, although everyone acknowledged that they happened with monotonous regularity. Two candidly admitted making more significant errors of judgement, the reasons why they thought these had occurred, and the impact on their confidence. Alan listened attentively to the tape, making notes.

Reflection Alan commented that the respondents must be exceptionally competent, to disclose their imperfections so freely. His new belief ('Everybody makes mistakes') strengthened, and he was able to begin to break the link between minor mistakes, serious errors of judgement, and personal failure. This began the process of undermining his excessively demanding assumption, thus reducing the pressure he placed on himself at work, which had contributed to triggering his depression.

Further work Alan still expressed concern that others might make 'lesser' mistakes than he did. Comparing mistakes he had made with mistakes mentioned in the survey helped to address this. He began to practice being more tolerant of his human imperfections.

Tips Alan's difficulties illustrate how negative core beliefs and related dysfunctional assumptions fuel depression. He took some time to feel comfortable with less demanding standards and to view himself less critically. (See also Experiment 10.5 and Chapter 20.)

Relapse and recurrence: planning for the future

Depression is a recurrent condition. Cognitive therapy has been shown to reduce relapse rates in the year following treatment by about 50%, but a continued risk remains (Hollon *et al.* 2002). Patients should be prepared from the outset to experience setbacks, and at the end of treatment it is important to identify possible triggers for relapse and to formulate an action plan detailing how to manage future episodes. Even so, patients can still slip into depression.

Experiment 10.10: short circuiting depression and hopelessness

Problem Christine came for cognitive therapy after being depressed for two years. She had also experienced depression in the past. Christine recovered with 12 sessions of therapy. However, three years later, she began to get depressed again. As her mood dipped, old patterns of thinking emerged (hopelessness and self-blame). She began to consider suicide as the only realistic option. Fortunately, she recognized this as a danger signal and re-contacted her therapist, albeit with little confidence that further sessions would help.

Target cognitions Here it comes again. I might as well give up—nothing will work, so what's the point of trying? I've failed again.

Alternative perspective In fact, Christine had good reason to feel low. Her husband had defrauded the company he worked for, and they had lost their house and their social circle. In the course of a long and painful session, a more hopeful alternative perspective was formulated: 'My depression is an understandable reaction to my circumstances, not a personal failure. The only way to find out if cognitive therapy will help again is to try it.'

Prediction If I try what worked last time, it might work again.

Experiment Christine hunted for the action plan she had prepared at the end of therapy. Along with the plan was an audiotape she had made—a message to herself which reminded her that she was likely to underestimate what cognitive therapy might do for her, and urged her to give it a try. She began activity scheduling to reduce rumination and increase access to enjoyable activities, and started the step-by-step process of tackling the real problems she faced.

Results Within a few days, Christine was feeling less depressed and hopeless.

Reflection Christine still had to face the major changes that had taken place in her life, but she felt in a better state to do so, with her therapist's continuing help and support.

Tips The onset of a new episode of depression can be insidious. Patients may not recognize what is happening until they are well down the road. It is crucial that end-of-treatment action plans incorporate ways of helping patients to be alert to early warning signals of depression and to avoid intensifying it by slipping into familiar patterns of negative thinking.

Distinctive difficulties

The nature of depression

Depression can make cognitive therapy a tough assignment. Patients are expected to engage actively in treatment, to carry out between-session self-help assignments, etc. Hopelessness, inertia, low energy, and lack of interest and motivation make this difficult. Labelling these problems as symptoms of depression is helpful. Associating them with specific negative thoughts reinforces the patient's grasp of the cognitive model of depression, encourages distance from thoughts and symptoms ('That's the voice of depression speaking—it may not be true'), and opens up opportunities for experiments.

Therapist contamination

Depressive negativity can make it hard for therapists to maintain optimism. Depression is an infectious disease: by the time a patient has repeated 20 times that nothing can possibly help, it may be hard for the therapist to remain convinced that cognitive therapy could make a difference. Again, keeping the model in mind is crucial.

Session frequency

Traditionally, sessions are twice weekly for the first 3–4 weeks, and once weekly thereafter. In moderate to severe depression, it is hard to carry the effects of a session forward over a whole week: the power of depression may overshadow initial interventions. Therapists are recommended to see patients twice weekly at the beginning of treatment. This may be difficult to organize, but patients are more likely to be able to transfer what they learn in session into their own lives, thus encouraging speedier recovery.

Cognitive deficits

Therapists must take cognitive deficits into account. Particular emphasis should be put on clear structure and action plans, being specific, and writing down predictions and the results of experiments. Otherwise, the value of the learning experience may be quickly dissipated by concentration and memory problems, and by pervasive negative biases.

High frequency of 'Yes, but . . . '

Depressed patients can always find reasons why an experiment will not (or did not) work, and is not (or was not) worth doing. Even what appear to the therapist to be positive results may be discounted (e.g. 'Yes, but anybody ought to be able to . . . ', 'What's so special about that?'). Therapists should expect this and, rather than being disconcerted, use it to consolidate the patient's understanding of the cognitive model (e.g. 'Look, there's another one of those'). 'Yes, but . . . ' can be tackled in the same way as any other negative thought.

Suicidal thoughts/hopelessness

Therapists working with depressed clients must always be alert to suicidal thinking and the possibility of suicidal behaviour. Hopelessness about the future is a crucial cue, and should be routinely monitored. If suicidal thinking is present, it must be tackled as a priority. Particular care should be taken in setting up behavioural experiments with people vulnerable to suicidal thinking, to ensure that tasks are manageable and that things that might go wrong are predicted and prepared for. Otherwise, apparent 'failure' can increase hopelessness.

Environmental reinforcement of negative thinking

Patients' friends and family may wittingly or unwittingly reinforce negative perspectives. A patient finally geared herself up to carry out a domestic task after weeks of procrastination. Her husband's response was, 'Well, that's very nice dear, but what about all the other things you've not got round to yet?' Taking over depressed people's responsibilities (out of a genuine wish to be helpful) may have a similar impact, magnifying their sense of uselessness. The solution to these problems depends on the reasons for them. Often meeting the people concerned, for an educational session or to involve them more closely in therapy (with the patient's agreement), is enough. Sometimes, however, such difficulties reflect serious problems in the relationship, which require attention in their own right.

Chronic/severe/inpatient depression

Activity scheduling is usefully enhanced with more chronic and severe depressions. Sessions may be shorter and more frequent, behavioural activation may continue for longer as the prime intervention, and tasks designed to undermine negative thoughts are likely to be smaller in scale than they would be with less distressed and disabled outpatients (e.g. five minutes of a single planned activity in a 24-hour period, to investigate 'I can't do anything', as opposed perhaps to planning half a day). These tasks may seem trivial, compared to the weight and scope of the depression, but 'a journey of 1000 miles starts with a single step'. Small steps can improve mood and help the patient move towards tackling bigger issues and life problems.

Related areas

Readers may find it useful to consult Chapter 11 (bipolar disorder) and Chapter 20 (low self-esteem).

Further reading

Beck, A.T., Rush, A.J., Shaw, B.F. and Emery, G. (1979). *Cognitive therapy of depression.* Guilford Press, New York.

Fennell, M.J.V. (in press) Depression. In: K. Hawton, P. Salkovskis, J. Kirk and D.M. Clark (ed.), *Cognitive behaviour therapy for psychiatric problems: a practical guide* (2nd end). Oxford University Press, Oxford.

Gilbert, P. (2000). *Overcoming depression* (2nd edn). Constable & Robinson, London.

Padesky, C.A. (1994). Schema change processes in cognitive therapy. *Clinical Psychology and Psychotherapy,* 1, 267–78.

Segal, Z.V., Williams, J.M.G. and Teasdale, J.T. (2002). *Mindfulness-based cognitive therapy for depression: a new approach to preventing relapse.* Guilford Press, New York.

Tales from the Front Line
Not for the faint-hearted

Sandra, who had a blood-injury phobia, worked excellently with her trainee therapist to learn the skills involved in applied tension, so as to reduce the chances of fainting at the sight of blood or injury. She decided she was ready to experiment with putting these skills into practice, and her therapist arranged for them both to visit the local hospital to have a blood sample taken. Sandra used her new skills so successfully that she felt fine – but her therapist fainted, suddenly and dramatically. She needed recovery time before they could return to base, feeling as if their roles had been reversed.

Subsequent discussion enabled this therapist to make excellent use of the experience. Sandra, who had been teased for fainting by her brothers, had a fundamental belief that she was stupid. However, she also believed that her therapist was not stupid, and seeing her faint changed her belief about herself at once. For herself, the therapist drew two conclusions: first "Don't assume that it's all going to go well", and second, "It's important to know where your limits are". On a second visit both of them were fine.

CHAPTER 11

Bipolar affective disorders

June Dent
Helen Close
Joanne Ryder

Introduction

Bipolar affective disorders are characterized by recurring episodes of mania
and depression, interspersed with periods of well-being. The American
Psychiatric Association defines an episode of mania as a persistently elevated,
expansive, or irritable mood lasting at least a week. It is accompanied by at
least three of the following symptoms: inflated self-esteem or grandiosity
(which can reach delusional proportions), decreased need for sleep, pressure
of speech or flight of ideas, distractibility, increased involvement in goal-
directed activities, and excessive involvement in pleasurable (but potentially
reckless) activities. These episodes significantly disrupt social and work function or require hospital treatment (DSM-IV-TR, APA 2000). Briefer mood
elevation, without severe symptoms such as delusions and without marked
social and occupational dysfunction, is defined as a hypomanic episode.
A mixed manic episode is when symptoms of both mania and depression
occur together.

In contrast, an episode of major depression occurs when a patient has
depressed mood or loss of interest or pleasure for two weeks. Five or more of the
following symptoms also need to be present: feelings of worthlessness, suicidal
thoughts, appetite or weight change, sleep changes, being agitated or slowed up,
loss of energy, and concentration difficulties (see Chapter 10 on depression).

A diagnosis of bipolar disorder (BP) is given when both major depressive
episodes and manic, hypomanic, or mixed manic episodes have featured. The
terms bipolar I and bipolar II are used to distinguish between disorders featur-
ing mania and hypomania.

Cognitive (and other) models

Until recently, cognitive models have had little impact on our understanding and
treatment of BP, which was historically regarded as a lifelong condition determined in large part by a patient's genetic inheritance. Treatment consisted of

medication, both during an acute episode and prophylactically, to prevent or moderate the frequency and severity of subsequent episodes (Scott 1995). However, the onset and course of BP have increasingly been linked both to external stressors and to cognitive and physiological vulnerabilities. Consistent with this is evidence that cognitive behavioural therapy in conjunction with medication may be effective in treating this client group (Lam and Wong 1997; Scott 2001).

It is widely acknowledged that stressful life events play a significant role in BP patients (for a review see Johnson and Roberts 1995) and that negative family interactions and attitudes predict relapse rates (Miklowitz *et al.* 1988). These findings have given rise to a number of biosocial models of BP which examine both inherited (and physiological) vulnerability and external stressors: so-called vulnerability–stress models. For example, people are thought to vary in their sensitivity to the effects of life stress on circadian rhythms (e.g. changes in sleep–wake cycle), and also in their ability to recover physiologically from life stress and return to a stable baseline. It has also been noted that BP patients exhibit relatively poor problem-solving skills (Scott *et al.* 2000), and may therefore experience greater difficulty in dealing emotionally and practically with life stress. This sensitivity to life events is thought to vary during the course of BP, with earlier episodes being more stress-related than later episodes.

Despite this knowledge about BP, it is not clear when and why life events and the subsequent disruption to circadian rhythms result in manic episodes and when they lead to depressive episodes, or indeed why a manic episode might become a depressive one. Beck (1967) suggests mania is a mirror image of depression. In contrast to the negative cognitive triad of depression (see Chapter 10, p. 206) there is a positive cognitive triad consisting of positive cognitive distortions concerning the self, the world, and the future. The self is viewed as lovable, powerful, and in control; the world has many possibilities, and experiences are viewed as being overly positive; and the future is one of unlimited opportunities. During mania, positive experiences are attended to, which in turn strengthens and maintains underlying beliefs and assumptions, influencing cognition, emotion, and behaviour. This framework is useful in clinical assessment and formulation, particularly in explaining how depressive or mania cycles are fuelled by the patient's thoughts about symptoms.

Studies have shown that people with BP have enduring beliefs regarding dependency, autonomy, and high goal attainment that are similar to those of unipolar depressed patients (Rosenfarb *et al.* 1998; Lam *et al.*, in press); their beliefs concerning perfectionism and need for approval are also greater than those of healthy controls (Scott *et al.* 2000). However, unlike unipolar depressed patients, beliefs about goal attainment are still apparent during remission from BP (Lam *et al.*, in press). Patients with BP also experience changes in self-esteem that seem to be mood-related (see reviews by Goodwin and Jamison 1990; Hayward *et al.* 2002).

Different cognitions are active in the manic and depressive cycles. During mania, positive interpretations of symptoms serve to exacerbate intense excitement ('I am amazing, I can do everything') and engagement in numerous activities (e.g. taking on more work, throwing all-night parties, etc.), which further disrupt sleep and eating. During depression, negative interpretations such as 'If I am not achieving people will consider me a failure' can lead to less engagement and withdrawal (e.g. not seeing friends) and sleep/appetite disturbance. Core beliefs ('I am special') and dysfunctional assumptions ('I need to let people see I am doing well') are active in maintaining both of these cycles: confirmed assumptions give rise to thoughts that fuel mania (e.g. 'I am doing well' and 'People can see I'm doing really well'), whereas disconfirmed or unmet assumptions promote thoughts and behaviour that maintain depressive cycles (e.g. 'I have failed—I mustn't let people see me'). These dysfunctional beliefs and assumptions may also be evident to a lesser extent during remission, when cognitive therapy usually takes place.

With respect to therapeutic interventions, the cognitive model (incorporating biological vulnerability factors) acknowledges a role for medication as well as a role for stress management, by promoting active coping. In particular, patients can learn effective ways to regulate their sleep, eating, and other patterns of activity, thereby compensating for their hypothesized inherited predisposition. Both medication and behavioural interventions (such as activity scheduling) can be employed during the early stages to prevent relapse into mania or depression. Cognitive therapy can also address:

♦ Unhelpful thoughts about symptoms that maintain the depressive and mania cycles

♦ Beliefs and assumptions associated with BP

♦ Beliefs about diagnosis, prognosis, medication, and stigma

As with cognitive therapy for depression, therapists initially work with thoughts about symptoms and go on to work with assumptions and beliefs. The remainder of this chapter will focus on cognitions specific to mania or to a diagnosis of BP. See Chapter 10 for an account of depressive cognitions and associated behavioural experiments.

Key cognitions
Typical thoughts associated with symptoms of mania

In the early stages of mania or hypomania, cognitions may be triggered by the external environment and by the early warning signs a patient is experiencing. For some people the onset of mania and hypomania can be a pleasurable experience: their mood improves, they feel energized, and they respond accordingly ('I feel great, I'm going to do lots of nice things'). However, others feel irritable and agitated ('Why can't people keep up with me?').

Most people have their own typical sequence of symptoms—racing thoughts, marked by a flood of ideas and often accompanied by pressure of speech, are common and may spiral into increased creative activity ('I have my best ideas when I'm high'); impulsiveness ('I'll sell the car today and go on holiday for six weeks'); grandiose thoughts about one's personal worth ('I'm the greatest!'); and a desire to behave more recklessly ('I must have sex now'). Thoughts may also relate to the patient's emotional state, such as irritability, or to physical symptoms, such as a reduced need for sleep ('I can manage on five hours' sleep a night').

Typical underlying beliefs and assumptions associated with bipolar disorder

More enduring themes often reported by BP patients, both during active episodes and in remission, include beliefs and assumptions concerning perfectionism (e.g. 'I need to do things to the highest standard'); a need for social approval (e.g. 'I need to put others first in order to be considered a good person'); autonomy (e.g. 'I must not rely on others'); and low self-esteem (e.g. 'I am worthless'). During remission, extreme goal attainment attitudes may also be apparent. These include assumptions such as 'I should always have complete control over my feelings' and 'I should be able to control what happens to me' (Lam *et al.*, in press). It is suggested that such beliefs may interact with the illness, influencing patients' behaviour and thoughts during a manic or hypomanic episode.

Patients with more dysfunctional attitudes have a more severe course of the illness than those with more benign patterns of thinking (Lam *et al.*, in press). Equally, it has been reported that cognitive dysfunction is greater in those patients who have had more episodes of illness and longer duration of illness (Scott *et al.* 2000).

Thoughts, assumptions, and beliefs about illness, stigma, prognosis, and medication

As with other severe and enduring mental illnesses, BP can be associated with secondary disabilities including loss of roles, decline in social status, threats to relationships, and stigmatization (see Hayward and Bright 1997). BP patients may overgeneralize their personal responsibility for their disorder (e.g. 'It's my fault I am ill'), and selectively attend to the good aspects of manic episodes whilst overlooking the risks (e.g. 'I can catch up with things when I go high'). Moreover, they may underestimate the likely efficacy of medication or the effect of non-compliance (e.g. 'Why should I take medication when I am well?') or catastrophize other people's reactions to them (e.g. 'No one will want to know me').

Behavioural experiments

> ◆ **Typical thoughts associated with symptoms of mania**
> *Experiment 11.1: testing the ability to control impulsiveness*
> *Experiment 11.2: engaging in pleasant activities without risky behaviour*
>
> Table 11.1: other experiments to test thoughts associated with symptoms of mania
>
> ◆ **Typical beliefs and assumptions associated with bipolar disorder**
> *Experiment 11.3: need for achievement—a survey experiment*
> *Experiment 11.4: need for autonomy—a discovery experiment*
>
> Table 11.2: other experiments to test typical underlying beliefs and assumptions associated with bipolar disorder
>
> ◆ **Beliefs about illness, stigma, prognosis, and medication**
> *Experiment 11.5: challenging a sense of hopelessness about prognosis and the future*
> *Experiment 11.6: discovering the extent of stigmatization surrounding BP—a survey experiment*
>
> Table 11.3: other experiments to test beliefs about illness, stigma, prognosis, and medication

Typical thoughts associated with symptoms of mania

Experiment 11.1: testing the ability to control impulsiveness

Problem One of David's early warning signs of mania was spending money on goods he didn't need. Over a period of a few days he could spend thousands of pounds of money he did not have. During one of his spending sprees he bought a sports car, a house, and booked several expensive holidays. This placed a considerable strain on his relationship with his wife and family, putting them in financial difficulties.

Target belief 'I can't do anything to stop this spending.'

Alternative perspective 'I can use self-management strategies to help me stop this.'

Prediction 'Next time I start to get high I will not be able to curb my impulse to spend too much.'

Details of experiment Strategies to manage impulsiveness were described to David, and it was proposed that he tried to use these strategies when he began to experience the urge to spend. The strategies proposed were the '48-hour rule' and 'second party advice'. In advance we agreed an upper limit that David could spend in any one day without concern: if he wanted to spend over this limit, he would delay the purchase for at least 48 hours (the '48-hour rule'). During this time it was hoped that he would be able to reflect on his plans. If he still had the urge to purchase the goods, then he would use the 'second party advice' strategy: asking someone he could trust – in this case his sister – to discuss the pros and cons of his proposed purchase.

Results of experiment David managed to complete the experiment next time he was getting high. He used the 48-hour rule and only once had to ask for advice from his sister.

Patient reflection David found it difficult to ask for help/advice from his sister, as he perceived feedback from others as critical when he was 'high'. He learned he could control his spending by agreeing a prearranged spending limit.

Follow-up experiments He continued to use the strategies and extended them to other areas of his life, such as asking his manager about work decisions when he realized he was becoming hypomanic.

Tips Ask patients in advance to discuss with their trusted person how to give feedback in a way that is acceptable and not perceived as antagonistic.

Experiment 11.2: engaging in pleasant activities without risky behaviour

Problem During the early stages of mania, Jane would become more socially active and want to 'party all night'. She would seek stimulating places and people to be with. Accompanying this was an excessive need to engage in pleasurable activities, which had the potential for serious consequences: in particular she would become sexually disinhibited. When she was in this state she found it difficult to hold conversations, her thoughts would race, her speech would speed up, and she became highly distracted, jumping from one thing to another.

Target belief 'In order to have a good time I have to draw attention to myself.'

Alternative belief 'I can have a good time without acting on my urges to attract attention to myself.'

Prediction 'If I go to the party and I don't do something unusual (e.g. undressing) nobody will notice me. I will not have a good time.'

Details of experiment Jane and her therapist agreed in advance how long she would stay at the party and how much alcohol she would drink (as both these influenced her need to party all night). Once at the party she would sit, rather than stand or dance, and engage in a conversation with the person she was sitting with. If she noticed she was speaking more rapidly, then she would do more listening than talking. She would sit on her hands if she started gesturing with them. Jane decided to assess how good the party had been by comparing it to other parties where she had drawn attention to herself.

Results of experiment Jane was able to sit until it was time to leave the party at the agreed time. She spoke to several people during the night, without doing things she would later regret, such as undressing.

Patient reflection She felt less 'speedy', was able to join in conversations, and felt people showed a genuine interest in the real Jane. She did enjoy the party as much as other parties she had been to.

Follow-up experiments Jane continued to practise this approach in other social situations, which provided her with more evidence that she could have a good time without painful consequences.

Tips Most bipolar patients enjoy their early stages of mania and find it difficult to rate their mood. It is helpful to introduce mood monitoring as early as possible in therapy. Patients are then more able to establish at what point on a $-10 / +10$ mood monitoring scale it is desirable for them to implement appropriate strategies to avoid serious consequences.

Table 11.1 Other experiments to test thoughts associated with symptoms of mania

Symptom	Cognition	Experiment	Result
Increased creativity	I have my best ideas when I'm high.	Kevin kept a log of his ideas for 3 months. He scored the quality of ideas (out of 10) both when high and when in remission.	He found that he had more ideas when high, but they were not always his best ideas. Kevin was able to review his belief and achieve a more balanced view.
Racing thoughts/ flight of ideas	I have lots of great ideas that I need to act upon now. I haven't enough time to carry them out.	Hector kept a record of his ideas. When his mood was more stable, he was able to prioritize which ideas were realistic and which were less so.	He found that some ideas were repetitive, some were unworkable, and some could be acted upon— though even those were not urgent.
Pressure of speech	Friends only enjoy my company when I'm talking quickly.	Fumi surveyed her friends as to how much they had enjoyed her company in three separate conditions: when she talked quickly, talked very little, and talked slowly.	Fumi found that her friends had enjoyed her company in all three conditions. She re-evaluated her thoughts and appreciated that her company was enjoyable regardless of how much she said.
Distractibility	I can't concentrate for more than 10 seconds; I may as well give up now.	Marge set herself graded experiments to write for up to 20 minutes per day, even if her mood was low or high.	Marge was able to write for at least 20 minutes about 5 days each week, whatever her mood. She reviewed her thoughts in line with this.

Reduced sleep	I should be able to manage on 5 hours' sleep a night.	(i) Robert surveyed other people's sleep patterns. (ii) He then monitored his own sleep, work, and mood pattern.	(i) The survey showed that most people like to have 7–8 hours per night and feel awful with less than 6 hours per night. (ii) He found that he worked better and had a more stable mood when he had more sleep.
Irritability	I should be able to do what I want.	Leroy agreed to keep a notebook to record all the decisions he wanted to make, and then to evaluate them when his mood was more stable.	By doing this he learned that he was better off delaying making decisions until his mood was more stable.
Risky behaviour (e.g. promiscuity)	I can never face going out again in this town because of what I've done when 'high'.	Camilla engaged in a graded experiment to reduce her avoidance of social situations and at the same time to enhance safety from sexual risks (e.g. going out with supportive, responsible friends).	She discovered she could go out when slightly high and not be promiscuous, providing she was with close friends. She endeavoured to go out only with friends when her mood was slightly high (and used second party advice to aid decision making).
Grandiosity	I'm too special to use a self-management group. I'm bound to be more interesting and knowledgeable than all the other participants.	James agreed to attend the group as a one-off experiment to test out his belief.	James learned some useful things at the group. He spoke to someone in the break whom he found to be interesting. He reviewed his thoughts and in fact attended the whole of the course. He discovered that other group attendees were also interesting to him.

Typical beliefs and assumptions associated with biopolar disorder

Experiment 11.3: need for achievement— a survey experiment

Problem Gerald had worked as a highly regarded scientist prior to having episodes of depression and mania. His BP diagnosis, plus physical health problems, had led him to leave this profession. He had not had a paid job since his first hospital admission. Throughout the course of therapy he was pursuing a career as a novelist.

Target belief 'I haven't achieved anything worthwhile since my first admission. People will judge me negatively for this.'

Alternative belief 'People do not judge others simply upon the number of papers they publish. Others may think I have achieved other worthy things in the past three years.'

Prediction In a personal life review and a survey of those who know me well, everyone will disregard the worth of anything except the academic work I did prior to my hospital admission.

Details of experiment First, Gerald and the therapist listed everything that Gerald had achieved in the last three years. The therapist used Socratic questioning and observed Gerald's style of disregarding his achievements. Gerald and the therapist then drew up some questions that he would ask his wife, brother, and some close friends. These were to be general at first (e.g. 'What do you think are my greatest achievements in life?'), then more specific ('Do you think I've achieved anything else?'), and finally, specific to the last three years ('Do you think I've achieved anything in the last three years?')

Results of experiment Friends and family all felt that his achievements not only included his scientific work but also: becoming a father, changing career, and coping with his diagnosis.

Patient reflection Gerald reflected that, despite the experiment, he still felt inclined to disregard these things as achievements. However, he acknowledged that not everyone would judge him purely upon the amount of papers he had published and that it was not helpful for him to continue to do this himself.

Tips This experiment was followed up with positive data logging to reinforce the change in beliefs about self and others (see Chapter 20 on self-esteem).

Experiment 11.4: need for autonomy—
a discovery experiment

Problem Since recovering from a manic phase in hospital, Ingrid felt that she had not resumed any of the household responsibilities. This made her feel useless and dependent upon other family members.

Target belief 'I am totally dependent upon other family members.'

Alternative belief 'Everyone in the household helps out. The extent of each person's tasks varies according to different individuals' needs at different times.'

Prediction 'I will discover that other family members will consistently carry out all of the household tasks.'

Operationalize prediction If this prediction is accurate, other family members will consistently carry out all of the household tasks. If the alternative belief is true, there will be variation in who does household tasks from day to day or week to week, and I will do my share.

Details of experiment Each family member kept a log of what they did for a week, in the first instance. The logs were brought into the therapy session and the tasks were tallied.

Results of experiment Ingrid was doing the highest percentage of household tasks.

Patient reflection Ingrid reflected that previously she had taken responsibility for all of the household tasks. She was comparing herself to this standard.

Therapist reflection Before this experiment, Ingrid was so convinced that she was not 'pulling her weight' that the experiment was set up with a view to helping her resume some of her share of tasks. In the event, this was not necessary.

Follow-up experiments Ingrid wanted to regain more control over household tasks (as she felt this was her role, whereas her husband was the breadwinner) and gradually increased her tasks to a level that felt manageable and not too stressful.

Table 11.2 Other experiments to test typical underlying beliefs and assumptions associated with bipolar disorder

Belief area	Theory A	Theory B	Experiment	Result
Perfectionism	If I don't do something perfectly, then I am a failure.	It's okay to do things less than perfectly.	(i) Sarah engaged in some activities that she was not perfect at (e.g. sport) just for fun.	(i) She recognized that this did not mean she was a failure.
			(ii) She later reviewed opinions of others about less than perfect achievements.	(ii) She recognized that the perfection standard was a standard that others didn't apply to her and she didn't apply to others.
			(iii) She then kept a record of doing things imperfectly.	(iii) Gradually, she became more relaxed in her approach to tasks.
Need for approval	I need to put others first in order to be considered a good person.	I need to take care of my own needs before I can attend to the needs of others.	John decided not to volunteer to befriend a new parishioner. In therapy, he role played an assertive response to the vicar, asserting his own needs.	The vicar acknowledged the importance of John prioritizing his own needs and agreed to ask someone else to do the task.

Beliefs about illness, stigma, prognosis, and medication

Experiment 11.5: challenging a sense of hopelessness about prognosis and the future

Problem William had a recent diagnosis of BP, which had delayed his career by a year. He had never had the intimate relationship that he desired. Although he was in remission over the course of therapy, there were subclinical fluctuations of depression, marked by thoughts that he had no chance of achieving the things he had hoped for in the future.

Target belief 'My life is blighted. People with a mental health problem never get the things they strive for (i.e. job, partner, family).'

Alternative belief 'Many people with a diagnosis of bipolar disorder have jobs, partners, and families. Many also go on to achieve worthwhile things. It is possible that I will too.'

Prediction 'If I am right, everyone with BP will be unemployed, single, and childless. If the alternative is true there will be the usual variations found in the population.'

Details of experiment Patient and therapist researched and surveyed people with BP as to whether they had careers, partners, and families. The therapist was able to provide some statistics, and the patient found some via the internet and self-help groups.

Results of experiment Both William and the therapist found the normal spread of careers, relationships, and families within a population of people with BP. They also discovered many high-profile people who had a BP diagnosis (e.g. Spike Milligan).

Patient reflection William felt less globally negative about his future.

Follow-up experiments This experiment was followed up with problem-solving strategies to direct his career path, and strategies for meeting more people so as to increase his chances of developing a relationship.

Tips Loneliness is a common feature in people with BP. We have found that cognitive therapy groups and self-help groups can be useful in initially reducing a sense of isolation.

Experiment 11.6: discovering the extent of stigmatization surrounding bipolar disorder—a survey experiment

Problem Susan had a recent diagnosis of BP. She was referred whilst in remission, with residual negative cognitions. At assessment, one of her main concerns was that she would not be able to tell her friends about her BP diagnosis. She was also concerned that she would not be able to make new friends unless they themselves had mental health problems.

Target cognition 'No one will want to know me with this diagnosis.'

Alternative perspective This was a discovery experiment, which started with no explicit alternative view but gradually led to an alternative theory, namely 'People do still want to know me'.

Details of experiment Initially, Susan joined a cognitive therapy skills group for people with BP. Following this, she and the therapist considered whether she should consider accessing self-help groups where discussions about informing others were held. In conjunction with this, a survey was conducted about people's attitudes to mental health.

Results of experiment Susan developed a network of friends, initially amongst people with a BP diagnosis. She gradually started to tell her friends about her diagnosis and would tell new people once trust was established. The survey led her to discover that many people without mental health problems had friends with mental health problems.

Patient reflection Susan reflected that she still had her initial fears about stigma in certain circumstances, but that on the whole they were greatly challenged. She also acknowledged that she had recognized some of her own prejudices about BP.

Tips This discovery experiment could have reinforced the target belief, as initially Susan did make contact with more people with a BP diagnosis. The fact that this had followed naturally from her decision to gradually explore what happened when she communicated with a range of people about her diagnosis was explicitly discussed with her.

Distinctive difficulties in cognitive therapy for bipolar affective disorder

Some adaptations need to be made to cognitive strategies to address the distinctive difficulties of BP. These include the changing presentation of patients with

Table 11.3 Other experiments to test beliefs about illness, stigma, prognosis, and medication

Belief area	Theory A	Theory B	Experiment	Result
About going high	Oh great, now I can catch up on missed time.	This discovery experiment only had an alternative theory after the experiment. This was that being high didn't help Sarah catch up.	Initially we reviewed the evidence regarding what Sarah had achieved over periods when high, and directly afterwards, compared to achievements over time when her mood was more stable. She also kept a prospective record of mood and achievements.	Over time, Sarah found that the benefit of achieving a lot in a few days was outweighed by costs of subsequent 'burnout' in following days. Over time she was able to see that a stable mood equated with more stable achievement.
About getting depressed	Oh no, here I go again, there's nothing I can do.	This discovery experiment led to the alternative theory: there are strategies I can use to prevent my mood declining.	When his mood started to dip, Peter experimented with different distraction and thought-challenging strategies.	Peter found that there were strategies that he could actively use to prevent his mood declining.
Beliefs about illness	It's my fault I'm ill.	There are many reasons why I have this diagnosis, most of which I had no control over.	Edward contacted the Manic Depression Fellowship and read some biographies of people with BP. He sought information regarding causes and maintenance of BP to test his alternative explanation.	Edward reviewed his belief and attained a less globally negative view about the causes of his BP.
Medication, compliance	Taking 6 tablets a day reminds me I'm ill. Other people don't need to take medication when they are well.	Other people do need to take medication when well. It is a way of preventing the illness.	Edward talked to some other people (with diabetes and epilepsy) who also had to take prophylactic medication.	He concluded that it would be more helpful to think that he took the medication to stay well.

BP, with periods of mania, depression, and subclinical mood fluctuations. This can affect patients, therapists, and the course of cognitive therapy. Furthermore, the different beliefs that are salient in episodes of hypomania, depression, and euthymia significantly contribute to the way that cognitive therapy can be applied, and the way that behavioural experiments are introduced and utilized. Finally, BP is an enduring disorder and therapists may need to guard against contamination by the sense of hopelessness. All of these difficulties emphasize the importance of a sound therapeutic relationship (Lam *et al.* 1999). Inexperienced therapists are encouraged to seek good supervision.

Changing presentation

Patients cannot readily engage with cognitive therapy, or any psychotherapy, when they are manic. Furthermore, patients recovering from mania have poor awareness of the benefits of therapy (Dell'Osso *et al.* 2002). Most cognitive therapy is therefore started during remission, when patients are more clinically stable (Lam *et al.* 1999; Scott 2002). However, clinically stable BP patients still display mood swings and subclinical fluctuations that are not necessarily the early signs of relapse (Molnar *et al.* 1988). Some patients react with alarm if they believe that they are getting depressed or, less commonly, that they are getting high (Lam *et al.* 1999). When this occurs, the patient (and sometimes the therapist) may be unwilling to engage in behavioural experiments that are perceived as risking emotional stability. Careful monitoring of mood and early warning signs can inform when, and at what pace, it is appropriate to proceed with behavioural experiments.

With patients recovering from a depressed mood, it is easy to get caught up in their relief at the improvement in their mood. There is a risk of encouraging patients to resume too many tasks too quickly, or to undertake behavioural experiments too quickly, thereby adding to their stress and tipping them into hypomania. This can be avoided by close monitoring of mood, the use of detailed relapse prevention strategies, such as being aware of the early warning signs and triggers to a potential episode of mania or hypomania, together with an action plan which may include self-monitoring, self-management, and self-medication. Some patients may welcome the early stages of mania. Inexperienced therapists may feel uncomfortable with helping patients to reduce pleasure seeking and dealing with patients' resistance to this. The typical cognitive therapist's role of building up pleasurable activities is replaced by encouraging patients to find alternative (less thrilling) activities in both the short and long term.

Patients becoming high might make over-optimistic assessments of their progress, and opt for early discharge (Scott 2002). The use of coping strategies to modify excessive behaviours significantly reduces the rate of manic relapse (Lam *et al.* 2001), so therapists need to offer prompt help to patients to apply mood-reducing strategies, such as taking additional medication. The changing presentation of BP necessitates therapist flexibility, as it is not always possible to follow a fixed format for this client group (Scott 2002).

Attitudes and beliefs

Common beliefs about social desirability, perfectionism, autonomy, and goal attainment may affect the way patients engage with cognitive therapy. Therapists may therefore need to take longer to engage these patients than those with unipolar depression (Scott *et al.* 2001) and take longer in preparing for appropriate behavioural experiments. Therapists need to be alert to the tendency of some patients to be 'good' patients and strive for the 'perfect' cure as an indicator of a broader belief system. Other patients' beliefs regarding the need to be independent and autonomous may explain why some BP patients have difficulty in acknowledging their negative feelings (Winters and Neale 1985); whilst others may wish to avoid discussing either their manic or depressive episodes (Scott *et al.* 2001).

By using behavioural experiments, therapists can encourage patients to try out behaviours that challenge the need to please, the need to get things right, the need to achieve, and the need to be independent. These beliefs can have positive as well as negative consequences, so Socratic questioning is used to explore their utility rather than directly refute them. Behavioural experiments are then used to test out alternative, more helpful beliefs. To change long-standing beliefs it may be necessary to carry out a series of behavioural experiments over an extended period.

Enduring disorder

BP is an enduring disorder which can often affect patients for the rest of their lives (Goodwin and Jamison 1990). Therapists need to acknowledge to patients that cognitive therapy does not necessarily aim for cure, but for acceptance, relapse prevention, and psychosocial improvement. It may not be appropriate to challenge distressing thoughts such as 'I need to take medication for the rest of my life' or 'I will have to tell my future employers that I've been seriously ill', since such thoughts may be justified. Also, some manic episodes may have resulted in tragic consequences, including accidents, financial losses, or family breakdown. Therapists can, with sensitivity, help patients appraise their life circumstances realistically, to modify catastrophic or dichotomous thinking such as 'I'm a failure because I have BP' or 'I'm only worth knowing when I'm high; when I'm low I'm worthless'.

Because of these difficulties, it is important to involve significant others, providing that this is acceptable to the patient. For example, relatives may be able to give information about early warning signs, help with reality testing, provide on-going support for patients coming to terms with their diagnosis, and help conduct behavioural experiments. For some patients, fear of talking to family members about their illness might itself be the subject of a behavioural experiment (for a case example, see Scott 2002). It is also important to help them communicate with other professionals involved in their care.

Related areas

The reader is specifically referred to Chapter 10 on depression for behavioural experiments on this aspect of BP. However, care needs to be taken before applying these strategies with patients with BP, because of the possibility of triggering a manic episode. The reader may also find useful experiments in Chapter 14 on insomnia and Chapter 20 low self-esteem. The following chapter on psychosis has useful experiments to deal with delusional beliefs, in addition to experiments regarding its enduring nature.

Further reading

Basco, M. and Rush, A. (1996). *Cognitive behavioral therapy for bipolar disorder.* Guilford Press, New York.

Lam, D., Jones, S., Bright, J., and Hayward, P. (1999). *Cognitive therapy for bipolar disorder: a therapist's guide to concepts, methods and practice.* Wiley, Chichester.

Scott, J. (2001). *Overcoming mood swings: a self-help guide using cognitive behavioural techniques.* Robinson, London.

Tales from the Front Line
Singing in the rain

A couple with sexual difficulties, who appeared to behave in a rather cold manner towards each other, was working on improving communication. He was a closet rubber fetishist, and she had said that she no longer found him attractive. However, their demeanour totally changed between two sessions. They had become open and affectionate. In the subsequent session they worked hard with the therapist to try to work out what had made the difference, and how to put the improvement onto a solid foundation. They could find no answers. They put their coats on and left. The therapist watched two rubberised macs, and two pairs of rubber boots disappear into the rain.

CHAPTER 12

Psychotic symptoms

Helen Close
Stefan Schuller

Introduction

Within the narrowest definition, psychotic symptoms are restricted to delusions or prominent hallucinations. Delusions are defined as 'erroneous beliefs that usually involve a misinterpretation of perceptions or experiences' (DSM-IV-TR; APA 2000), although it is acknowledged that prevailing cultural norms influence whether a belief is regarded as delusional. Hallucinations are defined as 'distortions or exaggerations . . . of perception' (ibid.).

Common symptoms of psychosis include hearing voices and holding delusional beliefs such as thinking you are being watched, that the television or newspapers are referring to you, or that your thoughts are being read. Thought processes may appear disordered and behaviour may be disorganized.

Although delusions and hallucinations are the most striking features, most people with psychosis will present with associated emotional disturbances such as depressed mood and anxiety. A range of associated impairments such as emotional flatness, poverty of speech, apathy, social withdrawal, and attentional deficits are also found. When such symptoms persist, secondary social disability is common.

Psychotic symptoms are usually episodic and a large percentage of patients will have more than one episode. Following recovery from the acute psychosis, many will have residual symptoms.

Due to the complex and multidimensional nature of psychotic disturbance, each person will differ markedly from the next (Fowler *et al.* 1995; Van Os *et al.* 1999). With so much diversity, a cognitive formulation can provide a useful framework for treatment.

Cognitive models

Various models have attempted to make sense of the disparate phenomena and anomalous experiences of people with psychosis. We shall highlight three key theoretical frameworks that inform clinical practice.

1 Vulnerability–stress models (e.g. Nuechterlein and Dawson 1984) suggest that longstanding biopsychosocial vulnerability interacts with more immediate stressors to trigger a psychotic episode. Triggers may include life events, stressful environments, or illicit drug use. This model implies the possibility of reducing vulnerability to relapse by moderating stress and promoting active coping.

2 The generic cognitive model of emotional disorder (Beck *et al.* 1979) can be used to construct a developmental formulation, integrating pre-disposing, precipitating, and maintaining factors in a way that guides treatment and helps psychotic patients make sense of their symptoms. Symptom maintenance cycles of cognitive and metacognitive appraisal, affect, and behaviour are crucial here, as are the roles of negative core beliefs and dysfunctional assumptions. In this context, behavioural experiments play a useful part in reducing avoidance and promoting reality testing.

3 An emerging body of research informs more specific cognitive models, exploring how psychosis impacts on perception and interpretation. For example, Fowler *et al.* (1995) view psychotic disturbance as a disorder in metacognitive processes: 'The central problem underlying many of the experiences and beliefs of psychosis [is] redefined as a problem in thinking, or judgment about one's own thoughts' (p. 43). Apart from causing distress and disrupting functioning, what gives thoughts a psychotic quality is their misattribution to an external source (e.g. 'He is putting aggressive thoughts in my head').

Developing these ideas, Garety *et al.* (2001) present a model which integrates contemporary psychosis research and is supported by empirical evidence. For someone with a vulnerability to psychosis, adverse environmental conditions may trigger emotional changes and disrupt cognitive processes of attention, perception, and judgement. If anomalous conscious experiences are then attributed to an external source, this may trigger emotional distress, physiological arousal, and a search for meaning This model can account for the occurrence of both delusions and hallucinations.

People with psychosis are also prone to jumping to conclusions, especially in relation to socially salient material: for example, a vulnerable person who is distressed and confused may interpret people randomly laughing in the street as laughing at him. A tendency to attribute negative outcomes externally, especially to other people, has also been described. Further, some patients are said to have compromised social understanding, with particular difficulty in judging the intentions of others. Together, these disruptions can mean that actions are experienced as unintended, thoughts appear to be broadcast or experienced as voices, or two unconnected events may appear to be causally linked.

Metacognitive beliefs about the dangerousness and power of hallucinations (Chadwick *et al.* 1996) and about the self (e.g. 'My voices telling me what to do means I am useless') can strengthen symptom maintenance processes through their influence on attentional biases, emotional distress, and avoidance strategies (Close and Garety 1998).

Dysfunctional schemas, often linked to early adverse environments and including themes of social humiliation and subordination, can also powerfully maintain psychotic symptoms.

Lastly, whilst isolation and avoidance are seen as maintaining factors in most mental health problems, psychotic clients can present with the most extreme and generalized forms of avoidance, to the point of cognitive, behavioural, and emotional 'shut-down' (Watkins 1997).

Key cognitions

Cognitive therapy in psychosis focuses on beliefs and thoughts that cause distress or interfere with a person's capacity to function. These can include beliefs about hallucinations and delusions, as well as about diagnosis, prognosis, medication, and stigma. It is also useful to work on 'non-psychotic' thoughts and beliefs (e.g. thoughts about acceptability or negative evaluation, as in social anxiety; see Chapter 7). Common cognitive themes include vulnerability to harm, social isolation, loss of control, inner defectiveness, and unrelenting standards (Fowler *et al.* 1995). Although clinically recognizable, these themes have yet to be validated through research. In this chapter three general categories of cognition are distinguished: delusional beliefs; beliefs about voices; and other problematic beliefs associated with psychosis.

Delusional beliefs

Persecutory beliefs lead patients to believe that they (or someone close to them) are being malevolently treated in some way (e.g. 'People are out to get me'). Grandiose beliefs reflect an inflated sense of worth, power, knowledge, identity, or special relationship to a famous person (e.g. 'I can control the world'). Other common delusions include thought insertion (e.g. 'My stepbrother puts these aggressive thoughts in my head'); thought broadcast (e.g. 'I can't go on public transport because everyone knows exactly what

I am thinking'); beliefs about telepathy (e.g. 'I know what you are thinking'); and delusions of reference (e.g. 'Magazines or newspapers are referring to me').

Beliefs about voices

Chadwick *et al.* (1996) describe typical beliefs about voices. Voices are often presumed to be powerful (e.g. 'I must obey my voice'): patients are often fearful of not complying with them and may believe that they have no influence over them. Many voices give the impression of knowing all about the hearer or of being omniscient (e.g. 'My voice knows my innermost thoughts').

Other important beliefs concern the origins and/or identity of the voices (e.g. 'The voice is my ex-wife, continuing to persecute me') and explanations for the voice experience (e.g. 'I hear them because I am bad'). In most cases, patients believe that individual voices reflect a desire to harm or help them. Malevolent voices may be seen as reflecting either an undeserved persecution or a deserved punishment. Benevolent voices reflect themes of protection, guidance, or special interest in the patient.

Other problematic beliefs associated with psychosis

Psychosis is often accompanied by secondary disabilities including loss of role, decline in social status, and threats to relationships. Fowler *et al.* (1995) note that some of these beliefs may be derived from problems commonly experienced by people with psychosis (e.g. a sense of failure may derive from difficulties in succeeding at work or in relationships). Beliefs about being doomed to social isolation or about inner defectiveness, (e.g. 'I'm a loser') are frequently observed, as are cognitions related to stigma (e.g. 'Others will know . . . and will think negatively of me'). Enduring negative self-appraisals have also been identified (Close and Garety 1998).

Accepting the pernicious stereotypes regarding psychosis can lead to demoralization, reduced social participation, and post-psychotic depression (Rooske and Birchwood 1998). Many patients present with a range of behavioural deficits ('negative symptoms'), which may be maintained by cognitions like 'No one will talk to me because I look mentally ill'. Such a thought might lead a patient to avoid going out, thus leading to greater anxiety, fewer opportunities for interaction, and subsequent social impoverishment. Other patients may actively avoid affect because of cognitions such as 'I must avoid intense feelings'.

Behavioural experiments

Delusional beliefs

Experiment 12.1: thought insertion

Problem As a child, David was bullied by his stepbrother Stephen. The brothers continued to have a difficult relationship as adults. When in Stephen's company, David reported experiencing aggressive thoughts. His explanation of this was that his stepbrother was putting these thoughts into his head.

Target cognition 'Stephen puts aggressive thoughts in my head.'

Alternative perspective 'I feel angry when I see Stephen because he bullied me throughout my childhood; perhaps the thoughts are my own angry thoughts.'

Prediction If the alternative perspective is true, then deliberately thinking about Stephen in the therapy session, when he is not around, might lead to similar angry thoughts.

Operationalizing prediction 'If I get angry thoughts in the session when I think about Stephen, this would support the alternative. The more similar the thoughts are to the thoughts I have when my brother is near, the more this new idea is supported.'

Experiment David wrote down the thoughts that he had when with his brother and passed them to the therapist. Then David was encouraged to think about his brother in session and describe the thoughts he had. These were also written down and compared to the first set of thoughts.

Results Both therapist and patient agreed that the two sets of thoughts were very similar.

Reflection David reflected that they must be his thoughts. The therapist empathized with him and encouraged him to appreciate that it is normal to have angry thoughts toward someone who has bullied you.

Experiment 12.2: mind reading

Problem Ruth believed that she could read other people's minds, including the therapist's. This led to a great deal of distress as she often 'read' other people's unpleasant thoughts about her.

Target cognition 'I can read people's minds. I know this because I can tell what my sister is thinking about; my friend rings when I am thinking about her; and I know when Dad's in a temper about things.'

Alternative perspective 'I am not able to read people's minds but I might be more attuned to people I am close to. Some people might be more predictable than others. I have a close friend who rings regularly and I might be good at predicting when that will happen. I might be sensitive to non-verbal cues, such as posture, gesture, etc. I might be worried that people are judging me.'

Prediction 'If I can read people's minds, then I should be able to read the therapist's mind.'

Operationalizing prediction If her first belief was right, Ruth would read the therapist's mind accurately. If the alternative view was right, Ruth might be able to read general non-verbal cues but not specific details.

Experiment The therapist was concerned that Ruth's belief might in some way bolster her self-esteem, so she explored how Ruth might feel if the new idea turned out to be more accurate. The pros and cons of each theory were discussed and Ruth was clear that it would be preferable if the target cognition was not accurate. The therapist then adopted a happy, thoughtful facial expression whilst thinking of something pleasant that she had written down. She then asked Ruth to guess what she was feeling and what her specific thoughts were. Ruth's guesses were also written down and compared to the therapist's thoughts.

Results Ruth could guess that the therapist was thinking about something positive but was not able to describe detailed thoughts.

Reflection Ruth and the therapist discussed how people may be sensitive to non-verbal cues which allow them to guess the general tone of someone else's thinking. It is also sometimes possible to predict what people might say from experience, rather than telepathy: 'You usually ring if we haven't met for over a week' rather than 'I knew you were going to ring because I read your mind'. Similarly, if we know someone's idiosyncratic behaviours, facial expressions, and style we may be able to guess, for example, 'You're thinking about Dad' (because you always wash up vigorously when you are thinking about him).

Further work Further attempts to read non-verbal cues (e.g. sad or amused facial expressions) were tested in session.

Tips This experiment can also be reversed for the patient who believes that others can read their thoughts. Here, significant others can be used if appropriate (e.g. 'Did you know I was thinking about Dad because you read my mind, or because I always behave like this when I think about Dad?')

Experiment 12.3: grandiose beliefs

Problem Jenny believed that she could control things simply by thinking about them. There was no time limit on this power, so if she thought about something and it happened many years later, she would still believe that this was due to her thoughts. Although it was frightening for Jenny to have this ability, it also made her feel powerful. Her main evidence for the belief was that she once wished dead someone who had mistreated her, and over a decade later the person died (of natural causes). A more recent example was when she found herself thinking that her parents' return from a holiday might be delayed. When they rang to say they were running late, she was 90% certain that this was due to her having thought about it.

Target cognition 'If I think about something it will happen.'

Alternative perspective 'I do not have this power. Sometimes things I think about happen by coincidence.'

Prediction Jenny's belief in the power of her thoughts extended to all areas. For example, she believed that if a coin were to be tossed, she would be able to control the side it would land on.

Operationalizing prediction It was agreed that as there were only two possible outcomes, Jenny would have a 50% chance of being correct just by chance. A figure was therefore agreed that would be a reasonable test of her powers: Jenny predicted that she would be able to predict every one of 50 coin tosses.

Experiment The therapist would toss a coin, following Jenny's prediction of the side it would land on. The therapist would check that Jenny was happy with her prediction before revealing the actual side. This would happen up to 50 times, but both Jenny and the therapist agreed they could stop the experiment if nothing further were to be gained.

Results Jenny opted out of the experiment. When the therapist again checked how Jenny would feel if her belief proved to be wrong, she decided that it would be too distressing.

Reflection Jenny acknowledged that although her 'power' caused her some distress, it also made her feel good at times. The therapist respected this but left the option open to explore it further, should there ever come a time when the costs of the belief outweighed the benefits.

Further work Were this experiment successful, the patient might feel able to test out her theory with more meaningful stimuli.

Tips This example highlights the need to regularly check with the patient, at each point in the experiment, the costs and benefits of testing the belief, and of being aware that there may be benefits to what may seem unrealistic or unhelpful ideas.

Beliefs about voices and other hallucinations

Experiment 12.4: challenging the omnipotence of voices

Problem Robert had dropped out of university and struggled subsequently to maintain employment or to have a sense of direction in life. He had hinted at feeling distracted by threatening and derogatory voices, but was reluctant to talk about these experiences.

Target cognition 'I can't talk to anyone about my voices; the voices will destroy me if I don't obey them.'

Alternative perspective 'The voices are a part of my own mind that I find 'too hot to handle' right now. I have often disobeyed the voices before and they haven't harmed me yet.'

Prediction 'If I tell my therapist some details about my voices, the voices will give me a hard time.'

Operationalizing prediction If the target cognition is right, then there will be an initial increase in distress, followed by punishment from the voices. If the

Table 12.1 Other experiments to address delusional beliefs

Target cognition	Alternative	Experiment	Result	Conclusion
Persecutory My colleagues are plotting against me. They all whisper at work.	Not everyone whispers. They are possibly friends with each other and whisper because we are not supposed to talk.	Monitor how many colleagues whisper. Keep a discreet tally. Check out whether they are friends.	Only two colleagues whispered. They spent their entire lunch break together.	The two people whispering are just friends.
Ideas of reference I often appear in magazines or on television.	My mind is playing tricks on me. It is one of the symptoms I get when I become unwell.	Look through magazines/watchTV and check with others whether they can see her.	Others did not note references to her on TV or in a magazine	It is not uncommon for me to literally take things too personally when I am unwell, and for my mind to play tricks on me.
Thought broadcast My baby daughter picks up my bad vibes when I look after her. She cries incessantly.	She is more familiar with my wife and is hungry for milk, which I can't give her.	Monitor the time that the baby cries when alone with mother and/or others. Note if baby stops crying when fed.	Baby stopped crying when being fed. Also crying times with others are similar to those with patient.	Babies often cry, usually they are hungry, uncomfortable, unwell, etc. It's not about me as a person.
Grandiose Andy believed he was a musical genius. He had not been accepted by bands, despite many auditions.This caused him distress and led him to neglect other things.	Although I am a good guitarist, this is not my only strength.It would be fruitful to explore other interests.	A tape of a few local guitarists' solos was compiled. A survey was conducted as to which was considered to be the best.	Andy's solo was rated as good but not as the best.	Andy was encouraged to feel positive about being selected as a good guitarist. Activity scheduling was used to increase confidence to engage in a range of pleasurable and meaningful activities. *Tip* This work was preceded by Socratic questioning exploring the pros and cons of needing to be 'special'.

alternative is right, there may still be an initial increase in distress, but it will be followed by feeling more relaxed or even exhausted towards the end of the session, rather than by punishment.

Experiment Robert agreed to describe the voices and tell the therapist about their identity during a session.

Results Robert noted that he only heard voices when concentrating on them. He described an initial increase in anxiety, as consistent with both theories, and then described a decrease in distress towards the end of the session, consistent with the alternative perspective.

Reflection 'What I was feeling was normal anxiety about telling another person about painful issues. My therapist can help me to ensure the anxiety goes down towards the end of the session, if I tell him openly what is going through my mind.'

Further work Experiments could be extended to other instances of 'disobeying' voices and noting the results.

Tips In order to disrupt possible preoccupation with painful memories, therapists need to adopt an empathic stance in session, offer normalizing attributions, and focus on the here and now towards the end of the session.

Experiment 12.5: running commentary voices (low self-esteem)

Problem For over 10 years, Hugo had heard voices giving a running commentary on his everyday actions. From the moment he got up he heard voices commenting on his usual routine in a way that sounded as if they were instructing him (e.g. 'Make a cup of tea . . . sit down . . . pick up the morning paper . . . read the headlines'). To Hugo, this meant that he was useless and needed his voices to guide him.

Target cognition 'I can't carry out the most simple everyday tasks without my voices to guide me—I must be useless.'

Alternative perspective 'I can do everyday tasks without my voices to guide me. Although the voices sound as if they are instructing, they may be simply commenting, and I can do things differently.'

Prediction Hugo's daily routine was very regular each day. We discussed ways that he might try to change it one morning, and whether the voices might comment on such a change. Hugo thought that it might be possible to change his routine but that it would be difficult, and that the voices might urge him to stick to it. However, if he did change the routine he would consider it a small success, and it would challenge his belief that he was useless.

Operationalizing prediction If Hugo was able to carry out a different routine, planned in collaboration with his therapist, he felt that this would give weight to the alternative theory. If the voices commented on the new routine then this would support the theory that they were simply commenting. If the voices urged him to return to his old routine, strategies such as using residential staff support to maintain the new routine were drawn up. Hugo was encouraged to consider that even a small change in his routine would give support to the new theory.

Experiment A new morning routine was drawn up in collaboration with Hugo and his key worker. It included the essential things that Hugo needed to do, but in a slightly different order. The experiment was conducted in his residential setting whilst his key worker was on duty.

Results As he had predicted, Hugo initially heard voices telling him to do things as usual. When he maintained the new routine, his voices resorted to a running commentary upon that.

Reflection Although his original belief conviction lessened, Hugo's core belief about his 'uselessness' remained intact. He was more able to entertain the notion that his voices reflected his thoughts and that the running commentary was probably a combination of habit and boredom.

Further work Given Hugo's reflections, a natural follow-on experiment was to test out the boredom theory by introducing more into his schedule. This intervention proved to be too difficult for Hugo to carry out, even with support.

Tips Even though the intervention as a whole was not entirely successful, Hugo was appreciative that he could reframe why he had 'running commentary' voices. Therapists need to be alert to these small but significant shifts for their patients.

Problematic non-psychotic beliefs

Experiment 12.6: low self-esteem and stigma

Problem Luke had expected to follow an academic career, but had not succeeded due to a number of episodes of psychosis. He was left with a number of negative symptoms and an impoverished lifestyle. His core belief was that he was a loser and that everyone around him knew it.

Target cognition 'It is obvious to everyone around me that I have a mental illness and that I look like a loser.'

Table 12.2 Other experiments to address beliefs about voices and other hallucinations

Target cognition	Alternative	Test	Result	Conclusion
Externality appraisal The voices I hear come from an external force.	These voices may be thoughts that I find too difficult and therefore I hear them as externally generated.	Check with significant others when hearing voices.	Others cannot hear the voices.	This suggests that they come from within me. Further work on understanding the content of the voice and its impact upon the patient.
Negative self-evaluations I can see the devil because I am bad.	Light levels, what I do at the time, and how I feel about myself at the time may influence these experiences.	◆ List personal strengths, involving survey of friends and family. ◆ Schedule absorbing activities, drawing on strengths. ◆ Monitor situations when visibility is poor and when alone. ◆ Compare frequency of visions and associated distress.	I only had the visions when it was hard to see clearly (e.g. twilight), and when I had nothing to do. I feel less 'spooked' by these visions now.	I sometimes feel that I am bad, like a self-prejudice. I must have been reading things into what I saw—it fitted with how I was feeling at the time. ***Tip*** Follow up with positive data log (see Chapter 20 on self-esteem).
Uncontrollability My abuser's voice comes and goes at will, to torment me.	My voices are more intrusive if something reminds me of my childhood.	I will bring on the voices by actively remembering certain childhood situations, and then gradually fade them out by concentrating on something else.	I had some control over the experience of voices.	I can control the voices to some extent by distracting myself. I feel safer now.

Alternative perspective 'I am self-conscious because of my experiences, but I just look like a regular guy to other people.'

Prediction That in an identity parade he would be picked out as the 'loser'.

Operationalizing prediction In a line-up of 10 people, observers would point him out as the loser. A minimum number of 10 observers would be needed and, for his initial thought to be confirmed, more than 50% of observers would need to pick him out.

Experiment Luke agreed to a full-length photograph being taken. It was put on a board with nine other volunteers' photos (also full-length). Luke was happy that they represented 'average guys on the street'. Over 20 people were surveyed and asked if anyone on the board was distinctive for any reason. They were also asked if anyone looked particularly successful or if anyone looked particularly like a loser. If this led to a negative response, Luke had requested that those surveyed be forced to pick out the two people who looked the most likely 'success' and the most likely 'loser'.

Results No one was particularly conspicuous in either direction. Two people took 20% of the vote each for looking more successful, and the 'loser' votes had a more even scatter. Luke picked up less than 5% of the vote (i.e. only one person, when forced, picked him out as looking like the loser).

Reflection Luke was extremely pleased with the result and the possibility that he appeared to look like a 'regular guy'.

Further work Luke was encouraged to notice how others looked in terms of dress, posture, movement, etc. He was encouraged to keep up a 'regular guy' look by maintaining self-care and adopting a more relaxed posture whilst out.

Tips This work was followed up by self-esteem (see Chapter 20 for more information) and anxiety management work.

Experiment 12.7: challenging affective avoidance

Problem Samantha had had a single psychotic episode five years ago but made a very limited recovery, presenting as overweight, lacking in energy, and with very flat affect. There was a suggestion in the notes that she had traumatic memories around the events leading to her admission. She had hit her father ('a disciplinarian') in the face and he had called the police to have her admitted.

Target cognition 'I have to avoid strong feelings or "rocking the boat" in order to avoid becoming unwell again.'

Alternative perspective 'Many factors that contributed to my crisis are no longer around (e.g. living abroad, a stressful job, a relationship breakdown). I do not need to avoid all emotional situations.'

Prediction 'Playing the piano used to be something I enjoyed, but I have avoided playing since my admission to hospital. If I play the piano for the first time after all these years it may upset me and I may lose control.'

Operationalizing prediction 'If the target cognition is right, I will feel anxious initially and then feel unable to concentrate on playing music, thinking instead about painful memories and worrying whether the feelings may get too strong—a bit like in the panic attacks I learned to cope with. If the other idea is right, I will also feel anxious initially but if I focus on the task in hand the feelings will not overwhelm me and I may end up enjoying it.'

Experiment Samantha agreed to try to concentrate on playing the piano (for at least 10 minutes, to enable a fair evaluation) and to note anxious thoughts and mood changes without catastrophizing.

Results She felt 'churned up' and frustrated at her poor technique; however, no major threat-related thoughts and feelings were noted. Then she felt some slight enjoyment and was glad she had had a go.

Reflection 'The mental health crisis has demoralized me and I felt I needed a thick skin. It now feels safe to let go a bit again.'

Further work Samantha was encouraged to show a range of feelings at the weekly residents' meeting and to note the results. No harsh responses like her father used to show were noted.

Tips A clear consideration of potential costs and benefits of the experiment needs to have been discussed, and one should only proceed if the patient agrees it is worth trying this out. (See Chapter 17 on avoidance of affect for more thoughts about this kind of problem.)

Experiment 12.8: withdrawal and social isolation

Problem Simon believed that his brain had become 'twisted' as a result of his being in intellectual conflict with his philosophy tutors. His description of this physical feeling sounded like physical tension. He believed that lying in bed all day thinking about philosophical questions would slowly untwist his brain, and he would then be able to resume his work in philosophy. His evidence for this was that he could physically feel his brain untwisting after lying in bed.

Target cognition 'Lying in bed all day thinking about philosophy untwists my twisted brain.'

Alternative perspective 'The twisting is physical tension that is maintained by ruminating about past events.'

Prediction If Simon were able to find alternative ways to relax and gain some pleasure and enjoyment from his life, this might also lead to 'untwisting'.

Operationalizing prediction This experiment would rely on Simon's self-reports as to how untwisted his brain felt after he had engaged in something that he had found either relaxing or pleasurable, or that gave him a sense of achievement. These activities included walking the dog, going to the pub for a drink, and cooking a meal. Simon commented that he would need to experience a lot of untwisting during these activities to challenge his initial belief.

Experiment Simon would try to build up a schedule of activities that gave him a sense of pleasure and achievement. The activities included some that might reduce physical tension, such as relaxation and sport. As Simon was reluctant to give up the time for ruminating, he would keep a written record of how much he felt his brain had untwisted (a) after activities and (b) after taking to his bed.

Results Simon struggled to add a new activity to his daily schedule. Family support did help, and he did report some untwisting. However, the lying in bed won out for him.

Reflection Simon acknowledged that he could untwist his brain by walking his dog, but lying in bed required less effort.

Tips Although this experiment did not serve to change Simon's theory, it did at least give him another framework to improve his mood. Activity scheduling became a useful strategy that he (and others involved in his care) employed when his mood was particularly low (see Chapter 10 on depression). It might also be useful to explore the wider pros and cons of lying in bed versus other strategies: although lying in bed certainly requires less effort, it may have other disadvantages, especially if it involves ruminating.

Distinctive difficulties in cognitive therapy with psychosis

Engagement

It can be difficult to engage people with psychosis within a therapeutic relationship. Many have been traumatized by their experiences; general behavioural disorganization and negative symptoms, such as poor motivation, may also make it difficult for patients to keep to appointments. Many fear relapse, which may lead to a 'sealing-over' recovery style in which patients try to cope by forgetting, or avoiding thinking about, their experiences. Therapists should

Table 12.3 Other experiments to address problematic non-psychotic beliefs

Target cognition	Alternative	Experiment	Result	Conclusion
Denial of difficulties I am not psychotic. Why should I stay in touch with services or take medication?	I do not like to remember being unwell. I want to obliterate my mental health problems. People I trust have told me I have appeared incoherent and a bit intimidating to others when ill.	Patient kept 'video diary' to self-monitor possible changes in mental health over time.	Patient noted changes consistent with theory B but felt defensive about admitting these. Therapist then helped chart crises against stressful life events to enhance sense of control and protect self-esteem.	When stressful things happen to me it does affect how I come across. I will try a few things that may help me to cope with stress (e.g. attend hearing voices group, take medication).
Non-adherence to prescribed medication My antipsychotic medication doesn't help (hence I don't take it).	It does help with the symptoms but also has some side-effects such as feeling groggy.	Monitor symptoms and adherence to medication. Note any patterns.	Patient noted an increase in positive symptoms when he didn't take medication regularly.	On balance it is better to take medication. Arranged psychiatric review to check out alternatives with fewer side-effects.
Fear-driven thought control strategies Songs in my head mean my psychosis is returning. I need to suppress them.	This has never been an early warning sign for me. It is common to have songs going around in your head. Blocking the song will only increase the anxiety.	Note song without judging it, or sing along.	Anxiety decreased, as did the occurrence of the songs.	The songs were discussed as being similar to (benign) intrusive thoughts. Thought blocking had led to an increase and alternative strategies were adopted.

Sense of defectiveness Talking to myself means I'm mad.	Talking to myself might remind me of my diagnosis, but it does not mean I am mad. Plenty of people talk to themselves.	Survey of public. Who talks to themselves? Do they notice if others do?	Many people talked to themselves. Some noticed others doing it. No one thought much of it.	It's OK to talk to myself. It is not seen as madness. This was followed with work helping the patient to come to terms with his diagnosis.
Social isolation No woman would ever want to have children with a man who has done the kind of 'mad' and unstable things I have done.	My despair is acute, but I have a fair prognosis. Other sufferers have managed to have caring relationships and families.	Introduced to co-operative older patient who tells freely of chaotic early years and of more recent consolidation.	This guy has done some pretty weird things when he was younger but he has his own family now.	If he can turn things around for himself, maybe I can too.

engage patients by taking a genuine interest in their problems, and developing an initial formulation that instils optimism and introduces behavioural testing as one of a number of ways forward.

Delusional beliefs

Collaborative enquiry helps to keep confrontation about beliefs to a minimum. Therapists can frame beliefs as patients' accounts of their experiences and tackle those beliefs that are either associated with distress or that interfere with the patient's ability to function.

Some delusional beliefs, such as believing that one is subject to secret service surveillance, can easily stay 'one step ahead' of reality testing and may, therefore, be difficult to disconfirm. Other beliefs (e.g. grandiose delusions) may serve to preserve vulnerable self-esteem, so that relinquishing the beliefs would result in a net loss for the patient. Therefore, particular attention needs to be given to all possible outcomes of behavioural experiments, and their implications for the patient (e.g. 'Let's say we somehow found this wasn't true, how would you feel?'). If severe distress or thought disorder occur during the experiment, the therapist should be available for debriefing, to make sense of the distress and revise coping strategies. Therapists also need to be wary of chance outcomes that might strengthen distressing delusions (e.g. the therapist guessing accurately what a patient is thinking about).

Vulnerability to in-session thought disorder

One should avoid behavioural experiments if patients are showing frank thought disorder or significant behavioural disorganization. One difficulty in working with psychotic patients is that when affect is high, cognitive disorganization and over-rehearsed biased and avoidant strategies are likely to be influential, limiting the patient's ability to generate more helpful beliefs without therapeutic assistance (Chadwick *et al.* 1994). This can reduce the patient's capacity to attend to relevant material and to remember the helpful aspects of the experiment. In order to guard against this, Chadwick *et al.* (1996) suggest the following adaptations:

- Establish a clear alternative belief that challenges the delusion from the outset.
- Clarify with the patient, in advance, precisely what has to happen for each belief to be supported or refuted.
- Establish a conceptual framework with patients first, enabling them to assimilate and make sense of empirical refutation.
- Involve significant others in reality tests to aid maintenance of gains.

We would add that it is helpful to gradually increase the difficulty of successive experiments, for example by getting other people to do an experiment first. Video recording of experiments can mitigate to some extent against selective attention and memory biases, as can writing down summaries of what happened in an experiment, what the implications of this are, and so on.

Enduring problems

For many patients, residual symptoms and vulnerability to psychotic relapse will be a lifelong problem. Cognitive therapy will not cure psychosis, but can aim to reduce demoralization, to provide more helpful coping strategies, and to help reduce relapse risk. A rehabilitative process therefore needs to underpin any attempts at reality testing through individual behavioural experiments, and therapists need to be well trained and supervised to be able to help patients manage their vulnerabilities in a sensitive yet purposeful way.

Therapists can become 'contaminated' by the hopelessness of patients who may struggle to maintain work, activity, relationships, etc. Behavioural experiments can be helpful here, by promoting a metacognitive shift, from the perspective of a chronic patient who feels threatened, vulnerable, and defeated, to the perspective of a hypothesis-testing, active individual, working towards their best possible recovery.

Other relevant chapters

As it is so important to target mood disturbance alongside psychotic symptoms, the reader may find it useful to consult Chapter 10 on depression and Chapter 7 on social anxiety. Further experiments on low self-esteem can be found in Chapter 20. Chapter 11 on bipolar disorder has some useful experiments for patients with enduring problems. Lastly, Chapter 17 on avoidance of affect offers useful ideas on disrupting symptom maintenance cycles.

Further reading

Chadwick, P., Birchwood, M. and Trower, P. (1996). *Cognitive therapy for delusions, voices and paranoia*. Wiley, Chichester.

Fowler, D., Garety, P. and Kuipers, E. (1995). *Cognitive behaviour therapy for psychosis: theory and practice*. Wiley, Chichester.

Nelson, H. (1997). *Cognitive behavioural therapy with schizophrenia*. Stanley Thornes, Cheltenham.

Morrison, A. (ed.) (2002). *A casebook of cognitive therapy for psychosis*. Brunner–Routledge, Hove.

Tales from the Front Line
You have the right to remain silent

A patient in her late 40s had a fear of using escalators in case she fainted and fell, resulting in injury and/or making a fool of herself. To test her predictions therapist and patient visited a shop with escalators. The therapist was to accompany her for the initial trials of riding up and down escalators and later stand at the bottom of the escalator with a promise that she would help if it became necessary. This was clearly being observed by the store's security system, because somewhere between the 10th and 15th time of descending the escalator, the store detectives arrested therapist and patient. They were told that they were acting suspiciously and taken to an office for questioning and to have their belongings searched. Whilst the therapist agonized over the dilemma of how to maintain patient confidentiality in such a situation, the patient, who had found the situation quite amusing, provided the necessary information voluntarily. As a result the therapist was able to negotiate permission to use the shop's facilities in future for treatment trials. The client did extremely well in treatment, but the therapist has since developed a strong suspicion she is being observed every time she walks into a shop.

CHAPTER 13

Eating disorders

Myra Cooper
Linette Whitehead
Nicky Boughton

Introduction

Eating disorders are serious and often life-threatening disorders. They are
common in young women and in women from majority cultures in the developed
West, but are by no means exclusive to these groups.

The main eating disorders identified in DSM-IV-TR (APA 2000) are anorexia
nervosa, bulimia nervosa, and eating disorder not otherwise specified (EDNOS)
(a mixed category which includes one specific subtype, binge eating disorder).
EDNOS now appears to be the most common diagnosis among those who present for treatment.

In anorexia nervosa, body weight is deliberately kept well below normal.
Anorexia nervosa patients fear weight gain and may 'feel fat'; they include a
subgroup who experience binge eating and purging. In bulimia nervosa, frequent binge eating is followed by inappropriate compensatory behaviour (e.g.
self-induced vomiting in the purging subtype or extreme fasting and exercise
in the non-purging subtype). Self-evaluation in bulimia nervosa is usually
very influenced by shape and weight. The EDNOS mixed category typically
includes those who share the relevant key features of anorexia nervosa or
bulimia nervosa, with one or two of the criteria for full diagnosis unfulfilled.
Binge eating disorder is characterized by binge eating (but not compensatory
behaviour), and concern about weight and shape is not an essential feature.

Anorexia nervosa

Anorexia nervosa patients restrict food intake and usually display unusual
behaviour around food and eating. This can involve eating only very small
amounts of food at a time or repeated checking of calorie content. Patients

*The authors are grateful to Anne Stewart who provided Experiment 13.4 (Helen).

may also check their body size and weight. They may be particularly interested in food and cooking, and are usually preoccupied with weight and shape. They are often depressed or low in mood, and commonly are anxious about food and eating (for example, they may worry all day about what and how much they will have to eat at supper). They may also experience interpersonal difficulties. Self-esteem is typically low, with a desire for achieving perfection in all the things they do.

Bulimia nervosa

Bulimia nervosa patients are often ashamed and embarrassed about their eating related behaviour (e.g. purging) and keep it a secret from those around them. They may also attempt to restrict their eating, check aspects of their weight and shape (e.g. weigh themselves frequently), and/or avoid them (e.g. by wearing loose clothing). They may be low in mood (usually less so than in anorexia nervosa), generally anxious and worried, and preoccupied with weight and shape. Self-esteem (as in anorexia nervosa) is low and there may also be interpersonal difficulties. A subgroup engage in self-harm or reckless (so called impulsive) behaviour.

Eating disorder not otherwise specified

Although little researched, most EDNOS patients resemble those with either anorexia nervosa or bulimia nervosa except that one or more of the DSM-IV-TR criteria for the disorder are not fulfilled. Patients with binge eating disorder are often overweight and commonly older than bulimia nervosa patients. Their binges are also more like normal meals in composition (but of similar calorie content to patient binges).

Cognitive models

The importance of cognition in anorexia nervosa and bulimia nervosa is well documented (Cooper 1997). Clinical experience suggests that those with a diagnosis of EDNOS who resemble these patients may also share some of their key cognitions. Relatively little is known about cognitions in binge eating disorder.

There are general and specific cognitive models of eating disorders. Two of the general models are the cognitive transdiagnostic model (Fairburn *et al.* 2003), which provides the conceptual framework for this chapter, and the schema model of Waller *et al.* (2004). Specific cognitive models have been developed for anorexia nervosa (Fairburn *et al.* 1999) and bulimia nervosa (Fairburn *et al.* 1986; Cooper *et al.*, in press) but not for EDNOS and binge eating disorder.

Experimental evidence supporting cognitive models of eating disorders is growing, though at this stage, with the exception of cognitive treatments for bulimia nervosa, there are few well-controlled outcome studies. The cognitive treatment developed by Fairburn and colleagues helps people with bulimia nervosa (Agras *et al.* 2000), and also appears to help many patients with binge eating disorder (e.g. Wilfley *et al.* 1993). However, while promising, outcomes indicate that approximately 50% of people may still be left with significant symptoms or an eating disorder diagnosis (Fairburn *et al.* 1995).

Key cognitions

Five key cognitive constructs form the framework for organizing the behavioural experiments in this chapter:

1 Overevaluation of eating, weight, shape, and their control
2 Mood intolerance
3 Core low self-esteem
4 Perfectionism
5 Interpersonal problems

All five are identified in Fairburn *et al.*'s (2003) transdiagnostic model, which provides a framework that encapsulates many of the organizing principles of other models.

While the five constructs of the transdiagnostic model provide a useful organizing framework for the behavioural experiments featured in this chapter, disorder-specific models tend to provide greater detail about the specific nature of the cognitions involved. For example, Cooper *et al.*'s (in press) model of bulimia nervosa identifies different types of automatic thought (positive thoughts, lack of control thoughts, negative thoughts, and permissive thoughts), different types of underlying assumption, and negative self beliefs that are unconditional and absolute.

The specific cognitions tested in the behavioural experiments outlined here are typical of those identified in disorder-specific models.

Table 13.1 contains examples of cognitions from each of the transdiagnostic categories, as well as types of experiment that may be undertaken. The sample cognitions are drawn primarily from theoretical accounts that contain detailed information on specific cognitions, including the accounts of Garner and Bemis (1982), Fairburn *et al.* (1986), Wolff and Serpell (1998), Cooper *et al.* (in press), Waller *et al.* (2004), and from our clinical work.

As may be seen in Table 13.1, the first category, *Overevaluation of eating, weight, shape, and their control* has been divided into four subcategories. The second, *Mood intolerance,* may include use of food and eating to cope with distressing feelings and thoughts. *Core low self-esteem* frequently includes beliefs

Table 13.1 Domains, typical cognitions, and sample experiments

Cognitive domain	Typical cognitions	Examples of experiments to test cognitions
Overevaluation of eating, weight, shape, and their control		
Thoughts about control of eating, weight, and shape	'I just can't control my eating; I can't help myself.' 'Eating means I lack self-discipline.' 'Being able to control your weight is a good thing.' 'Not eating means I am a superior person.' 'Controlling my eating is the one thing I can do really well.'	Graded experiments to establish and see if control can be achieved. Survey others' views about the meaning of eating and weight control.
	'Eating means I'll get fat or gain lots of weight.' 'If I don't weigh myself 10 times a day, my weight might balloon.'	Graded experiments to see if 'normal' eating results in actual weight gain over time (BN). Survey work on belief that normal weight entails 'fat'. Practise graded dropping of safety behaviours and monitor impact or frequency of feared outcome.
	'Eating will help me feel better, make the pain go away.' 'Not eating will stop me, or prevent me, from feeling bad.' 'Not eating means I'm doing better than other people.'	Test the truth of this by monitoring how long feeling better, or bad, lasts over a defined time period. Experiment with alternative solutions to test if they achieve similar benefits without the costs. Survey others' views about the meaning of not eating.
Eating, weight, and shape as acceptance by others	'If I get fat, others won't like me anymore.' 'If I get thinner, others will accept me more readily.' 'If I'm thin then people like me.' 'If I lose weight then people notice me.'	Survey others' views on the importance of weight and shape in general, and in relation to self. Graded weight gain and monitoring of others' reactions; survey of views (if very underweight).

Eating, weight, and shape as a means to self-acceptance	'If I gain weight, it means I'm a failure, no good, worthless.' 'If I lose weight, it means I'm a success.'	Survey others' views on the importance of weight and shape in general, and in relation to self. Graded weight gain and monitoring of others' reactions; survey of views (if very underweight).
Positive and negative thoughts about body image	'I'm so fat, I'm really overweight.' 'I can see my bones so I know I'll be noticed.' 'I look much more attractive now' (in context of extreme weight loss)	Monitor distress and belief in thoughts and experiment with reducing checking and avoidance behaviours to see if distress and belief subsequently reduce. Survey others' views (if own view is very distorted). Obtain and rate video feedback of self.
Mood intolerance		
Thoughts about control of feelings	'Distress will last forever, or keep getting worse and worse.'	Graded exposure to feelings and distress, and monitoring of these over a defined time period.
	'Getting upset means I'm out of control.' 'It's good to be in control of your feelings.'	Survey others' views on the meaning of distress and various feelings.
Core low self-esteem		
Core beliefs indicative of negative self-worth	'I'm no good . . . a failure . . . unlovable . . . stupid . . . can't cope . . . worthless . . . useless . . . out of control . . . ugly . . . greedy . . . lazy.'	Survey others' views on positive and negative qualities. Exposure to tasks and situations where belief will be challenged or (agreed) disconfirmatory evidence obtained.
	'If I'm not perfect, I'm a total failure.' 'If I'm not special or different, I'm worthless.'	Practise being 'not perfect', being average, and monitor others' reactions and own. Survey others' views on 'all or nothing' thinking—its advantages and disadvantages, application, in general and to self.

Table 13.1 (*Continued*)

Cognitive domain	Typical cognitions	Examples of experiments to test cognitions
Perfectionism		
Overevaluation of achievement	'I must do things really well.' 'I need to come top in class.' 'Being less than best isn't good enough.'	Reduce performance checking and avoidance, and monitor effect on beliefs and distress.
Interpersonal difficulties		
	'People won't take any notice of me if I tell them what I think.' 'If I say what I think others will be offended.'	Graded practice of assertiveness. Collect data on others' reactions and compare with predictions.
	'If I do what other people want they will like me.' 'I mustn't let anyone down.' 'Other people's needs are more important than mine.'	Graded practice of putting own needs first. Collect data on others' reactions and compare with predictions.
	'I don't fit in', 'Other people think I'm boring, dull, weird', 'No one likes me.' 'If other people knew what I was really like they would reject me.'	Survey others' views. Exposure to situations where (agreed) disconfirmatory evidence will be obtained.
	'If I get close to others they will control, hurt, abandon me.' 'I can't cope with adult sexuality.'	Graded practice of putting trust in other people. Collect data on others' reactions and compare with predictions.

about being ugly, greedy, and lazy—the latter two being particularly prevalent in anorexia nervosa. Such beliefs may be expressed as dichotomized thinking, or rapid switching between extreme negative core beliefs (examples of these are provided in the table). *Perfectionism* may take an extreme form, which has recently been termed clinical perfectionism (Shafran *et al.* 2002). *Interpersonal difficulties* are also often apparent. They may include unhelpful beliefs related to self-assertion, the priority of other people's needs, beliefs about social exclusion, defectiveness in the eyes of others, and beliefs about intimacy and sexuality.

Behavioural experiments

In this section, an example of a behavioural experiment is provided for each of the categories identified in Table 13.1:

◆ **Overevaluation of eating, weight, shape, and their control**
  Experiment 13.1: testing thoughts about control of eating, weight, and shape
  Experiment 13.2: testing thoughts about eating, weight, and shape as a means to acceptance by others
  Experiment 13.3: testing thoughts about eating, weight, and shape as a means to self-acceptance
  Experiment 13.4: testing positive and negative thoughts about body image

◆ **Mood intolerance**
  Experiment 13.5: testing thoughts about loss of control of feelings

◆ **Core low self-esteem**
  Experiment 13.6: testing core beliefs indicative of negative self-worth

◆ **Perfectionism**
  Experiment 13.7: testing thoughts about overevaluation of achievement

◆ **Interpersonal difficulties**
  Experiment 13.8: testing thoughts about interpersonal difficulties

---

Overevaluation of eating, weight, shape, and their control

Experiment 13.1: testing thoughts about control of eating, weight, and shape

Problem Sheila had a long history of severe eating disorder. She had managed to reach a normal weight but felt she could not allow herself anything that she would like to eat for fear of losing control.

Target cognitions If I allow myself to eat something I like the taste of, I'll be unable to stop myself bingeing. I'll have to make myself sick, which will confirm my belief that I'm a greedy, disgusting person.

Alternative perspective It is possible to eat a little of what you like, enjoy the taste, and find that you are quite satisfied and have no desire for more.

Prediction Sheila regularly had supper with Freda, who always provided a pudding which Sheila always refused. She was sure that:

1 If she agreed to have some pudding, Freda would be so surprised and pleased she would push her to have more, which Sheila would be unable to resist.
2 Once started she would have to finish the bowl. Then she would have to make herself sick. She and Freda would be disgusted.

Operationalize prediction When Sheila was next invited to supper, she would test the prediction by eating some pudding.

Experiment Sheila arranged to have supper with Freda and asked her to prepare some of her special rhubarb crumble. She agreed to meet with the therapist the following day for debriefing.

Results Although very nervous about trying the pudding, Sheila was able to enjoy the taste and felt a sense of relief that she was acting the same as the others at the table, by eating dessert. Freda did not comment on her eating the pudding and did not offer her more. Sheila enjoyed the meal and was satisfied that she had had enough.

Reflection Sheila was amazed to realise that Freda had been unaware of her struggle and was not interested in evaluating her via her eating habits. She was surprised to find she could stop eating and that she felt satisfied and in control. She commented that this was partly because she felt that she could take the risk in the first place as she was in a safe place with others who were not expecting her to struggle. It would be much more difficult at home with no-one else around. The experiment did highlight her unease at doing something she liked, and this was a further area to work on.

Further experiments Ideas for further experiments included trying the same experiment in different environments (e.g. a restaurant where she had to choose her food off a menu, a self-service buffet, and eating at home).

Tips Issues around losing control and negative evaluation are frequently apparent in both food *and* non-food situations (e.g. 'If I have too much fun, I'll lose control'). It is important to make these links, and for the patient to understand the general principle which may then be applied in similar experiments across the board.

Experiment 13.2: testing thoughts about eating, weight, and shape as a means to acceptance by others

Problem Cynthia successfully eliminated her bulimic behaviour in therapy, but still believed that other people would not accept her unless she was thin. When she put on weight during her first term, a friend of her father's commented on her weight gain. When she subsequently lost weight after strict dieting, her friends at university told her she looked 'lovely'.

Target cognitions I'm not worthy of being liked unless I am thin.

Alternative perspective I am worthy of being liked for who I am, not for how I look.

Prediction Cynthia predicted that if her friends were asked what they liked about her, they would focus on her appearance, and the fact that she was slim and athletic looking. She went rowing three times a week in all weathers to preserve this appearance (belief rating: 80%).

Experiment During the week, Cynthia asked half a dozen of her friends to write down what they saw as her positive qualities (this was easier than asking them to tell her to her face). She was somewhat embarrassed about doing this, but relieved to find that nobody objected or thought the request odd. Several of her closest friends knew that she was in therapy, and understood the importance of the exercise for her.

Results All Cynthia's friends listed personal qualities, and none of them mentioned her physical attributes. One or two of them mentioned that they thought she was rather hard on herself. Among the qualities listed were that she was fun loving, had a sense of humour, and was caring, loyal, and intelligent.

Reflection Cynthia's conclusion was that she was worthy, and that her friends accepted her for whom she was (belief rating: 90–100%). She described feeling 'released' from focusing on weight and shape. As her finals approached, she stopped rowing, and did not feel any anxiety about doing so. She also mentioned feeling more comfortable about eating with others.

Tips In this case, Cynthia accepted the results of her survey of her friends' views. Had she discounted the results as the product of politeness or kindness, as some more mistrustful patients do, it would have been important for her to seek more evidence of the genuineness of her friends' responsiveness to the personal attributes they had identified in her. In conducting a survey like this, it is also important to know something about the friends being surveyed. Some people with eating disorders associate principally with other sufferers, who may share similar attitudes about the importance of thinness. In such cases, a survey of this kind could be less helpful, and should be approached carefully, for instance, by considering that weight or shape might be one of the attributes mentioned, and thinking with the patient about whether this could reinforce their existing beliefs.

Experiment 13.3: testing thoughts about eating, weight, and shape as a means to self-acceptance

Problem Wendy was recovering from anorexia nervosa. She was trying to eat a wider range of foods.

Target cognitions If I eat a jacket potato with cheese it means I'm bad—useless, no good, out of control.

Alternative perspective It means I am trying to eat a healthier diet, to look after myself, to get better.

Experiment Wendy undertook a discovery-oriented survey experiment to see if she could gain any evidence to support the alternative perspective. She asked two close friends who knew about her difficulties with eating whether they thought that eating cheese with a potato at lunchtime was 'healthy' and might represent progress. She then tried eating cheese with her potato, and used the data collected from the survey and in-session thought challenging to confirm and support her alternative belief.

Results Wendy's friends both thought eating cheese with the potato was a sign of progress—a view reinforced by challenging her prediction in session with her therapist. Although anxious about eating cheese, she managed to eat a small amount on a prearranged day.

Reflection Wendy was reassured by the experiment. She reflected that paying attention to the data she had collected in and out of session, and the interpretations she was making, had helped to convince her that it was her thinking that was 'wrong', rather than eating cheese.

Follow-on experiments Wendy might continue to build up evidence that eating a wider range of foods is healthy, and expand her food choices.

Experiment 13.4: testing positive and negative thoughts about body image

Problem Helen had bulimia nervosa. She was living at home and studying for her final high-school exams. She was in her target weight range for age and height, but felt she was fat, and spent a lot of time in front of the mirror each day looking at her stomach from every angle.

Target cognitions If my stomach is flatter, I'll feel better and less depressed. Checking my stomach helps.

Alternative perspective Body image changes in different situations. Checking my body frequently will focus attention on it and leave me feeling more anxious about it.

Prediction If she limited the time she spent checking her stomach, she would become more anxious about her body image and feel worse about herself.

Experiment Over the next week, Helen continued to check her body six times a day, as usual, for three days, and then spent two days without checking. In the latter condition, she limited the time in front of the mirror to what she needed to brush her hair, apply make-up, etc. She monitored her level of concern about her body and her mood each morning, afternoon, and evening.

As Helen was anxious about not checking her body, she built in other activities to do instead of checking (e.g. ringing a friend, going out for a walk, listening to music). She also decided to approach the experiment in steps. Initially, she stopped checking for just part of the day, and then built up to a whole day, and then two days.

Results On days when she checked herself frequently, she was more anxious about her body and her mood was lower. Her general levels of satisfaction about her body depended on what she was doing. For instance, when she was out enjoying herself with her friends, she felt better. When she did not check herself and substituted other activities, her satisfaction with her body was higher.

Reflection Helen was truly surprised at the results, and at how much time was freed up to do other things.

Mood intolerance

Experiment 13.5: testing thoughts about loss of control of feelings

Problem Nicky had fallen into the habit of cutting herself or bingeing whenever she felt 'emotional'. She had managed to stabilize her eating for the most part, but found that she slipped back into bingeing and vomiting when things 'felt too much'.

Terry had recently sexually harassed Nicky. She felt unable to do anything about her feelings of violation and anger, and binged and vomited instead.

Target cognitions If I see Terry, he will sexually harass me, and I will feel powerless to stop him. I will feel like a fool, which will be unbearable, and I will have to binge to feel better.

Alternative perspective If I see Terry, when he starts to sexually harass me, I can tell him to stop, and this will leave me feeling better.

Prediction If I tell Terry to stop harassing me, he will deny it and I'll look a fool. This will be unbearable, so is to be avoided at all costs (belief rating: 90–100%).

Experiment On the next occasion that Nicky met Terry, she would get up and move away as soon as he started harassing her. She would take the action immediately, with minimum fuss and no discussion.

Results Nicky was surprised to find that when she acted decisively, feelings of anger and frustration were minimal. Terry was completely taken aback and made no attempt to humiliate her. Her feelings afterwards were quite bearable. No further action was necessary.

Reflection Nicky was amazed to discover she could affect her feelings by such a small action. She felt relatively secure in the belief that she had not made a fool of herself (40%) and that Terry was at fault. She noted that even if he had made her feel foolish, she didn't much care—at least she'd taken decisive action.

Follow-up experiments Nicky decided to try this with other acquaintances who were imposing their views on her. She quickly discovered that with straightforward feedback, they often backed off. No-one attempted to humiliate her, and her own feelings were quite tolerable.

Tips It is a good idea at first, in a situation like this, to choose people who are not so personally important, so that if the experiment does not go quite to plan, it will not feel so personally significant. Patients who think in an 'all or nothing' fashion may need reminding that actions can be taken discreetly, to avoid major confrontation. This means minimal feelings are evoked, and they avoid being overwhelmed.

Core low self-esteem

Experiment 13.6: testing core beliefs indicative of negative self-worth

Problem Karen had an 11-year history of bulimia and depression. In addition to bingeing and purging, she abused alcohol and self-harmed by cutting. She had also taken several overdoses. Despite having gained a first-class degree at university, she had an extremely poor opinion of herself.

Target cognitions I'm a failure. Other people must think I'm pathetic.

Alternative perspective I can be reasonably competent some of the time.

Prediction I'm bound to mess up whatever I do (belief rating: 100%). If I do well it's because the task was easy, or I was lucky, or anyone could have done it.

Experiment Karen observed her behaviour for a week to see if she could collect any evidence for her alternative belief that she was reasonably competent some of the time. She recorded this on a positive data log. She was highly sceptical, but willing to try.

Results Karen returned the next week having identified a number of items for her log. She had completed a questionnaire and a form to apply for a bank account. She had done some reading, housework, and voluntary work, mended one of her skirts, made some phone calls, written a letter with regard to her housing benefit, and organized a trip to see some friends.

Reflection Karen observed that it was good that she had had something to put in her log. However, she felt that the items were 'not sticking'. She discounted them by saying they were 'no great shakes anyway'. She couldn't allow herself to be pleased about such things, as she felt they highlighted what a long way she had to go. If she accepted that these were achievements she would be bound to live a 'bland and unfulfilling life'.

Follow-on experiments Karen's reactions to the experiment reflected her high standards for herself, which set her up to feel she was letting herself down in most situations. She continued the experiment for a longer period, re-reading her log on a daily basis to remind herself of the things she was accomplishing, however small.

Tips In the case of core low self-esteem, experiments may take longer to have impact than in the case of transient negative automatic thoughts. It is important not to abandon them prematurely if there is no immediate effect. The cumulative impact of many experiments repeated over time can be significant.

Perfectionism

Experiment 13.7: testing thoughts about overevaluation of achievement

Problem Susannah had a long history of anorexia and depression. Although she had now achieved a normal weight, she strove desperately to restrict her eating and felt deeply ashamed of her resulting feelings of hunger. She believed that eating made her wicked, greedy, dirty, and undisciplined. She also endeavoured to do things 'properly' in other areas of her life.

Target cognitions If I don't do things properly I'll be in big trouble. Doing things really well means succeeding. Not doing things really well means failing.

Alternative perspective If I continually strive to do things perfectly, I am constantly at risk of feeling I am failing, and my original enjoyment in carrying out the activity is lost.

Prediction Unless I strive really hard, I will do things badly, be criticized, and feel bad.

Experiment Susannah approached a short segment of her weekly yoga class with the aim of doing the poses to the extent that she felt comfortable, rather than straining in her usual manner in order to achieve perfection.

Results Susannah wasn't corrected any more than usual, and didn't feel she did the poses any worse than usual, though she did do them with less tension and strain.

Reflection She reflected that when she came to do the experiment she found it difficult to recall what was the point of doing yoga unless it was to do it 'properly'. She later reminded herself, from her therapy notes, that it could be for 'fun' or 'enjoyment'. She observed, after the experiment, that as one of the aims of yoga is to 'relax into' a pose, not straining was a 'good thing'. She hoped to keep on trying the new approach, and to extend it for longer into the class, as it seemed 'more comfortable'.

Follow-on experiments Susannah could practise applying a less perfectionistic approach to other non-eating-related areas of her life, before attempting to apply it to the eating domain.

Tips For patients who have eating disorders and clinical perfectionism, it may be more successful to address their perfectionism first, outside the eating arena, and then to extend the process of experimentation to the eating domain when they have experienced the benefits of lowering their punishing standards.

Interpersonal difficulties

Experiment 13.8: testing thoughts about interpersonal difficulties

Problem Jo had a relatively short history of anorexia. She had returned home after dropping out of college. She spent most of her time trying to make other people feel better and attempting to please them, in the belief that this was the only way to be happy herself. Unfortunately, this proved to be an impossible task, so she ended up feeling a failure and retreating to her anorexia for solace.

Target cognitions If I don't focus on making others happy, they will perceive me as a selfish, self-centred person and will have nothing to do with me. I will end up with no relationships at all.

Alternative perspective My friends and family may be relieved that I accept their feelings—positive and negative—at face value, without trying to turn them into something happy. They may appreciate not being controlled by my good intentions, and may even feel more able to approach me.

Prediction Each evening, mum expressed that she was feeling tired and sometimes fed up. Jo would always go into 'rescue' mode, telling mum why life was good, offering to do tasks to make her feel better, and trying to convince her that she really did not feel bad at all. She was sure that:

1 If she didn't do this, mum would feel hurt and rejected and be very upset.
2 The next evening mum would withdraw from Jo, and would want nothing to do with her. Jo would then feel very upset herself.

Experiment She would go home as usual that evening, and ask her mother about her day. If her mother expressed any distress, she would listen to her, resisting any temptation to 'make things better'. She would contain any of her own feeling of distress by e-mailing her therapist. She would repeat the experiment each evening as necessary.

Results Jo found the first night with her mother very difficult, as she herself felt very anxious. Her mother, however, did not show any additional stress or upset with Jo. Over the following few evenings, Jo's anxiety reduced and there were no signs at all from her mother that she felt rejected by Jo.

Reflection Jo found the experiment nerve wracking. However, she had not gone into rescue mode. Surprisingly, her mother seemed less pressurized, and ended up feeling better. Jo noted that it got easier for her to 'back off' as the experiment went on. There was no evidence at all for the belief that mum would reject her.

Further experiments Jo accepted that the next time to try out her new approach would be with a group of friends at the pub. She would try the 'listening' rather than the 'sorting' approach. This would then be extended to offering her opinions and stating her needs, rather than always waiting for the friends to take responsibility.

Tips It is often important to repeat these experiments many times to gradually erode original beliefs about being rejected. It is also necessary to work on alternative beliefs—in this case, that being happy and having friends is not just about pleasing others all the time.

Distinctive difficulties

Motivation and engagement

Motivation and engagement are commonly poor or ambivalent in patients with eating disorders, particularly anorexia nervosa, so it is important not to sacrifice emphasis on these merely to ensure specific techniques or strategies are implemented. In many cases it will be necessary to address motivation, engagement, and 'readiness to change' directly, as a preliminary aspect of treatment. Like interpersonal issues, they can all be framed and tackled within a cognitive framework. Important aspects are the person's beliefs about the advantages and disadvantages of change, the desirability of change, and the relative balance between these elements at the time of contemplating specific experiments. These are all likely to have a bearing on the timing (and likely success) of the experiments outlined in this chapter.

The therapeutic relationship

The therapeutic relationship has a particularly important role when working with this group. In many behavioural experiments, patients take great personal risks (as determined by their particular beliefs), and they are unlikely to do so without a trusting, open relationship.

Patients with eating disorders are often considered difficult to treat or hard to work with. Certainly their cognitions and beliefs may appear rigid and entrenched. Nevertheless, with a good, collaborative relationship (including a shared sense of humour!) and use of appropriately targeted and framed questions, beliefs can be uncovered and successfully challenged. Where a patient is proving 'difficult', use of empathy, summarizing, and a non-judgemental, open, and curious attitude can be enormously helpful. Close attention to what is unspoken, hinted at, or quickly mentioned but dismissed by the patient can also be useful. The support of a therapist, colleague, or supervisor experienced in working with eating disorder patients using cognitive therapy can be invaluable.

Illness identity

A strong illness identity is reflected in beliefs about the value of having an eating disorder, particularly in anorexia nervosa. It may be necessary to challenge these beliefs, or at least discuss their role in order to ensure successful intervention.

Treatment as a behavioural experiment

If there is a strong illness identity, the whole of treatment can be conceptualized as an overarching behavioural experiment. This can be discussed explicitly and, if appropriate, form a framework for treatment.

Sensitive and realistic beliefs

Some of the beliefs of patients with eating disorders are very personal or sensitive; some may be realistic. Personal, sensitive, and realistic beliefs will need careful and tactful handling, especially as many will involve relationships with family or a partner. Examples include: 'My partner will be critical if I gain weight', or 'My illness keeps the family together'. Others may involve a valued career (e.g. in cooking, dance, or fashion). With these kinds of belief the aim is not to challenge or set up a behavioural experiment to test the belief, especially if the predicted negative consequence may well result. Instead, one may need to look at the costs and benefits of change, and the resources that the patient has to make any change, if this seems desirable. Lack of resources to do this (which is not uncommon in these patients) may necessitate specific skills training.

Medical issues

Eating disorders may be associated with significant medical problems, so it is advisable to seek a medical opinion before embarking on cognitive therapy with a patient.

Other related chapters

As noted in the chapter, people with eating disorders often have underlying low self-esteem and interpersonal problems. So, Chapters 19 and 20 are highly relevant. Social anxiety, depression, worry, and avoidance of affect are also frequently accompaniments of eating disorders. So, Chapters 7, 10, and 17, that address these issues, may also be useful.

Further reading

Cooper, M.J., Todd, G., and Wells, A. (2000). *Bulimia nervosa: a client's guide to cognitive therapy.* Jessica Kingsley, London.

Fairburn, C.G. (1995). *Overcoming binge eating.* Guilford Press, New York.

Fairburn, C.G., Marcus, M.D., and Wilson, G.T. (1993). Cognitive behaviour therapy for binge eating and bulimia nervosa: a comprehensive treatment manual. In: C.G. Fairburn and G.T. Wilson (ed.), *Binge eating: nature, assessment and treatment.* Guilford Press, New York, pp. 361–404.

Freeman, C. (2000). *Overcoming anorexia nervosa.* Robinson, London.

Garner, D.M., Vitousek, K.M., and Pike, K.M. (1997). Cognitive-behavioural therapy for anorexia nervosa. In: D.M. Garner and P.E. Garfinkel (ed.), *Handbook of treatment for eating disorders* (2nd edn). Guilford Press, New York, pp. 94–144.

Tales from the Front Line
The cool on the hill

After careful preparatory work by his therapist, Tony, who had PTSD as a consequence of a severe car accident, was revisiting the accident site. In line with recent cognitive theories, the purpose of the behavioural experiment was to revisit the site of the trauma, in order to update the trauma memory by drawing distinctions between what happened then, and what the reality is now.

The initial accident had happened on a dark winter evening at the bottom of a hill, when an accelerating white van had crashed into the back of Tony's red Renault. The last thing Tony had seen were the headlights of another car coming through the back of his car, which ended up wrapped around the metal barrier dividing the two lanes.

The therapist and Tony took up their position at the bottom of the hill. First, the therapist asked Tony to close his eyes and visualize the accident. Then Tony was to open his eyes and see that his car was no longer on the barrier; that the barrier had been repaired; and that he was alive and in one piece.

Moments later, there was the sound of an accident. On the opposite lane, a white van had smashed into a red Renault. On the face of it, this might have been a disastrous confirmation of a belief that accidents like this happen regularly. Not missing a beat, the therapist took Tony over to see the accident (both drivers were unhurt) and carried on with the then versus now disconfirmation:

"What's different between today and what happened to you?"

"Is your car still wrapped around the metal on the central reservation?"

"Has the metal been replaced?"

"Are you now in one piece? What was the situation then?"

"Are you now just *watching* an accident, rather than being *involved* in one?"

"What's the difference between the accident that's just happened, and the one you were involved in? What does that tell you?"

When therapists are very clear about the purpose of behavioural experiments, even seemingly disastrous events can be turned to advantage.

CHAPTER 14

Insomnia

Melissa Ree
Allison Harvey

What is insomnia?

The term 'insomnia' does not refer to the night or two of poor sleep we all have now and then, especially associated with stressful life events. Insomnia is a difficulty of at least one month's duration involving problems getting to sleep, maintaining sleep, or waking in the morning not feeling restored. These disturbances must be severe enough to cause significant distress or impairment and they must not be fully explained by another sleep disorder (e.g. sleep apnea), mental disorder (e.g. bipolar disorder), substance (e.g. some antidepressant medications), or illness (e.g. asthma) (DSM-IV-TR, APA 2000). Insomnia is among the most prevalent psychological health problem, with chronic insomnia affecting approximately 9% of the population (Ancoli–Israel and Roth 1999).

Insomnia is defined subjectively. During the night, people with insomnia report consistently obtaining inadequate sleep, in terms of the amount and/or quality (this report of poor sleep *may* be based on an objective sleep deficit). People are also fearful of poor sleep because of its perceived disastrous consequences. As will be discussed later in this chapter, these honest and consistent reports of poor sleep are not necessarily reflected in estimates of objectively assessed sleep. During the day, people with insomnia report decreased ability to accomplish daily tasks, sleepiness, tiredness, difficulty functioning socially, impaired concentration, and memory problems. In addition, work absenteeism, increased use of medical services, and self-medication with either over-the-counter medications or alcohol are common among individuals with insomnia (Roth and Ancoli–Israel 1999).

There is high comorbidity between insomnia and other disorders, especially depression, anxiety, and substance abuse. Insomnia is often trivialized and considered to be a symptom of other disorders. Evidence is accruing, however, to suggest that insomnia is a risk factor for, and may even be causal, in the development of psychological disorders (Harvey 2001; Lichstein 2000). Accordingly, although this chapter is written with reference to individuals suffering from insomnia as the main or only presenting problem, we suggest that many of the ideas and experiments can be used with patients presenting with insomnia that is related to another psychological disorder.

Cognitive models of insomnia

Following pioneering work by Morin (1993), a number of theoretical models of insomnia have specified a role for unhelpful beliefs about sleep (Espie 2001; Harvey 2002a; Lundh 1998; Perlis *et al.* 1997). In a recent cognitive model, we have raised the possibility that a number of additional cognitive processes are important to the maintenance of insomnia. Specifically, that insomnia is maintained by a cascade of cognitive processes operating at night *and* during the day (Harvey 2002a). The key cognitive processes that comprise the cascade are worry, monitoring, thoughts/beliefs leading to safety behaviours, and perception of sleep.

Cognitive processes during the night

Taking the night-time cascade first, it is well documented that people with insomnia lie in bed worrying about not being able to get to sleep. This high level of worry triggers physiological arousal and distress. The combination of worry, arousal, and distress makes it more difficult to fall asleep and stay asleep. Further, when in an anxious state, people with insomnia selectively attend to or monitor their internal (e.g. body sensations) and/or external (e.g. the bedroom clock) environment for sleep-related threats. Monitoring for threat increases the likelihood of detecting random and meaningless cues that are then misinterpreted as threatening (Clark 1999). Monitoring, therefore, is likely to provide further cause for worry.

In an attempt to cope with escalating anxiety at night, people make use of safety behaviours such as suppressing all thinking (which may have paradoxical effects; Harvey, in press) or getting out of bed to drink a large whiskey (which may promote sleep in the short term but will result in poorer quality sleep and possibly a hangover the next morning). A simplified example of the proposed relationships between worry, arousal, monitoring, and safety behaviours is presented in Fig. 14.1.

As we have alluded to already, despite honest and consistent complaints of inadequate sleep, researchers who have monitored sleep using objective methods (e.g. polysomnography) have found that the difference between the sleep obtained by individuals with insomnia and good sleepers is less than expected (e.g. Chambers and Keller (1993) reviewed 14 studies and found an average difference of 35 minutes). In fact, many people with insomnia overestimate how long it takes them to fall asleep and underestimate how long they sleep in total (e.g. Bonnet 1990). These observations suggest that people with insomnia may

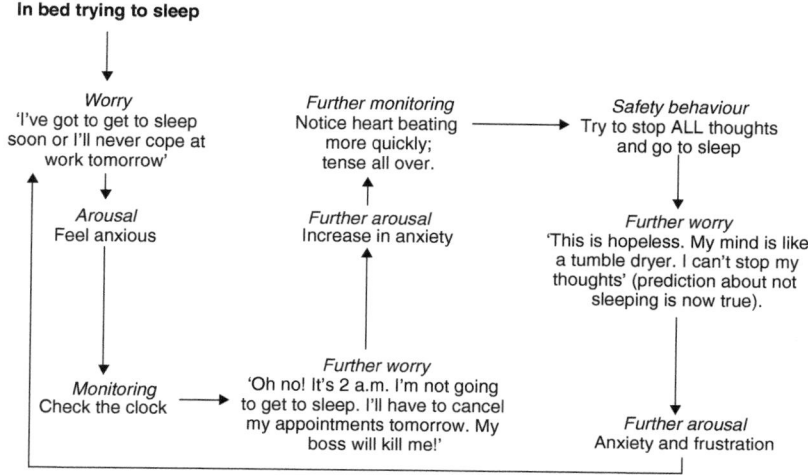

Fig. 14.1 Night-time cycle of insomnia.

believe that they slept much less than they actually did, perhaps in a similar way to people with anorexia nervosa who think they are overweight when actually they are underweight, and people with panic disorder who think they are having a heart attack when actually they are experiencing symptoms of anxiety.

It should be noted that because the moment of falling asleep is defined by the *absence* of memory, estimations of sleep are particularly vulnerable to distortion. The key point is that if an individual *perceives* they have not slept adequately, a further cause for worry is established. Further, if an individual wakes in the morning *believing* they have had inadequate sleep, this is likely to contribute to the cascade of daytime cognitive processes, as discussed below.

Cognitive processes during the day

It is proposed that parallel processes to those described for the night also operate during the day. On waking, people with insomnia often worry that they haven't obtained sufficient sleep. This worry in turn triggers arousal and distress, monitoring for sleep-related threat, and the use of safety behaviours. Each of these processes serve to maintain the insomnia: worry, arousal, and distress are likely to interfere with satisfying and effective daytime performance; monitoring is likely to increase the detection of ambiguous cues that are then misinterpreted; and the use of safety behaviours will maintain the belief that 'if I feel awful on waking it means I haven't slept enough and that I should take the day off work so as to catch up on sleep'. A simplified example of the proposed relationships between daytime and night-time cognitive processes is presented in Fig. 14.2.

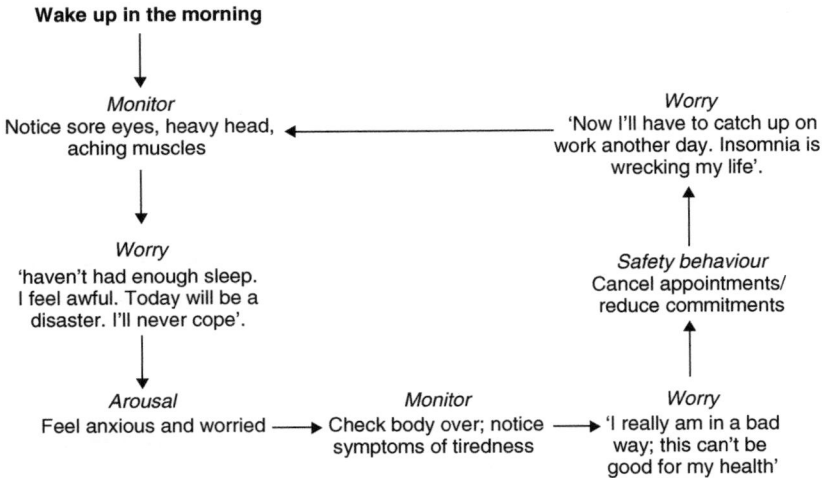

Fig. 14.2 Daytime cycle of insomnia.

It should be emphasized that although this approach highlights distorted perception of sleep as a key maintaining process, when an individual is trapped in the vicious cycles described above for a sufficient period, real sleep deprivation results. The cascade of cognitive processes serves to worsen night-time sleep and the extent of daytime impairment. In other words, the cognitive processes identified result in *perceived* impairment if sufficient sleep is being obtained, and they *worsen* the impairment if sufficient sleep is *not* being obtained.

Key cognitive constructs

Cognitive processes that maintain insomnia operate both during the day *and* the night, and include the following.

Unhelpful beliefs about sleep and tiredness

These beliefs relate to the amount of sleep required (e.g. 'I *must* get eight hours of sleep most nights', 'If I have to get up to go to the bathroom my night's sleep is wrecked'), fear of the short- and long-term consequences of insomnia (e.g. 'After a poor night's sleep, I know that I'll find it impossible to cope at work the next day', 'This is having serious affects on my physical health'), and loss of control over one's ability to sleep (e.g. 'When I have trouble getting to sleep, I should stay in bed and try harder', 'I'll go to bed early to ensure I get at least some sleep', 'I must actively control my sleep'). The Dysfunctional Beliefs About Sleep Scale (DBAS; Morin 1993) is a useful aid for identifying unhelpful beliefs about sleep.

Worry

Worry may be about a broad range of topics, especially the consequences of poor sleep for health and functioning, about having a poor night's sleep, and about losing control over the ability to sleep. Unhelpful beliefs about sleep will drive worry about the consequences of poor sleep.

Monitoring for sleep-related threat

Whilst trying to get to sleep, people with insomnia may monitor their body sensations for signs consistent with falling asleep, their body sensations and mental activity for signs inconsistent with falling asleep, the environment for signs indicative of wakefulness, the clock to see how long it is taking to fall asleep, and the clock to calculate how much sleep will be obtained. On waking, people with insomnia may monitor their body sensations for signs of poor sleep and the clock to calculate how many hours of sleep were obtained. During the day, people with insomnia monitor their performance and functioning, their mood, and their body sensations for signs of fatigue (Harvey 2002*a*).

Distorted perception of sleep and daytime impairment

As already stated, there is a significant subgroup of people with insomnia who believe that they have slept significantly less than they actually have. Also, people often assume that they can accurately gauge the quality of their sleep by how they feel on waking. Using feelings on waking to judge sleep quality is likely to lead to erroneous conclusions, as these feelings may be influenced by many factors. For example, patients often notice that if the day ahead involves hard, pressured work at the office they feel worse on waking relative to if the day ahead involves a relaxing outing with good friends. Importantly, for 5–20 minutes immediately on waking there is a period, known as sleep inertia, which is a transitional state between sleep and waking. During this time most people feel very tired and experience body sensations such as sore, heavy head and tired, heavy eyes. Monitoring at this time is likely to lead to misinterpretations of normal feelings of tiredness on waking (e.g. 'I had a terrible night's sleep last night'). It is also quite common for people with insomnia to overestimate the impact of poor sleep on daytime performance. They may rate their performance as far worse than it actually is.

Safety behaviours

Safety behaviours include overt and subtle attempts to cope with inadequate sleep and to increase control over sleep. A key point to note is that safety behaviours arise from beliefs/worries about sleep such as 'I can't cope without eight hours' sleep' or 'If I don't get to sleep I have to make up for it by napping or conserving my energy'. Unfortunately, safety behaviours serve to prevent disconfirmation of these beliefs and many have the effect of increasing the likelihood of the feared outcome (Salkovskis 1989). For example, safety behaviours can impact on:

- the regularity of the sleep cycle (e.g. sleeping late in the morning, napping during the day, going to bed early).
- getting to sleep (e.g. worrying over plans for the next day, telling oneself to stop worrying (which may, paradoxically, fuel unwanted thoughts), drinking coffee, engaging in vigorous exercise before bed).
- feelings of daytime sleepiness (e.g. taking the day easy, cancelling all appointments).
- the day being unpleasant or boring (e.g. avoiding other people, slowing down the pace of the day, reducing self-expectations).
- preoccupation with sleep (e.g. making plans based on how much sleep is obtained, keeping a calculation of the sleep obtained, formulating plans for catching up on sleep) (Harvey 2002b).

Behavioural experiments

The following section describes several examples of behavioural experiments, arranged under the five categories just discussed.

- **Addressing unhelpful beliefs about sleep and tiredness**
  Experiment 14.1: I have a fixed amount of energy that I must conserve
  Experiment 14.2: poor sleep is dangerous
- **Addressing worry**
  Experiment 14.3: expression of worries at the end of the day to aid sleep
- **Investigating distorted perception**
  Experiment 14.4: does tiredness noticeably affect my appearance?
- **Addressing monitoring**
  Experiment 14.5: manipulating symptom monitoring
  Experiment 14.6: manipulating clock monitoring
- **Addressing thoughts leading to safety behaviours**
  Experiment 14.7: Napping during the day

Addressing unhelpful beliefs about sleep and tiredness

Experiment 14.1: I have a fixed amount of energy that I must conserve

Problem Tom, a 45-year-old man, believed he had to plan his day carefully in order to conserve his energy. He believed that energy progressively drains away throughout the day and that the only way to generate energy is to sleep or rest. Accordingly, he tried very hard to conserve energy after a poor night's sleep. At work, for example, he would engage in mundane activities such as paperwork and data entry and would avoid meetings and socializing. This led to Tom's day being unpleasant, boring, and unproductive, as he avoided engaging in satisfying or enjoyable activities.

Target cognitions Energy is increased only by rest or sleep. I don't have much energy, so I need to take care to conserve it.

Alternative perspective There may be other factors than sleep that influence energy levels.

Prediction After a poor night's sleep, I will cope better and feel less fatigued and moody if I conserve my energy.

Experiment Tom agreed to trial an experiment for two days. On the first day he spent one three-hour block *conserving* energy, and then a three-hour block *using* energy. The following day he did this in the reverse order. After each three-hour block, Tom rated his fatigue, mood, and coping. Prior to the experiment, through careful questioning, we were able to understand what conserving energy meant for Tom. Examples included avoiding socializing with colleagues, setting work tasks at a slow pace, attempting only mundane tasks, not going out for lunch with work friends, and not returning phone calls. Time was also spent in the session brainstorming strategies for using energy. These included going for a 10-minute walk, returning all phone calls, arranging to have a coffee with a colleague, going to the water cooler to get a drink, and walking to a local shop to buy a magazine or snack. Tom rated his mood and fatigue on a form developed collaboratively in the session.

Results Tom found that his mood and energy were *improved* by 'using' energy.

Reflection 'Using' energy became synonymous with 'generating' energy. Tom learned that there are many factors that influenced his energy levels during the day. In particular, he concluded that his energy levels are like elastic; they can be stretched quite easily. This is in contrast to his original view that energy levels progressively deplete throughout the day.

Tip The evidence accrued during this experiment should be revisited in future sessions to reinforce the experience. Further, the use of energy-generating activities may need to be overtly adopted when feeling tired. If so, this will need to be supported with practice between sessions and discussion during the session (e.g. 'In what ways did you manage to generate energy?'). Retrospective experiments can also be useful (e.g. 'Can you think of a day after a poor night's sleep when you became energized sometime during the day, say if you had an exciting event on?')

Experiment 14.2: poor sleep is dangerous

Problem Jennifer was a 49-year-old woman with insomnia and generalized anxiety disorder. She had slept poorly for 20 years and she reported that her poor sleep exacerbated her tendency to worry. She came to believe that it was crucial to have eight hours' sleep (on most nights) in order to cope with daily stressors. In addition, Jennifer was concerned that a build-up of less than eight hours' sleep over several days would have very serious consequences for her emotional and physical health.

Despite a reduction in worry about sleep, and an improvement in sleep over the course of therapy, Jennifer remained anxious about nights of poor sleep. She was particularly concerned that if she slept badly on one night that this would trigger poor sleep on subsequent nights, leading to the 'build-up' referred to. The following experiment was conducted towards the end of treatment, when Jennifer was reasonably confident in her ability to manage daytime fatigue (e.g. challenging negative automatic thoughts, directing attention away from symptoms of tiredness, and using strategies to increase energy). Jennifer agreed that testing her beliefs about how much sleep she required may help to reduce her fear of poor sleep.

Target cognitions To function well the next day, I must get at least eight hours of sleep a night. Less than eight hours of sleep will have serious consequences for my health. If I go for more than three nights with poor sleep, I won't be able to cope with anything.

Alternative perspective I may be able to cope reasonably well after a poor night's sleep.

Predictions I won't cope, I'll feel awful, low, sick, tired, and I won't want to do anything or see anyone. If I aim to sleep for only six and a half hours, I'll end up sleeping much less. If I have one night of poor sleep this will trigger others.

Experiment Jennifer restricted her sleep to six and a half hours for one night. She did this by going to bed later than usual (she thought this would be more achievable than waking up early in the morning). She ensured that she would stay awake by arranging to see a group of her friends the evening before the experiment (this decision also served to make the experiment enjoyable and memorable). In order to assess Jennifer's predictions, a form was developed to help her monitor the effect of the experiment on her ability to cope, her tiredness, productivity, and mood. Jennifer also completed a sleep diary in the morning, immediately on waking.

Results Jennifer was surprised how well she coped with six and a half hours' sleep, and found that restricted sleep did not trigger poor sleep on subsequent nights.

Reflection I used to think I needed eight hours of sleep, but now I realize I can get away with seven. In fact, I only had six and a half hours for the last two nights and I actually feel fine.

See Table 14.1 for additional experiments to test unhelpful beliefs about sleep.

Addressing worry

Chapter 6 on generalized anxiety presents several examples of experiments to address worry that can be easily adapted for use with people affected by insomnia. One additional experiment is included here.

Experiment 14.3: expression of worries at the end of the day to aid sleep

Problem Kate was a 58-year-old successful business woman who had no time during the day to relax or unwind. She didn't take time for lunch or time to chat with a colleague. When she got home she immediately switched into what she referred to as 'mother mode' as she made her family dinner and helped her two children to do their homework and get ready for bed. By the time she got to bed, Kate was physically exhausted, but she found that she still had many issues from the day on her mind and was unable to stop planning and worrying about the following day. She agreed that a writing task, when she got home from work, might be a good way to put the day to rest before bedtime.

Target cognitions When I go to bed my mind is busy and full and there is no way to control it. I can't get all these thoughts out of my mind.

Alternative perspective Perhaps my mind is so full when I go to bed because I don't have time to think things through during the day.

Prediction Writing about my thoughts and feelings before bed may help me to sleep better.

Table 14.1 Further experiments to test unhelpful beliefs about sleep

Original belief	Alternative belief	Experiment	Result	Reflection
I've lost control over my ability to sleep. I must try to control it.	The more I try to control sleep, the more out of control it is.	On the first night, the patient does everything they can to control their sleep. On the second night, the patient drops all attempts to control sleep.	Actively trying to control sleep makes it worse. Sleep is an automatic biological process that does not need to be controlled.	The patient will learn the adverse effects of attempting to control sleep. Highlights that sleep is an automatic process.
It's not normal to have difficulty with sleep. Most people sleep about 8 hours a night.	Most people have trouble sleeping at least some of the time. It is not realistic to expect 8 hours' sleep every night.	Design a survey with the patient.* Administer it to as many people as possible.	The survey is likely to reveal that the majority of people get less than 8 hours of sleep, have some trouble with sleep when feeling stressed, and feel tired when they wake up and again after lunch.	The patient's expectations of sleep and daytime tiredness are adjusted, and anxiety about attaining 'perfect' sleep is reduced. Strategies for coping with poor sleep are generated.

* Questions might include:

1. How long, on average, does it take you to fall asleep?
2. What would be the maximum time it takes you to fall asleep?
3. How many hours of sleep do you think you need?
4. How many hours of sleep do you actually get?
5. Most people wake up in the night; how many times do you wake up, even if for a few seconds?
6. Do you ever find it difficult to get back to sleep (after waking up)?
7. Do you ever feel tired / lethargic when you wake up in the morning? Can you describe how you feel?
8. Do you ever feel tired during the day? Can you describe this?

Operationalized predictions Kate predicted that her sleep onset latency would reduce if she implemented the writing task. For the duration of the experiment Kate completed a diary, immediately on waking, in which she recorded how long it had taken her to fall asleep, how often she had woken during the night, how much sleep she had obtained in total, the quality of her sleep, and how anxious and worried she had felt when awake in the night.

Experiment Just after dinner, on alternate evenings, Kate wrote about her thoughts and feelings from the day and her plans for the following day. She carried out the experiment for one week. Whilst writing, Kate paid particular attention to working through her concerns and worries and expressing her feelings. She wrote for about 20 minutes each time.

Results Kate found the process of expressive writing helpful in organizing her thoughts and feelings and feeling more prepared for the following day. She felt less plagued by her 'racing mind' when in bed. The following week Kate adopted the writing as part of her routine.

Reflection The task emphasized to me how little time I usually take for myself, and how I try to push concerns away rather than face them. The thoughts are better on paper than in my head! After writing, I am less likely to have unwanted thoughts bothering me at night while I try to sleep.

Tip See Pennebaker (1997) for further information on writing interventions. Patients who do not like writing could be encouraged to talk to a friend or family member about their thoughts and feelings, or to even speak about their thoughts and feelings into a tape recorder.

Investigating distorted perception

Experiment 14.4: does tiredness noticeably affect my appearance?

Problem Suzie was a 32-year-old woman who was very concerned about the effect of her insomnia on her appearance. She believed that the effects of tiredness were very noticeable to others. As a consequence, she would cancel social engagements if she had not slept well, or would go along but stand in the background. She also worried greatly about sleeping the night before a social event. (Note that the experiments described in Chapter 7 on social phobia may be helpful for Suzie.)

Target cognitions I look shocking in the morning. Everyone can tell how tired I am by looking at me. I can't be as confident when I'm tired because I look terrible.

Alternative perspective Although I may not feel great when I am tired, this does not necessarily show in my appearance. It is unlikely that others can tell how much sleep I have had.

Predictions It is very noticeable to others when I feel tired.

Operationalized predictions If presented with an array of photographs taken on different days, people would easily be able to select the photograph in which I am most tired.

Experiment Suzie asked her partner to take photos of her every day for one week. The photos were taken at the same time of the day (just before leaving for work) and she wore a similar colour and make-up in each of the photos. Suzie also kept a sleep diary in which she estimated time slept and described how she felt at the time of the photograph (e.g. tired, lethargic, headache, lively). Suzie and the therapist asked four people each if they could pick the photo in which she looked most tired.

Results Most people either could not chose a photo, as they thought they all looked similar, or they chose a photo that did not correspond with the morning Suzie felt most tired.

Reflection Suzie came to see that her tiredness was more of a private experience than a public event, and that others were not able to detect the signs of tiredness she felt were so obvious.

See Table 14.2 for additional experiments to investigate distorted perception of sleep and daytime tiredness. See also Tang and Harvey (in press) for a powerful behavioural experiment designed to correct distorted perception of sleep, if an actigraph is available. (Actigraphs are watch-like devices, worn on the wrist, that measure movement and provide an objective estimate of how much sleep is obtained.)

Addressing monitoring

Experiment 14.5: manipulating symptom monitoring

Problem Ben was a 33-year-old man with a history of insomnia and depression. He focused a great deal of attention on his mood, energy, and performance throughout the day as a way of gauging his tiredness and whether he got enough sleep the night before. This internal focus amplified feelings of tiredness and contributed to concern about and preoccupation with sleep.

Target cognitions Monitoring helps me to keep a check on how I am doing and helps me to adjust my daytime activities accordingly. Monitoring my tiredness is automatic and I can't control it.

Table 14.2 Further experiments to investigate distorted perception of sleep and daytime tiredness

Original belief	Alternative belief	Experiment	Result	Reflection
Poor sleep makes me unable to concentrate and reduces my performance.	My concentration is not significantly impaired.	After deliberately not sleeping for more than 6.5 hours on the previous night, the therapist gives the choice of a card game (e.g. snap) or neuropsychological tests, both of which test concentration.	The patient performs as well as the therapist.	This means I can concentrate even when I have slept less than I would like.
I wake up at least 15 times in the night.	I'm not sure how many times I wake up. Sleep is really hard to estimate reliably.	Patient presses handheld counter every time he wakes up in the night.	The patient discovered that he woke between 0 and 3 times (i.e. that he sleeps better than he predicted).	The patient sees that sleep quality/quantity is hard to estimate, and that it is possible perceive sleep as worse than it really is.

Alternative perspective Monitoring actually makes me more likely to notice natural (and harmless) changes in my mood, energy, and performance, and makes me more likely to worry. I can choose not to monitor.

Predictions I won't be able to stop monitoring throughout the day. A focus on my mood, energy, and performance throughout the day helps me feel in control because I can check out what's happening. Focusing on external things will not make any difference.

Operationalized predictions Ben kept a diary of his mood, energy, and performance three times a day throughout the experiment. He predicted that these factors would be unaffected by any internal or external focus.

Experiment The therapist and Ben discussed specific ways both to monitor and not monitor for sleep-related symptoms. These were practised within the session. Ben was encouraged to direct his attention to the external environment by concentrating on sights, sounds, and smells around him. On the chosen day, Ben monitored sleep-related symptoms for two hours and then spent the next two hours *not* monitoring the sleep-related symptoms. This was repeated three times over the week. At the end of each period, Ben recorded how much he managed to be sleep focused (i.e. monitor) and not sleep focused (i.e. attend to the external environment). He also rated his mood, performance, and fatigue.

Results Ben felt better when he did not monitor his symptoms.

Reflection Ben realized that monitoring intensified his awareness of small fluctuations in his mood, energy, and performance. He also noticed that these fluctuations contributed to an exacerbation of tiredness.

Experiment 14.6: manipulating clock monitoring

Problem Madeline was a 36-year-old woman who had developed severe postnatal depression following the birth of her only child (two years ago). Although the depression remitted after six months, severe insomnia remained. At night, she monitored the clock in order to see how long it was taking her to fall asleep and to calculate the number of hours she had left to sleep. On waking, Madeline calculated the number of hours she had slept. She also used the clock as a means of 'proving' to herself how little sleep she was getting. For example, if she looked at the clock at midnight, she would conclude that she mustn't have slept since going to bed two hours earlier.

Target cognitions It is important for me to know how much sleep I have had so I can plan the next day.

Alternative perspective Watching the clock makes me worry more, which in turn interferes with me getting to sleep.

Predictions I won't be able to resist the urge to look at the clock; it will be really hard. It's a habit that I cannot break. I'll still find some way to calculate my sleep (e.g. by what was on the TV in the next room before falling asleep). Calculating how much sleep I get reduces my anxiety by letting me be prepared.

Operationalized predictions Madeline predicted higher anxiety levels when *not* looking at the clock and poorer sleep. She also predicted great difficulty in not looking at the clock.

Experiment As Madeline needed to be able to hear the alarm in the morning, she agreed to put the clock under her bed before turning out the light.

Results Removing the clock helped reduce Madeline's anxiety about sleep. She also felt that dropping clock monitoring helped her to sleep more soundly.

Reflection I didn't have any information to send me into panic mode while trying to sleep. This is so simple; I can't believe I wasn't doing this ages ago!

Addressing thoughts leading to safety behaviours

Experiment 14.7: napping during the day

Problem Belinda was a 46-year-old woman with longstanding insomnia. She had learned to cope with her daytime tiredness by taking naps. She would usually doze for 30–45 minutes on the sofa after getting up in the morning, and again for an hour or so in the evening in front of the TV. Belinda recognized that dozing may make it more difficult to get to sleep at night, but was concerned that she would find it hard to cope if she missed these rest periods.

Target cognitions I can't cope without my naps; I must nap in order to catch up on lost sleep.

Alternative perspective If I do not nap during the day, I will be able to cope, and my night-time sleep will improve.

Predictions Dozing reduces tiredness because it helps me catch up on lost sleep. Not dozing will lead to an increase in tiredness and poorer coping.

Experiment In the first week, Belinda did not make any changes. In the second week, Belinda attempted to abstain from dozing, regardless of the amount of sleep she had obtained on the previous night. Pleasant and engaging activities were scheduled for the times Belinda would ordinarily doze. Belinda found it difficult to stop napping, but was very motivated, so by the end of the week she had only dozed two times (in the week prior she had dozed 12 times). She kept a diary in which she recorded the frequency of naps, her tiredness, and how well she felt she was coping. In addition, questions were included in the diary so that Belinda could record what time she went to bed, how long it took her to fall asleep, awakenings during the night, and total sleep time.

Results Reducing naps was difficult but not impossible. Belinda ended up with more time in her week, hence she felt less stressed and more able to cope. In addition, in the latter half of the second week, Belinda's night-time sleep had started to improve.

Reflection Belinda concluded that most of the time she could cope without having a nap, and that the nap itself contributed to her poor night-time sleep and stress (because napping meant she didn't get as much done during the day).

Tips

♦ It is important to conduct this experiment over at least two weeks (a minimum of one week of napping and one week of no (or limited) napping). Looking at one day of not napping, for example, would not give the sleep cycle sufficient time to adjust to the new routine.

♦ In the short term, this experiment can result in patients feeling more tired. It is important to warn the patient of this potential short-term effect and encourage them to continue with the experiment.

♦ For older adults, a nap of less than one hour, before 3 p.m., may help overcome the natural tendency, with ageing, to sleep less at night (Morin *et al.* 1999).

See Table 14.3 for additional experiments to investigate the impact of safety behaviours.

Distinctive difficulties with behavioural experiments in insomnia

Most experiments need to be conducted between sessions

It is sometimes possible to complete behavioural experiments within a session. This is ideal, as it is more likely that the variables of interest can be investigated without the adverse impact of extraneous variables. In the context of insomnia,

Table 14.3 Further experiments to address safety behaviours

Original belief	Alternative belief	Experiment	Result	Reflection
Drinking lots of coffee is the only way I can get through the day.	Perhaps there are alternatives to drinking coffee. Coffee may actually be making my sleep worse.	Limit coffee to two medium-strength cups before 4 p.m. Try other energy-increasing strategies after 4 p.m.	Other strategies were as effective as coffee at increasing energy. Felt sleepier at bedtime.	Increased confidence that I can cope without coffee. Motivated to work out ways to increase energy, other than drinking coffee.
Talking or thinking about my insomnia will make it worse.	Talking about or thinking about my insomnia has minimal impact on my sleep.	Compare not talking about the insomnia for one week-end to talking, writing, and thinking about it for one weekend.	Thinking and writing about insomnia had no adverse effect.	Reduced motivation to try to suppress thoughts about sleep. (See Chapter 5 on OCD for behavioural experiments on thought suppression.)
I need alcohol to help me sleep.	Perhaps alcohol helps me get to sleep, but it worsens my sleep quality and means I wake up early.	No more than two standard drinks per day and no drinking within (at least) an hour of bedtime.	Took slightly longer to fall asleep at the beginning of the night but woke in the middle of the night less frequently.	No need to rely on alcohol to sleep.

however, most behavioural experiments have to be conducted *between* sessions. Where possible we would suggest that experiments conducted during the day-time be conducted within one day. If conducted over two days, the results can be attributed to sleeping better on one of the nights or to differences inherent to the days (e.g. 'the work I was doing wasn't so hard that day').

Different people need different amounts of sleep

Sleep research and sleep medicine are still in their infancy, such that the amount of sleep required and the function of sleep is still debated. One empirically supported view is that we obtain our 'core' sleep in six hours and any sleep we obtain over that is 'optional' (Horne 1988). It is also possible, however, that people differ in the amount of sleep they need to function. Hence, it is important to be sensitive to the potential for individual differences in the sleep need of patients. Behavioural experiments can be used to help the patient to work out their sleep need.

Excessive tiredness is associated with the risk of accident

It is important to note that people with insomnia have double the risk of an accident if they drive a motor vehicle or work in a context where they need to use a machine tool (Ohayon *et al.* 1997). As such, patients who do a lot of driving or work in an industrial environment should be warned to take regular breaks and make appropriate use of caffeine to maximize their safety.

Experiments should be timed carefully within treatment

The timing of behavioural experiments, within the treatment, is very important. This is particularly true for an experiment that involves patients purposefully restricting their sleep. This can be anxiety-provoking and should only be attempted when the patient has some confidence in their ability to cope following a night of restricted sleep. With a clear rationale, however, and supported by phone calls from the therapist on the evening prior to the experiment and the next day, patients derive enormous benefit. Behavioural experiments involving sleep restriction should not be scheduled for a night prior to a day when the patient will be engaging in activities where alertness is crucial for safety, such as driving.

Other relevant chapters

An important aspect of insomnia is worry about poor sleep and its perceived consequences. Additionally, people with insomnia often have an elevated level of generalized anxiety and worry. Experiments for excessive worry, and also beliefs about worry may often be relevant to insomnia treatment. See Chapter 6 on

generalized anxiety disorder. Experiments for depression, particularly behavioural activation (as people with insomnia frequently reduce their activity levels
in order to conserve energy), may also be relevant. See Chapter 10 on depression. Experiments for social anxiety may be helpful with people with insomnia
who are frequently very concerned about their appearance and social performance after a poor night's sleep, triggering social anxiety and withdrawal. See
Chapter 7 for experiments for social anxiety. Avoidance of affect can be an
important issue to tackle in people with insomnia. One account of insomnia is
that it arises, at least partly, from inadequate emotional processing during the
day. See Chapter 17 for relevant experiments. Also, experiments on health anxiety (see Chapter 4) may be important for those people with insomnia who
believe that their poor sleep may have serious physical health consequences.
Finally, experiments testing the effect of thought suppression may be useful for
people who might attempt to suppress unwanted thoughts during the night; see
Chapter 5 on obsessive-compulsive disorder.

Acknowledgements

The authors gratefully acknowledge David M. Clark, Ann Hackmann, and
Martina Mueller for their contributions to experiments reported in this chapter. This work was supported by the Wellcome Trust (grant no. 065913).

Further reading

Espie, C.A. (2001). Insomnia: conceptual issues in the development, persistence, and
treatment of sleep disorder in adults. *Annual Review of Psychology,* **53,** 215–43.

Harvey, A.G. (2002*a*). A cognitive model of insomnia. *Behaviour Research and Therapy,*
40, 869–93.

Lundh, L–G. (1998). Cognitive-behavioural analysis and treatment of insomnia.
Scandinavian Journal of Behaviour Therapy, **27,** 10–29.

Morin, C.M. (1993). *Insomnia: psychological assessment and management.* Guilford Press,
New York.

Perlis, M.L., Giles, D.E., Mendelson, W.B., Bootzin, R.R. and Wyatt, J.K. (1997).
Psychophysiological insomnia: the behavioural model and a neurocognitive
perspective. *Journal of Sleep Research,* **6,** 179–88.

Tales from the Front Line
Ineffective ways of killing oneself

Behavioural experiments don't always work out the way you might expect, but upon reflection may still produce substantial cognitive change.

Kerry had been referred with panic disorder. She was pre-occupied with the idea that the sensations she experienced in her panic attacks were a sign of a serious physical abnormality, and that she could die in an attack. The therapist was conducting an in-session behavioural experiment in which she was asked to read pairs of words representing her panic-related thoughts in an attempt to demonstrate that the main problem was her fearful thoughts, rather than a physical abnormality. Kerry had been quite emotional before the task. She took one look at the sheet—the first pair was 'Breathless-Suffocate'—and said: "I don't think I can do this, I'm feeling too breathless". However, the therapist got her as far as the fifth pair, 'Palpitation-Dying', whereupon she stopped, and pushed the paper away. She looked very anxious and said she didn't want to carry on reading.

"You look as though you are feeling anxious. Is that right? What's going through your mind right now?" enquired the therapist.

"Its just occurred to me that if you can get breathless by reading the word breathless, by the same token, you can die by reading the word Dying."

The therapist was surprised by this response and gave a rather muddled explanation of why this would not happen. The experiment had not had its intended effect but, as usual, the patient was asked to listen to the session tape as part of homework.

At the start of the next session, reviewing the homework, Kerry commented: "I can't believe how stupid I was".

"In what way were you stupid?"

"Thinking that if I said the word, Dying, that I'd die."

"Why's that stupid?"

"Well, I've got friends in the funeral business, they think about dying all the time, and they're not dead. And anyway, when I listened to the tape, I noticed I said you might die by reading the word Dying—and I didn't die."

The therapist proceeded with therapy. The next task was to consider the amount of times that Kerry had had the thought that she might die, but had not died. They worked out that with about 10 panic attacks a day over a period of 10 years this had amounted to some 36,000 occasions!

"What do you make of that?" asked the therapist.

"Well" said Kerry, "it wouldn't be a good way of killing myself, would it."

CHAPTER 15

Physical illness and disability

Amy Silver
Christina Surawy
Diana Sanders

Introduction

This chapter covers conditions in which physical health and ability to function
are compromised. Physical illness and disability impact on many aspects of
life, and adjustment may be difficult. We include problems resulting from
diagnosable medical diseases such as diabetes, cancer, and multiple sclerosis,
difficulties following surgery, and the complex mental and physical interactions that occur in conditions such as chronic fatigue syndrome (CFS) and
irritable bowel syndrome (IBS) for which no medical cause can be found.
From the wide range of potentially relevant conditions, we have selected commonly encountered difficulties, in order to clarify issues and principles that
can be generalized to other physical problems.

Cognitive models

The psychological impact of illness and disability is broad. People face challenges
in adjusting to variable functioning, managing their condition, and maintaining
independence and previous roles (Holman and Lorig 2000). A number of models are valuable in understanding physical health problems and in clarifying how
people make sense of, and respond to, illness. Illness representations (beliefs or
schemas) guide people in giving meaning to their condition. Leventhal *et al.*
(1992) identify beliefs about diagnosis and symptoms, seriousness, duration,
cause (e.g. genetic or viral), and the value of medical treatment. Illness representations influence coping style, behaviour change, treatment compliance, the
emotional impact of health problems, and patient outcome, including both
physical and mental well-being (Roesch and Weiner 2001).

Psychological difficulties such as anxiety and depression are common
amongst people with physical health problems and can be understood using
current cognitive models (see, for example, Chapter 3 on panic disorder,
Chapter 4 on health anxiety, Chapter 10 on depression, and Chapter 20 on
low self-esteem). Knowledge about self-focus, safety behaviours, cognitive

distortions, and avoidance or denial of emotion, helps us to understand processes that maintain many conditions, for example, the low or fluctuating levels of activity that occur in CFS, after surgery, and in chronic pain (White 2000). Cognitive models have also been developed for specific problems including eczema and psoriasis (Papadopoulos and Walker 2003), cancer (Moorey and Greer 2002), and less clearly diagnosable conditions such as CFS (Surawy et al. 1995), IBS (Toner et al. 2000), chronic pain (Main and Spanswick 2000), and premenstrual syndrome (Blake 1995).

Key cognitions

Negative automatic thoughts

The meanings attached to being ill or disabled can affect mood and self-worth, leading to unhelpful coping strategies and safety behaviours. They commonly concern loss of identity (e.g. 'I'm not the person I was') and the judgement of others (e.g. 'Everyone thinks I should be better by now'). Such thinking may be associated with low mood and helplessness. It can lead to withdrawal from friendships and social activities, as can the fear that others will not know how to react (for example, to changes caused by the illness). Similarly, thoughts about changes in role and loss of function can influence self-esteem and trigger low mood (e.g. 'I'm not doing anything useful any more').

In many conditions, particularly those for which there is no adequate medical explanation, fearful predictions about symptoms can lead to unhelpful coping strategies. For example, 'This pain means I'm getting worse' could result in avoidance, excessive resting, self-monitoring, or over-reliance on aids such as walking sticks and wheelchairs. Conversely, when coming to terms with ill health, overriding the body's signals to stop or slow down might become a way of maintaining self-esteem and keeping difficult emotions at bay. Coping is also influenced by thoughts about the future (e.g. 'I'm never going to get better'), about ineffectiveness (e.g. 'Nothing I do will make a difference'), and about peers, which can interfere with self-medication, particularly in young people (e.g. 'My friends will think I'm odd if they see me inject myself with insulin').

Key cognitions and behaviours associated with different conditions are summarized in Table 15.1.

Core beliefs and dysfunctional assumptions

Beliefs and assumptions that emerge in the face of illness and disability may originate in early experience (e.g. being criticized as lazy unless doing something useful, having to be responsible and self-sufficient from an early age). People may have had difficult experiences of dealing with pain, illness, and death in the family (e.g. not having emotions validated or heard; parents

Table 15.1 Key concerns in specific conditions

Condition	Cognitions	Safety behaviours
Irritable bowel syndrome	I might lose control of my bowels.	Avoid places with no toilets. Empty bowels repeatedly.
	There is something wrong with my guts.	Seek medical reassurance. Read about bowel conditions (e.g. cancer).
Chronic fatigue syndrome	I need to rest or I'll do myself harm.	Excessive resting, avoiding activity.
	People think there's nothing wrong with me or I'm just lazy.	Using walking aids, avoiding socializing, pushing self too hard.
Chronic pain	Pain is a warning signal to stop. Pain is dangerous.	Gradual withdrawal from activities.
	I'll never get better. If it gets worse, I'll never cope.	Constant monitoring of pain level.
Heart disease	I'm going to have a heart attack and die.	Avoid raising heart rate (e.g. through exercise, sex, excitement).
Diabetes	Self-medicating makes me stand out from others, is tedious, and/or shameful.	Hide concerns about insulin injections. Irregular medication use.
Cancer	My life is over. There's no point in trying.	Unhelpful denial. Withdrawal. Stops trying to cope.
Post-surgery	If I move, I'll cause damage.	Avoid movement and physiotherapy.
	My scars are ugly, shameful.	Cover scars, which inhibits healing. Avoid social contact.

being dismissive or fussing too much) or in contact with medical professions (e.g. unclear explanations of illness or procedures).

Beliefs and assumptions relating to illness, self-worth, and coping ability trigger negative thoughts, drive mood and coping behaviour, and undermine motivation (e.g. 'Either I am fully functioning, or ill and unable to do anything'). Assumptions such as 'I should always be able to cope' can lead people to reject offers of help and to become socially isolated. Physical illness can have a profound impact on self-esteem, and assumptions such as 'I'm no good if I can't go to work' may surface.

Assumptions leading to avoidance of painful feelings can be especially problematic (see also Chapter 17 on avoidance of affect). Difficult issues avoided include: acknowledging changes in function, role, identity, or friendships; a sense of being somehow to blame for the illness; and fear of being overwhelmed by emotion. Fear of expressing feelings can follow concerns about not being understood, being alienated, or being labelled as weak. It can interfere with adjustment and lead to unhelpful behaviour such as social withdrawal or safety behaviours. Suppression of emotion can cause physical tension and symptoms such as fatigue or pain. Unhelpful strategies employed to avoid facing painful feelings include keeping busy to the point of exhaustion, sleeping excessively, putting on a 'brave face', and keeping cheerful.

Behavioural experiments

Behavioural experiments can be used to test out unhelpful cognitions (e.g. 'Exercise is harmful for people with heart disease'), and to build up support for new ideas (e.g. 'I am a strong and competent person, despite my physical problems'). Some people have no access to alternative interpretations. For example, people who have negative stereotypes of illness and disability (e.g. 'Becoming disabled means life is not worth living'), and then become ill or disabled themselves, may find it difficult to know what to believe. Discovery experiments can help them to identify alternative perspectives, to be tested and strengthened through further experiments.

In this section, we describe a range of experiments designed to tackle the themes identified above. Additional suggestions will be found in the accompanying Tables.

- ◆ **Managing changes in functioning**
  Experiment 15.1: incorporating breaks in activity
  Experiment 15.2: incorporating positive experiences

  Table 15.2: additional experiments

- ◆ **Investigating others' reactions**
  Experiment 15.3: being open about disability

  Table 15.3: additional experiments

- ◆ **Exploring the meaning of symptoms**
  Experiment 15.4: normalizing symptoms
  Experiment 15.5: finding a benign explanation for symptoms

  Table 15.4: additional experiments

- ◆ **Strengthening sense of identity**
  Experiment 15.6: perceived disappearance of identity
  Experiment 15.7: identity defined by physical appearance

- ◆ **Examining the effects of safety behaviours**
  Experiment 15.8: dizziness and avoidance of movement
  Experiment 15.9: regulating bowel movements

  Table 15.5: additional experiments

Managing changes in functioning

Experiment 15.1: incorporating breaks in activity

Problem Bill had a history of CFS. He always had to complete tasks, regardless of how he felt. This was part of a see-sawing pattern of over-activity, exhaustion, and subsequent under-activity, driven by self-criticism.

Target cognitions If I stop, I'll find it impossible to return to the task and I'll achieve much less. I should carry on until it is finished, no matter how I feel.

Alternative perspective Taking breaks will refresh me. Perhaps I'll finish the job anyway, especially if I'm less hard on myself.

Experiment Despite concern that completing his tasks would be frustratingly slow, Bill experimented with taking regular breaks (e.g. having a wander round the garden) whenever he felt mentally fatigued. To curb self-critical 'shoulds', in-session work was done to find less harsh alternatives (e.g. 'I am feeling tired. What can I choose to do now?'). Bill recorded how refreshed and how tired he felt at the end of each day, and how much work he had completed.

Results Bill noticed that, after a break, he felt refreshed and returned to his tasks feeling less driven. He achieved as much as he had when not taking breaks, and felt less exhausted.

Reflection Bill saw that using fatigue as a cue to choose whether to continue or to take a break, rather than as a cue for self-criticism, made it easier to pace himself.

Tips Sometimes it is better to take breaks at regular intervals rather than breaks based on feelings; people are not always good judges of how fatigued they are.

Experiment 15.2: incorporating positive experiences

Problem Penny, a single mother of two, was referred for low mood and excessive tiredness. Two years ago she had been diagnosed with cancer and had had a double mastectomy, reconstructive surgery, and removal of her ovaries. Soon afterwards, she ignored medical advice and returned to work. She believed that she needed to meet the expectations others had of her.

Target cognitions I haven't time to look after myself—others' needs are greater, and taking time for myself takes time away from them.

Alternative perspective If I look after myself, I will enjoy things more and be less depressed and exhausted.

Prediction Going out for the day with my friend will make me stressed and guilty that I haven't done my chores. I'll take it out on my children.

Experiment Penny arranged to go window-shopping with a friend. She rated her belief in the target cognition, and her mood, before and after her day out.

Results Penny had a good day out. Her mood was significantly better than on days when she was doing chores or working, and she was actually nicer to the children. Her enhanced mood gave her energy and something other than work and children to talk about to her friends. In session, she then planned time for herself during the week.

Reflection On her day out, Penny felt guilty. During the following therapy session, she saw that nothing bad had happened as a result of leaving her chores for one day—in fact, when she did them the next day, she achieved more than normal. She reflected that time for herself was an important part of being a good mother, and actually made her more efficient.

See Table 15.2 for further experiments related to changes in functioning.

Investigating others' reactions

Experiments concerning being open about limitations and difficulties include revealing physical problems, and admitting to painful emotions and being unable to cope as well as the patient would like (see also Chapter 17 on avoidance of affect, and Experiment 20.8 in Chapter 20 on low self-esteem).

Experiment 15.3: being open about disability

Problem Klaus had rapid onset visual impairment and was registered blind. He did not want to use a stick or tell anyone he was visually impaired. His activity levels had drastically reduced, and his mood was very low.

Target cognition By trying to appear sighted, I will maintain my quality of life.

Alternative perspective If I explain to people that I can't see, I will be able to do more.

Prediction If others notice that I can't see, they will pity me and be patronizing, or they might tease me and give me wrong information. I will be hurt by their comments or their tone of voice, as it will highlight what I've lost.

Experiment Klaus and his therapist went out during a therapy session to catch a bus that Klaus had used before (but not since) his vision had declined. When a bus arrived, Klaus asked someone at the stop or the driver what number bus it

Table 15.2 Managing changes in functioning

Target cognitions	Alternative perspective	Experiment	Results
If I cannot do things for other people, I'm no good.	People may value me for other reasons and have different expectations of me.	Make a list of what I value in myself and other people. Ask friends and family what they value in me. Check out expectations. Keep a log of signs of appreciation not concerned with achievement.	There are other aspects to me that are still OK, despite my illness. I value them and so does my family (e.g. my ability to listen, sense of humour, honesty).
I should be doing more to look after the house.	I'm doing all I can, given my physical condition.	Discovery experiment to explore whether family think I'm doing enough.	No one expected me to do more, but we all felt something needed to be done. Worked out a rota together. My family are happy with what I do, but I still have a lingering doubt that I should be doing more to be worthwhile. *Further work:* survey—what would other people expect me to do? What would people expect of themselves in a similar situation?
Because of my limitations, I cannot do what I used to do. So, there's no point in doing anything. If I start something I'll feel more disheartened.	There are activities I could still get pleasure from. Trying some would be a start. Who knows, I might feel better once I get going.	Work out some new and adapt some old activities, which might be pleasurable or give some small sense of achievement. Plan times in the day to carry them out. *Remember:* don't expect to be able to do everything as before. Rate mastery and pleasure for each activity. *Or:* keep an activity diary to monitor actual levels of activity.	Patient chose activities based on previous enjoyment of gardening (e.g. reading books, planning changes in the garden, and ordering seeds from catalogues). He planned what help he needed in the garden to enable him to do more. This helped to get him going and gave him a sense that it was worth doing something. He was heartened—he could still do small things he had discounted, and enjoy them.

was. The therapist and Klaus rode only one stop, and then got off and repeated the experiment with the next bus.

Results Klaus asked seven people what number bus it was or where the bus was going. Each one gave him the correct information. Two people spoke very clearly and loudly, which Klaus interpreted as patronizing. However, this could be tolerated, as he still got the information he wanted. He felt confident that he could catch a bus home from the therapy session, rather than getting a taxi as usual.

Reflection Klaus realized that others did not always respond as he predicted, and that pretending he was not disabled might not after all be the best way of being able to do what he wanted.

Further work In therapy sessions, Klaus worked out a hierarchy of situations in which he still feared people might pity, tease, or mislead him if he displayed his visual impairment. Initially, the top of the hierarchy was being out on a Saturday night in town and asking drunk people for directions, but in fact this was not something he would have done previously anyway. A more realistic high-risk situation was going to a new pub and asking for the toilets. Through a sequence of behavioural experiments, Klaus explored his hierarchy for homework.

Tips People with new-onset loss of vision can be extremely anxious when conducting this kind of experiment. It is helpful to do preparatory in-session cognitive work and role play to increase their confidence in coping with difficult situations. Initially, it may be helpful to use therapist-guided experiments; later, between-session experiments will encourage independence. It could also be helpful to use a survey to explore real attitudes to the visually impaired, and ask people how they might actually respond if approached for information.

See Table 15.3 for further experiments related to investigating others' reactions.

Exploring the meaning of symptoms

Experiment 15.4: normalizing symptoms

Problem Mark experienced a range of medically unexplained symptoms and difficulties with memory and concentration (e.g. forgetting what he wanted to buy when he got to a shop). He was very anxious about his symptoms and the effect they were having on his life. Neurological assessment showed that his memory was functioning normally.

Target cognitions I am having abnormal memory lapses. There must be something wrong with my brain (belief rating 80%).

Table 15.3 Investigating others' reactions

Target cognition	Alternative perspective	Experiment	Results
Wheelchair users Now that I am in a wheelchair, it will be harder to co-ordinate where to go out in the evening. People will not want to make the effort to think about my needs.	People will make the effort to think about appropriate places to go.	Say yes to an invitation to go out. Explain my needs for wheelchair access.	Went out with friends to wheelchair-accessible places. When we encountered steps without a ramp, friends lifted the chair, and seemed to enjoy the challenge. *Tip:* many places are not wheelchair-accessible, and people do meet obstacles and unhelpful attitudes. Experiments and information gathering (e.g. reading about issues/campaigns for wheelchair users) can help patients discover that most people are happy to help, and lack of access is a general problem, not a criticism.
Skin conditions People will stare and whisper when they see my skin, and I will feel bad.	None	In session, the patient closed her eyes and imagined being in a café with people staring and whispering about her skin.	Initially, she felt embarrassed and saw herself becoming red and sweaty. As the imagined situation continued, people stopped staring and returned to their own activities. Her anxiety went down. She realized that people might stare and whisper, but this was manageable. She then felt confident to try further experiments in real situations.
Post-surgery If I admit how difficult I find it to cope, and that I still feel upset sometimes, no one will understand.	If I confide in others, they may be sympathetic, and I may feel less pathetic.	Talk to a trusted friend, after role playing alternative responses in session and considering whether feeling like this was justified, given what she had gone through.	Managed to talk to friend, who was sympathetic. Another person nearby, however, proceeded to advise her on self-help. Felt relieved, and less isolated, but still just as pathetic. *Further work:* contacting others who had had similar operations, reading about adjustment to major surgery, questioning the value of giving weight to others' opinions, and gradually working out less demanding standards for coping and a kinder perspective on herself.

Alternative perspectives Other healthy people, who do not have problems with their neurological functioning, have similar memory lapses (belief rating 10%). There may be a number of explanations for them.

Prediction If asked, other people will not report similar memory problems.

Experiment The therapist conducted a survey, asking members of staff in her department specific questions:

1 What sort of memory lapses have you experienced over the past week?
2 Do these happen regularly?
3 What do you think are some of the reasons why these might occur?

Results Mark was very surprised at the range of responses, particularly since they came from 'fully functioning' clinicians and secretarial staff. He thought that many of the experiences reported were more 'ridiculous' than his own. Reflections on why these occurred included 'I was thinking about something else', 'I was preoccupied, busy, ahead of myself', 'Sometimes I just make mistakes', 'Feeling tired'. This helped him to re-evaluate his idea that there was something wrong with his brain. His belief in the target cognition reduced from 80% to 20%, and his belief in the alternative perspective increased from 10% to 90%. People's explanations for their memory lapses strengthened the idea that there might be many alternatives to his original hypothesis, including simply not knowing.

Reflection Mark realized that memory lapses are very common even in healthy, normal people. He went on to monitor mistakes made by people in his social circle and family, which reinforced his new perspective.

Experiment 15.5: finding a benign explanation for symptoms

Problem Trevor had had a myocardial infarction (MI) five years ago. Since then he had experienced episodes of chest pain which had been fully investigated and were not angina. He was supposed to take regular exercise, but every time he experienced a twinge in his chest, he stopped and rested or took medication (against medical advice).

Target cognitions Chest pain during exercise means another attack of angina and a possible heart attack (belief rating 70%).

Alternative perspective Chest pain is not always angina and does not mean I am going to have another heart attack (belief rating 30%). The pain means I am unfit, and I have to keep exercising despite the symptoms.

Prediction If I carry on exercising when I'm getting the pains, they will get worse and I'll do myself damage—another heart attack, or worse.

Experiment Trevor started an exercise programme developed by the cardiac physiotherapist, beginning with 10 minutes' gentle walking and gradually increasing speed over two weeks, up to 20 minutes' brisk walk daily.

Results Trevor noticed some pains in his chest initially, but these went away after a few days. After a few weeks, he began to feel fitter and better overall. His belief in the target cognition reduced to 40%, and his belief in the alternative increased to 50%.

Reflection Trevor realized that he was getting pains because he was taking unaccustomed exercise, focusing on every sensation, and breathing more deeply. He needed to exercise more, starting gently and working up over time. As he got fitter, he would not notice pains so much, and eventually they would go away.

Tips Many experiments used to treat panic are also helpful to patients with non-cardiac chest pains (e.g. the hyperventilation provocation test). The therapist will need to help patients to examine anxieties they have about doing these experiments.

Some activities (e.g. hyperventilation, sudden exertion) are medically contraindicated for people with heart conditions. However, for many post-MI patients, rehabilitation involves significant exercise, so it is important not to be over-cautious and thus feed patients' fears. If in doubt, seek medical advice.

See Table 15.4 for further experiments related to exploring the meaning of symptoms.

Strengthening sense of identity

The following experiments are useful when people feel that their sense of who they are has been overshadowed by illness. Given that people are in a new situation, it is difficult to know how others might respond and how to develop a new sense of self. Discovery experiments can help people to formulate new perspectives.

Experiment 15.6: perceived disappearance of identity

Problem Josie had a recent diagnosis of multiple sclerosis (MS), had gradually become more disabled, and needed to use a wheelchair. Her mood was low, and she had an image of herself as a tiny disappearing spot enclosed within a large sphere, the illness.

Table 15.4 Exploring the meaning of symptoms

Target cognition	Alternative perspective	Experiment	Results
Chronic pain			
Unless I stop moving when I experience pain, I will make it worse and this will lead to more damage.	Pain is not dangerous.	Stay with the pain and the activity. See what happens.	The pain continued but did not get any worse. I was able to do more and nothing catastrophic happened.
Chronic fatigue			
Experiencing tiredness and headaches after I've been studying means I am ill and need to go to bed, or I will make myself much worse.	The symptoms may be caused by doing too much of one activity, not general exhaustion. If I did something else like going for a walk, I might feel more refreshed.	Next time, go out to the pub for a short time and see friends, rather than go to bed.	Enjoyed going to the pub. Energy level boosted. Symptoms such as headache and tiredness can be dealt with in ways other than rest.

Target cognitions There is nothing left of the old me, and I will continue to disappear. Other people think I am a different person now.

Alternative perspective I have many enduring characteristics, which are still there even though I can't do the same things.

Experiment Josie and her therapist discussed the idea that thoughts are not facts, and that how people see things is affected by low mood. She agreed to take a first step towards checking this out by asking her husband two questions: 'What have you noticed is the same about me since the diagnosis?' and 'What have you noticed is different?' Josie did not know what her husband would say, but felt he would be truthful.

Results Josie's husband was surprised by the questions. He had not thought she was different in any way, except that she was clearly feeling depressed. Josie also asked a close friend the same questions. She gave almost exactly the same response, saying that she felt very sad for Josie, but still saw her as the same person as before.

Reflection Josie felt that perhaps she had become stuck in negative thinking, but hoped she could now adopt a wider perspective when the thought arose.

Further work Josie recorded when the thought recurred and used the results of the experiment to challenge it. With her therapist, she also worked on another concern: how to conduct herself in a wheelchair. In her wheelchair, she was physically lower than other people. This prompted a sense of inferiority. She felt that she could not ask for help or express her opinion, as people would carry on talking as if she wasn't there. She believed people were sorry for her and did not relate to her as the person she used to be. In a series of experiments, she practised behaving assertively, as she had been perfectly able to do before. This increased her confidence, raised her mood, and boosted her self-esteem so that, after a few weeks, her original image changed to a pair of overlapping circles, one being the illness and the other being her.

Experiment 15.7: identity defined by physical appearance

Problem Following a transplant, Jane had to take medication, including steroids. These caused facial hair growth, and her face developed a moon shape. She felt this changed her identity and she did not want to 'face' her old friends. As she could not find any alternatives to this idea, she and her therapist decided to conduct a discovery experiment.

Target cognitions I don't look nice any more and people will not see me as the same person. Other people look more or less the same throughout their lives.

Alternative perspective People will still see me as the same person. Appearance changes throughout a person's life, but they remain the same person.

Predictions If I see people, I look so different that they will not think I am the same person any more. My friends will react differently to me—they will blush or sound awkward.

Experiment Jane met a few of her friends and closely observed their reactions to her. Then she recruited them to help in the experiment, collecting photographs of themselves at different stages of their lives, and looking at them together to identify changes and how they felt about them.

Results Jane's friends were unanimously pleased to see her and behaved exactly the same towards her as before. Most said she looked very healthy and that, despite looking 'different', she was the same person as before. The photograph session revealed that most had gone through many changes. For example, through pregnancy, one friend had grown more facial hair and put on significant weight. They had all changed over time, but were still 'the same people'.

Reflection Jane decided that it is a fact of life that people change over time, but they are still 'themselves'. These changes make people as they are, and are part of their histories.

Tips Many physical health problems involve significant changes in appearance. It is important not to question whether change has happened or not, but rather to work on its meaning. Experiments involving changes in appearance can be conducted using photographs. For example, a digital camera can be used to take photographs of the patient, and observe how appearance changes depending on clothes, make-up, and time of day.

Examining the effects of safety behaviours

Experiment 15.8: dizziness and avoidance of movement

Problem Rena was referred from the neurology department for persistent vertigo and dizziness. Medical investigations showed deficits in her vestibular system, leading to mild balance problems. These were exacerbated by Rena's avoidance of movements that provoked feelings of vertigo or unsteadiness and of physiotherapy exercises designed to help her balance. If she woke up feeling at all 'off', she would rest during the day as much as possible, only attempting normal activities if she felt completely well.

Target cognitions If I feel unsteady or dizzy, I must avoid head movements which will make the dizziness worse and do me some damage. I cannot tolerate even the slightest dizziness. I'll have a terrible fall.

Alternative perspective I will feel unsteady sometimes, but avoiding movement means that my vestibular system will not adapt and compensate—I will not learn to balance and will make the problem worse. If I make myself dizzy it will only last a short time, and gradually get better the more I do.

Prediction If I move around more I will get more and more dizzy and I will feel worse.

Experiment Rena practised head movements designed to provoke dizziness, first sitting down in a safe place, then standing up, and then gradually moving her head around even when feeling dizzy.

Results Initially the exercises provoked dizziness and Rena felt sick. However, the feelings only lasted a short time, and she felt better afterwards. After a week or so, the exercises provoked less dizziness, and she was able to progress to standing up, moving around, walking whilst moving her head around, and turning in circles. Each time the symptoms quickly went away as her balance system compensated and adjusted. She did not fall, discovering that her eyes and muscles kept her steady even when feeling dizzy.

Reflection Rena noticed that while movement was unpleasant at first, the more she did, the better she felt. She concluded that slight dizziness was tolerable and was a prompt to move around.

Tip Experiments need to be conducted within safe limits, as some dizzy patients have been so avoidant of movement that they may risk staggering or falling if challenged too quickly. It is important to check that patients have had full physical investigations for the causes of the dizziness and, if necessary, to work with a physiotherapist (c.f. Yardley and Redfern 2001).

Experiment 15.9: regulating bowel movements

Problem Mark had a 15-year history of IBS. He could only go out to places with easily accessible toilets because he feared losing control of his bowels in public. His life had become very restricted. He allowed himself to go out only for short periods, after spending a long time trying to empty his bowels.

Target cognitions If I get any sensations from my bowels, I am going to lose control immediately. I must always get to a toilet or I will have an accident. I need to make sure that my bowels are completely empty before I go anywhere.

Alternative perspectives I can develop control over my bowel sensations. Part of the problem is that I have been straining and altering bowel function. If I empty my bowels regularly, further sensations are likely to be anxiety or sensations that will recede with time.

Experiment At home, Mark practised good bowel habits, regularly emptying his bowels at the same time each day and not allowing himself to strain. He did not respond to further bowel sensations, but timed how long they took to go away.

Results At first, the bowel sensations seemed overwhelming, but Mark found that they receded after 20 minutes or so. After a few weeks of practising at home, he experimented with going out and found once again that, if he waited, bowel symptoms receded.

Reflection Mark realized that part of the problem was that he had altered normal healthy bowel habits by rushing to the toilet and straining at the slightest sensation. He noted that it was very difficult to lose control of his bowels and learned that, if he waited, the sensations went away. He decided to continue developing healthy bowel habits, no longer straining, and not responding to 'inappropriate' sensations.

Tips It helps to explain to clients that bowels have sphincters designed to control how they function, and that messages from the bowel can be altered by repeated straining and hypervigilance (Toner *et al.* 2000). People who have used safety behaviours such as checking or straining for a long time may indeed have altered bowel function leading to episodes of loss of control. In this case, bowel re-training exercises may be necessary. Patients initially feel safer conducting experiments at home, with a toilet close by, but it is important to encourage them to start experimenting in public as soon as possible. Therapists should be vigilant for safety behaviours such as covertly checking for toilets, clenching, and carrying spare clothes (see also Chapter 3 on panic).

See Table 15.5 for further experiments related to examining safety behaviours.

Distinctive difficulties
Engagement
People with medically unexplained symptoms may find engagement in psychological therapy difficult. They may believe that their symptoms are not taken seriously, especially if professionals, friends, or family have given the impression that they think 'It's all in the mind'. They may feel they have not done enough to help themselves, or find it hard to face emotions associated with loss or sense of failure. Some may have a vested interest in proving psychological approaches do not work, to strengthen the case for physical treatment. They may see psychological treatment as irrelevant or secondary to their main, physical problems. Furthermore, since behavioural experiments require patients to take risks, their potential benefits must be clear.

Table 15.5 Examining the effects of safety behaviours

Target cognition	Alternative perspective	Experiment	Reflection
Chronic pain			
If I rest when I notice a symptom, I will feel better and prevent further pain or harm.	Symptoms are normal reactions to adjusting to a new level of activity. It means my body is getting stronger and fitter.	Graded exercise programme, together with symptom management (e.g. distraction, relaxation).	Pain is not to be feared.
Over-use of motility aids			
If I use a walking stick, I will feel less pain and others won't expect so much of me.	I feel more pain walking with a stick because I walk awkwardly. I can tell other people that I can't do certain things.	Try walking without a stick and monitor what happens to the pain (first practise different ways of walking in the session). Practise assertiveness.	Although it hurts, I walk with a straighter back without the stick and my shoulders ache less. Other people were more responsive to me because I wasn't causing a fuss.

Genuine adversity

It is important to take the time to hear patients' stories, to understand their views of their problems, and to acknowledge that they have been dealing with difficult and distressing conditions. It takes time to build up trust, to create shared formulations (Sanders 2000; Moorey and Greer 2002), and to clarify what therapy can offer: we cannot guarantee to take physical symptoms away, but we can tackle unhelpful thinking and behaviour that fuels distress. Some of these tasks can be presented as experiments. Indeed, therapy itself can be seen as a discovery experiment: therapist and patient together explore psychological factors maintaining symptoms and distress, working in a spirit of curiosity and collaboration.

Recognizing limits

Therapy needs to be adapted in accordance with patients' physical problems and disabilities. People with motility problems may be physically or socially restricted, and using other people or social situations as a source of experimental information may be limited. The world does present challenges to people with disabilities—social prejudices and restrictions in access. Many people's 'negative' ideas are in fact accurate (c.f. Moorey and Greer 2002). Experiments must always be realistic, rather than impossible tasks, attempting to disprove accurate perceptions.

Difficulty expressing emotions

Some patients find talking about emotions unfamiliar or difficult. They may have spent much time going through the medical system, focusing on physical symptoms, and introducing emotional and psychological issues can be alarming. Therapists need to go gently, using open questions (e.g. 'Can you tell me more about that?') and reflections (e.g. 'That sounds really tough'). It is particularly important not to put words into patients' mouths, as they may feel undermined. Again, experiments can be used to explore the effects of discussing emotional issues.

Change and adjustment

Some people are nervous about change. Patients with chronic pain or fatigue, for example, are understandably cautious about embarking on anything that might make them worse: 'I don't want to jeopardize progress'. The diagnosis of any illness, whether medically explicable or otherwise, inevitably requires a process of adjustment. After a clear diagnosis such as cancer or MS, many people go through a period of sadness, grief, or anger, and feeling out of control. They must also face the functional aspects of coming to terms with illness and the changes it brings (Moorey and Greer 2002). This may cause problems if people do not accept that they are 'allowed' to feel upset.

Discovery experiments (e.g. contacting self-help groups and looking at reputable web sites) can reveal what others go through in similar circumstances. With conditions such as CFS or unexplained pelvic pain, the process of adjustment may be arrested by the search for a diagnosis. Equally, adjustment to changes in function is more difficult for those whose self-esteem depends on being strong and coping well, and for perfectionists. Negative self-schemas, especially common in people with unexplained physical symptoms, mean that behavioural experiments may have to be done over and over again before they 'bite'.

Other relevant chapters

Patients with chronic disability or illness can share concerns with patients with panic disorder (see Chapter 3), social phobia (see Chapter 7), and health anxiety (see Chapter 4). Ill health often affects self-esteem (see Chapter 20) and can lead to depression (see Chapter 10). Avoidance of affect may also be a key feature (see Chapter 17).

Further reading

Fennell, M.J.V. (1997). Low self-esteem: a cognitive perspective. *Behavioural and Cognitive Psychotherapy*, **25**, 1–25.

Mayou, R., Bass, C. and Sharpe, M. (ed.) (1995). *Treatment of functional somatic symptoms.* Oxford University Press, Oxford.

Moorey, S. and Greer, S. (2002). *Cognitive behavioural therapy for people with cancer.* Oxford University Press, Oxford.

Sanders, D. (1996). *Psychosomatic problems.* Sage, London.

Toner, B., Segal, Z.V., Emmott, S.D. and Myran, D. (2000). *Cognitive-behavioural treatment of irritable bowel syndrome.* Guilford, New York.

White, J. (2000). *Cognitive behavioural therapy for chronic medical conditions.* Wiley, Chichester.

Worden, W. (1991). *Grief counselling and grief therapy* (2nd edn). Routledge, London.

Tales from the Front Line

It never rains but it pours

A severely depressed young woman was becoming less withdrawn and beginning to recover some optimism. She had a history of family disruptions, and during her school days she had experienced an apparently endless series of unlucky events which had left her believing that she was accident-prone, and singled out for catastrophe. Her therapist was sceptical.

The patient tested her prediction about expected catastrophes by engaging in more 'normal' daily activities to see whether she encountered an unusual number of catastrophes. The flat she had agreed to look after whilst a friend was on holiday was burgled whilst she was out shopping. On the way back from visiting her uncle she came across a road traffic accident, had to phone the emergency services, and stayed to look after the driver, who died before the arrival of the ambulance. She saw her car being vandalized in the car park as her train drew out of the station. Her therapist (almost) gave up planning behavioural experiments . . .

CHAPTER 16

Acquired brain injury*

Joanna McGrath
Nigel King

Introduction

This chapter provides some conceptual and practical resources for two main groups of practitioners working with people who have acquired brain injury (ABI):

1 Cognitive therapists who would not consider themselves specialists in the area of neuropsychology or rehabilitation

2 Rehabilitation professionals who wish to improve their application of cognitive therapy, especially behavioural experiments, to this group of patients

Behavioural experiments are particularly appropriate for these patients, whose ability to engage with both the theory underpinning cognitive therapy and the intellectual demands of the therapy sessions themselves, is limited by neuropsychological impairment (Hibbard *et al.* 1990; Whitehouse 1994; Kinney 2001). Moreover, it is not necessary to be an expert in the field of neuropsychology to apply cognitive therapy techniques, including behavioural experiments, to the benefit of people with ABI.

This chapter focuses on the specific issues of ABI (a subgroup within the more general class of organic brain pathology). The key characteristics of ABI are:

◆ A sudden-onset cerebral event in adulthood in the context of previously normal brain function

◆ Psychological, and often physical, impairment of varying type and degree

◆ A non-progressive course

◆ An initial relatively rapid recovery followed by a slower phase, with full recovery of past function very rarely achieved

....

*Behavioural experiment 16.6 was contributed by Audrey Daisley.

The most common causes of ABI are closed head injury (due to road traffic accidents, assaults, or falls); stroke; subarachnoid haemorrhage; cerebral hypoxia (secondary to prolonged cardiac arrest, near drowning, hypoglycaemia, carbon monoxide poisoning); cerebral infections (meningitis, encephalitis), and tumours. Brain injury can thus affect anyone, at any age.

Cognitive model

Doing psychological work with people who have organic brain injury or disease is often seen as a highly specialist field, which entails sophisticated knowledge of neuropsychology, and is dominated by psychometric assessment. Indeed, the presence of organic brain pathology is still sometimes given as a reason for not applying psychological treatment approaches, including cognitive therapy. One, usually unstated, reason for this may be the assumption that if psychological symptoms are 'caused' by brain pathology rather than by psychological mechanisms, then the treatment approach must primarily address the brain pathology, and a psychological approach may be both irrelevant and ineffectual.

In fact, the situation is at once more simple and more complex than this. Psychological processes (e.g. grief) remain highly important even in the context of abnormal brain function, and deserve to be addressed directly in their own right. However, it is also true that some of the specific neuropsychological impairments resulting from brain injury (e.g. memory problems and concrete thinking) can present specific challenges to the delivery of cognitive therapy, and these need to be addressed thoughtfully and creatively. So, while the situation of people with organic brain pathology is more complex than that of people without organic brain pathology, and formulating problems may make special demands of the therapist, the basic cognitive model (Beck 1976) and techniques are no different from those applied to any other group.

The main psychological issues facing people with ABI are essentially threat, loss, and restriction in multiple life domains, and a reduced psychological capacity to cope with these because the central cognitive processor has itself been affected.

Brain injury can have a direct effect on physical appearance, sensorimotor skills, higher cognition, emotional experience and control, and communication ability. These effects combine to underpin behavioural changes (e.g. forgetfulness, unsteady and clumsy walking pattern, increased emotionalism, and loss of independence in personal care). These in turn can result in dramatic changes to roles and relationships (e.g. reduced employability or marital and family breakdown). The person with ABI is often struggling with a very difficult psychosocial situation but is not able to bring previous coping strategies (such as physical activity, spending time alone, reflection, problem solving, talking to others) into play because these coping strategies have themselves been compromised by the brain injury.

Any psychological therapeutic approach to the problems of people with brain injury must, therefore, take into account:

- Premorbid core beliefs, underlying assumptions, aspirations, and preferred coping style (which may have been highly functional and may still be assets)
- The circumstances of the injury, which may in itself have been psychologically traumatic
- Current psychosocial situation
- Current physical and psychological impairments and disabilities
- Current appraisals

The levels of psychological distress in people with brain injury (and their families) are high (Gainotti 1993), although identifying formal psychiatric disorder in this population is fraught with methodological problems (see, for example, House 1992). The degree of distress expressed may not appear excessive in view of the person's circumstances. It may be based on accurate appraisal. For instance, there may be risk of further brain injury from recurrent strokes or hydrocephalus or epilepsy, which makes going out or engaging in physically demanding activities or choosing to live alone, genuinely risky; or poor balance may make mixing in crowded situations likely to result in a fall; or there may be a good deal of real social rejection related to attitudes to disabled people; or the person may have lost, overnight, the chance of realizing cherished career ambitions, financial security, and key relationships.

This, at first sight, presents a difficulty to the cognitive therapist who is used to challenging the patient's 'catastrophic' interpretations of, for instance, ambiguous bodily sensations or the social behaviour of others. A cognitive approach is nevertheless still applicable in these situations, but some inventiveness is required. The focus of intervention is less on testing out the situation itself than reflecting on the relative costs and benefits of the strategies the patient is using to manage it, such as persistent avoidance or defensive aggression (see the experiments that follow for further details of this approach).

Having noted that the situation of people with brain injury is often dire, and that their reactions are often understandable, it is also important to point out that they can make errors in appraising their situation and respond in ways that appear excessive or inappropriate. This may occur for all the reasons that are familiar to the mental health practitioner. However, faulty appraisal may also occur because of specific cognitive deficits. For instance, a man with a memory problem may have the cognition, 'My girlfriend hasn't been to visit me—she must have dumped me', purely because he does not recall the visits she actually made; or a woman with visual perceptual problems may start to avoid car travel because she thinks, 'It's not safe to travel with my husband—he's a bad driver', based on her distorted experience of speed and the proximity of other vehicles.

Key cognitive constructs

ABI constitutes a major change to a past fundamental schema—the old or normal self (McGrath and Adams 1999). Thus, a lot of the concerns of the brain-injured person relate to a basic longing to return to this state, to re-establish a sense of personal identity. Personal identity is a highly complex notion, varying between individuals. Yet it is possible to identify common themes, relating to its maintenance or re-establishment, that preoccupy people with ABI. The first is a desire to be healthy again and to avoid relapse—to be rid of, or at least to be able to control, symptoms (see Experiments 16.1 and 16.2). A second theme is the desire to return to previous levels of function—the ability to carry out meaningful tasks (see Experiments 16.3–16.5). A third is the desire to be acceptable to other people and to manage relationships (see Experiments 16.6 and 16.7). These latter two themes relate to the desire to be 'normal' as perceived by self and others.

People with ABI respond to difficulties with symptoms, level of function, or social relationships in a number of characteristic ways. Some deny the extent of their problems in these areas. This may itself arise from a specific type of organically based cognitive deficit—anosognosia (Prigatano and Schacter 1991) (see Experiment 16.4), or it may be a purely psychological response (see Experiment 16.5). Others openly express enormous fear at the prospect of not being 'normal', and this means that dysfunctional approach behaviour (running before they can walk, taking on tasks that are beyond them) is at least as common as dysfunctional avoidance behaviour (see Experiment 16.1). These people need to be protected from demoralizing failure experiences, and instructed to slow down and reduce their expectations. This sets the tone of many behavioural experiments. Others have given up hope of being 'normal', and present with more depressive concerns, often focusing on issues of low self-esteem and impoverished personal identity (see Experiment 16.6).

Whether working at the level of automatic thoughts, underlying assumptions, or core beliefs, a key task of the therapist should be actively to present the patient with the possibility that life is worth living in the context of lost cognitive and physical function. This may challenge strongly held core beliefs and values (Prigatano 1991), and makes existential demands of the therapist as well as the patient.

Behavioural experiments

The behavioural experiments presented in this chapter can be seen as examples of the following categories.

- **Beliefs about symptoms**
  Experiment 16.1: how to manage symptoms
  Experiment 16.2: origin of symptoms
- **Beliefs about functional abilities**
  Experiment 16.3: overpessimistic beliefs
  Experiment 16.4: overoptimistic beliefs related to poor insight (cognitive problem)
  Experiment 16.5: overoptimistic beliefs related to denial (emotional problem)
- **Beliefs about social situations**
  Experiment 16.6: social presentation
  Experiment 16.7: using self-advocacy

Beliefs about symptoms

Experiment 16.1: how to manage symptoms

Problem Brian, a 49-year-old computer programmer with an army background, had a subarachnoid haemorrhage while out jogging. He made a good physical recovery over several months, but remained prone to cognitive fatigue. He returned to part-time work, but became distressed as he found himself less and less able to cope with work demands. In the past he had coped with adversity by pushing himself and trying harder. This fitted in well with the army culture and had usually resulted in him successfully overcoming setbacks. However, in his present circumstances it led to a vicious cycle in which he became more fatigued and frustrated. The therapist advised him to pace his activity and take small breaks during the working day, but he was unconvinced that this would be effective and described the strategy as 'throwing in the towel'.

Target cognitions More effort equals more success. No pain, no gain. If I don't keep pushing myself then I'm a defeatist. Double the problem, double the effort.

Alternative perspective Success doesn't necessarily mean doing everything I did before the brain haemorrhage. I do have some limitations now, and trying harder can make things worse.

Prediction I will get more effective work done if I use my strategy of trying harder. I will get less effective work done if I try taking small breaks as advised.

Operationalizing the prediction Measure the actual time spent on task and amount of effective work under two conditions (see details of experiment).

Preparation for the experiment Didactic education about the cognitive effects of brain injury and socratic dialogue about acceptance of his limitations had little direct effect. However, it was sufficient to lead him to agree to conduct the behavioural experiment.

Experiment Though highly sceptical, Brian measured the amount of time spent effectively on tasks for two weeks under each of two conditions. The first used his preferred strategy of just trying harder until he was so tired that he had to stop work for a very long rest or go home. The second involved him taking a 10-minute break every hour whether he felt like it or not.

Results The records indicated that the second strategy was associated with significantly more effective work.

Reflection Brian reflected that he had begun to see winning in terms of 'being maximally effective', rather than about putting in maximum active effort; disciplining himself to rest could be seen as a type of effort in itself. 'I can only do my best and that may involve doing things differently from before.'

Tips This approach can be used with patients who have to manage fatigue arising from a variety of causes including multiple sclerosis, anxiety or depression, and chronic fatigue syndrome.

Experiment 16.2: origin of symptoms

Problem Daniel was recovering from a severe head injury, which had left him with some problems with memory and concrete thinking and marked problems with speed of information processing. He had returned to live at home with his wife and two small children. He went back to work on reduced duties from Monday to Thursday, and was at home with the children on Fridays. He started to develop severe headaches and feelings of depersonalization and derealization, which got worse as the week progressed.

Target cognitions The headaches are caused by a late complication of the brain injury, perhaps a bleed inside the brain. The periods of depersonalization are post-traumatic epileptic seizures.

Alternative perspective (suggested by therapist) My cognitive stamina is reduced. When there are too many cognitive and physical demands, my brain becomes tired. The headaches and other symptoms may be a signal that I am asking too much of myself at this stage in my recovery.

Prediction If the target belief is true then reducing the cognitive demands made on me should make no difference. If the alternative belief is true, then it will lead to a reduction in my symptoms.

Operationalizing the prediction The weekly routine, including work pattern, was changed to include more cognitive rest.

Preparation for the experiment Close liaison with the medical team was important to establish that a direct physical cause for the symptoms was less likely than the target belief.

Experiment With the agreement of his employers, Daniel worked Monday, Tuesday, Thursday, and Friday. This built in a mid-week break from work so that he could spend time alone on a day that the children were out at nursery.

Results There was an almost immediate cessation of all symptoms.

Reflection Daniel expressed relief that the symptoms did not seem to be due to life-threatening complications of brain injury. He reflected on the unexpectedly close relationship between cognitive deficits and physical symptoms, and described an increased sense of control over his own life and health. On the other hand, the more leisurely weekly timetable was a source of some frustration, as he did not see this level of activity as congruent with his view of himself.

Further work Daniel and his wife were able to use the principles from this experiment to monitor the course of recovery, and to pace the resumption of activities, using the return of these symptoms as an indication of situations in which he was functioning at his current limits.

Tips This approach can also be used with symptoms of irritability, anxiety, and panic, where brain injured patients may fear that they are 'going mad' or undergoing permanent 'personality change'. Often such symptoms are responses to situational demands in the context of cognitive impairment.

Beliefs about functional abilities

Experiment 16.3: overpessimistic beliefs

Problem John had a stroke, which left him with a paralysed left arm and weak left leg. The sensation on the left side of his body was generally reduced, so that he could not feel the ground under his left foot. His balance was poor. He was learning to walk again with a physiotherapist. Even though he was desperately keen to be able to walk independently, he became very frightened in the physiotherapy sessions, and avoided any exercises that required him to bear weight on his left side.

Target cognitions My balance is very poor, and my brain has been damaged and is vulnerable. I am likely to fall over. If I fall I will tip over onto my head and be unable to protect it. My brain, which is already fragile, will be hurt further. Once I have fallen I won't be able to move, so I will be lying there injured and helpless on the ground. (Core belief: any hope of recovery and getting back to normal will be dashed.)

Alternative perspective My balance, though not normal, is improving. Although my left foot and leg are no longer able to feel the floor, I am safer than I feel. My likelihood of falling is low, though not zero. Having had a stroke does not make your brain more vulnerable to the effects of impact. Falling is not likely to damage my head. I can control how I fall and protect myself. I can get up if I fall. Taking risks is part of the process of getting better. If I don't take risks, I will ensure my physical safety but I will not make the progress that is so important to me.

Predictions If the target beliefs are true then (a) I will regularly fall in physiotherapy sessions when I practise walking, (b) it will not be possible for me to learn to fall 'safely' and to get up from the ground, and (c) I would hear or find out about cases of people whose heads have been damaged by falling after stroke.

Operationalizing the predictions Observational data were collected from physiotherapy sessions. John was given information about the actual vulnerability of the brain. Controlled falling was incorporated into the physiotherapy programme.

Preparation for the experiment The therapist endorsed those aspects of John's perceptions that were accurate. His experience needed to be validated before the dysfunctional components were challenged, particularly because the difference between the situations of John and the fit, able-bodied therapist was considerable. It was acknowledged that he was indeed more vulnerable, weaker, with poorer balance than before the injury. With John's permission, the physiotherapist was made aware of the degree of fear involved. She was then able to approach the experiment not merely as a motor skill training exercise, but with full understanding of its psychological implications.

Experiment John recorded in a diary the occasions on which he actually fell, or felt that he was going to fall in physiotherapy. Information was given to him via medical textbooks and Stroke Association literature. John was encouraged to question his consultant neurologist about the risk to his head. He was also encouraged to discuss his fear of falling with other patients who were more advanced in physiotherapy, and who could provide an incentive and role model for him. Getting up from the floor, and then controlled falling was practised. Initially, the cognitive therapist modelled the technique with the physiotherapist.

Results John found that the probability of falling in physiotherapy was zero, and that he could steady himself and avoid falling more successfully than he had thought. He was reassured by the explicit discussion of the actual effects of the stroke on his brain, and met other stroke survivors who had experienced falls with no long-term ill effects (that is, his health beliefs were modified). He noted an improvement in his competence through the achievement of increasingly ambitious physiotherapy goals. He learned to fall in a controlled way and to get up from the floor.

Reflection John talked in terms of gaining a relationship of trust with his physiotherapist, which enabled him to attempt risky activities, and beginning to know and to trust his own body again, while understanding its limitations. He described feeling stronger and less vulnerable, so that the degree of perceived risk was reduced.

Further work Similar experiments to do with safe walking, falling, and getting up can be attempted, in a graduated way, in other environments such as the ward, the patient's home, and on the street. In some ways this is part of normal physical rehabilitation—the rehabilitation programme can be turned into a series of behavioural experiments aimed at increasing confidence, the pace determined by the degree of anxiety involved.

Tips Falls and injury cannot be eliminated; anyway, this is not desirable. The aim is not for patients to see life as risk-free, but to tolerate a certain amount of increased risk in their lives. When a fall or physical setback occurs, this can be used as the focus of therapy. Patient and therapist can examine whether the consequences were as catastrophic as might have been predicted, or whether the fall was worth experiencing because it happened during an otherwise pleasurable activity such as shopping for clothes in town.

Experiment 16.4: overoptimistic beliefs related to poor insight

Problem Jason, who had a small landscape gardening business, sustained a severe head injury, which included focal damage to the frontal lobes. He had marked cognitive problems, but only partial awareness of these, despite clear feedback to the contrary given by family, friends, and clinicians. Within two months of the injury he was expressing a determination to return to work as soon as possible. He could not be persuaded that significant cognitive impairment did exist, and that his return to work at this point was not likely to be successful, which might put his business at risk.

Target cognitions I'm OK; I don't have any problems with thinking. I have recovered. I'm completely back to normal. I'm totally ready to return to work.

Alternative perspective (a) (generated by Jason) I may still have some problems; (b) (generated by therapist) being unaware of problems may be a problem in itself.

Predictions If I am right about my recovery, I will have no problems in carrying out some work tasks under supervision. If I am really not ready to go back to work, I will have problems in carrying out these tasks.

Operationalizing the predictions Jason and his boss on a work simulation rehabilitation project agreed on criteria for successful task performance.

Preparation for the experiment Preparation involved ensuring that the work simulation was realistic and meaningful to Jason. This included having a 'boss' who could give realistic feedback, using video recording as necessary.

Experiment Jason joined a work party of patients with ABI who were doing light horticultural work at a local National Trust park. His 'boss' was the head groundsman.

Results Jason coped well with the light horticultural work, so his prediction was partly confirmed. However, when it was his turn to make the tea for the 15 people involved, he was unable to plan, initiate, and remember enough of the task to complete it. His colleagues were consequently unable to have their tea break.

Reflection Jason was able to see very clearly that he had failed at a significant component of the work simulation. He reflected, 'If I can't organize a tea break, I certainly can't manage my business at this time' and 'I now realize I've got some problems'. His more realistic appraisal of the situation paved the way for a much slower, graduated, and ultimately successful return to work.

Further work The therapist needed to support Jason emotionally as the effects of task failure were demoralizing (see 'Distinctive difficulties' section).

Tips It is important to stress that the results of this sort of experiment apply to the present time only. The process of recovery from severe head injury takes at least two years, and just because return to work is not possible at one point in this process does not mean that it will not be possible at a later time. Both realism and hope need to be encouraged.

Experiment 16.5: overoptimistic beliefs related to denial

Problem Nicola sustained a severe head injury in a car accident in the summer term of her second year at university. She did not sit her second year examinations, primarily because she was in hospital for treatment of the significant orthopaedic injuries also sustained in the accident. She returned home, made an excellent physical recovery, and was coping well with normal family life during the long vacation. Both she and her family felt that she was ready to resume her studies in the autumn, and she was desperately keen to put the accident behind her. Their plan was for her to sit her second year examinations on her return, and then to complete her final year as normal. However, her neurologist was more cautious, and referred her for a neuropsychological assessment.

Target cognitions I've got some minor problems with reduced concentration and fatigue, but these won't interfere significantly with my studies. The doctors are being overly pessimistic about my brain injury—look at my physical recovery; it was quicker than they expected. I know myself better than anyone else does.

Alternative perspective (generated by therapist) Even though I've made a good physical recovery, my cognitive problems may still be significant. It's normal for the brain to recover more slowly than the rest of the body. Most people with severe head injury take some time to get back to studying. Even though my brain is coping well with everyday life, it may not be ready yet to cope with the heavy demands of studying.

Predictions I will be able to complete psychological tests with no problems and achieve satisfactory scores.

Preparation for the experiment The general procedure and the nature of the tests involved in a neuropsychological assessment were carefully explained to Nicola.

Experiment A neuropsychological assessment, lasting about 120 minutes and involving cognitively demanding tests, was carried out. While the scores obtained on the tests were important, the procedure also functioned as an exploratory behavioural experiment in which Nicola could test the limits of her own cognitive capacities for the first time since her accident.

Results Nicola performed well on the tests for the first 30 to 40 minutes, but was so fatigued after that time that she felt unable to complete the assessment, even when an additional break was offered.

Reflection While initially demoralized, Nicola was able to reflect, 'I knew in the back of my mind that I was kidding myself', 'I need to plan around the possibility that I may not finish my degree next year', 'Maybe the doctors were right about this part of my problems after all, and their advice may be sensible'. These changed cognitions paved the way for Nicola to plan a third year of light studies with support from her personal tutor. She completed two modules over the year, and successfully passed her second year examinations. She extended her time at university by one year and completed her degree.

Tips Neuropsychological assessments, and assessments by other rehabilitation professionals, can be set up as behavioural experiments, with predictions about outcome, and discussion of implications prior to and after the assessment. This can greatly enhance their utility for patients.

Beliefs about social situations

Experiment 16.6: social presentation

Problem Dave sustained a severe head injury three years previously in a cycling accident. In addition to problems with memory and concentration, he had reduced initiation and decreased ability to approach people and start conversations. He also had a left-sided weakness, mainly affecting his arm, with his hand held in a 'fist-like' position with the arm rigidly across his body. His gait pattern was clumsy and rigid. He described frustration, embarrassment, and lowered self-esteem. He found social situations particularly difficult. Recently, while in a crowded local pub, Dave had 'hooked' a woman's handbag on to his left arm when trying to get to the bar. The woman had become upset and called him a thief. Her boyfriend was verbally abusive and threatened violence. Since then Dave refused to visit the pub and started to avoid other situations, such as city-centre shops, where there were crowds of people.

Target cognitions My left arm is likely to hook up other bags in future, and there will be more arguments and embarrassment. Because of this incident, and because of my disabilities, people now think I'm a hard man, a thief, and a weirdo. They will see me as looking for trouble and steer clear of me.

Alternative perspective The incident with the woman's handbag was probably a fluke, just an unfortunate one-off. It has never happened before and is unlikely to happen again. I think the woman backed into me, so she may have been partly responsible. The event was probably not widely discussed in the pub because arguments do happen from time to time when it is crowded. The regulars know I have had a head injury, and if I take time to explain my situation they will be interested and supportive.

Predictions When I enter the pub I will not attract undue attention or trouble, and it will in fact be difficult for me to hook people's bags on to my arm.

Operationalizing the prediction Visit pubs and other busy places and deliberately stand close to people when attempting to pass through crowds. Engage strangers in conversation rather than avoid them.

Preparation for the experiment Dave participated in extensive role play prior to the first experiment. There was discussion and rehearsal of the appropriate level of self-disclosure, and techniques for initiating conversations. There were also some more supportive sessions focusing on issues of body image and identity. Since Dave's difficulties with initiation were primarily due to damage to the frontal lobes, and not purely due to anxiety, this remained a significant problem which required continuing management.

Experiments Dave went to his local pub on two quiet afternoons and attempted to engage someone in a conversation that involved him talking about himself. He returned there on two busy evenings and made an effort to hook bags as he passed close to people.

Results Dave was able to strike up a conversation on two occasions, and found that the listeners were interested in his situation. He had not been able to hook up any handbags, and had not been aware of attracting undue attention from customers, even when he had bumped into someone, having lost his balance.

Reflection Dave reported surprise and pleasure at the interested reactions of strangers and felt this experience had given him confidence to explain himself in the future. He expressed relief that he had not had a repeat of the handbag situation, especially as he had been almost 100% certain that it was likely to recur. He concluded that the woman involved must have had a good deal of responsibility for the situation. He felt it unlikely that he would be faced with a similar situation again.

Further work Dave was able to use this experimental approach to other avoided social situations, including shopping, attending college, and dealing with his solicitors. In all these situations he had worried about what other people thought of him.

Tips This approach can also be used with individuals with other disabling physical conditions (e.g. tremor, which may be perceived by others as a sign of alcoholism).

Experiment 16.7: using self-advocacy

Problem Fred sustained a severe head injury in a motorbike crash. He had no major physical problems. However, his memory was poor, his speech was slow and rather flat, and his speed of processing information was slow. He came from a violent background, and since the injury had significant problems with angry outbursts. Despite this, he was doing well, and obtained a work placement in a large retail store, where his job was to take receipts from customers and give them the item they had purchased which would be delivered to him on a conveyer belt. He had no control over the rate at which customers arrived at his counter. There was no clear queue. Quite often customers complained because goods took longer than expected to arrive. When things got pressurized he would lose his temper, and there were incidents in which he shouted and swore at customers or other staff. His support worker suggested that he explain his condition to these people so that they would make less demands of him.

Target cognitions I know my problems with temper outbursts are because my head injury has made me slow at processing stuff, but if I tell people about it, it can only make things worse. They'll think I'm a spastic (that's what I used to think about disabled people before this happened to me).

Alternative perspective People can be quite understanding if they are given a reason for something. If I tell them what my problem is, I will be managing the situation, it won't be managing me.

Predictions If the target belief is true, then when I tell people what my problem is they will be abusive towards me. If the alternative belief is true, then they will be sympathetic and allow me to handle the situation my way.

Operationalizing the predictions Fred agreed a form of words that he would say when too many demands were being made of him at work: 'I've had a head injury, my short-term memory has been affected, and I can only do one thing at a time. Please be patient and I will deal with you when I have finished with this customer.'

Experiment Fred used this strategy in the work situation. His support worker spent some time observing him and recording what happened, to aid Fred's memory of events.

Results When Fred used this technique, customers agreed to wait their turn. No customer was verbally abusive towards him, and staff gave him some space. There were no more incidents in which he lost his temper.

Reflection Fred was surprised that the technique had worked so well and described an increased sense of self-respect in the work setting. On the other hand, he said that he deeply resented being in a situation in which he had to use such techniques. He did not feel that he could use a technique like this with his friends or partner; its usefulness was confined to interactions with strangers.

Tips Self-advocacy is reported here as a means of reducing angry outbursts, but it is not primarily an anger management technique. It is an important skill for people with disabilities, especially those with communication or cognitive problems. Feeling confident in using the technique requires behavioural experiments that are aimed at challenging the belief that others will respond unhelpfully to people who draw attention to their disability. Unfortunately, negative attitudes to people with disability remain fairly widespread in society. The experiments may first need to be carried out in a protected or artificial environment. The less friendly, real world calls for experiments that allow for rejecting or abusive responses to the disabled person.

Distinctive difficulties

Working with people who have a medical condition

There may be risks associated with some behavioural experiments with certain patients (e.g. inducing a seizure or further stroke, or adversely affecting motor function). Close contact with the patient's general practitioner and, if relevant, medical consultant and physiotherapist should ensure the construction of appropriate experiments. In general, significant medical risks are rare.

Working with people who have cognitive impairment

Where possible, the patient's cognitive problems should be identified by means of an assessment carried out by a clinical neuropsychologist. It is also essential to interview the patient and a relative or friend to gain information about everyday cognitive function.

Behavioural experiments may need to be relatively less demanding to take into account reduced cognitive stamina (almost ubiquitous in any condition affecting the brain) and physical limitations. Patients with memory problems whose reading ability is intact can be greatly helped by the use of diaries, written records of the rationale of the treatment approach, and flashcards to use *in situ*, reminding them of cognitive techniques. Their rate of learning will be slow, so more experiments and more therapy sessions may be needed to achieve an effect comparable to that of a person with normal memory function.

Patients with damage to the frontal lobes can often have difficulties in executive function. This can show itself as rigid and concrete thinking styles and as difficulty initiating thought and action. The style of cognitive therapy here needs to be highly directive, especially in generating alternative perspectives on problems, as these patients can get stuck in particular ways of thinking and acting. They also benefit from forced choice rather than open-ended questioning because of their problems in generating thoughts and ideas from scratch.

In general, cognitive problems are at their worst during times of emotional arousal and distress. This may affect the degree of arousal that therapist and patient are prepared to tolerate in a behavioural experiment.

Formulation: a wide range of factors which may contribute to a problem

It is important to be aware of the danger of misattributing behaviour to emotional factors when it is due to cognitive impairment *and vice versa*. For instance, a person may show rigid adherence to a particularly negative view because of depressed mood, executive impairment, or a combination of both; another may have problems with irritable and aggressive behaviour because of anger at her situation or because of cognitive overload, or both; another person may deny any problems in his abilities or relationships because of psychological denial or an organically based lack of awareness, or both; another may struggle to complete homework tasks due to memory impairment or motivational factors, or both. Teasing these issues out can be very difficult (see Prigatano 1999), but it is an enormous help for the therapist at least to be aware of the issues, and potential alternative formulations of the problem.

It is important not to fall into the trap of attributing all problems to the brain injury. Some may have predated the injury; some may have happened anyway. A fairly common scenario is for a mother with ABI to attribute the deterioration in her relationship with a teenage daughter to her own inadequacy and acquired disability, idealizing the early childhood relationship from a time when she was able-bodied. Normalizing the changes that occur in parent–child relationships over time can be immensely helpful in this type of situation.

Recognizing emotional behaviour

It is important to be alert to signals of emotion in these patients. Some people are highly expressive, but others can appear 'flat' and subdued because of their disability, unable to use body language, facial expression, or tone of voice to convey emotion. They may be highly aroused and distressed, but this may only become evident on careful questioning.

On the other hand, excessive or exaggerated emotional reactions, such as weeping or anger outbursts can also occur. These may be mediated through a general loss of emotional control arising directly from the brain injury. Such excessive reactions are rarely meaningless and may reflect genuine concerns of the patient (McGrath 2000), but they need to be recognized for what they are, and managed as part of a general cognitive therapeutic approach.

Experiments in which the results are potentially distressing

Where insight difficulties or denial of disability are present, the nature of the cognitions to be tested is the opposite to that most commonly encountered in adult mental health work. The overly positive beliefs of some brain-injured patients may be just as maladaptive as the overly negative beliefs of the adult mental health patient. They may result in short term positive mood but longer term distress due to excessive failure experiences for which the patient is unprepared. Experiments which challenge positive, perhaps defensive, cognitions may consequently require more sensitive handling and careful follow-up, as they often lead to a reduction in positive mood.

Experiments that 'don't work'

The degree of certainty of the outcome of behavioural experiments in this group is often significantly reduced. An experiment may be as much for the benefit of the therapist as it is for the patient. It may, for example, test both the patient's potential lack of insight and consequent overestimation of his fitness, or the potential underestimation of fitness by the therapist due to the limitation in ecological validity of psychometric assessment instruments.

Sometimes the results of a behavioural experiment seem clearly to contradict the target cognition and support an alternative belief, yet patients will persist in holding on to their original belief because they claim that the experiment was not a good test of the belief in question. This commonly occurs when the issue is the patient's overestimation of level of function. For instance, failing to complete a simulated work task in the time allocated is attributed to the task being a poor simulation of the real work environment rather than to changed ability levels. Conversely, patients who are convinced that they have become so disabled that their lives are no longer worthwhile may dismiss the positive outcome of a behavioural experiment as trivial when compared with their previous level of social and occupational function. Such a patient might move from, 'I'm so disabled that I can't even put my own socks on' to, 'So—I did an experiment and found I *could* put my own socks on—big deal!'

It is vital to get clear agreement that the experiment is a reasonable test of the belief before carrying it out. However, patients may change their mind later, claiming that they only realized that the experiment was flawed after they had begun to participate. It is possible to ask patients to construct a better experiment. They may respond by setting unrealistically stringent conditions, so that it is easy for them to rationalize evidence that challenges their beliefs by saying that the experiment did not meet their original conditions.

The problem here is not with the experiments themselves but with patients' approach to them, welcoming the experimental method exclusively as a means of confirming their existing world view, and not a means of modifying it. This indicates that this world view, or the view of self, is at once highly cherished and deeply threatened. Behavioural experiments on their own will not address the core issues for these patients, who may benefit from a schema-focused approach to their psychological therapy and a multidisciplinary approach to their rehabilitation in general (McGrath and Adams 1999).

Other relevant chapters

The following chapters are likely to contain material that is helpful in working with people with ABI: Chapter 6 on generalized anxiety disorder; Chapter 7 on social anxiety; Chapter 9 on post-traumatic stress disorder; Chapter 10 on depression; Chapter 15 on physical health problems; and Chapter 20 on low self-esteem.

Further reading

Gass, C.S. and Brown, M.C. (1992). Neuropsychological test feedback to patients with brain dysfunction. *Psychological Assessment, 4*, 272–7.

Khan–Bourne, N. and Brown, R.G. (2003). Cognitive behaviour therapy for the treatment of depression in individuals with brain injury. *Neuropsychological Rehabilitation, 13*, 89–107.

McGrath, J. and Adams, L. (1999). Patient-centred goal planning: a systemic psychological therapy? *Topics in Stroke Rehabilitation, 6*, 43–50.

Prigatano, G.P. (1999). *Principles of neuropsychological rehabilitation.* Oxford University Press, New York.

Williams, H.W., Evans, J.J. and Fleminger, S. (2003). Neurorehabilitation and cognitive-behaviour therapy of anxiety disorders after brain injury. *Neuropsychological Rehabilitation, 13*, 133–48.

Tales from the Front Line
Not a fertile idea

Sean, a 20-year-old medical student, had partially recovered from his first psychotic episode. All those involved in his care became concerned when Sean became increasingly unwilling to take his anti-psychotic medication. On further discussion it became clear that Sean had grown convinced that the medication would threaten his fertility, a concern not easily dispelled by numerous educational chats with staff. Upon discovering that Sean owned (and knew how to use) a microscope, the team psychologist asked Sean, "What do you think might be happening to your sperm?" "Dead", came the unequivocal reply. "Is there any way of checking that?", enquired the psychologist. "Sure thing", said Sean, looking sheepish.

A few days later as the psychologist arrived for a team meeting she was greeted by groans and dirty looks. Unaccustomed to such a reception she sought to discover the source of the team's malcontent. Team members replied in unison, "You put the idea in his head, now you make him stop".

CHAPTER 17

Avoidance of affect

Gillian Butler
Christina Surawy

Introduction

People who avoid affect avoid feelings and emotions. This means that they avoid experiencing feelings and expressing feelings, and they may also avoid provoking the experience and the expression of feelings in others. As is common in people who experience strong anxiety, avoidance is provoked by fear. Feelings in all their manifestations have become a source of threat, and the possibility of experiencing them, showing them, talking about them, or eliciting them in others induces a sense of vulnerability.[1]

People who avoid affect attempt to reduce perceived risks and use safety behaviours which dampen feelings down internally. Common safety behaviours include distraction, joking, intellectualizing, changing the topic, and disengaging. More dysfunctional, emotionally numbing safety behaviours include dissociating, binge eating, drinking, drug taking, and deliberate self-harm.

Those people who have a poorly developed vocabulary for feelings may find it hard to distinguish one from another and to recognize these feelings in themselves as well as in others.

Avoidance of affect is not a diagnosis, but occurs in many disorders. It is particularly common in avoidant personality disorder, social anxiety, and health anxiety; it is often described by people who have suffered from abuse, violence, or emotional neglect, and by some with binge eating disorder. Common consequences include difficulties in forming and keeping relationships, low self-esteem, and increases in physical, as opposed to psychological, symptoms.

---

[1]We have omitted reference here to psychopathy and narcissism in which reduced affect is conceptualized in terms of poor empathy rather than avoidance.

Cognitive models

The general principles applied in therapy are consistent with Beck *et al.*'s (1985) notion that anxiety arises when perceived threats outweigh perceived resources (internal and external) for dealing with them. Internal threats, such as the sensations associated with emotional arousal, are particularly important. Resources for dealing with such threats, in order to keep feelings hidden or to keep their expression within supposed limits of acceptability, are likely to be perceived as inadequate. For a detailed account of avoidance of affect as it occurs specifically in avoidant personality disorder, see Padesky and Beck (2003*a*).

General cognitive features

Anxiety is about what might happen, but has not yet happened, so typical cognitions reflect an element of uncertainty and are often rather vague: 'If this goes on, I'll lose it', 'This feels horrible; I need to get away'. Other people often feel too close for comfort. Themes of threat, risk, and danger predominate, leading to anxiety-provoking expectations and predictions: 'I'll be shown up', 'I won't be able to handle this'. These are important, but can be hard to verbalize, and may sound more like a 'felt sense' that occurs when exposed to something strange but alarming, than a thought.

People who avoid affect show three kinds of cognitive biases. First, attentional biases determine what is noticed. They include hypervigilance and selective attention to signs of emotion, in oneself and in others (e.g. noticing sensations, the tone of voice others use, or their frowns). Second, interpretations are consistent with underlying attitudes: 'I'm not safe here', 'It is wrong to let your feelings show'. Third, selective and state-dependent memory both confirm and endorse the biases: remembering being scolded for crying or being bullied for getting angry; memories of feeling pain and receiving a cold, rejecting response; or memories of being bewildered by feelings for which one had no name. Memories may be encapsulated in a powerful sense of being at risk and specific meaning-packed images or dreams.

In extreme cases, giving voice to the fears (verbalizing thoughts, expectations, predictions, assumptions, ideas, attitudes, etc.) threatens to bring feelings with it, and is also avoided. Negative automatic thoughts are especially hard to identify when the behaviours associated with them have been successful. Stifling feelings of hostility, or of affection, reduces the risk of becoming 'emotional'. So cognitions may be hard to access, and patients may deny having relevant thoughts, as if they have shut down the links between cognition and emotion. Being asked to 'open up' is for them like entering unknown, and potentially dangerous territory. They give the impression of thinking 'I can't go there', 'I mustn't let this happen', without being able to put such thoughts into words.

For such people the content of underlying beliefs may relate closely to their fear of affect so that activating, or threatening to activate, them will be associated with intense distress. Then people go out of their way to avoid doing or saying anything that feels even slightly emotional. A hint of anger, or of friendliness, may be sufficient to trigger a massive retreat, and make it hard subsequently to explain their experiences to the therapist.

Patients' reports also suggest that their attention may be diverted towards other aspects of experience such as activities, achievements, verbal behaviour, or physical sensations. A significant subgroup pay attention to physiological rather than psychological aspects of emotion, and their cognitions focus correspondingly on bodily changes and discomfort.

Hypotheses about aetiology

We suggest that avoidance of affect typically derives from:

- ◆ Experience: e.g. belonging to a family in which talking about feelings is not customary or acceptable; painful or traumatic events that produce discomfort with feelings, such as humiliation, criticism, betrayal, rejection, bullying, cruelty, etc.

- ◆ Genetic or biological variation: e.g. in speed of arousal or sensitivity to physiological changes.

- ◆ Cultural factors, determined for example by race, nationality, gender, age, or religion. These influence the degree and type of emotional expression that is considered acceptable within a particular group. Avoidance of affect occurs in some people when cultural norms are threatened.

- ◆ Post-traumatic stress disorder following specific (Type I) trauma, which is often associated with symptoms of emotional numbing.

Key cognitions

Although anxiety about affect can be described as instinctive, and specific cognitions may apparently be absent, three kinds of cognitive factors play a central role in its maintenance. Behavioural experiments can be devised for tackling each of these.

The meaning of having feelings

People who try to dampen down or stifle their feelings, especially negative ones such as anger or sadness, presumably do so partly because of what experiencing emotions means to them. Typical meanings include being weak, being liable to lose control or be overwhelmed, and being unable to cope. Experiencing feelings may seem to be impossible without precipitating a 'catastrophe' such as sliding into deep depression or becoming violently angry. Images, memories, and nightmares often reflect these meanings. They may be based on painful and traumatic experiences such as being bullied, criticized, excluded, or exploited, and they may be derived from what is considered acceptable within the boundaries of gender, family values, or culture.

Assumptions about the sort of person who experiences emotion, or about the values associated with certain feelings, are often culturally accepted (e.g. 'A strong person should not have feelings which are disturbing or difficult', 'It is bad to feel jealous or angry', or 'It is wrong not to feel affectionate and grateful').

The meaning of expressing feelings

Thoughts associated with talking about or showing emotion are often related to beliefs about the perceptions others may have should this happen (e.g. the fear of being evaluated as weak, silly, childish, a burden, or incomprehensible). Beliefs may also reflect how others are expected to feel or behave in response to expression of feelings (e.g. they will be upset or unable to handle it; dismissive, rejecting, or controlling; hostile, aggressive, or abusive).

The self-protective rules and assumptions that govern behaviour link with low self-esteem, and with a sense of being painfully exposed and vulnerable. Dominant themes concern acceptability and behaviour that will lead to rejection or humiliation: 'Others will discover the real me if I open up, and reject me'. People may have good evidence for their assumptions and beliefs from their experience, family values, and culture: 'If you get close you will get hurt', 'No-one wants to know how I feel. No-one cares', 'People will take advantage if you show any sign of weakness', 'Being emotional is completely unacceptable and wrong', 'It is shameful to admit to feeling unconfident/scared/sad', 'Disagreements should be kept hidden', 'Men should be able to hide their sadness'.

People who disclose or talk about emotion may be assumed to be weak, immature, controlling, gossipy, or 'out of order' in some way. Misconceptions may exist about how others experience and deal with feelings: 'No-one else seems to feel this distressed', 'Everyone else can control themselves better than me'.

Confusion about affect

Being unable to label feelings or understand their significance causes confusion and uncertainty, and gives rise to a wide variety of cognitions. It is as if people know that something is missing without knowing what; or as if an important dimension of experience is impaired or unavailable. Then it can be hard to understand what others mean by what they say or to interpret their facial expressions, communications, and behaviours. Recognizing that something that is routine for others is fraught with difficulty for oneself has an impact on self-opinion. Patients who avoid affect may think of themselves as weird, different, unacceptable, or defective.

People who do not understand the relevance of emotion, or find it hard to label what they are feeling or to distinguish one state of high arousal from another, may focus predominantly on the bodily sensations that accompany arousal, and complain of physical ailments at times of stress, worry, or sadness. They are often puzzled, irritated, or insulted by the suggestion that psychological factors are relevant, and confused in the face of emotional experience in general—their own, or that of others—without knowing how to respond to it.

When emotional distress remains frequent (e.g. in some cases of borderline personality disorder), people can be unable to distinguish between different types of high arousal (excitement, anticipation, fear, terror) or between different ways of 'feeling bad'. They may confuse signs of physical illness with emotional distress, and more readily seek medical, rather than psychological, help (or social support) when in need. Extreme fear of intense feelings can lead people to disengage from them, to dissociate, binge eat, drink, or self-harm.

Some people are scared of all unfamiliar feelings, including positive ones. For them, emotional arousal, positive or negative, is strange, alarming, or disconcerting, and any degree of arousal may be experienced as intense. This can be understood in a variety of ways, leading to different kinds of behavioural experiment. For example, it might reflect a normal response to novelty, or it might be an understandable consequence of the experience of being hurt or exploited by people who were also a source of love, care, or support. Behavioural experiments that help the person to ascertain the implications of current ambivalence in relationships can be clarifying, and reduce confusion.

Behavioural experiments

◆ **Changing thoughts about having feelings**
  Experiment 17.1: grounding affect in sensation
  Experiment 17.2: testing fear of consequences
  Experiment 17.3: fear of feeling worse

Table 17.1: further suggestions for changing thoughts about having feelings

◆ **Changing thoughts about expressing feelings**
  Experiment 17.4: changing lifelong habits
  Experiment 17.5: anticipated rejection
  Experiment 17.6: assumptions about being pathetic

Table 17.2: further suggestions for changing thoughts about expressing feelings

◆ **Reducing confusion about affect**
  Experiment 17.7: a 'felt sense' of discomfort
  Experiment 17.8: accepting intense feelings
  Experiment 17.9: culture-specific confusion
  Experiment 17.10: unfinished business

Table 17.3: further suggestions for reducing confusion about affect

---

Behavioural experiments may be devised to explore thoughts, assumptions, or beliefs, and single experiments may be relevant to all three aspects of cognition. For example, experiments involving interactions with others may provoke feelings and provide opportunities for expressing feelings and for reducing underlying confusion.

General considerations:

◆ For people who avoid affect, thoughts as well as feelings may be shadowy, and the purpose of the experiment may be to identify and clarify cognitions.
◆ Talking about feelings instead of expressing them is a common safety behaviour.

Changing thoughts about having feelings

The main purpose of these experiments is to help people to accept their feelings and to feel more comfortable with them; to foster more functional adaptation. It is not to trigger high affect in the session.

Experiment 17.1: grounding affect in sensation

Problem Whenever Pru felt criticized or hurt, she automatically went into a state of dissociation, described as 'going out of my body', in which she could not speak and felt physically weak. Her experience may also have been that of intense anxiety. It was impossible in therapy to work with either feelings or thoughts at the core of her problems.

Target cognition Experiencing hurt is too painful and I need to escape. (This was more a felt sense than an articulated belief.)

Alternative perspective If I find a way of staying with the emotion, then it might help me to deal more effectively with the way I respond to feeling criticized or rejected.

Prediction Staying with the sensations will make me very upset. The pain will get more and more intense and I'll have to go out of my body, and stay out of my body, for even longer.

Experiment The therapist and Pru agreed to talk about an occasion when she had felt criticized in the session. As soon as she started to go out of her body (clutching at the chair, looking pale and limp), the therapist asked her to focus on each part of her body in turn, suggesting that she concentrate on what she was experiencing physically, starting with her feet and legs.

Results Pru was able to stay more connected to her experience as she felt it in her body, rather than escaping from it by going out of her body. After several sessions of doing this, Pru described a deep pain in her abdomen which she was able to stay with for the first time.

Reflection Discovering that her predictions were wrong helped Pru to work more cognitively with her difficulties. Tolerating the pain in her abdomen taught her that she could respond more constructively than by escaping. As she built on the experience of grounding herself in physical sensations, she started to talk more easily about emotions.

Further work Pru practised this skill whenever she noticed that she was reacting in her usual way to emotional upset (the main trigger being the sensation in her abdomen). She practised staying with sensations daily, using a tape, for several weeks. Later she worked on assertiveness in response to both emotions and cognitions.

Tip Staying with bodily sensations as a way of relating to strongly experienced emotion is one aspect of mindfulness-based cognitive therapy (MBCT, Segal *et al.* 2002), and may also be useful.

Experiment 17.2: testing fear of consequences

Problem Anna came from a strict religious background in which self-sufficiency and stoicism were encouraged. She was referred with chronic fatigue syndrome (CFS). She kept constantly busy to keep difficult thoughts and feelings at bay.

Target cognition If I allow in or explore negative thoughts and emotions, I will become depressed and more tired and unable to carry on with my housework and looking after the children.

Alternative perspective If I develop strategies to identify and challenge my difficult thoughts and emotions, I will feel less like they are in control of me, and more like I am in control of them. Avoiding them might also make me more tired by pushing me into overexerting myself and being unable to relax.

Prediction Anna thought that if she gave any space to experiencing and exploring her emotions and thoughts she would feel depressed and fatigued and be less able to function physically (e.g. look after children, do house-work).

Experiment Over three weeks, Anna experimented with recording (rather than avoiding) her negative thoughts and emotions (e.g. 'I'm a failure', 'I'm not good enough'), her activities, and her level of fatigue (rated 0–5). In the sessions she challenged and questioned the thoughts.

Results Anna quickly saw the benefit of challenging the thoughts that accompanied her low mood, and her belief in her concern about being overwhelmed diminished from 80% to 30%. She used the information from exploring her thoughts in session to plan her day, and her fatigue ratings fell from an average of 4 to 3.

Reflection Anna realized that dealing with difficult thoughts and feelings, rather than avoiding them, helped her to complete tasks through better planning and feeling less tired. She also achieved a greater sense of control over her life and an understanding of the role of psychological factors in CFS.

Tip Experiments of this sort are useful with any patients who doubt the relevance of psychological factors.

Experiment 17.3: fear of feeling worse

Problem Josh believed that facing his loneliness would lower his mood to the extent that he would need in-patient treatment.

Target cognitions I will become depressed if I allow myself to feel lonely instead of distracting myself by working.

Alternative perspective Feelings of loneliness can be worked with constructively. This was a tentative hypothesis, as Josh had no idea how this could be done.

Experiment Josh recorded his emotions and thoughts and began to work on practical strategies to deal with the loneliness by signing up for evening classes.

Result His feelings of loneliness became somewhat more tolerable as a result of changing his behaviour and talking about them in the sessions. Further experiments tested Josh's assumption that he always needed to feel and behave in a jolly way, to be the 'life and soul', to be liked by others—which kept him from going out to meet people. His mood improved slowly as he worked on his relationships and emotions.

Reflection Strong negative feelings are less frightening if one can work with them.

Table 17.1 lists additional suggestions for experiments.

Table 17.1 Further suggestions for changing thoughts about having feelings

Thought to be tested	Suggested experiments	Potential value
I've got to stop this getting worse.	Let it come and let it go (e.g. using MBCT, distraction, working to accept feelings as normal).	Discovering that, although it feels bad, the feeling moves on, decreases, and eventually dies away.
I have to keep talking (or keep occupied) to keep my feelings in check.	Graduated periods of quiet or relaxation without being busy.	Learning to pay attention to feelings without shying away from them.
The only way to stop these bad feelings is to eat (or drink or sleep or cut).	Name the feelings and write them down; talk to someone; work at self-soothing and (functional) distraction. Later, work out how to make sense of the feelings in terms of the past.	Building up functional ways of dealing with feelings; discovering that avoiding the feelings makes them more frightening.
Allowing myself to feel something positive (happy, excited, interested, pleased) is too scary. I can't let it go on.	Attend to the feeling and give it a name. Relax into it. Later: work out what makes better feelings feel so dangerous. Are they associated with painful experiences?	Although it feels strange I can get used to it. Good feelings pass too. It's normal for them to come and go. No need to get depressed when they go
It's best not to go there ('felt sense' rather than a thought). It can be followed by joking, changing the topic, intellectualizing, etc.	In-session experiments— return to the topic, explore the meaning or origins, try describing the sensations, reflect own feelings, etc.	Aim for discovery that own feelings, and those of others, can be trusted as a source of information and means of relating to others.

Changing thoughts about expressing feelings

Experiment 17.4: changing lifelong habits

Problem Jackie had been brought up in a family in which all feelings (good and bad) were suppressed, and in which she was ostracized and punished for expressing them. The punishment was worse if the expression had been public (i.e. outside the family home). Neither of her parents showed any affection to her or her siblings. Jackie was unable to talk to her husband, children, or GP about her feelings.

Target cognition Talking about feelings is wrong, shameful, and leads to rejection.

Alternative perspective Talking about feelings will reveal whether it matters, and whether it makes a difference to how I feel.

Preparatory work Jackie recognized that she needed to try expressing different feelings, in different settings, in different ways. First, she learned how to identify her expectations and to make predictions about the impact of putting her feelings into words in therapy. She applied the lessons learned in therapy first in her family, and then extended the practice outside the family.

Predictions and experiments In summary, Jackie did four main experiments spread over six weeks:

1 In therapy, she spoke for the first time about the events surrounding a neighbour's death that she thought revealed her callousness. She predicted that this would disgust anyone who heard the story, including the therapist.

2 She told a cousin how sad she felt about her childhood, and that she was scared of showing her true feelings. She predicted that he would be bored and quickly close the conversation.

3 Despite predicting that her son would shrug her off, she gave him a hug as he left for school.

4 She told her GP that she was worried about recent headaches. She predicted he would dismiss her worries as 'psychological' and be irritated with her for wasting his time.

Results Jackie's predictions were wrong: she was neither rejected nor shamed, and her tentative conclusion was that maybe others thought differently about showing feelings than she did.

Reflection She remained uncertain about what was acceptable, and she realized that it would take practice before she would be able to express emotions without feeling apprehensive and vulnerable. She tried to find words for a new, more helpful belief that fitted with her observations. Her first attempt was 'Being myself is alright'.

Further work Jackie kept a positive data log based on her new belief. The therapist took care to ensure that she practised expressing feelings that could lead to disagreements or anger (especially within the family). It was necessary, repeatedly, to refer to the formulation of her problems in terms of the products of painful experiences rather than in terms of her inherent inadequacy or badness.

Tip Patients may find this type of work exhausting and benefit from a slow pace.

Experiment 17.5: anticipated rejection

Problem Sandy was concerned about disclosing her true feelings, believing that saying that she was upset, particularly to people that she knew well, would lead to automatic rejection.

Target cognitions If I tell my friend that I am puzzled and upset because she has not spoken to me and seems to be avoiding me, she will get angry and blame me, and our friendship will end.

Alternative perspective She may react differently and be prepared to listen. If I don't say how I'm feeling, I will continue to feel horrible and our friendship will suffer anyway.

Prediction Sandy was unsure whether her target cognitions or the alternative perspective were more likely (this was a discovery experiment).

Preparation for the experiment Sandy predicted her friend's possible reactions, and discussed how she might respond. She role played what she wanted to say in the session and practised speaking in an assertive but considerate and understanding way.

Experiment Sandy told her friend how she felt and why.

Results Her friend initially became angry, saying that she had a lot of problems to deal with and could do without any others. Sandy felt uncomfortable at first, then felt better that she had at least expressed herself. Later, the friend came round and said how important the friendship was to her and they talked again.

Reflection Saying what I feel may not always end a relationship. It can make me feel better to bring things out into the open, and can add a new dimension of understanding to a friendship.

Tip This kind of experiment would be harder for someone with strongly negative self-schema. It may need to be repeated in different situations, and could be followed by asking the patient to obtain feedback from the person they fear will reject them. This kind of fear can also be tested using surveys, patients could use imaginal role play to rehearse a range of responses, or they could list reasons for the rejecting behaviour and distribute them on a pie chart.

Experiment 17.6: assumptions about being pathetic

Problem Six months after a difficult operation, Jean was still adjusting to periods of feeling unwell and tired. She felt she should be back to normal by now, and avoided talking to friends about how miserable she felt.

Target cognition and prediction I can't tell anyone how I really feel because they will think that I should be over it by now and that I'm pathetic.

Alternative perspective There may be some people who like to know how I feel so they can be helpful and feel closer to me, rather than judge me. I can choose to whom and how much I disclose.

Experiment Jean chose a reasonably close friend and told her that she felt miserable at times, that she thought she ought to be better by now, and that it was pathetic not to be and to feel fed up.

Results Jean's friend said she was glad to have been told and had realized that something was wrong but had felt unable to help. She had no view as to whether Jean should be better by now as she did not know the normal time scale for recovery. The friend also said that anyone who had been through so much must find it difficult to cope at times and she did not consider it pathetic.

Reflection Jean concluded that she had no evidence from this friend that she was pathetic and should be feeling better. She followed it up by contacting others who had had similar operations and by gradually disclosing her feelings to more people.

Table 17.2 lists additional suggestions for experiments.

Reducing confusion about affect

Experiment 17.7: a 'felt sense' of discomfort

Problem Harry relied on his work for his sense of value, and had few friendships. After work, when mentally and physically exhausted, he felt a strong sense of discomfort from which he escaped by going to bed.

Target cognition I'm uncomfortable. I need to go to bed. (This was more a 'felt sense' than an articulated thought.)

Table 17.2 Further suggestions for changing thoughts about expressing feelings

Thought to be tested	Suggested experiments	Potential value
If I say something angry, I will lose it and get violent.	Tune in to anger early. Practise assertive methods of expressing anger.	Discovering that the feeling is not dangerous, and that talking can clarify issues and sometimes resolve them.
It's best to pretend I'm OK even when I'm not. Talk about something else.	Own up to my feelings instead. Start by saying: 'I feel . . .'.	Discover that people could usually tell something was wrong, without knowing what it was
Old assumptions about self-disclosure: e.g. it's a sign of weakness, of not coping.	Survey by patient and/or therapist of opinions about self-disclosure.	Normalize expression of feelings.
New assumptions: e.g. If I am more open and friendly, others will be more pleasant and caring to me.	Series of experiments, startingwith easier people and less intense feelings.	Increasing fluency and variety of expression; confidence and friendship.
Once I start—crying, feeling sad, feeling angry—it will never stop.	Practise (e.g. using imagery or verbal methods) eliciting feelings,expressing them, and moving on.	Discovering how to control both experience and expression (resolving confusion about feelings as mysterious, etc.).

Alternative perspective Understanding the discomfort may provide ideas about how to develop a more helpful response to it.

Experiment The therapist evoked the sense of discomfort in the session by focusing on a recent event. They planned to investigate it together.

Results Harry described an image of being in a deep pit with no way out, and he drew the image. He first remembered similar feelings when he was teased at school and could tell no one about it, and concluded: 'I'm not liked', 'I'm no good', 'There's no way of stopping this'. The experiment enabled him to link this image to his current wish to blot out discomfort quickly. These meanings were used to give tentative labels to the emotions: fear, sadness, and hopelessness.

Reflection Knowing what the feelings are and where they come from makes them less confusing and less frightening.

Further work Harry practised focusing on the feelings by representing them in drawings rather than retreating to bed. He learned to distinguish exhaustion and fatigue from emotional distress, and this work helped him to tackle his self-critical thinking and (slowly) to widen his range of out-of-work activities.

Experiment 17.8: accepting intense feelings

Problem Sarah had a diagnosis of borderline personality disorder, felt severely distressed, and became increasingly out of control after her college tutor said about a piece of her work: 'That's interesting, but it wasn't quite what I meant'. She was bombarded by a stream of (familiar) thoughts—'I can't ever do anything right', 'This is horrible', 'I can't control this'—and wished to burn herself. She said she knew the feelings would stop if she did.

Target cognitions I deserve to be punished. I'm bad and useless. I can't handle this. I have to stop these feelings somehow.

Alternative perspective The feelings are frightening and reminiscent of the past—hence the need to stop them. However, avoiding paying attention to them means that they remain confusing, and the self-destructive cycle continues.

Experiment Sarah undertook a discovery experiment to see what would happen if she paid attention to her feelings. She planned to tune in to them as early as possible, and to try to give them a name. Rather than hurt herself, she would try to acknowledge the severity of her pain and decide how to look after herself (just as she would look after someone else who was in pain).

Results She was able to interrupt the cycle that led to self-harming behaviours rarely at first, but this gradually became easier.

Further work Sarah extended the range of ways in which she explored her feelings (drawing, writing, etc), so as to discover what they meant. During the next stage, Sarah learned how and when to seek help and comfort, and increased her self-soothing skills.

Reflection (reached after extended practice) I don't believe in punishment as a way of teaching anybody anything, including me. It doesn't help.

Experiment 17.9: culture-specific confusion

Problem Mike's partner Rachel complained that he seemed either to be completely unresponsive or unpredictably explosive. Mike sought help because their relationship was at risk, and because his explosiveness was also causing problems at work. As therapy progressed it became clear that he had few words for feelings, and experienced his outbursts as unpredictable and puzzling.

Target cognitions and prediction I don't think I have feelings. I feel blank most of the time. I wouldn't know how to recognize them.

Experiment Mike undertook a discovery experiment to determine if his target cognitions were true. In the session, together with the therapist, he made a list of emotion words. During the next week, as often as possible, and in as many different situations as possible, he ticked off those which came up in himself, and marked in another way those that he noticed in someone else (at home, at work, or on the television).

Results In the first week he could only find signs of feelings 'coming up' in others. However, gradually, he became better at finding them in himself, especially when the experiment was repeated during a therapy session. Mike commented that he had not realized before that so many feelings were mixed, and this helped him to understand why it was hard to name them.

Reflection Mike was astonished to discover how often feelings came up in his life, and how many different ones he experienced. He said that previously the 'normal' ones had been like shadows, and that he had lived in dread of them as potentially overwhelming or explosive.

Experiment 17.10: unfinished business

Problem Ruth and her older brothers had been neglected by their mother all their lives, emotionally and physically. When her mother died, Ruth was unexpectedly distressed. She described herself as inconsolable, and could not understand why, as she had thought she had left the past behind 15 years ago. She had started having nightmares in which she felt overwhelmed by desperation and hopelessness.

Target cognitions I'm terrified of these feelings. They could make me founder completely. I can't let them surface.

Preparation for experiment Prior to the development of an alternative perspective, Ruth and her therapist reviewed her early history, searching for the experience of similar feelings. She remembered countless moments of feeling a similar kind of 'despair', together with specific memories from her childhood.

Alternative perspective (in outline) Ruth was grieving for her lost childhood, and had now to accept that she would never know more about why the neglect had happened, or be able to question her mother further.

Prediction Expressing feelings will help to resolve them.

Experiments Ruth explored a variety of ways of expressing her feelings. She wrote letters to her mother in which she expressed desperate, hopeless, and confused thoughts and feelings. She said things that she had never dared say previously. She spoke to her brothers about their shared memories, but in order to do so had to overcome the habitual style of affectless communication adopted by the whole family. Although little was said, this allowed Ruth to understand why she found her feelings so confusing. She went with one brother to visit her mother's grave, and she read about grieving. Finally, she recognized deep hidden resentments that her mother was, after death, still causing her so much pain. Experiments to change her lifestyle in ways she had always wished to, but never dared try, helped at this stage to resolve her anger, and to help her feel that she could move on.

Reflection Ruth chose the experiments herself, and may have had a sense of what she needed to do first to initiate the emotional processing. She came to realize that her sadness was profound, but not after all too confusing to understand or too overwhelming to face. Her nightmares ceased.

Table 17.3 lists additional suggestions for experiments.

Distinctive difficulties

Bombardment

Using a 'barrage' of Socratic questions when talking with patients about their feelings may feel like being subjected to the Spanish Inquisition. Other useful methods include: using statements ('I would like to hear more about that'); reflections that help patients think about what they have just said; and comments about feelings ('That sounds disappointing', 'Hearing about that makes me feel quite angry').

Discomfort

Unless comfortable with the experience and the expression of emotions within therapy, patients may drop out or attend reluctantly. Therapists should be sensitive to non-verbal behaviour (body posture, tone of voice, etc.), and to placement of furniture. If chairs are too close or placed face to face, it is hard to look up without making eye contact and feeling threatened. Painful early experiences can make it hard to trust or to form relationships, so interpersonal issues within therapy should be considered early, and included in the formulation.

Table 17.3 Further suggestions for reducing confusion about affect

Thought to be tested	Suggested experiments	Potential value
It's best not to think. Just do what seems best.	Stop to think, and pay attention to the feelings that emerge.	Breaking a habit learned in childhood: 'If you don't think about it, it won't hurt'.
Feelings aren't important.	Record feelings, thoughts, and consequences (i.e. Does this feeling make me want to do (or say) anything? Does it affect my life in some way?) Use thought records.	Linking behaviour and thoughts with feelings, and evaluating their importance.
I can't put my feelings into words	Watch video clips and help the patient to name feelings from posture, expression, etc. Practise exaggerating these and naming them until they become familiar.	Learn the signals and practise giving approximate names.
I never know what my partner is feeling.	Try asking them: 'What are you feeling?' Make a guess on the basis of how they look. Think: 'If I was in their shoes, how would I feel?'	Discover that knowing the feelings helps to explain their behaviour, etc.
I can't sort one feeling out from another.	Use specific examples. Try to label feelings in terms of context, physiological cues, thoughts, memories, etc.— When your wife shouted at you, what did you notice in your body? What was your posture like? Can you demonstrate? Have you seen other people looking like this? If so, what do you think they were feeling? Have you felt like this before? When?	Learning to identify feelings in terms of distinctive markers that people can look out for (and then act on).

Shutdown

Emotional withdrawal may be a better indication of (potential) belief activation than 'hot cognitions'.

Intensity

Experiencing a wider range of emotions, and more intense emotions than usual, can be alarming. Cooling down methods can help patients tolerate intense feelings and persist with the work (e.g. moving in and out of feeling states, working on the white board or on paper, or using written material and drawings).

Memory

Counterschematic material is easily forgotten. After an unusual emotional interaction (e.g. a row, sharing some personal information), someone who avoids affect may not remember details, even when the physiological after-effects, such as tension or severe apprehension, are still present. To initiate a search for this material it is important to understand the type of information that someone typically screens out. Positive data logs can also be helpful and can generate specific memories, which are then more easily accessible than are the general impressions which tend to be formed when people have learned to detach themselves from painful experiences (Williams *et al.* 1999).

Dreams

Disturbing dreams are commonly reported. Identifying the feelings present and the meanings conveyed can contribute to the formulation, and provide a focus for further work. Processing them and re-examining their implications can reduce the impact of the dreams.

Enmeshment

Opportunities for change may be missed when the patients' beliefs mesh with those of therapists (e.g. neither feels comfortable with expressing anger, or both come from a culture which values a 'stiff upper lip'). Supervision and reflective practice skills are essential.

Decision making

Reduced access to feelings makes it harder, not easier, to make decisions and, for example, to assign weights to pros and cons (Goleman 1996). Acknowledging feelings, and developing a vocabulary for them, facilitates decision making. It also helps to imagine the consequences of particular decisions, including (with help if necessary) feelings about them.

Others

Those people who are confused about the feelings of others can find it hard to work out why people act the way they do. Learning how to use empathy is valuable.

Worry

Worry can be understood as a way of avoiding strong affect and the imagery associated with it (see Chapter 6).

Other relevant chapters

Avoidance of affect crosses diagnostic categories. With respect to anxiety disorders, it is especially relevant to generalized anxiety disorder (Chapter 6), social anxiety (Chapter 7), health anxiety (Chapter 4), and unexplained physical health problems (Chapter 15). Eating disorders (Chapter 13) and self-injurious behaviours (Chapter 18) often involve behaviours designed to reduce or control affect; and emotional numbing is one of the features of post-traumatic stress disorder (Chapter 9).

Further reading

Beck, A.T. (1996). Beyond belief: a theory of modes, personality and psychopathology. In: P. Salkovskis (ed.), *Frontiers of cognitive therapy*. Guilford, New York.

Gilbert, P. (1998). Shame and humiliation in complex cases. In: N. Tarrier, G. Haddock, and A. Wells (ed.), *Cognitive therapy for complex cases*. Routledge, London.

Greenberg, L.S., Rice, L.N. and Elliot, R. (1993). *Facilitating emotional change: the moment by moment process*. Guilford, New York.

Leahy, R.L. (2001). *Overcoming resistance in cognitive therapy*. Guilford, New York.

Safran, J.D. (1998). *Widening the scope of cognitive therapy. The therapeutic relationship, emotion and the process of change*. Aronson, New York.

Tales from the Front Line
It's a mad world

A patient with severe PTSD had expressed serious concerns that he would be "locked up" if anyone ever witnessed him having a dissociative flashback. The therapist had witnessed several such episodes, but her reassurance on this point had largely been disbelieved. During a therapist-guided *in vivo* session in a park the patient had a dissociative flashback. Whilst the therapist tried to reconnect him with the here and now, a man cycled by, staring. He was persuaded to move on, but returned shortly afterwards with a wad of tissues in his hand, which he attempted to pass to the patient. The cyclist ignored the therapist's increasingly desperate requests to move on, and became cross. Saying: "I just hate b***** women who go around upsetting blokes". Probably aided by the commotion, the patient reconnected with reality, staring at the tissues proffered in front of his nose. Eventually the cyclist was persuaded to move on. Afterwards the patient concluded, with a little smirk, that the cyclist must have thought, "I was being ditched by my girlfriend", and decided, "if that's what I look like when I have a dissociative flashback it can't be all that bad". His belief that he looked mad evaporated.

CHAPTER 18

Self-injurious behaviour

Helen Kennerley

Introduction

An enormous range of terms is used to describe intentional behaviours that are damaging to a person. These include terms for those behaviours which are meant to be lethal (e.g. attempted suicide), those which might not be intended to kill (e.g. deliberate self-harm, parasuicide, self-mutilating behaviour), those which communicate pleasure (e.g. masochism, self-stimulation), or behaviours which aim to gain attention (e.g. Munchausen's syndrome, malingering).

The presentation of self-injurious behaviour (SIB) is also varied. It may present in a direct way, causing an immediate impact on a person (e.g. suicide attempts, self-mutilation through cutting or burning); it may present indirectly, effecting damage over a period of time (e.g. high-risk activities, such as practising unsafe sex or chronic alcoholism). Some self-injury reflects an isolated incident, while some is repetitive and/or chronic. Some behaviours are impulsive, while some are well planned and anticipated with satisfaction or excitement. Self-injury can be associated with psychotic episodes, although much is not. For many, self-harming behaviour reflects a transient period of distress, whilst for others it is an important indicator of mental health problems and suicide risk.

Thus, self-injurious behaviours are extensive and can have a range of functions, and many different terms are used to describe them (Suyemoto 1988). Lack of consensus about the definition complicates generalization across both theoretical and treatment studies: however, useful models have been devised which aid our understanding of SIB. For example, Walsh and Rosen (1988) suggest that self-injury comprises a continuum of behaviours of varying severity. At one extreme are physically, socially, and psychologically benign behaviours (e.g. ear piercing, nail biting, minor cosmetic surgery); at the other are those which involve severe physical damage, are socially unacceptable, and reflect marked psychological disturbance (e.g. amputation).

In a recent survey of adolescents, 7% reported an act of deliberate self-harm in the preceding year (Hawton *et al.* 2002). In this study, self-harm was more common in females than males (11.2% vs 3.2%)—a similar finding to an earlier survey of university students, which showed that 11% of females and 5% of males had practised self-harm by cutting or other means (Sell and Robson 1998). It is important to appreciate that deliberate self-harm can be a dangerous behaviour even when death is not intended and, untreated, deliberate self-harm may precede suicide (Hawton *et al.* 1999).

Several reviews of SIB and its management exist. Horrocks and House (2002) have produced a particularly concise overview.

Understanding self-injurious behaviour

The most commonly proposed functions of self-injurious behaviour are intrapsychic, interpersonal, and physiological. A helpful understanding is suggested by Vanderlinden and Vandereycken (1997) who propose that the functions of self-mutilation span a continuum from 'positive' through to 'negative'. At the positive end of the spectrum is the goal of 'relaxation' achieved, for example, through enjoyment of pain or tension, or via relief through dissociation or a fall in blood pressure. At the negative end of the spectrum is 'self-destructiveness', with goals such as killing oneself or rendering oneself unattractive. Points between these extremes commonly reflect the attainment of attention or stimulation or punishment.

Vanderlinden and Vandereycken also note that a self-injurious behaviour might serve more than one function simultaneously. Thus, a woman might cut herself and thus simultaneously satisfy goals of self-punishment, of catharsis, and of dissociation. Such a form of self-injury is likely to be very compelling. However, the same self-injury could carry different meanings at different times.

Dissociation, whether psychological or somatic, is commonly associated with intentional self-injury. Often, the purpose of self-injury is to achieve a dissociated state which promotes a profound distraction from psychological and/or physical distress, or which provides a gratifying state of elation or detachment. Interestingly, self-injury is also used, by some, as a means of escaping from a dissociated state, breaking out of the experience of depersonalization or derealization or out of a flashback, for example.

Key cognitive constructs

It is generally accepted that self-injurious actions are preceded by cognitions which drive and facilitate engagement in an otherwise unacceptable act, and that the individual has, at that time, an impoverished range of cognitive and behavioural options. Therefore, the route to self-injury is unobstructed.

Thus, the key to helping those who self-injure is in helping them to discover:

1 The function(s) of the action(s).

2 The belief system(s) supporting the action(s).

3 The beliefs about the consequences of those actions. Conclusions drawn about the consequences of SIB may either encourage or discourage further injury.

Relapse following initial improvement is common and managing it requires a good understanding of 'Why do I continue to do this?' Exploration of 'What do I get out of it?' and 'What would be so bad about not doing it?' generally reveals assumptions and predictions which are testable. Not all the beliefs relevant to SIB lend themselves to behavioural testing, but grasping the wider cognitive framework will help a person to better understand 'Why me?' and 'Why do I continue to do this?'

It is of note that SIB is very much a cognitive-*behavioural* problem and, in addition, the person who self-injures is often helped by developing alternative ways of responding to distress, and then field-testing them.

Key cognitions

Cognitions relevant to SIB generally fall into four categories which interact to maintain the pattern of self-injurious behaviour (see Fig. 18.1). Only the first three are amenable to behavioural testing.

1 *Fundamental beliefs* and associated assumptions that are consistent with self-injury, such as: 'I'm bad and I deserve to hurt', 'I am nothing and it doesn't matter what happens to me', 'I hate myself—I should be punished', 'The world is cruel and spiteful—I should get out', 'Others are superficial and selfish: no-one is going to be there for me'. These support the action of self-harm by either undermining self-concept such that self-injury is tolerable and acceptable, and/or by sanctioning self-harm directly. Such cognitions can be the powerhouse driving urges to self-injure.

2 *Facilitating beliefs* Immediate permission-giving statements which enable a person to find the behaviour acceptable at times of stress. They include assumptions and predictions such as: 'I cannot tolerate this feeling and there is no other way to deal with it', 'It's okay to do this because this is the last time that I'll hurt myself', 'Don't think about it—just do it. It will feel good', 'I have to cut, it's the only way to stop the urge', 'This will make them listen to me', 'This is the only way to show how I really feel', 'There is no other enjoyment in my life—I deserve this'. Without such facilitating cognitions, the person is unable to sanction an otherwise unacceptable behaviour and the behaviour will not occur. The urge or craving might exist but will not be

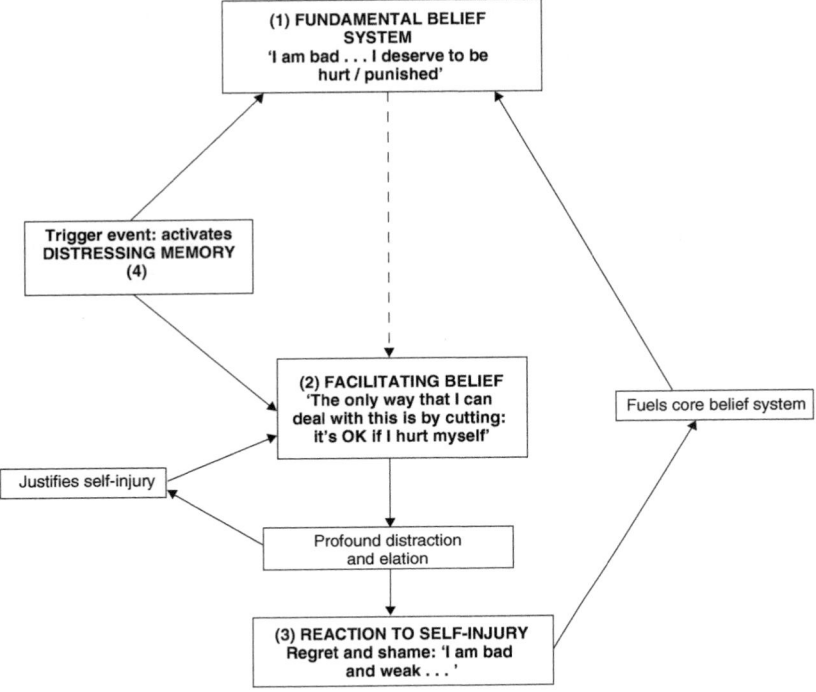

Fig. 18.1 The maintenance of self-injurious behaviour.

transformed into action unless it can be endorsed. These cognitions often readily lend themselves to behavioural testing and tackling them can be the most expedient means of managing self-injurious behaviours.

3 ***Reactions to self-injury*** These can fuel the problem either by feeding the negative fundamental belief system (e.g. 'This proves that I am bad/weird/weak/worthless') or by providing support for facilitating beliefs (e.g. 'It *does* feel good', 'This *is* the only way that I can cope', 'This *did* make them sit up and listen'). These statements often close a vicious circle for those who self-injure, rendering them vulnerable to further incidents of self-injury.

4 Finally, ***flashbacks and other intrusive recollections*** of traumatic and/or painful events can drive the sufferer to self-injure in order to distract or to dissociate from the distress. A common assumption of the person who self-injures is that there is no other way of managing these intrusions. These cognitions play a role in self-injury but, in themselves, are not amenable to behavioural testing.

Behavioural experiments

♦ **Fundamental beliefs**
  Experiment 18.1: challenging hopelessness
♦ **Facilitating beliefs**
  Experiment 18.2: tolerating pain
  Experiment 18.3: recreating belonging
  Experiment 18.4: eliciting help
  Experiment 18.5: managing anger
♦ **Reactions to self-injury**
  Experiment 18.6: reviewing the consequences

Behavioural experiments can be an effective way of testing the predictions which facilitate or enable self-injury. Below are four case examples of this: Lucy, Richard, Saul, and Alison. In each case, the index prediction represents only one aspect of the patient's many problems, and in each case, in-session experiments preceded those carried out *in vivo*.

The majority of experiments address the facilitating beliefs, without which the self-harm would not occur. This is because this level of cognition exists in the form of an assumption which readily lends itself to behavioural testing and which can often yield rapid results. However, each of these patients also harboured powerful and extreme core beliefs which were not necessarily modified via facilitating beliefs, and which continued to undermine their functioning. In each case, it was necessary to address the problem core beliefs more directly. Experiment 18.1 illustrates how behavioural testing can play a part in this.

Fundamental beliefs

Experiment 18.1: challenging hopelessness

Problem Lucy was a 23-year-old in-patient who used self-inflicted wounding as a strategy to manage painful and frightening physical sensations. Her repeated experience of physical, emotional, and sexual abuse had left her with a fundamental hopelessness and helplessness. This fuelled her vulnerability to self-injure as she felt unable to change her habitual response to stress—namely, self-harm.

Target cognitions I am impotent—I cannot make a difference.

Alternative perspective I can make choices and I can make a difference.

Prediction If I look for evidence that I can make sound choices and make a difference to my life or the lives of others, I will find nothing.

Operationalizing the prediction When I am unsure of what to do, or when I am asked to do something, I will stop to consider what I prefer or what I think is best. I will assert my choice and see what happens.

Experiments

1 Activity scheduling each morning in order to prompt making decisions about the day.

2 Brief assertiveness training exercises to help her recognize and assert her views.

3 Recording the outcome of making a decision in a data log. Lucy recorded the circumstances of her decision making, the factual outcome, and what relevance this had to her alternative belief.

4 Weekly rating of her confidence in the new, alternative belief (0–10 scale).

Results

In session: assertiveness training and role play in the sessions increased Lucy's confidence that she could both ask for more time to consider her decisions and, if necessary, say 'no'.

Between sessions: developing a routine of activity scheduling each day was already familiar to Lucy and she readily re-established this. Maintaining a data log was also relatively easy for her as she was practised at diary keeping. However, accepting her achievements was less easy and, in the first week, she had downgraded and dismissed those achievements which she was able to recognize, and there seemed to be many for which she had not given herself credit. Her confidence rating in the alternative belief was 2/10. With practice, she became more adept at noticing the positive consequences of her decision making and she became more proficient in accepting her achievements. Over a period of three months, her confidence in the new belief steadily rose to 8/10.

Reflection Lucy noted that this exercise had less initial impact than those which tested predictions about self-harm, and she had to combat her hopelessness about continuing with the task. Nonetheless, she persevered over several months and gradually built up a genuine belief that she had both the ability and the right to make decisions, and that many of these were of consequence. This fuelled her resolve to use coping strategies other than self-harm and, in addition, enhanced her interpersonal skills.

Further work Although Lucy successfully challenged her personal beliefs about impotence, her progress was not without setbacks. She discovered that whenever she was criticized in her decision making or she felt that the outcome was not good, her old beliefs regained intensity and she had to work hard to challenge them. Nonetheless, with each setback she generated more challenges to her old personal belief and, over time, the new outlook was strengthened. However, Lucy's 'impotence' beliefs were not the only fundamental cognitions that underpinned her self-injurious behaviour, and other core belief systems (e.g. 'I am bad and should be punished' and 'This body is disgusting and should be disfigured') had to be addressed too.

Facilitating beliefs

Experiment 18.2: tolerating pain

Problem Lucy's painful and frightening feelings were chronic, but at times would increase in intensity so as to become unbearable. She would then self-injure. The mediating mechanism linking self-injury and relief was psychological and somatic dissociation: self-injury promoted an out-of-body experience and a (transitory) sense of elation and calm.

Target cognitions I cannot tolerate this feeling and the only way to make it go away is by cutting myself.

Alternative perspective I can manage this bad feeling in other, less damaging ways.

Prediction If I avoid cutting, but try something else instead, I will not be able to bear the feelings.

Operationalizing the prediction When the feeling becomes unbearable (intensity rating 10/10), I will do something other than cutting myself—something that is not harmful to me—and see if I can tolerate it.

Experiment

1 Develop a modified relaxation/imagery exercise which enables the patient to achieve mental and somatic relaxation.
2 Rehearse the exercise so that it can be readily evoked.
3 Use this 'relaxation exercise' in response to the 'bad feelings'.

Results

In session: guided application of the exercise resulted in the intensity of the 'bad feelings' dropping to 1/10. Without therapist guidance, the rating rose to 6/10.

Between sessions: in the first week of trials, the intensity of 'bad feelings' steadily decreased to a range between 2/10 and 5/10. This level was 'tolerable' and the patient did not self-injure.

Reflection Lucy reported: 'The exercise is not as effective as cutting in switching off the bad feelings: in fact, it doesn't stop the bad feelings completely. However, I have learned that I don't have to cut to gain *some* relief, and that I can cope with the feelings if I can reduce their intensity. I have learned that, hard as it is, I can manage these feelings myself. I feel more confident and I don't feel such a victim now.'

Further work Over time, with increasing use of the exercise, the intensity ratings became consistently lower and the incidence of self-injury dropped to zero. However, at times of stress, the 'bad feelings' were more difficult to reduce, and the patient learned to accept these feelings. She also learned to use the exercise to help her combat other impulsive behaviours (such as binge eating) and manage her general stress levels.

Experiment 18.3: recreating belonging

Problem Richard was 37 and reclusive. He intermittently inflicted pain to his genital and anal area in order to recreate a sense of belonging. As a child, he had been physically and emotionally neglected by his parents and bullied at school. A neighbour befriended him when he was nine years old and began to sexually abuse him a year later. The abuse was painful and distressing, but the relationship remained Richard's only source of companionship and affection during his adolescence. In his loneliest moments as an adult, he rekindled a sense of affection and friendship by causing very specific pain to himself.

Target cognitions I need to feel wanted and loved—I can only do this by restimulating old memories through self-abuse.

Alternative perspective There are other ways to feel wanted and loved.

Prediction If I don't injure myself, I won't be able to remember my times with Ralph, the loneliness won't go away, and I will kill myself.

Operationalizing the prediction When I feel so lonely that I feel suicidal, I will focus on other ways of feeling wanted and cared for.

Experiment

1 Compile a log of all the occasions when someone indicated affection.
2 Review memories of people, other than Ralph, showing affection, however slight.
3 Statements and images collected in this way would form the basis for an alternative possibility for Richard to reflect on when he felt lonely and uncared for.

Results

In session: the therapist helped Richard to identify relevant experiences, then prompted him to record and note what each indicated about his relationships with others. For example, in a routine review of his week, the therapist thought that Richard might have failed to consider that a colleague's offer to take on some of Richard's backlog of work could indicate kindness and concern—Richard had actually perceived it as a veiled criticism. The therapist helped him to identify this positive event and then to reflect that the colleague had chosen to be helpful towards Richard.

Between sessions: with this coaching, Richard slowly became more adept at perceiving helpfulness, friendliness, and concern, and he became increasingly proficient in recalling friendly incidents from his past. In fact, he made up a scrapbook of photographs, letters, and positive data logs that helped him to bring these incidents to mind vividly.

After several months, Richard had developed a more positive attitude towards his relationships both past and present. He felt less depressed and lonely, and on the occasions that he felt isolated and at risk of self-harm, he reviewed his scrapbook and resisted resorting to self-injury.

Reflection on experiment Initially, Richard made little headway in trying to record and recall times when others indicated affection. He showed the 'blind sight' for positive data that is common amongst patients with chronic and profound negative beliefs. As Richard progressed with the data logging exercises, his interpersonal beliefs and expectations grew more positive and he became less vulnerable to SIB. The task was actually targeting some of the fundamental beliefs which underpinned his self-injury. In addition, behavioural changes followed his shift in beliefs: his social confidence improved and he began to have more friendly interactions. Thus, although he was able to resist strong urges to self-harm by reviewing his scrapbook, the urges had already decreased in frequency and the targeted problem behaviour had reduced.

Further work Richard's urges to self-harm continued to diminish, his social confidence grew, and he became less reclusive. However, this then raised further issues for him such as deficits in his social skills, uncertainty about his sexuality, and grief over the 'lost' years. These too were resolved in therapy.

Experiment 18.4: eliciting help

Problem Saul was 28 years old and had used self-inflicted wounding as a strategy to communicate his need and to elicit care since his early twenties. His depression and sense of hopelessness were both severe and chronic: he anticipated that no-one would listen to his pleas and so he never asked for help directly. His most common form of self-injury was inflicting a few very deep cuts with a Stanley knife, which were usually treated in the A&E unit at a local hospital.

Target cognitions I need to be cared for, and the way to make others realize this is to badly injure myself.

Alternative perspective I can elicit care by asking for help.

Prediction If I don't cut, no-one will take me seriously and make time for me, despite my pleas.

Operationalizing the prediction When I need help from others, I will first ask for help and see what happens.

Experiment

1 Clarify criterion for seeking help—namely, when his distress reached 7.5 on a 10-point scale. In this way he would ask for help before he became so desperate that he was unable to function socially.

2 Develop a contact list of potential helpers ranging from professional to social.

3 Devise a series of statements to use when asking for help.

4 Rehearse and role play asking for help. Develop social skills and confidence.

5 Devise contingency plans in case help is refused or unavailable.

Results

In session: in role playing asking for help, Saul's confidence that he would be listened to rose from 5% to 85%.

Between sessions: he practised asking for help in a number of emotionally neutral situations. For example, he asked a librarian to help him find a book; a shop assistant to help him find a department in the store; a pedestrian for directions to a particular building. When the first instance of needing emotional help arose, he turned to his contact list and rang a friend. The friend was unavailable and he turned to his second friend, who was available to help him. Saul was able to assert his needs clearly and his friend visited Saul immediately. There was no incident of cutting, but Saul did experience great disquiet and a continued craving to cut himself.

Reflection Saul reported that, although he was pleased that he had found an acceptable, alternative means of communication which he was able to use, and which was having a positive impact on his formerly negative interpersonal beliefs ('Others will not be there for me/listen to me/take me seriously'), he was disappointed that he felt so unsettled and 'edgy' when asking for help and that he still had urges to self-injure.

Further work Over a period of months, Saul asked for help on several occasions and was met with a supportive response by friends and professionals. In the past he had often been treated unsympathetically by staff in A&E who, for example, sutured his wounds without anaesthetic and who were critical of him for 'wasting their time'. Now, he was no longer subject to such punitive attention. His behaviour changed rapidly, his interpersonal beliefs shifted, and there were no further episodes of direct self-injury. It seemed that his initial discomfort had largely related to the novelty of the situation; it diminished as he gradually become more comfortable and confident in seeking help.

However, it also became apparent that, for him, cutting served two other purposes which further explained his enduring disquiet. One function he described as 'the melodrama in my life', which had imbued him with a transitory sense of being special. The other function had been an expression of anger and an intention to distress and disturb those who had not cared enough for him. Further work focused on helping him develop a sense of being adequate and on extending his communication skills. In addition to this, he had also achieved a profound sense of depersonalization after inflicting deep lacerations, and he later turned to alcohol misuse to try to recreate this dissociated state at times of stress. This became a further focus of treatment.

Experiment 18.5: managing anger

Problem Alison was 43 years old and single. She used a variety of self-inflicted wounding behaviours in order to manage sporadic feelings of anger. The mediating mechanism linking self-injury and relief was emotional dissociation, which was rapid and profound: after cutting or burning, she felt 'nothing'.

Target cognitions Unless I space out, I'll become so angry that I will really hurt someone—I might even kill a person.

Alternative perspective I can accept and be in control of my angry feelings.

Prediction If I don't cut, I won't be able to space out, and I will be overwhelmed by anger and I will hurt someone.

Operationalization When I begin to feel angry I will stay with it, using anger management strategies, and see if I can tolerate it.

Experiment

1 Develop and rehearse anger management strategies, including distraction skills which could be substituted for cutting if the patient felt overwhelmed by her feelings.

2 Develop a graded hierarchy of situations which provoke anger.

3 Anger management in imagination.

4 Anger management *in vivo*.

Results

In session: Alison systematically worked up a hierarchy of increasingly provocative images. The therapist guided this graded exposure to an increasing intensity of anger, which resulted in Alison being able to discriminate and tolerate angry feelings in imagination.

Between sessions: initially, the patient used active anger management, in the form of cognitive challenging, when low levels of anger were provoked, and employed distraction when she felt unable to manage or tolerate the feelings. Gradually, she became more confident that she could deal with her angry reactions and she used distraction less and less.

Reflection Alison reported that learning to stand back, review the situation, and use anger management techniques taught her that she could handle strong emotions—not just anger. She said that she no longer feared them, and that she had the reassurance that *if* she were faced with an overpowering situation, she could use distraction rather than cutting to 'space out'.

Further work Over time, the patient became more confident and able in both managing her anger and in managing other powerful emotions, such as grief, which she had avoided in the past. The self-injury which was aimed at 'spacing out' ceased. However, her use of self-injury was complex and, in some other situations, she still had to combat very strong urges to harm herself. Further work focused on helping her to distinguish the function of self-harm in other contexts (e.g. as a means of dissociating from painful memories) and to devise safer, alternative reactions to substitute for self-harm.

Reactions to self-injury

Experiment 18.6: reviewing the consequences

Problem There were times when Alison could not curb her impulses to self-injure. She relapsed, and perceived this as confirmation that she was a 'misfit/weird'. This fundamental belief rendered her vulnerable to further self-injury because it was coupled with the assumption that there was, thus, no point in curbing her urge to self-harm.

Target cognitions I am a misfit. I'm weird, so I might as well hurt myself.

Alternative perspective I am a regular person in many ways.

Prediction I cannot challenge the belief that I am a misfit because it is fact.

Operationalization I will keep a log of all the times that I show that I am a regular person. Entries will support the possibility that I am not a misfit.

Experiment

1 Develop criteria for 'regular person', to ensure that they are realistic, unambiguous, and achievable.
2 Compile a positive data log of evidence that 'I am a regular person'.
3 Test the inevitability of continued self-injury by presenting an argument that 'I am a regular person'.

Results

In session: the therapist coached Alison in the skill of identifying and reflecting on experiences that were consistent with 'I am a regular person'. She struggled at first, but gradually became more able to recognize experiences which challenged her longstanding negative belief about herself.

Between sessions: over several weeks, Alison managed to build up a sufficient body of experience to persuade her that she might not be a misfit—although she did not strongly believe this. Her belief that she was, indeed, a regular person rose from 5% to 60%. Nonetheless, she held this new possibility firmly enough for her to generate a coping statement which prevented her from continuing to self-harm once she had initiated self-injury. She reminded herself: 'I feel weird because I am so upset, not because I am weird. I've done a weird thing to try to deal with my distress, but this does not mean that I am weird. I am a regular person who has had extreme experiences and who sometimes has extreme feelings.'

Reflection Alison was dissmissive of evidence that suggested that she was not a misfit and, at first, she was unable to record any positive data. It was necessary to devise practical solutions to help her retain relevant information. She agreed to carry a piece of paper and pencil with her so that she could record key information quickly—before she had a chance to discard it. She remained highly skilled at dismissing positive experiences, but she did agree to retain entries in her data log even if she rejected them later. Over time, these entries actually became more plausible to her and served to reinforce her new perspective.

Further work Alison's coping statement became an important part of her relapse management plan. When she lapsed into unhelpful behaviour (and not only SIB), she reminded herself of the message, and she managed to recover rather than slipping into relapse. The more often she resisted repeated self-injury, the more 'regular' she felt, and her positive belief ratings steadily rose.

Distinctive difficulties

The complexity of the cases

All these patients had complex and chronic difficulties and the exercises described addressed only one aspect of a range of problems. With such cases it can be particularly helpful to tease out discrete and manageable problems and, where possible, devise relatively simple interventions that can be generalized to other problem situations. However, it is necessary to keep the 'bigger picture' in mind at the same time—namely, a conceptualization of the interplay of intrapsychic, interpersonal, and physiological aspects of a person's current experiences. This will help in generalizing useful strategies to other situations, in better understanding relapse, and in keeping a sense of structure to the therapy. In summary, keep it simple, but keep the case conceptualization in mind.

Keeping the 'bigger picture' in mind

Once an experiment has been achieved, clarify and reinforce the wider implications; ask 'Now you've done this, what does it tell you? What does it say about you? What have you learned from this? What might you do next time?' Revisit and revise the conceptualization as you shift to a more positive picture, and use the experience to develop a comprehensive and personal relapse management plan.

The role of physiology in SIB

Many forms of self-injury have a significant physiological impact which can play a powerful role in the maintenance of self-injury. Physical trauma results in the release of high levels of endogenous opiates, the effects of which can become addictive; blood letting dramatically reduces blood pressure and can precipitate a rapid and deep sense of tranquillity; substance misuse (drugs, alcohol, food) can result in the development of cycles of craving and satiation; self-starvation can cause biochemical changes which trigger elation and dissociation. These effects need to be taken into account in devising realistic treatment approaches.

Insufficient preparation

Try to anticipate difficulties and to prepare for them. The application of behavioural experiments often requires preliminary work, for example, motivational counselling to enhance engagement; continuum work to address the patient's dichotomous view of 'success' and 'failure' of their efforts; positive data logging to help them keep sight of their achievements. This was the case for both the women described in this chapter. Insufficient preparation can mean that the patient risks 'failing' in the assignment and, although perceived failure can be managed within therapy, there is the risk that it will demotivate and/or undermine the fragile patient. The groundwork for behavioural experiments can be extremely time-consuming, but it can be seen as an investment, and such additional work is usually relevant to other aspects of a patient's difficulties too.

Making change safe and possible

We often ask patients to engage in a task that is both difficult and which is perceived as risky, so we need to explore ways of making the task as achievable as possible. Sometimes, simply asking 'What do you think might make this easier for you? Is there anything else that we might do to help you go through with this?' can produce very helpful pointers and solutions.

A contract helped Lucy to engage in her difficult assignments. For her, a commitment made to the therapist helped her to overcome her resistance to try something new. For Alison, however, a contract would not have been helpful: at the time of crisis, it would have meant little to her and breaching it would have, later, fuelled her low self-esteem. For her, engagement in a difficult task was made easier by the quality of the therapeutic relationship which had been established over several months. Both also benefited from simple additions to therapy, for example, both used cue cards which acted as an *aide-mémoire* at times of high stress and both had thought through, and planned for, the worst case scenario.

Making sure distraction is working for the patient

Both Lucy and Alison used a form of distraction, and there is always the risk that a distraction technique can serve the purpose of avoidance. Therefore, the therapist must check out the patient's perception of the use of distraction. Is it viewed as a means of managing a problem or of side-stepping it? Is it used as a technique for overcoming a difficulty or as a permanent crutch? Is it helping or hindering progress? For both women described here, being able to distract themselves from frightening experiences which had previously overwhelmed them, was perceived as an indication of their being able to take control, of having choices, and becoming stronger.

Understanding schema-driven problems

Those who engage in SIB very commonly present with difficulties under-pinned by rigid fundamental belief systems which undermine progress. An appreciation of the nature and role of schemata in the development and main-tenance of psychological problems can help the therapist better understand the nature of the problem and its resistance to change. Each of the patients described here benefited from a schema-based conceptualization of their difficulties. It helped us to understand their vulnerability to SIB and their resistance to change. The schemas which were relevant to SIB also played a part in undermining other aspects of their functioning—aspects of their life, such as their social functioning, which then benefited from the schema change effected by the self-injury focused work.

Finding an appropriate substitute

Self-injury can trigger deep relaxation, profound dissociation, or even exhila-ration and is, thus, very compelling. It can be difficult to find an appealing and acceptable alternative. However, unless the substitute response meaningfully reflects the function of the unwanted behaviour, it is unlikely that the person who self-harms will be drawn to it at times of craving. So, it is crucial that the therapist and patient work together to devise alternative responses that will 'match' the function of the unwanted behaviour, even though this may be in a less immediate, less exciting, less thrilling way. For example, tension-releasing self-injury needs to be substituted by a tension-releasing safe alternative; attention-seeking SIB should be replaced by more adaptive communication; dissociation-provoking SIB can be replaced by less harmful distraction techniques.

Most patients find that the safer substitutes are considerably less compelling than the self-injurious behaviours, and it is reasonable to prepare them for this. Sometimes, the alternative response serves only to take the edge off an urge to self-harm, which then gives the patient an opportunity to continue to cope in a more adaptive way.

Managing relapse

Relapse is a common feature of compulsive behaviours. Progress in therapy is often a process of repeated relapse management, with each setback offer-ing an opportunity to understand better the personal meaning of SIB and the idiosyncratic approach which will best meet a patient's needs. Relapse management guidelines should be introduced from the outset so that the patient can learn to analyse, learn from, and predict setbacks. In this way, over the course of therapy, a patient can build up a very personal and com-prehensive management plan.

Tackling multi-impulsive behaviours

Frequently, patients who self-injure have complex histories and presentations, and it is not unusual for them to develop a repertoire of coping strategies which include other compulsive behaviours such as substance misuse or excessive spending. Thus, therapists need to be alert for the development of multi-impulsive behaviours and to regularly review the patient's repertoire of coping strategies. Overall, there are two guidelines for tackling apparent 'symptom substitution' of multi-impulsive behaviour. First, the therapist should be diligent in encouraging patients to generalize from their therapy successes. In this way, they are helped in developing the skill of applying their coping skills more widely and can, for example, use the strategies which have helped them overcome impulses to self-harm to deal with impulses to overspend. Secondly, therapists might need to identify and tackle the fundamental belief systems that underpin these related impulsive acts.

Addressing the risk of death

The possibility of death arising from self-injury has to be borne in mind at all times. An act can be lethal by design or by accident, and therapists should continually assess risk, be prepared in methods for handling it, and seek supervision for their work.

Other related chapters

Many of the cognitive-behavioural conceptualizations and techniques which are relevant to helping those who suffer from other psychological problems, such as depression or social anxiety, can also be of benefit to the patient who self-injures, and can be used to enhance and augment therapy.

Depression The understanding and management of depression is particularly relevant, as the patient who self-injures often struggles with low self-esteem and depressed mood. (See Chapter 10.)

Post-traumatic stress disorder It is not uncommon for self-injury to be used as a means of dealing with flashbacks which are characteristic of Type I and/or Type II trauma. An understanding of post-traumatic phenomena can aid the therapist working with SIB. (See Chapter 9.)

Personality disorder Borderline personality disorder, particularly, is often associated with self-injury, and can present a further challenging dimension to the therapy. (See also Chapter 17.)

Substance misuse Eating disorders, and drug and alcohol misuse can contribute to a repertoire of self-injurious behaviours or can exist in parallel. (See Chapter 13.)

Further reading

Beck, A.T., Freeman, A., *et al.* (1990). *Cognitive therapy of personality disorders.* Guilford Press, New York.

Kennerley, H. (1996). Cognitive therapy of dissociative symptoms associated with trauma. *British Journal of Clinical Psychology,* 35, 325–40.

Marlatt, G.A. and Gordon, J.R. (1985). *Relapse prevention.* Guilford Press, New York.

Walsh, B.W. and Rosen, P.M. (1988). *Self-mutilation. Theory, research and treatment.* Guilford Press, New York.

Vanderlinden, J. and Vandereycken, W. (1997). *Trauma, dissociation, and impulse dyscontrol in eating disorders.* Brunner Mazel, New York.

Tales from the Front Line
You psychologists can read minds, can't you?

Lisa had a strong conviction that people could read her thoughts. To test this Lisa agreed to think about what she had done the previous evening and the therapist would try to read her thoughts. Although the therapist discussed with Lisa that an inaccurate guess would be evidence against her belief, the therapist was so convinced that her guess would be inaccurate that she failed to discuss what would happen if she guessed correctly. To her astonishment, the therapist correctly guessed that Lisa's boyfriend had been to stay and that she had been to the pub and had a beer. Fortunately, Lisa was able to laugh at this and could discuss with her therapist other reasons why she would have accurately guessed how she had spent her evening. Subsequent attempts at reading Lisa's thoughts proved that the therapist had not missed her vocation in life.

CHAPTER 19

Interpersonal difficulties*

Paul Flecknoe
Diana Sanders

Introduction

Traditionally, treatment protocols in cognitive therapy have focused on specified disorders, such as panic disorder, social phobia, depression, or obsessive-compulsive disorder. Behavioural experiments dealing with interpersonal and relational issues can be an intrinsic part of therapy for these problems. For example, therapy with depressed patients who avoid social activity may involve behavioural experiments testing the consequences of increasing social contacts or testing specific beliefs such as the notion that their work colleagues do not like them. Cognitive therapy for social anxiety involves many interpersonal behavioural experiments aimed at testing beliefs and assumptions about the self and others in interpersonal situations (see Chapter 7).

Interpersonal issues are also relevant in other ways in cognitive therapy. Some patients seek cognitive therapy explicitly because of relationship difficulties, where interpersonal problems become the main therapeutic focus. Interpersonal issues, such as dependence, can be a feature of working with patients with personality disorders, and a direct focus on interpersonal beliefs and assumptions is a necessary part of effective therapy. Some of these patients have difficulties in relationships without knowing why, and seek treatment initially for other problems. Interpersonal difficulties then become the main focus later on in therapy. The therapeutic relationship itself is interpersonal, and often where there are difficulties in the therapeutic relationship, process issues can be understood and formulated in terms of interpersonal beliefs. For example, patients with beliefs and assumptions to do with trust may have difficulties in forming any therapeutic relationship; those inclined towards dependency may become overly dependent on

*The authors would like to acknowledge the contribution of Dr Helen Jenkins who provided some of the behavioural experiments described in this chapter.

the therapist, which may, for example, impede therapeutic collaboration. These processes can be directly observed within the therapeutic relationship, which in turn may become an arena for interpersonal behavioural experiments.

The experiments in this chapter cover a potentially wide area, ranging from those which are an intrinsic part of working on another primary problem, through to those which arise out of dealing with difficulties in the therapeutic relationship and in relationships more generally. The common theme is that all the experiments relate to beliefs about relationships and interpersonal situations. Related issues brought to cognitive therapy include problems with intimacy, assertiveness, and relationship formation and maintenance. Interpersonal beliefs are often connected with specific interpersonal styles, such as a tendency to be hostile, defensive, critical, overly compliant, or always trying to entertain or amuse other people. These styles are seen as behavioural consequences of the underlying beliefs, and experiments can therefore include deliberately changing these styles and assessing the consequences of this change.

Cognitive models

Two models seem to have relevance to this area. First, Beck *et al.*'s (1979) generic cognitive model can be applied to beliefs about relationships themselves. The relevant core beliefs, assumptions, and negative automatic thoughts are therefore those which are concerned with relationships. Example core beliefs might include 'intimacy is dangerous' or 'relationships are always abusive'. Dysfunctional assumptions might include 'If I tell people what I think, they'll reject me', 'If I'm not always in control, I'll be attacked' or 'If I am criticized, it means I am a terrible person'. These beliefs lead the person to behave in ways that prevent disconfirmation of the beliefs and to perceive information in a biased way that tends to fit with and strengthen the original beliefs. For example, the person who believes that 'intimacy is dangerous' might avoid intimate relationships and selectively attend to experiences and evidence that supports this belief. These are all features of the generic cognitive model, but applied specifically to interpersonal beliefs. Experimenting with new ways of behaving in interpersonal situations is an important part of working on those beliefs.

The second useful model is the cognitive-interpersonal framework suggested by Safran and Segal (1990). This integrates interpersonal theory with the cognitive model, and suggests that the interpersonal responses of others may contribute to maintenance processes. This idea is particularly useful in circumstances where people are engaged in repetitive relational patterns which seem to confirm their interpersonal beliefs. For example, patients who believe that they will be rejected in close relationships may have had a series of rejecting partners or friends, and this confirms and strengthens their interpersonal beliefs. They may in some way 'choose' friends who are more likely to reject them, or in their friendships, act in such a way as to make friends more likely to reject them. One patient, for example, became very angry and hostile if she felt a friend was letting her down in any way, such as changing an arrangement to meet. She would give the friend 'a good telling off' for letting her down, so that people were reluctant to make arrangements with her in the future, thereby confirming her original belief that people reject her.

Safran and Segal suggest that a person's interpersonal behaviour tends to invite or 'pull' a predictable response from others, which is then confirmatory of their original beliefs. This interpersonal maintenance process is expected to occur inside and outside the therapy relationship in situations where interpersonal schema are activated, and is therefore considered an appropriate target for therapy. By identifying the belief that is linked to this interpersonal style, behavioural experiments can be devised whereby the patient deliberately experiments with different interpersonal behaviours, and collects information about the responses of others.

Key cognitions

Essentially, any beliefs, assumptions, and thoughts that refer to relationships and interpersonal situations are of relevance. Some core beliefs may relate directly to relationships, such as 'I am bad at relationships' or 'Other people let me down'. Often, interpersonal beliefs involve a synthesis of beliefs about the self and others, and so interpersonal dysfunctional assumptions seem particularly relevant, as they represent a combination of these elements—for example, 'I am a bad person; if people get to know me they will find out how awful I am and reject me' or 'I am an evil person; if people get close, then I'll cause them damage'. In these cases, it may be easiest to target the interpersonal assumption rather than the core belief. Many of these beliefs have relevance inside and outside the therapeutic relationship, and (once sufficient trust has been established) the therapeutic relationship can provide a 'safe' place to identify and test them out.

Patients who hold these beliefs also engage in different kinds of interpersonal safety behaviours which maintain beliefs, as in other kinds of problems such as panic disorder (see Chapter 3) or social anxiety (see Chapter 7). In some cases they simply prevent disconfirmation—for example, the person who fears revealing herself will avoid disclosing personal details to others. In other cases, the safety behaviour actually can lead to confirmation of the original belief (e.g. the patient who expects hostility, behaves in a hostile manner, and tends to receive a hostile reception as a result). In this way it is possible to conceptualize a problematic interpersonal style as a type of safety behaviour.

The behavioural experiments in this chapter are categorized according to broad common interpersonal themes. They are not intended as an exhaustive list, but to provide a framework for organizing different kinds of experiments in this area. With the exception of interpersonal style, each category reflects a grouping of common cognitions relating to themes observed in clinical practice. The interpersonal style category reflects interpersonal safety behaviours that tend to confirm underlying beliefs. Although the beliefs may be quite varied, the organizing principle here is that the patient has a problematic interpersonal style and much confirmatory evidence for the belief. In many cases, experiments within each category can be conducted both within and outside the therapeutic relationship.

Categories of beliefs

Trust

Beliefs about trust essentially relate to whether or not another person can be relied upon to react or behave in a certain way in a given situation. With negative beliefs about trust there is often an expectation of being hurt or betrayed if the person places trust in others (e.g. 'If I confide in someone, they can't be trusted not to tell other people' or 'If I show my vulnerability, other people will exploit or harm me'). In other cases, problematic beliefs relate to excessively rigid or globalized beliefs about trust (e.g. 'People can either be trusted or they can't' or 'If someone lets you down once, they can never be trusted again'). Many interpersonal experiments involve a degree of trust, and so this category of belief may be relevant to all the others.

Intimacy

Beliefs in this category are usually concerned with the consequences of revealing hidden aspects of the self to another person. Interpersonal beliefs about intimacy may relate to core beliefs about the self and others (e.g. 'If people got to know the real me, they would find out how bad I am and reject me'). Patients may also have beliefs about how intimate relationships are developed. For example, the person who believes that relationships are deepened by always presenting a flawless persona might experiment with sharing vulnerability and assessing the relational consequences of this.

There is some overlap between trust and intimacy experiments, especially when the belief about intimacy reflects more general beliefs about trust. In these cases, the results of the experiments can be related to both categories.

Assertiveness

This category includes beliefs about the relative importance of the patient's versus others' needs (e.g. 'Other people's needs are more important than my own'). They may involve beliefs specifically about assertiveness (e.g. 'If I speak up and say what I want, other people won't like me and I will be rejected'). Experiments often involve behaving more assertively and the person assessing the interpersonal consequences. Specific problems arise when people swing between passive and aggressive styles and find it hard to strike a balance. This usually reflects beliefs such as 'If I don't get absolutely what I want, there's no point in trying'. In these cases, experimenting with negotiation and compromise may help, bearing in mind that low self-esteem (see Chapter 20), and anxieties about relationship formation and maintenance may also be present.

Interpersonal style

Patients may have specific interpersonal styles which cause difficulties in relationships (e.g. being hostile, defensive, critical, compliant, or demanding). Patients' specific interpersonal styles may relate to core beliefs and assumptions about the self and others (e.g. 'I must always be on my guard to protect myself from attack' or 'I am a boring person, and will only be liked if I try and entertain people all the time'). Experiments involve different interpersonal styles. For example, the person who believes she always has to entertain others to be liked, might experiment with being quieter or simply listening to other people.

Authority and power

Patients may have difficulties in relationships with those in authority which relate to beliefs about the meaning of being told what to do by others or the meaning for oneself of being in a hierarchical relationship with others. Example beliefs include 'If I let other people tell me what to do, it means I am a weak person' or 'If I accept someone else's authority, I'll end up being totally controlled by them'. Experiments can include exploring both the meanings and the consequences of accepting the authority of others. For example, a person who struggles with those in authority and believes that one should always resist being told what to do in order to maintain the respect of other people, could undertake a survey to explore this issue.

Behavioural experiments

- **Interpersonal trust**
    Experiment 19.1: disclosing personal information
    Experiment 19.2: discovering meanings of trust
- **Intimacy**
    Experiment 19.3: showing vulnerability to other people
- **Assertiveness**
    Experiment 19.4: experimenting with saying 'no'
    Experiment 19.5: expressing criticism
- **Interpersonal style**
    Experiment 19.6: dropping an interpersonal safety behaviour
- **Power and authority**
    Experiment 19.7: dealing with criticism

It is important to be aware when setting up experiments involving interactions between people, that interpersonal situations contain some degree of unpredictability. It is therefore necessary to prepare the patient for an unexpected or unwanted response, through discussion and role play in the session. For example, a patient who receives a negative reaction to a personal disclosure might find it useful to consider how to respond assertively to this, and avoid personalizing or overgeneralizing. This is especially important when the person is trying to make changes to their behaviour in established relationships where there might be an entrenched pattern of reciprocal responses. In such cases, it is likely that the other people in the interpersonal 'dance' will be likely to exert some pressure on the patient to change back to the old interactional style (Lerner 1997).

The therapy relationship can be used as a relatively safe laboratory for interpersonal behavioural experiments, which can then form the basis for new beliefs, to be consolidated and generalized to other interpersonal settings. The therapeutic relationship also provides an opportunity for 'spontaneous' experiments, which occur naturally as part of the relationship but which can be explicitly identified as a source of data to test beliefs. This also makes it possible to get immediate feedback and to reflect on the experiment as soon as possible.

To work on interpersonal issues within the context of the therapeutic relationship, it is important to have developed a collaborative agreement to include this as part of the therapy before setting up formal experiments. Both therapist and patient need to agree on the beliefs to be tested and on details of the experimental test. For example, a therapist had to cancel two appointments unexpectedly, because of illness and the second because of an unrelated and unexpected funeral. The patient's belief about trust, 'People always let me down and reject me', was strongly activated by this, leading her to feel angry, hurt, and rejected. When they met, patient and therapist explored the meanings in terms of two hypotheses: the old belief ('People let me down and reject me') leading her to feel upset and low, versus a new belief ('People do have to change appointments and I do feel let down, but they are not rejecting me—sometimes unexpected things happen'). In session, she role played discussions between these two beliefs, reviewing the evidence for and against them and the feelings they aroused in her. This enabled her to conclude that 'People cancelling appointments does not always mean they are rejecting me'.

Interpersonal trust

When underlying beliefs about trust are formulated in fairly global terms (e.g. 'Other people cannot be trusted'), it is useful to help the patient consider what they would be trusting the other person to do or not to do in a given situation. This helps clarify the exact prediction in a given interpersonal situation, and helps the patient to see trust on a continuum rather than in an all-or-nothing way. It may also be of value to conduct experiments testing the notion that trust is an all-or-nothing concept, and to consider the possibility that different people may be trusted in different ways depending on one's relationship with them and the context.

Experiment 19.1: disclosing personal information

Problem Philippa had a history of severe physical and sexual childhood abuse. She had symptoms of post-traumatic stress disorder, depression, and agoraphobia. At a key point in therapy, the issue of whether to disclose details of flashbacks from her childhood sexual abuse became highly relevant. While she was clear that it would be of value for her to disclose these, she was concerned about the therapist's reaction.

Target cognition I can't trust anyone enough to tell them the details of my abuse. If I tell them, they will be disgusted, overwhelmed, and will never want to see me again.

Alternative perspective Someone might be moved or affected by how badly I was abused, but will not reject me or be unable to hear about it.

Prediction Philippa thought that if she did disclose details of her abuse flash-backs, the therapist would leave the room to be physically sick, and would not return or offer further sessions (belief rating 90%).

Experiment To write down details of one flashback in session, and allow the therapist to read it. Observe the therapist's reaction and ask for feedback. To promote a sense of safety, it was emphasized that Philippa could pause or stop the experiment at any time. The meaning of different kinds of therapist response and the need to talk about this before the end of the session was discussed in advance. For example, the discussion included how Philippa could ask questions to distinguish between the therapist wanting to be sick and the therapist simply reacting or being affected by the material. It was agreed that the best way to do this was simply to ask for honest feedback.

Results The therapist read a brief written account of one of Philippa's flashbacks. He was not sick and did not leave the room. The therapist admitted to being appalled that adults can treat children this way, but did not feel differently about wanting to continue working with Philippa.

Reflection Philippa became visibly relieved as the session continued and felt that the experiment had helped disconfirm the idea that the therapist would be unable to stand hearing about the details of her abuse and would therefore reject her (belief rating 20% at the end of the session).

Tips As the vehicle for this experiment was the therapeutic alliance, it was essential that a strong positive alliance had already been formed. It was also helpful to allow time for discussion both before and after the session and to emphasize to Philippa that she had control over the experiment. The importance of not overgeneralizing the results of this experiment was also discussed, since these were highly personal, sensitive issues. This led to a useful discussion about only disclosing sensitive material in trusting, secure relationships.

Experiment 19.2: discovering meanings of trust

Problem Laura was referred for help with low self-esteem and problems in maintaining relationships. She often ended new or recently-formed relationships, usually when she felt the other person had let her down or betrayed her trust in some way.

Target cognition People can either be trusted totally or not at all. If someone lets you down, it means that they can't be trusted at all.

Alternative perspective Laura could not think of an alternative hypothesis so the experiment was conducted with a view to discovering other possibilities.

Prediction Even a slight doubt about someone will make me want to break off the relationship. I'll never be able to hang on in there once doubts start.

Experiment Laura's therapist undertook a survey of a small number of colleagues and friends. Each person was asked to think of five people in their own lives, and rate their degree of trustworthiness on different dimensions (e.g. 'look after my children', 'confide in emotionally', 'turn up on time for dates'). They were also asked whether any of these people had ever let them down and, if so, what effect this had had on the level of trust, and how this had been repaired.

Results It was clear from the survey that the participants trusted different people, to different degrees, depending on the area of inquiry. For example, trusting someone to turn up on time was not the same as trusting them with an emotional confidence. It was also clear that most participants could recall examples of having been let down, but were usually able to recover from this.

Reflection After listening to the results of the survey, Laura said she now thought that trust was 'lots of things' rather than 'just one thing', and realized that it was possible to trust different people in different ways. She also became curious about the possibility of repairing trust, even if she had been let down. This led her to conduct a specific experiment with a new friend who had let her down. She was tempted to terminate the relationship but persisted with it instead.

Tips This was a discovery experiment, to compare an overgeneral and polarized belief with the day-to-day behaviour of other people as reported in the survey. It is worth noting that the old belief may have performed a protective function for Laura in that it prevented her from the possibility of being hurt any further if she were let down once in a relationship. It might have been useful, therefore, to help Laura develop her own criteria for when it would be wise and protective to end a relationship that was proving emotionally damaging to her.

Intimacy

Most intimacy experiments involve testing the notion that there are aspects of the self that are shameful or unacceptable to other people. It is valuable to prepare the patient for both positive and negative reactions to disclosure, by using role-play techniques. It is also useful to consider the exact meaning of a negative reaction for the patient. It is common for people to believe that a negative reaction in a specific situation signifies a permanent, global, negative judgement about them, and will lead to the termination of any further relationship.

Experiment 19.3: showing vulnerability to other people

Problem Hilary, a 39-year-old woman with social phobia, depression, and low self-esteem, had always tried to conceal any perceived weaknesses or difficulties from other people, even her close friends and husband. As a result, she had a reputation as a 'superwoman' who could handle everything and who had no difficulties, which left her feeling alone and unsupported when she experienced periods of difficulty or distress. Therapy identified her 'superwoman' image as a safety behaviour, protecting her from her beliefs and fears of rejection, but also preventing her finding alternative beliefs.

Target cognition If other people see my weaknesses or vulnerability, they will ridicule and reject me. It would damage my relationships if people were to see this part of me.

Alternative perspective Everyone has some vulnerability. If I share mine, perhaps I could get support from other people.

Prediction Hilary predicted that if she disclosed to her friend that she got very anxious about her presentations at work, then the friend would distance herself from her and their relationship would be damaged.

Experiment Hilary agreed to drop her usual safety behaviour and confide in a longstanding friend that she was experiencing anxiety about work-related presentations. She believed that the friend would provide honest feedback about this issue, and agreed to ask her for her reaction.

Results Hilary confided in her friend when they went out for coffee, as agreed. The friend expressed amazement that Hilary got anxious about anything, as she seemed so confident. She also volunteered that it made her feel relieved, as she sometimes felt intimidated by Hilary's apparent invulnerability, and talked about some of the things that she sometimes felt anxious about.

Reflection Hilary said that the experiment had made her realize how other people might perceive her as invulnerable. This was in stark contrast to how vulnerable she felt inside. She also thought that the conversation had deepened her friendship rather than damaged it, and this provided a starting point for other experiments to generalize her new idea that intimacy could often be developed by sharing vulnerability rather than by concealing it.

Tips It was useful to reflect beforehand on how the therapy to date had also been an implicit test of this belief, as Hilary had gone into depth about her vulnerabilities and difficulties with the therapist. We used Socratic questioning to elicit Hilary's own reactions to other people sharing vulnerabilities with her, highlighting her double standards, since she would feel sympathetic and interested with other people. Careful consideration was given to which friend Hilary would confide in. We looked for a close, longstanding friend who she felt would give her honest feedback, and who did not seem to hold similar beliefs to Hilary.

Assertiveness

Experiment 19.4: experimenting with saying 'no'

Problem Mary, a 56-year-old who had experienced two heart attacks, had been told to take things more easily in life, but remained very driven—she worked part time, but had always taken work home with her, and took on many problems of her friends and family. She felt like 'everyone's dustbin' but was unable to say 'no' to other people. Her neighbour, in particular, used to drop in regularly and expect Mary to drop what she was doing and listen to her problems.

Target cognition I must always help out others in need. If not, they will think badly of me and never speak to me again. Others' needs are more important than my own.

Alternative perspective If I carry on like this, I will be ill again. Other people are responsible for their own problems. I can say 'no' and still keep on with my friendships.

Prediction If I say 'no' to my neighbour, she will think I'm being rude, storm out, and never speak to me again. That would be more stressful than just listening, yet again.

Experiment Mary planned a one-hour rest period each day, which was usually interrupted by things to do. She planned to try and protect this time assertively from interruptions. Her neighbour came round just as Mary was about to rest. She told her she was busy, but could see her the following morning for coffee for half an hour.

Results Her neighbour did indeed flounce off upset that she was unable to talk about her problems. Rather than feeling upset about this, Mary thought her neighbour was being very selfish, and felt annoyed with her but pleased she had been firm. Later on, the neighbour dropped her a note to apologize, and invited Mary round to her house for coffee the following morning. Mary went round, but kept to her half-hour limit.

Reflection Mary's new perspective following the experiment was that 'I can say 'no' to others, and need to do this more to look after myself'.

Tips To prepare for experiments like this one, it may be necessary to do initial cognitive work about the relative importance of one's own versus other's needs. The reactions of others to new boundaries in relationships are unpredictable— in this case, the neighbour may well have taken offence and ceased the relationship—so it is necessary to prepare the patient for different outcomes.

Experiment 19.5: expressing criticism

Problem Adam was in therapy for help with depression and would often miss sessions and then return the next week saying he forgot the session time. The therapist gently enquired about this pattern, and Adam said that he had not attended because something the therapist had done or said had made him feel annoyed or angry. He had felt misunderstood or not listened to, and, not wanting to volunteer this at the time, had missed sessions because he was still feeling annoyed with the therapist.

Target cognition If I express anger or dissatisfaction, then the other person will get angry and reject me.

Alternative perspective If I express how I am feeling at the time, then there might be a chance to discuss it and resolve things straight away.

Prediction Adam predicted that if he expressed his anger or dissatisfaction with facets of therapy, the therapist would get fed up with him and discharge him from therapy prematurely.

Experiment The therapist and Adam agreed that Adam would try to let the therapist know when he felt angry or annoyed at key moments in the therapy. It was also agreed that this would form part of end-of-session feedback, when the therapist would specifically enquire if there had been any moments in the session that had been difficult for Adam.

Results Adam was able to indicate moments in the therapy during which he felt angry, and these were usually related to feeling misunderstood. The therapist used this feedback to explore the meaning of these moments to Adam. This provided an opportunity to acknowledge Adam's feelings and also to clarify misunderstandings or misperceptions on the part of both Adam and the therapist.

Reflection Adam became more positive about the therapy and started to attend more regularly. He reflected that communicating his feelings to the therapist had led him to feel better understood and had improved the therapy relationship. He concluded that communicating his feelings directly was an important part of building a positive relationship, rather than something that would lead to rejection.

Tips The initial inquiry into the meaning of Adam's pattern of missing sessions had to be handled sensitively, since it could also have led him to feel criticized and annoyed. It was also important for the therapist to be able to respond non-defensively when Adam disclosed his feelings. It was useful here to focus on the meaning of these incidents for Adam, rather than to take them as criticisms of the therapy or therapist.

Interpersonal style

Experiment 19.6: dropping an interpersonal safety behaviour

Problem Rhaji had bipolar disorder and presented for therapy with interpersonal problems, feeling very isolated from other people. He believed that he always had to be the 'life and soul' of a social situation, and always had to avoid social situations when he was low and unable to 'entertain' other people.

Target cognition If people get to know the real me, they will find out that there is nothing there. To get people to like me, I have to entertain them all the time.

Alternative perspective I am a mixture of different things, like most people, and can be quiet with people as well as jolly. Most people have their ups and downs, and it is OK to be myself.

Prediction If I am quiet, and just make small talk, no-one will be interested in me and I'll be left alone.

Experiment Rhaji went to the pub when feeling quite low, and made small talk with his friends, chatting on a low-key level rather than being the 'life and soul' of the evening. He monitored the reactions of others, and noted how many people were still talking to him and taking an interest in him by the end of the evening.

Results Rhaji's friends treated him normally, and as many people as usual were interacting with him by the end of the evening. In some cases, he felt people seemed more interested in him than usual, since they asked him more questions. He felt he had a good evening, no-one walked away or left him alone, and he found out more things about his friends by listening to them more. They all arranged to meet again later in the week.

Reflection I can be myself, and maybe people like me more when I am quieter. I felt more connected to my friends and learned more about them, rather than them having to listen to me all the time.

Power and authority

Experiment 19.7: dealing with criticism

Problem John, a 47-year-old kitchen salesman, had been in therapy for depression. He recently returned to work, and the new manager was quick to criticize his staff for any perceived mistakes. John reacted very badly to criticism, immediately becoming angry and defending himself, which led to bad feeling between him and his manager.

Target cognition If anyone in authority criticizes me, I need to defend myself, otherwise they will think that I am weak and not up to the job. If I let someone in power see me as weak, I'll be picked on more and more.

Alternative perspective There may or may not be truth in the criticism. I am allowed to make mistakes; it is part of being human and does not mean I am weak.

Prediction If I don't defend myself, my manager will see how weak I am and pick on me even more.

Experiment The next time I am criticized, listen carefully to what is said and do not react. Allow myself one hour to think about it and decide on my response.

Results John made an error in a customer's order, forgetting to order a tap. The manager heard about the mistake and told John off about it, saying he had to be more careful otherwise he would have to think about his job. John listened to his manager, then agreed with him that it was a mistake and explained how it had come about. He apologized to the manager, and to the customer. Later on, his manager apologized to John for over-reacting to a small error.

Reflection By listening to the criticism and accepting that I made a mistake, nothing blew out of proportion. My manager seemed to respect me more for taking his criticism and listening to it. Listening to criticism did not make me weak, and my manager became less critical rather than picking on me more.

Tips The key issue in this experiment was that John had a rigid rule for responding to all criticism, whether or not it was justified, as an attempt to protect himself from further attack. In this case, careful discussion suggested that the criticism often was justified, but only to a degree. If the criticism had not been justified at all, it might have been relevant to consider appropriately assertive responses to this.

Distinctive difficulties

Generalization

When using the therapeutic relationship as a laboratory to test or develop new beliefs, we need to consider how and when the patient generalizes to other situations. The patient may be comfortable experimenting with disclosing depressed feelings to the therapist, but remain convinced that all other people will be hostile or dismissive if they were to disclose feeling low to them. It can be helpful to construct a list of situations in which experiments can be conducted, using discrimination and judgement about when interpersonal disclosure is helpful. For example, it may be appropriate for a patient to tell close friends about difficulties with low mood, and expect them not to gossip, but less appropriate to indiscriminately disclose personal information to work colleagues.

Specificity to therapy

It is important to be wary of assuming that patients' interpersonal difficulties expressed in therapy are always characteristic of those occurring elsewhere, or vice versa. The therapeutic relationship is in many ways a unique relationship, and interpersonal issues expressed there may be unique to that setting or to the patient's reaction to the therapist in particular. If interpersonal difficulties arise within the therapeutic relationship, it is important, therefore, to discuss with the patient whether this is a problem that occurs elsewhere, or whether it only occurs with the therapist. For example, a patient telephoned to cancel an appointment because he said that he had not done his homework and did not want to attend until he had done it 'properly' and 'up to standard'. The therapist encouraged him to come to the session anyway, guessing that beliefs about needing to please other people, or to be compliant with them, could be relevant. On discussion, they discovered that doing what he was told, or doing things properly, were not general themes in the patient's life, but the therapist strongly reminded him of a rather critical primary school teacher who would consistently tell him he did not do his homework 'properly' or 'up to scratch'. Once this was identified, and the patient was able to disentangle the therapist from the memories of the abrasive teacher, the issue no longer caused difficulties.

Practising new interpersonal styles

In some cases, experiments involve patients trying out new interpersonal styles as well as new behaviour. In order to conduct the experiments, it may be necessary to consider whether the patients have the relevant skills in their behavioural repertoire. For example, the patient might not know how to behave assertively and, in addition, doing so might not be congruent with the relevant belief system. In some cases, it may be necessary to learn how to behave assertively (e.g. saying 'no' or stating needs clearly), rehearsing and role playing such skills within therapy sessions, and then using them in safe social situations such as with a trusted friend. As the patient becomes more confident with the new skill, he can then experiment with using them flexibly, in different situations.

Therapist interpersonal beliefs

Given that many of these beliefs can manifest themselves in the therapeutic process itself, and that therapists' responses may be a key part of the change process, it is also important that therapists have good awareness of their own interpersonal assumptions and beliefs, which may inadvertently contribute to the maintenance of a problem. Safran and Segal (1990) describe a process of 'decentering', in which the therapist becomes a 'participant observer' within the therapeutic relationship, 'stepping outside' the immediate experience and thereby not only observing the experience but also changing it. This helps the therapist to identify the thoughts, assumptions, and beliefs that are activated when difficulties occur, and to step back, rather than continuing to be 'hooked' by them.

Teasdale (1997) describes the processes of acting and thinking, and observing the self acting and thinking: in essence, being mindful of what is occurring in an interpersonal context in order to identify unhelpful beliefs and behaviours. It can at times be very difficult to spot interpersonal patterns, particularly when working with patients with complex problems, such as those with personality disorders. Good supervision and use of audio and video tapes can be valuable resources in helping therapists reflect on their own contribution to the in-session interpersonal process.

Other related chapters

Interpersonal difficulties can be part of many of the problems discussed in this book. Of particular relevance are Chapter 20 on low self-esteem, Chapter 7 on social anxiety, and Chapter 17 on avoidance of affect, where interpersonal problems may be primary or secondary. People with depression can experience problems related to social withdrawal and loss of social confidence, so Chapter 10 is also useful.

Further reading

Beck, A.T. (1988). *Love is never enough*. Harper and Row, New York.

Leahy, R. (2001). *Overcoming resistance in cognitive therapy*. Guilford Press, New York.

Lerner, G.H. (1997). *The dance of anger: a woman's guide to changing the pattern of intimate relationships*. Harper Collins, New York.

Sanders, D. and Wills, F. (1999). The therapeutic relationship in cognitive therapy. In: C. Feltham (ed.), *Understanding the counselling relationship*. Sage, London, pp. 120–38.

Waddington, L. (2002). The therapy relationship in cognitive therapy: a review. *Behavioural and Cognitive Psychotherapy*, 30, 179–91.

Tales from the Front Line
A bit of a tight spot

Janet was referred for CBT for claustrophobia. After assessment it was still very unclear what Janet actually experienced in relation to small spaces, and in particular what worrying thoughts accompanied the emotional response. She had avoided such experiences for so long that she had no recent experiences to draw on. To address this problem, Janet agreed to take part in an experiment that involved locking the office door by turning the key on the inside. It was planned to leave the door locked only for as long as Janet could cope in order to investigate her response.

Janet quickly became anxious once the door was locked and requested that it be unlocked. Unfortunately the door had jammed and no amount of wrestling with it would budge the lock. The office was of reasonable size, but it only had two small windows at head height. A call was made to hospital porters to try to open the door. Quickly Janet's worrying thoughts became extremely clear. On learning that the door had jammed, she immediately started to hyperventilate and rushed to the window where she proceeded to take very deep breaths. She remembered as a girl being repeatedly held under the bedclothes by her older brothers and thinking she was going to suffocate. She feared that if she experienced claustrophobia now, she would lose control and seriously attack someone. It was unclear who was more relieved when after 20 minutes the porters managed to open the door.

CHAPTER 20

Low self-esteem*

Melanie Fennell
Helen Jenkins

Introduction

Low self-esteem means a negative sense of self. It may be openly expressed ('I'm useless', 'I don't matter', 'I'm a failure'), or it may be an underlying sense of inadequacy or worthlessness that is hard to put into words. Low self-esteem is neither an axis I emotional disorder nor a personality disorder (DSM-IV-TR, APA 2000), but rather an element of many different presenting problems.

The relationship between low self-esteem and presenting problems varies (Fennell 1998; Fennell in press). It may be an *aspect* of the presenting problem, which rights itself once that problem is successfully treated (e.g. low self-esteem as a feature of depression). It may be a *consequence* of other problems (e.g. generalized loss of confidence resulting from longstanding anxiety, or a radical shift in self-perception following experience of trauma). Again, treating the primary problem often restores self-esteem. Finally, it may act as a *vulnerability factor* for other problems (e.g. depression, eating disorders, social anxiety). In these cases, resolving the presenting problem without addressing the underlying negative sense of self may leave people vulnerable to future difficulties. Here, low self-esteem must be tackled in its own right.

Cognitive models

A cognitive model of low self-esteem is presented in Fig. 20.1. This forms the basis for a treatment programme combining established methods for working with anxiety and depression with ideas from cognitive therapy for longstanding, complex problems and personality disorders. At every stage, behavioural experiments are crucial, ensuring that belief change does not remain an intellectual exercise but is grounded in direct experience and the transformation of emotion.

---

*The authors would like to thank Dr Roz Shafran for contributing Experiment 20.6.

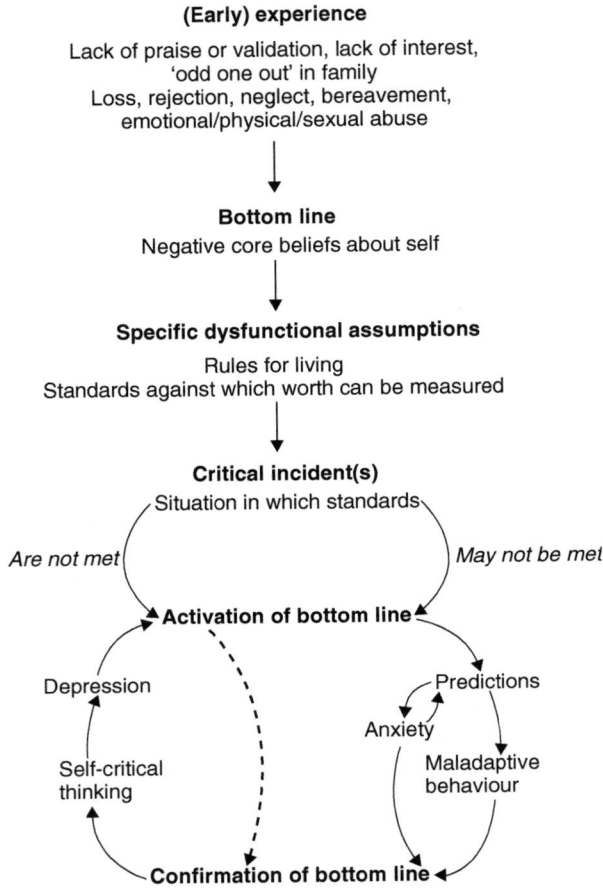

Fig. 20.1 A cognitive model of low self-esteem (based on Fennell 1997).

The model suggests that experience leads to negative beliefs about the self (the 'bottom line'), others, and the world. Based on these beliefs, the person develops operating strategies or guidelines for living (conditional dysfunctional assumptions). Elizabeth, for example—whose parents failed to praise her, always expected more, and sent her to a highly academic school—saw herself as 'not good enough', others as critical and demanding, and life as a competitive business. In order to conceal her shortcomings, avoid criticism, and feel reasonably satisfied with herself, she adopted a strategy of working extremely hard and avoiding challenges where she doubted her ability to achieve excellence. This strategy was encapsulated in her assumptions: 'I must always give 110%', 'If I work hard, I'll be above criticism', and 'Better not to try than to fail'. So long as she could act in accordance with these all was well, despite an underlying sense of precariousness and unease.

Thus, dysfunctional assumptions allow people to maintain self-esteem, so long as their terms are met. However, problems arise if the person encounters a situation (a critical incident) where the terms of the assumptions either *are not met* (there is no doubt about it) or *might not be met* (the outcome is uncertain). Elizabeth had difficulties if, for some reason, she could not perform to her usual standard (the terms *were not met*), or could not escape a challenge which she feared would be beyond her capacity (the terms *might not be met*).

When outcome is uncertain, the response is an anxious one. Activation of the bottom line triggers negative predictions (e.g. 'I'm going to make a mess of this') and symptoms of anxiety. The symptoms may generate further predictions (e.g. 'I'm going to lose it'). Additionally, people often resort to unhelpful behaviours (avoidance, safety behaviours) which prevent disconfirmation of their predictions or create a sense of a 'near miss' even if the situation does turn out well. Anxious preoccupation may genuinely disrupt performance (e.g. the mind goes blank). Even apparently positive outcomes may be ignored or discounted rather than used to reassess the negative perspectives (e.g. 'I managed it by the skin of my teeth—but next time . . . '). Thus, subjectively, the bottom line is confirmed. Self-critical thinking and hopelessness follow, and mood dips. This may be short-lived, but could escalate into clinical depression. Depressed mood ensures that a negative sense of self and negative predictions remain active, closing the circle.

This sequence, a response to uncertainty, contains elements of both anxiety and depression. If, however, people encounter situations where the terms of their assumptions *are not met* (there is no uncertainty), they may head straight for self-critical thinking and depression without intervening anxiety (the dotted line in Fig. 20.1). Many people fluctuate between these two routes, with corresponding shifts in emotional state.

Key cognitions

Negative core beliefs about the self lie at the heart of low self-esteem. This means that cognitive therapists wishing to understand and work with low self-esteem can draw on theoretical concepts and clinical interventions already available in the literature (e.g. Beck *et al.* 1990; Padesky 1994; Young *et al.* 2003).

The everyday expression of beliefs about the self depends not only on the content of the beliefs themselves, but also on the person's beliefs about others and the world. So, for example, the belief that one is weak and inadequate, allied to the belief that others are judgemental and hostile, will incline a person towards avoiding others lest the inadequacy be exposed. The same belief, allied to the idea that others are kind, helpful, and strong, will lead towards dependency (Beck *et al.* 1990, pp. 54–5).

Interacting beliefs about the self, others, and the world lead to patterns of perception, interpretation, and behaviour that confirm their apparent truth. Information-processing biases make people alert to experiences consistent with pre-existing negative beliefs, and quick to screen out, discount, and misinterpret information that contradicts them. Self-defeating behaviour may involve acts consistent with the person's negative beliefs, attempts to avoid their activation, or overcompensation (Young 1990). So, a man who believes he is unlovable may neglect himself, avoid intimate relationships for fear of rejection, or be unassertive and self-sacrificing to an extent that provokes rejection. Each of these strengthens his belief that he is unlovable. The implication for treatment is that patients need to become aware of processes that perpetuate their negative beliefs, including information-processing biases and self-defeating behaviours, and learn ways of overcoming these.

Cognitions contribute to low self-esteem at three levels:

1 Core beliefs about the self (the bottom line), which interact with beliefs about others and the world.

2 Conditional dysfunctional assumptions, which encapsulate the rules that must be obeyed if self-esteem is to be protected.

3 Negative automatic thoughts (anxious predictions and self-criticism), which maintain the problem.

Generally speaking, treatment first aims to disrupt maintaining processes by teaching people to identify, question, and test situation-specific negative automatic thoughts. At the same time, work begins on building a more balanced sense of self, for example by monitoring positive qualities and learning to treat oneself as a person worthy of respect and care. During this process, underlying assumptions and beliefs often come into focus, and work on the specifics can begin to undermine them. Therapy then builds on day-to-day changes by tackling assumptions and beliefs in their own right.

Behavioural experiments are a powerful means of tackling cognitions at all three levels. Furthermore, an experiment carried out at one level will often produce change in others, provided the therapist makes the links explicit. Elizabeth, for example, experimented with only giving 80% to an assignment. This allowed her to test a specific prediction: 'My boss will reject it'. However, it was also an opportunity to road test an alternative to her '110%' rule, and to begin finding out whether people are indeed always critical and demanding. Therapists can ensure that such links are made by asking questions like 'How does this specific experience relate to your assumption that . . . ?', 'What alternative rule might be more realistic and helpful?', 'How does this particular incident relate to your beliefs about . . . ?', 'What alternative perspectives might make better sense of what we observed here?'. Thus, specific experiments can be used to undermine old beliefs and assumptions and to construct new ones right from the beginning of treatment.

Behavioural experiments

♦ **Negative automatic thoughts**

Testing anxious predictions

> *Experiment 20.1: the meaning of mistakes*
> *Experiment 20.2: lack of assertiveness*

Countering self-criticism

> *Experiment 20.3: assertive defence of the self*

Increasing self-acceptance

> *Experiment 20.4: treating oneself with care*

♦ **Unhelpful assumptions**

Perfectionism

> *Experiment 20.5: testing the consequences of lowering standards*
> *Experiment 20.6: doing something for the pleasure of it*

Underestimating abilities

> *Experiment 20.7: sense of incompetence*

Expressing emotions

> *Experiment 20.8: showing emotion is a sign of weakness*

♦ **Re-evaluating the bottom line**

> *Experiment 20.9: enduring low self-esteem*
> *Experiment 20.10: low self-esteem following recent trauma*

We would like to re-emphasize the value of relating specific experiments to broader issues (assumptions, beliefs). Equally, work on assumptions and beliefs should always be solidly grounded in changes in moment-to-moment thoughts, feelings, and behaviour.

Negative automatic thoughts

Testing anxious predictions

Experiment 20.1: the meaning of mistakes

Problem John had a niggling sense of inadequacy. He seemed to make a lot of mistakes, and lived in fear that someone would notice them.

Target cognition Making mistakes is a sign of inadequacy.

Prediction If someone notices a mistake I make, they will think less of me.

Experiment First, John carefully observed people at work and elsewhere to see how frequently they made mistakes. He recorded mistakes he noticed, and whether he considered the person who made the mistake to be inadequate. The following week, John deliberately made a number of small mistakes at work (e.g. not returning a phone call). He ensured that these mistakes were noticed, and observed the reactions of his boss and his colleagues.

Results John discovered that making mistakes was common, even in people he considered competent. For example, he observed a confident and articulate television news presenter lose his way on the autocue and look at the wrong camera. There were no adverse reactions to mistakes John made. For instance, a colleague simply reminded him to make the 'forgotten' phone call.

Reflection John realized that making mistakes is normal, even for competent people. His own 'mistakes' showed that people were more tolerant than he anticipated.

Further work John began to search for and record evidence consistent with a tentative new bottom line: 'I am competent'. This drew his attention to positive aspects of himself which he had simply ignored, and his confidence in himself began to grow.

Tips This case shows how small experiments, testing specific predictions, can be used as a first step to questioning assumptions (breaking the link between mistakes and inadequacy) and creating a new bottom line.

Experiment 20.2: lack of assertiveness

Problem Annie believed she was inferior. She was convinced that if she asked anyone to take account of her needs, they would refuse.

Target cognitions If I ask for what I want, people won't want to know me any more.

Prediction If I ask my boss to change my shift so I can go to a friend's fortieth birthday party, I will be told I am selfish and ought to put the team's needs first.

Experiment Annie would ask to change her shift. She would watch carefully for any sign that her colleagues thought her selfish or treated her as inferior. She and her therapist worked out different reactions she might get (including her worst case scenario), and rehearsed how she might respond. Annie felt reasonably confident with her therapist, but felt too nervous to make her request at the team meeting as planned. In the next session, she decided that it would be easier to speak to her team leader alone. This she was able to do, carefully watching the team leader's reactions.

Results Annie felt very anxious before speaking to her team leader, and was not sure she could do it. The team leader seemed a little irritable, and Annie was tempted to chicken out, but the thought of having to tell her therapist stiffened her resolve. In fact, the team leader was happy to change Annie's shift, treated her as an equal, and wished her a good time.

Reflection Annie was pleased with herself. The reactions she expected were not forthcoming. However, she was still not convinced that the same thing would happen in other situations.

Further work Annie's sense of inferiority had a long history. She needed to repeat the experiment many times, asking for people's time and attention in different situations. Only then was her sense of inferiority undermined.

Tips The first experiment (speaking out in front of the team) was too hard for Annie. Experiments, while extending the patient's range, must be manageable or they may lead to demoralization. Small steps are often the best way forward, especially in the case of chronic difficulties. The experiment also illustrates how patients' belief systems can affect the therapeutic relationship. Annie later admitted that she had agreed to the first experiment because she was afraid to displease her therapist. Therapy itself then became an experiment in expressing her needs.

Countering self-criticism

Self-criticism contributes to low mood and reinforces negative beliefs about the self. Classical cognitive therapy methods can be used to tackle it (e.g. questioning self-critical thoughts, exploring the advantages and disadvantages of self-criticism). Enactive methods such as 'assertive defence of the self' (Padesky 1997) enhance the emotional impact of these interventions. This involves not simply writing down alternatives to critical thoughts, but assertively talking back to the critical voice.

Experiment 20.3: assertive defence of the self

Problem Gemma had to wear thick spectacles as a child. Her schoolmates called her 'speccy four-eyes' and hid her glasses. She grew up feeling there was something wrong with her as a person. She learned to make herself inconspicuous, believing that otherwise people would ridicule her and she would be unable to defend herself.

Target cognition There's something wrong with me.

Predictions If people notice me, they will think I'm stupid and abnormal, and there's nothing I can do about it.

Experiment Through a sequence of experiments, initially with her therapist, and then alone, Gemma discovered that people mostly paid little or no attention to her, even when she deliberately acted oddly. She also began to question self-critical thoughts, and to note daily examples of her own qualities and strengths ('positive data logging', Padesky 1994). Although she started to feel better about herself, she still feared the 'one in a million person' who would be contemptuous if they noticed anything unusual about her, and doubted her ability to stand up for herself.

The therapist noted down, word for word, Gemma's predictions about what the 'one in a million person' might think: 'You're stupid', 'You must be abnormal', 'There's something wrong with you'. She asked Gemma to say these things to her, and reacted as Gemma might herself react ('You're right. I am'). Then she asked Gemma to repeat the rude remarks, and this time responded more assertively: 'No, I'm not stupid or abnormal, and there's nothing wrong with me'. Gemma liked this new approach. She said that now, if someone did speak to her like that, she would know what to do. The therapist rather doubted this, and suggested that they reverse roles: the therapist would be the 'one in a million person' and Gemma would defend herself.

Results When it came to the point, Gemma's mind went blank. The therapist came out of role briefly to coach her ('No, I'm not stupid . . . '). Gemma warmed to the part, and began to defend herself. The therapist gave way when Gemma had responded assertively. Gemma found this new way of reacting stressful and difficult, so they tried it again. This time she needed no coaching, and the therapist was quickly silenced. Finally ('third time lucky'), Gemma zapped the therapist almost instantly, and they both collapsed in fits of laughter.

Reflection Gemma commented 'That was great!'. She discovered two important things. First, she could defend herself effectively. Second, hearing her own thoughts spoken aloud by the therapist helped her to realize how extreme they were— and she said that life was too short to spend time with people who thought like that.

Tips It is important that patients realize, when the therapist speaks in the critical voice, that this is only an act. This may sound obvious, but critical thoughts often reflect painful experiences, and it may be difficult for patients not to be affected by them. It may be helpful for therapists to repeat that they are voicing patients' own thoughts, not saying anything they personally believe. Equally, sensitive debriefing is important.

Patients often go blank when it is their turn to speak assertively, even when the therapist has just modelled what to do. Usually, brief coaching primes an assertive response. If not, or if the patient becomes upset, the therapist will need to explore what speaking assertively might mean. It could be that distressing memories have surfaced, or that there is some taboo on self-defence.

Assertive defence of the self kills several birds with one stone: it enacts effective answers to self-critical thoughts; it may also enact an assertive response to the person whose voice is reflected in the thoughts (e.g. a parent or teacher); it puts the critical voice in perspective by demonstrating how outrageously rude it is; and it is energizing and empowering, and thus emotionally powerful.

Increasing self-acceptance

Self-neglect and other self-defeating behaviours can play a significant role in perpetuating low self-esteem. The following experiment illustrates how *acting as if* one deserves affection and respect can encourage more adaptive behaviours, increase self-acceptance, and even prompt more kindly and respectful behaviour from others.

Experiment 20.4: treating oneself with care

Problem Ian's problems included longstanding low mood and low self-esteem. He neglected himself by not eating regularly, abusing alcohol, ignoring his financial difficulties, and not doing anything that he might enjoy.

Target cognitions I'm worthless. Nobody cares about me.

Alternative perspective If I learn to care for myself this may help me to feel better about myself, and maybe people will show more interest in me.

Experiment Ian reduced his alcohol intake, addressed his financial difficulties, cooked himself healthy meals, and scheduled potentially enjoyable activities (including visits to the cinema, cafes, and a pottery class). This experiment was carried out over several weeks, and was combined with activity scheduling (see Chapter 10, p. 210, on the use of activity scheduling in depression).

Results Ian reported a marked improvement in his mood and self-esteem. His new activities brought him into contact with new people and provided more opportunities for him to receive positive feedback.

Reflection Ian concluded that little things could make a real difference to how he felt, and that self-neglect maintained his low self-esteem. When asked about the implications for his view of himself, he said he saw himself as being 'an average sort of bloke' who could enjoy himself and be liked and cared for by other people.

Tips This experiment shows how activity scheduling can be used to help address low self-esteem as well as depression. It can be combined with a positive data log (e.g. Ian recorded evidence of positive feedback). Encouraging behavioural change through the use of experiments may help foster curiosity and increase motivation in people who feel hopeless about themselves.

Unhelpful assumptions

Perfectionism

Experiment 20.5: testing the consequences of lowering standards

Problem Mark's perfectionist standards were slowing him down so much that he was missing deadlines for his university course work and was at risk of failing the course. He believed he had to read everything on the reading list, and understand it all. He put off essay writing and analysed every sentence in detail as he wrote. He was anxious about his work, and his sense of failure and lack of time for relaxation contributed to low mood. Underlying his difficulties was his belief that he was not very capable and must work extremely hard in order to be good enough.

Target cognitions I need to work extremely hard in order to be good enough.

Prediction Unless I read and understand everything on the reading list, my essay will not be good enough and I will fail.

Preparation for the experiment Before experimenting with lowering his standards, Mark talked to his peers about their study methods and the time they typically spent on essays. He discovered that most people read only five or six references (as recommended by the course) and did not always understand everything they read. They usually spent less than half the time he did on an essay.

Experiment Mark selected six references off the reading list for his next essay and tried to spend a similar amount of time on his essay as his peers. He wrote the essay as if it was a rough draft to help reduce procrastination.

Results Mark spent around an hour more than he planned on his essay, but met the deadline and took several hours less than normal. The essay passed and he was awarded a mark at least as good as his average.

Reflection Mark concluded that perfectionism and working extremely hard did not necessarily help him to write good essays. In fact, it actually interfered with the flow of his ideas and slowed him down. His therapist encouraged him to consider the implications of the experiment for his judgement of his abilities. Mark was able to entertain the possibility that he might be as capable as his peers.

Further work Mark found the outcome of this experiment encouraging, but his perfectionist tendencies were well established, and he returned to his old studying habits when the work seemed more complex. He needed support in order to test what happened when he applied his new standards to more challenging assignments.

Experiment 20.6: doing something for the pleasure of it

Problem Fiona often started activities but gave them up unless she excelled in them. For example, she gave up playing the violin when she realized she would not be a professional musician. Over time, she stopped trying new things because she worried that others would think that trying to do something beyond her capabilities meant that she thought too much of herself. She then became self-critical and distressed, which sometimes led to her cutting herself.

Target cognitions Unless I'm absolutely certain that I'm going to be good at something, I shouldn't bother trying.

Alternative beliefs If I might enjoy something, it might be worth giving it a try.

Predictions I won't enjoy drawing because I might not be good enough and I'll definitely be anxious. I'm better off not trying new things.

Experiment Fiona would attend a 'friendly' art class with people of all levels of ability. She agreed to attend on a specific day and to bring a friend with her. She rated her moods and thoughts before and after attending the class and compared them with her moods and thoughts before and after avoiding an activity (auditioning for an orchestra).

Results Fiona was definitely anxious and did not want to go to her art class. Her friend encouraged her. Once there, she found that the people were not those that she usually mixed with, and didn't care what they thought of her. During the evening, she began to enjoy herself. She was able to accept that she was not particularly good or bad at drawing. Afterwards, she felt good about herself for trying something new. In contrast, although she had felt less anxious when she avoided the audition, later she felt worse about herself, more depressed, and more self-critical.

Reflection Fiona realized that not trying new activities because she might not excel was unhelpful. Her mood improved when she tried something new— even if she was not the best among the group. Although she was more anxious at first, her anxiety soon decreased. She agreed that simply trying a new activity was valuable in its own right, and led to her feeling better about herself than telling herself that she couldn't be bothered.

Tips Fiona's all-or-nothing thinking was a clue to her perfectionist tendencies, even though she was not actively striving for success, as is typical of people with perfectionism.

Underestimating abilities

Viewing oneself as incompetent or inadequate, and underestimating one's ability to cope, can lead to avoidance of opportunities and challenges, which in turn maintains lack of self-esteem. Experiments that involve testing out negative predictions about learning new tasks and coping with challenges can help people build a more realistic view of their abilities.

Experiment 20.7: sense of incompetence

Problem Kate viewed herself as incompetent and a slow learner, and underestimated her ability to cope with challenges. Learning new things caused her a lot of anxiety, and she would avoid it if possible. This prevented her from developing self-confidence. When she heard that she must learn how to use new computer software at work she considered resigning, assuming that she would find it impossible.

Target cognitions If I try to learn new things, I shall fail.

Alternative perspective Sometimes things are easier than I expect—for example, learning to drive. Perhaps this is another example of me underestimating myself.

Prediction I will never learn to use the new computer software. If I try, I will be so anxious I won't remember anything I am told.

Experiment Kate arranged for a colleague to spend half an hour showing her how to use the new computer software, and then attempted to use it independently.

Results Kate was very anxious, but found she could remember more than half of what she had been shown. She needed a little help when she first used the computer independently, but it was not as difficult as she had expected.

Reflection Kate concluded that she could remember things better than she had predicted. This was another example of underestimating her abilities. However, she discounted the results of the experiment somewhat by referring to the computer software as 'idiot proof'.

Tips Educating Kate (prior to the experiment) about schema maintenance processes, using the prejudice model (Padesky 1993*b*), helped her to accept the results of the experiment. She noticed how she automatically downgraded her performance, and how normally this made it hard to give herself credit for her achievements.

Further work Kate began to identify and test out negative predictions about her abilities on a daily basis. These experiments, which she recorded in a positive data log, generated more evidence that she was 'competent and capable'.

Expressing emotions

Experiment 20.8: showing emotions is a sign of weakness

Problem Pete grew up in a family where controlling emotions and being strong and independent were highly valued. These abilities served him well, and he saw himself as strong and competent. However, there came a time when his wife developed a chronic illness, his children needed time and attention, and, as the family breadwinner, he had to continue to work. Pete became increasingly stressed. He coped by ignoring his feelings. When this did not help, he began to see himself as weak and pathetic. Being referred for cognitive therapy confirmed this idea.

Target cognitions Showing emotions is a sign of weakness. I should be able to cope (belief: 100%).

Predictions If I ask for help and support, I will be rejected (belief: 90%). If I show my feelings, I will fall apart (belief: 100%).

Experiment Pete rather reluctantly agreed to experiment with breaking the rules by being more open about how he felt and by asking for help. He asked a friend to pick the children up from school, instead of trying to do it himself. He also told his wife a little about how he had been feeling.

Results Pete's friend was happy to pick up the children from school. She commented that he must be under a lot of pressure at the moment, and he admitted that he was feeling very stressed. She encouraged him to ask for more help when he needed it. His wife was very loving and supportive. She had noticed how uptight he was, but didn't know how to help. As far as falling apart was concerned, Pete did become quite upset when he started talking about his feelings, but afterwards he felt as if a weight had been lifted off his shoulders.

Reflection Both Pete's predictions were disconfirmed. His belief in his assumption fell to 35%. He recognized that he still needed to work on it, but could see that showing feelings and asking for help, far from being a sign of weakness, are effective ways of caring for oneself and making relationships closer and deeper.

Tips Unhelpful assumptions can have a direct impact on therapy. Pete's rule made it difficult for him to resolve his problems and to engage with the therapist. In many ways, however, it was useful to him. The aim, therefore, was not to remove it altogether, but to make it more flexible, so that his sense of strength and competence incorporated the idea that expressing feelings is human, and that no one can manage without help all the time.

Re-evaluating the bottom line

Negative beliefs about the self are often formed during childhood and adolescence, and may be deeply rooted and repeatedly rehearsed. The first case described below falls into this category. Sometimes, however, low self-esteem can develop much later in life. The second case exemplifies this.

Experiment 20.9: enduring low self-esteem

Problem Alan was teased at school because he came from a background unlike that of his classmates. As an adult, he still saw himself as 'weird' and 'boring', and felt he had to conceal his true self. Consequently, he rarely talked about his work, his interests, or his leisure pursuits. He came for help with social anxiety and recurrent low mood.

Target cognitions I am weird and boring.

Prediction If I talk openly about myself, people will think I am weird and boring and will not want to spend time with me. They will be right (belief: 80%).

Experiment In session, Alan would talk about himself for 5–10 minutes to a small group of people and ask them for feedback, using a short questionnaire he had devised with his therapist:

- How weird did you think Alan was?
- How boring did you think Alan was?
- Would you have liked more time to talk to him?

Each answer was rated on a 0–100 scale ('not at all' to 'extremely'). Alan also rated his own performance, and wrote down the ratings he thought people would give him. After the experiment, his ratings were compared with those of his audience. In the following session, Alan and the therapist watched the videotape of the session, so that he could judge for himself how 'weird' and 'boring' he was. The therapist instructed him to observe himself as if he were another person towards whom he felt well disposed, rather than getting caught up in how he felt at the time and in old patterns of self-criticism.

Results Alan's predictions were disconfirmed. He predicted that the audience would see him as 30% weird and 30% boring; none of their ratings were close to that. All three said they would have liked more time to talk to him ('We were just getting started'). When Alan watched the videotape of the session, he saw that he appeared neither weird nor boring, and his ratings came into line with those of his audience. He could also see from their non-verbal behaviour (nodding, smiling, asking questions) that they were genuinely interested and engaged in what he had to say.

Reflection Alan realized that, if he talked openly about himself, he would find out for himself whether people were interested. They would find it easier to get to know him, and he would find it easier to get to know them. Some people would not be interested in him, but that didn't mean there was something wrong with him. His belief in this new perspective was 75%, and his belief in his original prediction fell to 20%.

Further work Alan's doubts about himself had been present since early childhood, so it would be astounding if a single experiment were enough to change them permanently. Talking about himself and observing the outcome became a recurrent homework assignment over a number of weeks. In addition, he began keeping a positive data log of encounters where people reacted to him with interest and acceptance, and discovered he had been ignoring many pleasant encounters and noting only those which (to his mind) confirmed his negative sense of self.

Tips It should not be assumed that longstanding low self-esteem can only be helped by long-term treatment. Alan made substantial changes within the context of short-term, focused cognitive therapy. Before this experiment, he had already worked on social anxiety (see Chapter 7). He had experienced the power of behavioural experiments, and had built up a friendly, trusting relationship with his therapist. This created a solid foundation for transforming his fundamental sense of himself.

Experiment 20.10: low self-esteem following recent trauma

Problem Irina, a devout Christian, was viciously raped by an acquaintance. She was a virgin, and strongly believed that sexual intercourse should be saved for marriage. She felt deeply ashamed of what had happened, and believed that it had permanently destroyed her worth as a person. In contrast, before the rape, she had seen herself as good and worthwhile.

Target cognitions After what happened to me, I am not worthy of a decent man. I am ruined (spoiled, contaminated, dirty).

Predictions Irina believed that anyone to whom she confided her story would agree with her perspective—that is, they would think she was ruined. This would be especially true of other Christians.

Experiment Irina was too frightened and ashamed to canvas opinion herself, so the therapist carried out a survey on her behalf. The details were worked out in collaboration with Irina. Ten men and women were consulted, including six devout Christians. The therapist described Irina's situation and her current view of herself, and asked:

- ◆ Do you agree with Irina's opinion of herself? What is your own opinion of what happened?
- ◆ What would your perception be of what she's gone through? How would you expect her to feel—her vulnerabilities; the impact on her life? How would you behave as a result?

Replies were audiotaped and transcribed, and Irina listened to the tape as well as reading the transcription. The therapist repeatedly asked her how what she heard fitted with the reactions she had predicted.

Results All those surveyed responded with sympathy and horror. They placed the responsibility for what had happened squarely on the rapist, and emphatically did not agree with Irina's evaluation of herself.

Reflection Irina was astonished by what she heard. She noted that people were not judgemental or rejecting. Perhaps she did not need to be so hard on herself, and could begin to consider confiding in others.

Further work This experiment introduced an element of doubt into very powerful, distressing negative beliefs about the self. However, on its own it was not enough to persuade Irina to adopt a kinder perspective. In addition, she needed to experiment with confiding in people she was close to and returning to church (a support network she had abandoned). She also needed to work on her own beliefs about the rape.

Tips A survey carried out by the therapist is a good way of tackling guilt and shame. For patients, such information gathering involves a frightening degree of self-exposure; therapists have no comparable investment in the answers. The therapist's supportive warmth and matter-of-factness in themselves communicate a refusal to endorse the patient's negative view. Audiotaping participants' responses to questions is a good way of increasing their credibility. The patient will hear emotional reactions in people's tone of voice—in this case, horror, compassion, and disbelief.

Distinctive difficulties
Treatment difficulty

Beware of assuming that negative self-statements *necessarily* indicate beliefs requiring long-term therapy. They may be primarily mood-dependent, or reflect the demoralizing impact of another presenting problem. Treating presenting problems first will make this clear. Even if self-doubt predates the presenting problem, substantial changes often occur in a relatively short space of time. However, entrenched negative beliefs about the self may only yield to more lengthy interventions.

Decentring

Engaging patients in behavioural experiments is difficult if they believe their negative attitudes to themselves reflect hard fact: 'I *am* . . .'. The possibility that these beliefs are simply opinions—and may (like other opinions) be misguided, unhelpful, or wrong—provides a framework within which therapy becomes an extended exploration of an alternative perspective: 'I *believe* I am . . .'.

Information-processing biases

Even well designed and implemented experiments can fail—their results ignored, discounted, or misinterpreted. In-session experiments are particularly helpful in this regard, as the therapist can:

◆ Ensure that predictions are recorded in careful detail, so that patients cannot easily move the goalposts after the event.

◆ Prepare patients for a range of outcomes.

◆ Be alert for cognitive biases ('Yes, but . . . 's', disclaimers, non-verbal signs of doubt).

◆ Teach patients to be aware of them too, without buying into them ('Oh look, I just did it again').

Emotional change

Patients with entrenched negative beliefs sometimes respond to verbal interventions with 'I see what you mean, but I don't *feel* any different'. Behavioural experiments, for the reasons outlined in Chapters 1 and 2, optimize the chances of transforming new 'head' knowledge into action-based, emotionally grounded 'heart' learning.

Multi-level change

If specific experiments are not clearly related to broader beliefs and assumptions, they may appear trivial. Additionally, opportunities to undermine old perspectives and create and strengthen new ones through specific, here-and-now experiences will be missed.

Word for word

In surveys, use patients' own language (e.g. 'weird', 'abnormal', 'evil', 'not human'). Audiotaped surveys communicate respondents' emotional reactions—extreme language, which patients may firmly believe, often elicits audible incomprehension and disbelief.

The environment

Environmental factors are incorporated into the model at the developmental phase, and as triggering events. They may also contribute to confirmation of the bottom line and, unless taken into account, hinder patients from generalizing new learning to the real world. Examples include bullying (at school or at work); abuse; criticism; excessive support encouraging dependency; societal prejudice; adverse circumstances; and systems which have little sensitivity to individual need or where autonomy is undermined (including well-meaning mental health-care services).

Other related chapters

Low self-esteem is associated with a wide range of presenting problems. Readers may be particularly interested to consult Chapter 10 on depression, Chapter 7 on social anxiety, Chapter 13 on eating disorders, Chapter 12 on psychosis, Chapter 18 on deliberate self-harm, and Chapter 19 on interpersonal problems.

Further reading

Fennell, M.J.V. (1997). Low self-esteem: a cognitive perspective. *Behavioural and Cognitive Psychotherapy*, 25, 1–25.

Fennell, M.J.V. (1998). Low self-esteem. In: N. Tarrier, A. Wells, and G. Haddock (ed.), *Treating complex cases: the cognitive behavioural therapy approach*. Wiley, Chichester.

Fennell, M.J.V. (1999). *Overcoming low self-esteem*. Robinson, London.

McKay, M. and Fanning, P. (1992). *Self-esteem*. New Harbinger Publications, Oakland, CA.

Padesky, C.A. (1994). Schema change processes in cognitive therapy. *Clinical Psychology and Psychotherapy*, 1, 267–78.

Tales from the Front Line
Flying by the seat of your pants

Jen, who had a fear of flying, was her trainee therapist's very first patient. Together they followed the protocol to the letter, and both were delighted with the progress Jen made. For her last behavioural experiment, Jen arranged for the chief instructor of a local flying school to take her and the therapist on a half-hour trip in a small three-seater plane. On a hot summer afternoon Jen and her therapist were shown round the outside of the plane, and the instructor then invited the therapist to come along for the ride. She climbed into the back, and watched while both Jen and the instructor put on earphones and checked that they could communicate with the control tower and with each other. Neither of them could see or hear the therapist sitting quietly behind them. Nor could the therapist hear what they said to each other over the engine noise.

Once in the air the instructor let Jen take control and her confidence grew visibly. She circled the airport and headed out – directly over the village where the therapist lived. A thunderstorm was brewing. Black clouds were fast approaching. The plane lurched and bumped, but Jen, with the instructor in dual control, carried confidently on. As the storm began to break they turned back. To the therapist's consternation the plane suddenly veered round at an astonishing angle right over her home, where she saw her children rescuing their toys from the garden. A terrifying trip back to the airport ensued. The plane tipped unpredictably this way and that and seemed, as far as the therapist was concerned, to be entirely at the mercy of increasingly strong gusts of wind. Once they had landed, taking in a few unexpected jumps and hops, Jen emerged smiling and happy. The instructor turned to the therapist and said: "Well, the only sign of emotion I saw was in the *back* seat!"

CHAPTER 21

Behavioural experiments: at the crossroads

Christine Padesky

Do not go where the path may lead,
go instead where there is no path and leave a trail.

Ralph Waldo Emerson

The crossroads are where all paths meet, traditionally a place for assembly, social interchange, and exchange of knowledge and goods. Today, they are often highways, heavily travelled because of their utility and speedy convenience. This chapter highlights how behavioural experiments are the crossroads of cognitive therapy. They are prime opportunities for exchanging knowledge and speedy paths to therapeutic change. Crossroads also can be a point of divergence from which new trails are blazed. Speculation on the future of behavioural experiments within cognitive therapy points to trails yet lightly travelled.

Behavioural experiments as the crossroads
Professional and personal science

This text beautifully illustrates the empirical nature of cognitive therapy. Succinct summaries in each chapter provide readers with a digest of current theoretical and empirical knowledge regarding each problem focus. Cognitive therapy treatment protocols are detailed that mark the leading edge of empirical knowledge regarding each topic. For therapists, these chapter reviews ground the described behavioural experiments within a broader scientific framework.

For patients, however, behavioural experiments *are* the science. Patients bring the healthy scepticism to experiments that true experimental science requires. They, more than therapists, are likely to question conclusions formed and press for more data before toppling a tightly held theory. Informed by a therapist's understanding of psychology's scientific knowledge base, behavioural experiments are designed to help patients use their own life as a laboratory, so they can derive personal scientific knowledge from analysis of life events. In these ways, behavioural experiments form the crossroads of professional and personal science.

Analytical and experiential knowledge

As highlighted in Chapter 1, behavioural experiments provide a meeting ground for discourse between knowledge derived from the rational mind and from the more intuitive, emotional mind (that is grounded in subjective phenomenological experience). Cognitive therapists sometime err in giving too much weight in therapy discussions to rational arguments ('head'). Patients often err in anchoring their conclusions in subjective experience filtered through biases in information processing and distortions of memory ('heart'). The four-stage learning model outlined in Chapter 2 and illustrated throughout the book provides a frame that can help ensure therapists and patients balance and value both types of information.

The importance of helping 'head' and 'heart' to reach consensus is highlighted by findings in experiments conducted by Epstein and his colleagues. When the emotional consequences of decisions and behaviours are increased, rational processing of information takes a back seat to experiential processing. The first thoughts that occur to people in times of misfortune are most likely to rise from the experiential mind. And when there is a conflict between 'head' and 'heart', information that comes from the heart is generally more compelling (Epstein 1994). Thus, to help ensure lasting change, it is important the experiential mind is truly convinced of new beliefs. Case examples throughout this book eloquently demonstrate how repeated experiments can and must be done to explore and answer all the reservations of the experiential mind.

Old and new beliefs, behaviours, emotional responses

Behavioural experiments create an intersection for old and new beliefs. Similarly, behavioural experiments often mark the transition between old and new behaviours as well as old and new emotional responses to events. As is clear in preceding chapters, cognitive therapists hope that a patient who enters a series of behavioural experiments following the path of old beliefs emerges on a different path of new belief. The quality of the new beliefs, behaviours, and emotional reactions derived will be affected by the relevance of the experiments designed and the care with which therapist and patient analyse and extract learning from what is observed.

The authors of the *Oxford Guide* provide excellent models for how to design behavioural experiments to test pivotal beliefs, rather than tangential beliefs. As is clear, behavioural experiments can involve great time and perceived risk for patients, and sometimes therapists too. Thus, it is important to choose experiments that are likely to make a relevant and significant difference for the patient's well-being. Each chapter offers meaningful help to therapists by identifying common cognitive themes and beliefs that are central to the problem discussed. Readers are encouraged to examine these cognitions to see if any appear pivotal to the maintenance of a particular patient's problems.

In addition, therapists are challenged to develop their guided discovery skills. As illustrated in each chapter, skilful and dogged guided discovery can uncover invaluable patient observations. Focusing patient attention on the relevant details revealed can lead to evidence palpable enough to convince the experiential mind. One is left with the impression that several behavioural experiments, expertly designed and debriefed, significantly influence learning more than dozens of experiments half-heartedly designed and inadequately analysed.

Therapist as collaborative ally

Cognitive therapy has long championed the idea that therapist and patient should be active collaborative partners in therapy (Beck *et al.* 1979). Therapists often coach patients to do behavioural experiments on their own, between sessions. As described in this book, behavioural experiments can challenge therapists to collaborate with patients by crossing the invisible line between therapy office and broader world. The Oxford group encourages therapists to leave the office and become experimental allies whenever adopting this role facilitates learning.

Each therapist needs to judge the professional boundaries appropriate to his or her own community, professional affiliations, and legal restrictions, and to each patient relationship. Yet a powerful picture emerges from case examples that observation of therapist experiments in the real world can pave the way for rapid patient learning and subsequent patient risk taking. Audiotaped therapist-conducted surveys provide patients with normative information they might hesitate to gather on their own. Therapist activities such as these can provide a positive or negative crossroad in the therapy relationship. A therapist stance of curiosity, empirical interest, and compassionate exploration of patient beliefs contribute to patient perception of these experiences as therapeutic rather than boundary crossings.

New trails ahead

Individual therapists

The most promising trails often go unrecognized until explored. The *Oxford Guide* shows cognitive therapists new ways to design and debrief behavioural experiments. The vivid samples offered should encourage them to use behavioural experiments more often, with greater precision, and with more thorough examination of patient observations and learning. Therapist readers now need to do their own behavioural experiments to test whatever reservations or questions linger about the utility of this powerful therapy tool.

Several chapters in this book specifically address use of behavioural experiments with patients diagnosed with personality disorders. In addition to treating problems associated with particular personality disorders (e.g. avoidance, self-injurious behaviours, interpersonal difficulties), there is a growing literature that suggests cognitive therapy can effectively treat the personality disorder itself (Beck *et al.* 2003). Behavioural experiments play a key role in this treatment (Beck *et al.* 2003; Mooney and Padesky 2000; Padesky 1995). As modelled in previous chapters, cognitive therapists help patients with personality disorders to identify alternative beliefs prior to embarking on behavioural experiments. This is particularly important because the absence of viable alternative beliefs is considered a maintenance factor of these disorders (Padesky 1994).

Behavioural experiments have a clear advantage over purely verbal interventions when treatment focus is a personality disorder. Target symptoms are interpersonal behaviour patterns maintained by beliefs deeply grounded in emotionally laden experiences. Patients with personality disorders are generally certain that their central maintaining beliefs are absolutely true. Thus, verbal questioning of beliefs can be construed as a sign that the therapist does not understand or care about the patient's welfare. The curious, experimental approach illustrated in this *Oxford Guide* can enhance the collaborative relationship considered fundamental to successful transformation of personality. As patients with personality disorders engage fully in behavioural experiments, they learn to adopt more flexible beliefs, behaviours, and strategies that increase interpersonal success.

Cognitive therapy researchers

It is remarkable there is little research on behavioural experiments given the central role they play in treating so many disorders. On the other hand, the paucity of research is a great opportunity for new discovery. Qualitative comparisons of different types of behavioural experiments (e.g. observational, active, discovery) can be made to see if some experiments are associated more strongly than others with positive treatment outcomes. Empirical studies could evaluate what qualities of therapeutic debriefing (e.g. use of guided discovery, focus on patient observations) influence patient learning and change. Patient factors that influence behavioural experiments are also important to identify, especially to understand which factors enhance the efficacy of this therapeutic method.

Cognitive therapy: new trails

For a broad spectrum of problems, cognitive therapy offers one of the best roads to recovery and relapse prevention (DeRubeis and Crits–Christoph 1998; Hollon and Beck 2003). As this *Oxford Guide* suggests, behavioural experiments play a beneficial role in each cognitive therapy application developed to date. What is the future of cognitive therapy? What role will behavioural experiments play in this future?

As long as cognitive therapy is grounded in empiricism, it will evolve (Padesky and Beck 2003*b*). Cognitive therapy treatments and use of behavioural experiments should improve in upcoming years, hopefully informed by empirical research. There are likely to be more diverse methods for delivering cognitive therapy through print, electronic media, and even video games (Padesky 2002). There will be greater focus on applications for children (c.f. Friedberg and McClure 2002) and modifications for particular cultural groups. In addition to an emphasis on therapy for individuals or couples, new attention is likely to be given to family therapy, group therapy (c.f. White and Freeman 2000), applications within communities (including prevention programmes), and administration of cognitive therapy via guided self-help programmes (c.f. Greenberger and Padesky 1995). Each new or expanded cognitive therapy application is likely to include, or even emphasize, use of behavioural experiments because they potentiate learning and change.

In addition, the topical attention of cognitive therapy is likely to continue to expand beyond its current focus on psychiatric disorders. Seligman, a leading proponent of the positive psychology movement, has challenged psychology to apply its scientific knowledge to enhance positive human qualities rather than simply addressing human problems (cf. Seligman and Csikszentmihalyi 2000). Cognitive therapy is well poised to meet this challenge. Positive psychologists propose that we can build a psychology that will help people become happier, more altruistic, resilient, kind, compassionate, and courageous.

Positive qualities, behaviours, and moods are influenced by beliefs just as surely as negative ones. What better way to develop and refine positive qualities than through behavioural experiments? As cognitive therapy contributes to positive psychology in the years ahead, behavioural experiments will not only test beliefs but also help evaluate the individual and social consequences of behaviours, decisions, and values.

Conclusion

Readers of this *Oxford Guide* will gain a broad perspective on the state of the art for the theory, processes, and practical use of behavioural experiments in cognitive therapy. Practitioners who emulate the model articulated will discover, through their own experience, the depth and breadth of learning that can emerge from creative use of behavioural experiments. Hopefully, this book also will inspire researchers. In the history of cognitive therapy, ideas published become ideas researched.

Behavioural experiments provide an intersection for professional and personal science, patients' analytical and experiential minds, old and new beliefs/emotions/behaviours, and patient learning inside and outside the therapy office. With such a rich convergence, it is not surprising that behavioural experiments play a central role in cognitive therapy for so many diverse problems. As cognitive therapy continues to evolve, behavioural experiments are likely to be found at the crossroads.

References

Abramson, L.Y., Alloy, L.B., Hogan, M.E., Whitehouse, W.G., Donovan, P., Rose, D.T. *et al.* (2002). Cognitive vulnerability to depression: theory and evidence. In: R.L. Leahy and E.T. Dowd (eds.). *Clinical advances in cognitive psychotherapy: theory and application.* Springer, New York.

Agras, W.S., Walsh, T., Fairburn, C.G., Wilson, G.T. and Kraemer, H.C. (2000). A multicentre comparison of cognitive behavioral therapy and interpersonal psychotherapy for bulimia nervosa. *Archives of General Psychiatry,* 157, 459–66.

American Psychiatric Association (2000). *Diagnostic and statistical manual of mental disorder* (4th edn, text revision). American Psychiatric Association, Washington DC.

Ancoli–Israel, S. and Roth, T. (1999). Characteristics of insomnia in the United States: results of the 1991 National Sleep Foundation Survey. I. *Sleep,* 22 (**Suppl 2**), S347–S353.

Arntz, A. and van den Hout, M. (1996). Psychological treatments of panic disorder without agoraphobia: cognitive therapy versus applied relaxation. *Behaviour Research and Therapy,* 34, 113–21.

Barlow, D.H. (1988). *Anxiety and its disorders.* Guilford Press, New York.

Basco, M.R. (2000). Cognitive-behavior therapy for bipolar I disorder. *Journal of Cognitive Psychotherapy,* 14, 287–304.

Baxter, H. (2003). An exploratory qualitative investigation of clients' views regarding behavioural experiments within the context of CBT. Unpublished manuscript, Oxford Doctoral Course in Clinical Psychology, Oxford.

Beck, A.T. (1963). Thinking and depression: 1. Idiosyncratic content and cognitive distortions. *Archives of General Psychiatry,* 9, 324–33.

Beck, A.T. (1964). Thinking and depression: 2. Theory and therapy. *Archives of General Psychiatry,* 10, 561–71.

Beck, A.T. (1967). *Depression: clinical, experimental, and theoretical aspects.* Hoeber, New York. Republished as *Depression: causes and treatment.* University of Pennsylvania Press, Philadelphia.

Beck, A.T. (1970). Cognitive therapy: nature and relation to behavior therapy. *Behavior Therapy,* 1, 184–200.

Beck, A.T. (1976). *Cognitive therapy and the emotional disorders.* International Universities Press, New York.

Beck, A.T., Emery, G. and Greenberg, R.L. (1985). *Anxiety disorders and phobias: a cognitive perspective.* Basic Books, New York.

Beck, A.T., Freeman, A. and associates (1990). *Cognitive therapy of personality disorders.* Guilford Press, New York.

Beck, A.T., Freeman, A., and associates (2003). *Cognitive therapy of personality disorders* (2nd edn). Guilford Press, New York.

Beck, A.T., Rush, A.J., Shaw, B.F., and Emery, G. (1979). *Cognitive therapy of depression.* Guilford Press, New York.

Beck, A.T., Sokol, L., Clark, D.A., Berchick, R. and Wright, F. (1992). A crossover study of focused cognitive therapy for panic disorder. *American Journal of Psychiatry,* 149, 778–83.

Beck, J.S. (1995). *Cognitive therapy: basics and beyond.* Guilford Press, New York.

Bennett–Levy, J. (2003a). Mechanisms of change in cognitive therapy: the case of automatic thought records and behavioural experiments. *Behavioural and Cognitive Psychotherapy,* 31, 261–77.

Bennett–Levy, J. (2003b). Reflection: a blind spot in psychology? *Clinical Psychology,* July, 16–19.

Bernal, G. and Scharron del Rio, M. (2001). Are empirically supported treatments valid for ethnic minorities? Towards an alternative approach for treatment research. *Cultural Diversity and Ethnic Minority Psychology,* 7, 328–42.

Blake, F. (1995). Cognitive therapy for premenstrual syndrome. *Cognitive and Behavioral Practice,* 2, 167–85.

Bonnet, M.H. (1990). The perception of sleep onset in insomniacs and normal sleepers. In: R.R. Bootzin, J.F. Kihlstrom, and D.L. Schacter (eds.). *Sleep and cognition.* American Psychological Association, Washington DC, pp. 148–58.

Borkovec, T.D. (1994). The nature, functions and origins of worry. In: G.C.L. Davey and F. Tallis (eds.). *Worrying: perspectives on theory, assessment and treatment.* Wiley, Chichester.

Borkovec, T.D., Alcaine, O. and Behar, E. (in press). In: R.G. Heimberg, C.L. Turk, and D.S. Mennin (eds.). *Generalized anxiety disorder: advances in research and practice.* Guilford Press, New York.

Borkovec, T.D. and Newman, M.G. (1999). Worry and generalized anxiety disorder. In: P. Salkovskis (ed.). *Comprehensive clinical psychology (vol. 6).* Elsevier, Oxford, pp. 439–59.

Borkovec, T.D., Newman, M.G., Lytle, R. and. Pincus, A.L. (2002). A component analysis of cognitive-behavior therapy for generalized anxiety disorder and the role of interpersonal problems. *Journal of Consulting and Clinical Psychology,* 70, 288–98.

Brewin, C.R. (1996). Theoretical foundations of cognitive-behavior therapy for anxiety and depression. *Annual Review of Psychology,* 47, 33–57.

Brewin, C.R. (2001). A cognitive neuroscience account of post-traumatic stress disorder and its treatment. *Behaviour Research and Therapy,* 39, 373–93.

Brewin, C.R., Dalgleish, T., and Joseph, S. (1996). A dual representation theory of posttraumatic stress disorder. *Psychological Review,* 103, 670–86.

Broscarino, J.A. (1997). Diseases among men 20 years after exposure to severe stress: implications for clinical research and medical care. *Psychosomatic Medicine,* 59, 605–14.

Brown, T.A. and Barlow, D.H. (1992). Comorbidity among anxiety disorders: implications for treatment and DSM-IV. *Journal of Consulting and Clinical Psychology,* 60, 835–44.

Butler, G. (1998). Clinical formulation. In: A.S. Bellack and M. Hersen (eds.). *Comprehensive clinical psychology.* Pergamon, Oxford, pp. 1–24.

Butler, G. (1999). *Overcoming social and anxiety and shyness.* Constable Robinson, London.

Butler, G. and Hope, T. (1995). *Manage your mind.* Oxford University Press, Oxford, pp. 173-91.

Cameron, C.M. (1997). Information processing approaches to phobias. In: G.C.L. Davey (ed.). *Phobias: a handbook of theory, research and treatment.* Wiley, Chichester.

Chadwick, P., Birchwood, M. and Trower, P. (1996). *Cognitive therapy for delusions, voices and paranoia.* Wiley, Chichester.

Chadwick, P., Lowe, C., Horne, P. and Higson, P. (1994). Modifying delusions: the role of empirical testing. *Behavior Therapy*, 25, 35–49.

Chambers, M.J. and Keller, B. (1993). Alert insomniacs: are they really sleep deprived? *Clinical Psychology Review*, 13, 667–82.

Clark, D.M. (1986). A cognitive approach to panic. *Behaviour Research and Therapy*, 24, 461–70.

Clark, D.M. (1989). Anxiety states: panic and general anxiety. In: K. Hawton, P.M. Salkovskis, J. Kirk, and D.M. Clark (eds.). *Cognitive behaviour therapy for psychiatric problems*. Oxford Medical Publications, Oxford, pp. 52–96.

Clark, D.M. (1996). Panic disorder: from theory to therapy. In: P.M. Salkovskis (ed.). *Frontiers in cognitive therapy*. Guilford Press, New York, pp. 318–44.

Clark, D.M. (1997). Panic disorder and social phobia. In: D.M. Clark and C.G. Fairburn (eds.). *The science and practice of cognitive behaviour therapy*. Oxford University Press, Oxford, pp. 121–53.

Clark, D.M. (1999). Anxiety disorders: why they persist and how to treat them. *Behaviour Research and Therapy*, 37, S5–S27.

Clark, D.M. (2002). A cognitive perspective on social phobia. In: W.R. Crozier and L.E. Alden (eds.). *International handbook of social anxiety*. Wiley, Chichester, pp. 405–30.

Clark, D.M., Ehlers, A., McManus, F. *et al.* (in press). Cognitive therapy versus fluoxetine in generalized social phobia: a randomized controlled trial. *Journal of Consulting and Clinical Psychology*.

Clark, D.M., Salkovskis, P.M., Hackmann, A., Middleton, H., Anastasiades, P. and Gelder, M. (1994). A comparison of cognitive therapy, applied relaxation and imipramine in the treatment of panic disorder. *British Journal of Psychiatry*, 164, 759–69.

Clark, D.M., Salkovskis, P.M., Hackmann, A., Wells, A., Ludgate, J. and Gelder, M. (1999). Brief cognitive therapy for panic disorder: a randomized controlled trial. *Journal of Consulting and Clinical Psychology*, 67, 583–9.

Clark, D.M. and Wells, A. (1995). A cognitive model of social phobia. In: R.G. Heimberg, M.R. Liebowitz, D.A. Hope, and I. Schneier (eds.). *Social phobia: diagnosis, assessment, and treatment*. Guilford Press, New York, pp. 69–93.

Close, H. and Garety, P. (1998). Cognitive assessment of voices: further developments in understanding the emotional impact of voices. *British Journal of Clinical Psychology*, 37, 173–88.

Clum, G.A. and Knowles, S.L. (1991). Why do some people with panic disorder become avoidant? A review. *Clinical Psychology Review*, 11, 295–313.

Conway, M.A. (1997). Introduction: what are memories? In: M.A. Conway (ed.). *Recovered memories and false memories*. Oxford University Press, Oxford, pp. 1–22.

Cook, M. and Mineka, S. (1989). Observational conditioning of fear to fear relevant versus irrelevant stimuli in rhesus monkeys. *Journal of Abnormal Psychology*, 98, 448–59.

Cooper, M.J. (1997). Cognitive theory in anorexia nervosa and bulimia nervosa: a review. *Behavioural and Cognitive Psychotherapy*, 25, 113–45.

Cooper, M.J. (2003). *The psychology of bulimia nervosa: a cognitive perspective*. Oxford University Press, Oxford.

Cooper, M.J., Todd, G. and Wells, A. (in press). A cognitive theory of bulimia nervosa. *British Journal of Clinical Psychology*.

Davey, G.C.L. (1994). The 'disgusting' spider: the role of disease and illness in the perpetuation of fear of spiders. *Society and Animals*, 2, 17–24.

Davey, G.C.L. (1997). A conditioning model of phobias. In: Davey G.C.L. (ed.). *Phobias: a handbook of theory, research and treatment*. Wiley, Chichester.

Davey, G.C.L. and Tallis, F. (1994). *Worrying: perspectives on theory, assessment and treatment*. Wiley, Chichester.

Dell'Osso, L., Pini, S., Cassano, G. *et al.* (2002). Insight into illness in patients with mania, mixed mania, bipolar depression and major depression with psychotic features. *Bipolar Disorders*, 4, 315–22.

DeRubeis, R.J. and Crits–Christoph, P. (1998). Empirically supported individual and group psychological treatments for adult mental disorders. *Journal of Consulting and Clinical Psychology*, 66, 37–52.

Dewey, J. (1938). *Experience and education*. Collier Books, New York.

Dobson, K.S., Backs–Dermott, B.J. and Dozois, D.J.A. (2000). Cognitive and cognitive behavioral therapies. In: C.R. Snyder and R.E. Ingram (eds.). *Handbook of psychological change*. Wiley, New York, pp. 409–26.

Dugas, M.J., Gagnon, F., Ladouceur, R. and Freeston, M. (1998). Generalized anxiety disorder: a preliminary test of a conceptual model. *Behaviour Research and Therapy*, 36, 215–26.

Edwards, D.J.A. (1989). Cognitive restructuring through guided imagery: lessons from gestalt therapy. In: A. Freeman, K.S. Simon, H. Arkowitz, and L. Beutler (eds.). *Comprehensive handbook of cognitive therapy*. Plenum, New York, pp. 283–97.

Ehlers, A. and Clark, D.M. (2000). A cognitive model of post-traumatic stress disorder. *Behaviour Research and Therapy*, 38, 319–45.

Eliot, T.S. (1917). *Prufrock and other observations*. Faber and Faber, London.

Ellis, A. (1962). *Reason and emotion in psychotherapy*. Lyle Stuart, New York.

Engelkamp, J. (1998). *Memory for actions*. Psychology Press, Hove.

Epstein, S. (1994). Integration of the cognitive and psychodynamic unconscious. *American Psychologist*, 49, 709–24.

Epstein, S. and Pacini, R. (1999). Some basic issues regarding dual-process theories from the perspective of cognitive-experiential self-theory. In: S. Chaiken and Y. Trope (eds.). *Dual-process theories in social psychology*. Guilford Press, New York, pp. 462–82.

Espie, C.A. (2001). Insomnia: conceptual issues in the development, persistence, and treatment of sleep disorder in adults. *Annual Review of Psychology*, 53, 215–43.

Eysenck, H.J. (1952). The effects of psychotherapy: an evaluation. *Journal of Consulting Psychology*, 16, 319–24.

Fairburn, C.G., Cooper, P.J. and Cooper, Z. (1986). The clinical features and maintenance of bulimia nervosa. In: K.D. Brownell and J.P. Foreyt (eds.). *Physiology, psychology, and treatment of the eating disorders*. Basic Books, New York, pp. 389–404.

Fairburn, C.G., Cooper, Z. and Shafran, R. (2003). Cognitive behaviour therapy for eating disorders: 'transdiagnostic' theory and treatment. *Behaviour Research and Therapy*, 41, 509–28.

Fairburn, C.G., Norman, P.A., Welch, S.L., O'Connor, M.E., Doll, H.A. and Peveler, R.C. (1995). A prospective study of outcome in bulimia nervosa and the long-term effects of three psychological treatments. *Archives of General Psychiatry*, 52, 304–12.

Fairburn, C.G., Shafran, R. and Cooper, Z. (1999). A cognitive-behavioural theory of anorexia nervosa. *Behaviour Research and Therapy*, 37, 1–14.

Fava, G.A., Rafanelli, C., Grandi, S., Conti, S. and Belluardo, P. (1998). Prevention of recurrent depression with cognitive behavioral therapy. *Archives of General Psychiatry,* 55, 816–20.

Feeley, M., DeRubeis, R.J., and Gelfand, L.A. (1999). The temporal relation of adherence and alliance to symptom change in cognitive therapy for depression. *Journal of Consulting and Clinical Psychology,* 76, 574–82.

Fennell, M.J.V. (1989). Depression. In: K. Hawton, P. Salkovskis, J. Kirk and D.M. Clark (eds.). *Cognitive behaviour therapy for psychiatric problems: a practical guide.* Oxford University Press, Oxford.

Fennell, M.J.V. (1997). Low self-esteem: a cognitive perspective. *Behavioural and Cognitive Psychotherapy,* 25, 1–25.

Fennell, M.J.V. (1998). Low self-esteem. In: N. Tarrier, A. Wells, and G. Haddock (eds.). *Treating complex cases: the cognitive behavioural therapy approach.* Wiley, Chichester.

Fennell, M.J.V. (1999). *Overcoming low self-esteem.* Constable Robinson, London.

Fennell, M.J.V. (in press). Depression. In: K. Hawton, P. Salkovskis, J. Kirk, and D.M. Clark (eds.). *Cognitive behaviour therapy for psychiatric problems: a practical guide* (2nd edn). Oxford University Press, Oxford.

Foa, E.B. and Kozak, M.J. (1986). Emotional processing of fear: exposure to corrective information. *Psychological Bulletin,* 99, 20–35.

Foa, E.B. and Rothbaum, B.O. (1998). *Treating the trauma of rape. Cognitive-behavioral therapy for PTSD.* Guilford Press, New York.

Fowler, D., Garety, P. and Kuipers, E. (1995). *Cognitive behaviour therapy for psychosis: theory and practice.* Wiley, Chichester.

Freeston, M., Rheaume, J. and Ladouceur, R. (1996). Correcting faulty appraisals of obsessive thoughts. *Behaviour Research and Therapy,* 13, 459–70.

Friedberg, R.D. and McClure, J.M. (2002). *Clinical practice of cognitive therapy with children and adolescents.* Guilford Press, New York.

Gainotti, G. (1993). Emotional and psychological problems after brain injury. *Neuropsychological Rehabilitation,* 3, 259–77.

Garety, P., Kuipers, E., Fowler, D., Freeman, D. and Bebbington, P. (2001). A cognitive model of the positive symptoms of psychosis. *Psychological Medicine,* 31, 189–95.

Garner, D.M. and Bemis, K.M. (1982). A cognitive-behavioral approach to anorexia nervosa. *Cognitive Therapy and Research,* 6, 123–50.

Gillespie, K., Duffy, M., Hackmann, A. and Clark, D.M. (2002). Community based cognitive therapy in the treatment of post-traumatic stress disorder following the Omagh bomb. *Behaviour Research and Therapy,* 40, 345–57.

Glaser, B.G. and Strauss, A.L. (1967). *The discovery of grounded theory.* Aldine, New York.

Goleman, D. (1996). *Emotional intelligence.* Bloomsbury, London.

Goodwin, F. and Jamison, K. (1990). *Manic depressive illness.* Oxford University Press, Oxford.

Greenberger, D. and Padesky, C.A. (1995). *Mind over mood: change how you feel by changing the way you think.* Guilford Press, New York.

Grey, N., Young, K., and Holmes, E. (2002). Cognitive restructuring within reliving: a treatment for peritraumatic emotional 'hotspots' in post-traumatic stress disorder. *Behavioural and Cognitive Psychotherapy,* 30, 37–56.

Hackmann, A. (1998). Cognitive therapy with panic and agoraphobia: working with complex cases. In: N. Tarrier, A. Wells, and G. Haddock (eds.). *Treating complex cases: the cognitive behavioural therapy approach.* Wiley, Chichester.

Hackmann, A., Clark, D.M. and McManus, F. (2000). Recurrent images and early memories in social phobia. *Behaviour Research and Therapy*, 38, 601–10.

Hackmann, A., Surawy, C. and Clark, D.M. (1998). Seeing yourself through others' eyes: a study of spontaneously occurring images in social phobia. *Behavioural and Cognitive Psychotherapy*, 26, 3–12.

Harvey, A.G. (2001). Insomnia: symptom or diagnosis? *Clinical Psychology Review*, 21, 1037–59.

Harvey, A.G. (2002*a*). A cognitive model of insomnia. *Behaviour Research and Therapy*, 40, 869–93.

Harvey, A.G. (2002*b*). Identifying safety behaviors in insomnia. *Journal of Nervous and Mental Disease*, 190, 16–21.

Harvey, A.G. (in press). The attempted suppression of pre-sleep cognitive activity in insomnia. *Cognitive Therapy and Research.*

Harvey, A.G., Clark, D.M., Ehlers, A. and Rapee, R. (2000). Social anxiety and self-impression: cognitive preparation enhances the beneficial effects of video-feedback following a stressful social task. *Behaviour Research and Therapy*, 38, 1183–92.

Harvey, A.G., Watkins, E., Mansell, W. and Shafran, R. (2004). *Cognitive behavioural processes across psychological disorders: a transdiagnostic approach to research and treatment.* Oxford University Press, Oxford.

Hawton, K., Houston, K. and Shepperd, R. (1999). Suicide in young people: a study of 174 cases, aged under 25 years, based on coroners' and medical records. *British Journal of Psychiatry*, 175, 1–6.

Hawton, K., Rodham, K., Evans, E. and Weatherall, R. (2002). Deliberate self-harm in adolescents: self report survey in schools in England. *British Medical Journal*, 325, 1207–11.

Hawton, K., Salkovskis, P., Kirk, J. and Clark, D. (1989). *Cognitive behaviour therapy for psychiatric problems.* Oxford University Press, Oxford.

Hayward, P. and Bright, J. (1997). Stigma and mental illness: a review and critique. *Journal of Mental Health*, 6, 345–54.

Hayward, P., Wong, G., Bright, A., and Lam, D. (2002). Stigma and self-esteem in manic depression: an exploratory study. *Journal of Affective Disorders*, 69, 61–7.

Heimberg, R.G. (2002). Cognitive-behavioural therapy for social anxiety disorder: current status and future directions. *Biological Psychiatry*, 51, 101–8.

Heuer, F. and Riesberg, D. (1992). Emotion, arousal, and memory for detail. In: S–A. Christianson (ed.). *The handbook of emotion and memory: research and theory.* Lawrence Erlbaum, Hillsdale NJ, pp. 151–80.

Hibbard, M.R., Grober, S.E., Gordon, W.A. and Aletta, E.G. (1990). Modification of cognitive psychotherapy for the treatment of post-stroke depression. *The Behavior Therapist*, 13, 15–17.

Hollon, S.D. and Beck, A.T. (2003). Cognitive and cognitive-behavioral therapies. In: M.J. Lambert (ed.). *Garfield and Bergin's handbook of psychotherapy and behavior change: an empirical analysis* (5th edn). Wiley, New York, pp. 447–92.

Hollon, S.D., Thase, M.E. and Markowitz, J.C. (2002). Treatment and prevention of depression. *Psychological Science in the Public Interest*, 3, 39–77.

Holman, H. and Lorig, K. (2000). Patients as partners in managing chronic disease. *British Medical Journal*, **320**, 526–7.

Horne, J. (1988). *Why we sleep: the functions of sleep in humans and other mammals*. Oxford University Press, Oxford.

Horowitz, M.J. (1997). *Stress response syndromes. PTSD, grief, and adjustment disorders*. Jason Aronson, Northvale NJ.

Horrocks, J. and House, A. (2002). Self-poisoning and self-injury in adults. *Clinical Medicine*, **2**, 509–12.

House, A. (1992). Management of mood disorder in adults with brain damage: can we improve what psychiatry has to offer? In: P.J. Cowen and K. Hawton (eds.). *Practical problems in clinical psychiatry*. Oxford University Press, Oxford.

Ingram, R.E., Miranda, J. and Segal, Z.V. (1998). *Cognitive vulnerability to depression*. Guilford Press, New York.

Janoff–Bulman, R. (1992). *Shattered assumptions: towards a new psychology of trauma*. Free Press, New York.

Johnson, S. and Roberts, J. (1995). Life events and bipolar disorder: implications from biological theories. *Psychological Bulletin*, **177**, 434–49.

Keijsers, G.P.J., Schaap, C.P.D.R. and Hoggduin, C.A.L. (2000). The impact of interpersonal patient and therapist behavior on outcome in cognitive-behavior therapy. *Behavior Modification*, **24**, 264–97.

Kemmis, S. and McTaggart, R. (2000). Participatory action research. In: N.K. Denzin and Y.S. Lincoln (eds.). *Handbook of qualitative research* (2nd edn). Sage, Thousand Oaks CA, pp. 567–605.

Kessler, R.C., Sonnega, A., Bromet, E., Hughes, M., and Nelson, C.B. (1995). Post-traumatic stress disorder in the National Comorbidity Survey. *Archives of General Psychiatry*, **52**, 1048–60.

Kessler, R.C., Walters, E.E. and Wittchen, H.U. (in press). The epidemiology of generalized anxiety disorder. In: R.G. Heimberg, C.L. Turk, and D.S. Mennin (eds.). *Generalized anxiety disorder: advances in research and practice*. Guilford Press, New York.

Kinney, A. (2001). Cognitive therapy and brain injury: theoretical and clinical issues. *Journal of Contemporary Psychotherapy*, **31**, 89–102.

Kolb, D. (1984). *Experiential learning: experience as the source of learning and development*. Prentice Hall, Englewood Cliffs NJ.

Ladouceur, R., Dugas, M.J., Freeston, M.H., Leger, E., Gagnon, F. and Thibodeau, N. (2000). Efficacy of cognitive behavioural treatment for generalized anxiety disorder: evaluation in a controlled clinical trial. *Journal of Consulting and Clinical Psychology*, **68**, 957–64.

Lam, D., Bright, J., Jones, S., Hayward, P., Schuck, N., Chisholm, D. *et al.* (2000). Cognitive therapy for bipolar illness—a pilot study of relapse prevention. *Cognitive Therapy and Research*, **24**, 503–20.

Lam, D., Jones, S., Bright, J., and Hayward, P. (1999). *Cognitive therapy for bipolar disorder: a therapist's guide to concepts, methods and practice*. Wiley, New York.

Lam, D. and Wong, G. (1997). Prodromes, coping strategies, insight and social functioning in bipolar affective disorders. *Psychological Medicine*, **27**, 1091–100.

Lam, D., Wong, G., and Sham, P. (2001). Prodromes, coping strategies and course of illness in bipolar affective disorder—a naturalistic study. *Psychological Medicine*, **31**, 1397–402.

Lam, D., Wright, K., and Smith, N. (in press). Dysfunctional assumptions in bipolar disorder. *Journal of Affective Disorders.*

Layden, M.A., Newman, C.F., Freeman, A. and Morse, S.B. (1993). *Cognitive therapy of borderline personality disorder.* Allyn and Bacon, Boston.

Lerner, G.H. (1997). *The dance of anger: a woman's guide to changing the pattern of intimate relationships.* Harper Collins, New York.

Leventhal, H., Diefenbach, M. and Leventhal, E.A. (1992). Illness cognition: using common sense to understand treatment adherence and affect in cognition interactions. *Cognitive Therapy and Research*, 16, 143–63.

Lewin, K. (1946). Action research and minority problems. *Journal of Social Issues*, 2, 34–46.

Lichstein, K.L. (2000). Secondary insomnia. In: K.L. Lichstein and C.M. Morin, *Treatment of late-life insomnia.* Sage, California, pp. 297–320.

Linehan, M.M. (1993). *Cognitive-behavioural treatment of borderline personality disorder.* Guilford Press, New York.

Lundh, L–G. (1998). Cognitive-behavioural analysis and treatment of insomnia. *Scandinavian Journal of Behaviour Therapy*, 27, 10–29.

Mahoney, M. (1974). *Cognition and behavior modification.* Ballinger, Cambridge.

Main, C.J. and Spanswick, C.C. (2000). *Pain management: an interdisciplinary approach.* Churchill, Edinburgh.

McGrath, J. (2000). A study of emotionalism in patients undergoing rehabilitation following severe acquired brain injury. *Behavioural Neurology*, 12, 201–7.

McGrath, J. and Adams, L. (1999). Patient-centred goal planning: a systemic psychological therapy? *Topics in Stroke Rehabilitation*, 6, 43–50.

Meichenbaum, D.B. (1977). *Cognitive-behavior modification: an integrative approach.* Plenum, New York.

Miklowitz, D., Goldstein, M., Nuechterlein, K., Snyder, K., and Mintz, J. (1988). Family factors and the course of bipolar affective disorder. *Archives of General Psychiatry*, 45, 225–31.

Molnar, G., Feeney, M., and Fava, G. (1988). Duration and symptoms of bipolar prodomes. *American Journal of Psychiatry*, 145, 1576–8.

Mooney, K.A. and Padesky, C.A. (2000). Applying client creativity to recurrent problems: Constructing possibilities and tolerating doubt. *Journal of Cognitive Psychotherapy*, 14, 149–61.

Moorey, S. and Greer, S. (2002). *Cognitive behavioural therapy for people with cancer.* Oxford University Press, Oxford.

Morgan, H. and Raffle, C. (1999). Does reducing safety behaviours improve treatment response in patients with social phobia? *Australian and New Zealand Journal of Psychiatry*, 33, 503–10.

Morin, C.M. (1993). *Insomnia: psychological assessment and management.* Guilford Press, New York.

Morin, C.M., Coecchi, C., Stone, J., Sood, A. and Brink, D. (1999). Behavioral and pharmacological therapies for late-life insomnia: a randomized controlled trial. *Journal of the American Medical Association*, 281, 991–9.

Murray, C.L. and Lopez, A.D. (1998). *The global burden of disease: a comprehensive assessment of mortality and disability from disease, injuries and risk factors in 1990 and projected to 2020.* Harvard University Press, Boston.

Nathan, P. and Gorman, J.M. (2002). *A guide to treatments that work*. Oxford University Press, New York.

Nolen–Hoeksema, S. (1991). Responses to depression and their effects on the duration of depressive episodes. *Journal of Abnormal Psychology*, 100, 569–82.

Nuechterlein, K. and Dawson, M. (1984). A heuristic vulnerability/stress model of schizophrenic episodes. *Schizophrenia Bulletin*, 10, 300–12.

Obsessive-Compulsive Cognitions Working Group (1997). Cognitive assessment of obsessive-compulsive disorder. *Behaviour Research and Therapy*, 35, 667–81.

Ohayon, M.M., Guilleminault, C., Paiva, T., Priest, R.G., Rapoport, D.M., Sagles, T. *et al.* (1997). An international study on sleep disorders in the general population: methodological aspects of the use of the Sleep-EVAL system. *Sleep*, 20, 1086–92.

Organista, K., Munoz, R. and Gonzalez, G. (1994). Cognitive behavioural therapy for depression in low income and minority medical outpatients: description of a program and exploratory analyses. *Cognitive Therapy and Research*, 18, 241–59.

Öst, L.G. (1997). Rapid treatment of specific phobias. In: Davey, G.C.L. (ed.). *Phobias: a handbook of theory, research and treatment*. Wiley, Chichester.

Öst, L.G. and Sterner, U. (1987). Applied tension: a specific behavioural method for treatment of blood phobia. *Behaviour Research and Therapy*, 25, 25–30.

Padesky, C.A. (1993a). *Socratic questioning: changing minds or guided discovery?* Paper presented at the European Congress of Behavioural and Cognitive Therapies, September, London.

Padesky, C.A. (1993b). Schema as self-prejudice. *International Cognitive Therapy Newsletter*, 5/6, 16–17.

Padesky, C.A. (1994). Schema change processes in cognitive therapy. *Clinical Psychology and Psychotherapy*, 1, 267–78.

Padesky, C.A. (1997). A more effective treatment focus for social phobia? *International Cognitive Therapy Newsletter*, 11, 1–3.

Padesky, C.A. (2002). The client as architect of change. In: T. Scrimali (ed.). *Cognitive psychotherapy toward a new millennium*. Kluwer Academic/Plenum Publishers, New York.

Padesky, C.A. and Beck, J. (2003a). Avoidant personality disorder. In A.T. Beck, A. Freeman, D.D. Davis (eds.). *Cognitive therapy of personality disorders* (2nd edn). Guilford Press, New York.

Padesky, C.A. and Beck, A.T. (2003b). Science and philosophy: comparison of cognitive therapy (CT) and rational emotive behavior therapy (REBT). *Journal of Cognitive Psychotherapy*, 17, 211-24.

Padesky, C.A. with Greenberger, D. (1995). *Clinician's guide to mind over mood*. Guilford Press, New York.

Padesky, C.A. and Mooney, K.A. (1999). Underlying assumptions: rules that bind and blind. Workshop presented at Camp Cognitive Therapy VII, Palm Desert CA, February.

Papadopoulos, L. and Walker, C. (2003). *Understanding skin problems*. Wiley, Chichester.

Pennebaker, J.W. (1997). Writing about emotional experiences as a therapeutic process. *Psychological Science*, 8, 162–6.

Perlis, M.L., Giles, D.E., Mendelson, W.B., Bootzin, R.R. and Wyatt, J.K. (1997). Psychophysiological insomnia: the behavioural model and a neurocognitive perspective. *Journal of Sleep Research*, 6, 179–88.

Persons, J.B. (1993). Case conceptualization. In: K.T. Kuehlwein and H. Rosen (eds.). *Cognitive therapy in action: evolving innovative practice*. Jossey–Bass, San Francisco, pp. 33–53.

Power, M.J. and Dalgleish, T. (1997). *Cognition and emotion: from order to disorder.* Psychology Press, Hove.

Power, M.J. and Dalgleish, T. (1999). Two routes to emotion: some implications of multi-level theories of emotion for therapeutic practice. *Behavioural and Cognitive Psychotherapy,* 27, 129–41.

Prigatano, G.P. (1991). Disordered mind, wounded soul: the emerging role of psychotherapy in rehabilitation after brain injury. *Journal of Head Trauma Rehabilitation,* 6, 1–10.

Prigatano, G.P. (1999). *Principles of neuropsychological rehabilitation.* Oxford University Press, New York.

Prigatano, G.P. and Schacter, D.L. (1991). *Awareness of deficit after brain injury.* Oxford University Press, New York.

Rachman, S.J. (1980). Emotional processing. *Behaviour Research and Therapy,* 18, 51–60.

Rachman, S.J. (1997). The evolution of cognitive behaviour therapy. In: D.M. Clark and C.G. Fairburn (eds.). *The science and practice of cognitive behaviour therapy.* Oxford University Press, Oxford, pp. 3–26.

Rachman, S.J. (2002). Fears born and bred: non-associative fear acquisition? *Behaviour Research and Therapy,* 40, 121–6.

Rachman, S.J. (2003). *The treatment of obsessions.* Oxford University Press, Oxford.

Rachman, S.J. and Bichard, S. (1988). The overprediction of fear. *Clinical Psychology Review,* 8, 303–18.

Rachman, S.J., Craske, M., Tallman, K., and Solyom, C. (1986). Does escape behaviour strengthen agoraphobic avoidance? *Behavior Therapy,* 17, 366–84.

Rachman, S.J. and Hodgson, R. (1974). I. Synchrony and desynchrony in fear and avoidance. *Behaviour Research and Therapy,* 12, 311–18.

Roemer, L., Borkovec, T., Posa, S. and Lyonfields, J.D. (1991). Generalized anxiety disorder in an analogue population: the role of past trauma. Paper presented at the annual meeting of the Association for the Advancement of Behavior Therapy, New York, November.

Roesch, S.C. and Weiner, B. (2001). A meta-analytic review of coping with illness: do causal attributions matter? *Journal of Psychosomatic Research,* 50, 205–19.

Rooske, O. and Birchwood, M. (1998). Loss, humiliation and entrapment as appraisals of schizophrenic illness: a prospective study of depressed and non-depressed patients. *British Journal of Clinical Psychology,* 37, 259–68.

Rosenfarb, I., Becker, J., Khan, A., and Mintz, J. (1998). Dependency and self-criticism in bipolar and unipolar depressed women. *British Journal of Clinical Psychology,* 37, 409–14.

Roth, T. and Ancoli–Israel, S. (1999). Daytime consequences and correlates of insomnia in the United States: results of the 1991 National Sleep Foundation Survey. II. *Sleep,* 22 (Suppl 2), S354–S358.

Safran, J.D. and Muran, J.C. (2000). *Negotiating the therapeutic alliance: a relational treatment guide.* Guilford Press, New York.

Safran, J.D. and Segal, Z.V. (1990). *Interpersonal process in cognitive therapy.* Basic Books, New York.

Salkovskis, P.M. (1985). Obsessive-compulsive problems: a cognitive-behavioural analysis. *Behaviour Research and Therapy,* 23, 571–83.

Salkovskis, P.M. (1988). Phenomenology, assessment and the cognitive model. In: S. Rachman and J. Maser (eds.). *Panic: psychological perspectives.* Lawrence Erlbaum, New Jersey, pp. 111–36.

Salkovskis, P.M. (1989). Cognitive-behavioural factors and the persistence of intrusive thoughts in obsessional problems. *Behaviour Research and Therapy*, 27, 677–82.

Salkovskis, P.M. (1991). The importance of behaviour in the maintenance of anxiety and panic: a cognitive account. *Behavioural Psychotherapy*, 19, 6–19.

Salkovskis, P.M. (1994). Principles and practice of cognitive-behavioural treatment of obsessional problems. *Praxis der Klinischen Verhaltensmedizin und Rehabilitation*, 26, 113–20.

Salkovskis, P.M. (1996). The cognitive approach to anxiety: threat beliefs, safety-seeking behaviour, and the special case of health anxiety and obsessions. In: P. Salkovskis (ed.). *Frontiers of cognitive therapy*. Guilford Press, New York, pp. 48–74.

Salkovskis, P.M. (1999). Understanding and treating obsessive-compulsive disorder. *Behaviour Research and Therapy*, 37, S29–S52.

Salkovskis, P.M. and Bass, C. (1997). Hypochondriasis. In: D.M. Clark and C.G. Fairburn (eds.). *Science and practice of cognitive behaviour therapy*. Oxford University Press, Oxford, pp. 313–39.

Salkovskis, P.M., Clark, D.M., Hackmann, A., Wells, A. and Gelder, M.G. (1999*a*). An experimental investigation of the role of safety-seeking behaviours in the maintenance of panic disorder with agoraphobia. *Behaviour Research and Therapy*, 37, 559–74.

Salkovskis, P.M., Forrester, E., Richards, H.C. and Morrison, N. (1999*b*). The devil is in the detail: conceptualising and treating obsessional problems. In: N. Tarrier, A. Wells, and G. Haddock (eds.). *Treating complex cases: the cognitive behavioural therapy approach*. Wiley, Chichester, pp. 46–80.

Salkovskis, P.M. and Warwick, H.M. (1986). Morbid preoccupations, health anxiety and reassurance: a cognitive-behavioural approach to hypochondriasis. *Behaviour Research and Therapy*, 24, 597–602.

Sanders, D. (2000). Psychosomatic problems. In: C. Feltham and I. Horton (eds.). *Handbook of counselling and psychotherapy*. Sage, London, pp. 515–25.

Schön, D.A. (1983). *The reflective practitioner*. Basic Books, New York.

Scott, J. (1995). Psychotherapy for bipolar disorder: an unmet need? *British Journal of Psychiatry*, 167, 289–92.

Scott, J. (2001). Cognitive therapy as an adjunct to medication in bipolar disorders. *British Journal of Psychiatry*, 178, (Supplement), S164–8.

Scott, J. (2002). Cognitive therapy for clients with bipolar affective disorder. In: A. Morrison (ed.). *A casebook of cognitive therapy for psychosis*. Brunner–Routledge, Hove.

Scott, J., Garland, A., and Moorhead, S. (2001). A pilot study of cognitive therapy in bipolar disorders. *Psychological Medicine*, 31, 459–67.

Scott, J., Stanton, B., Garland, A., and Ferrier, N. (2000). Cognitive vulnerability in patients with bipolar disorder. *Psychological Medicine*, 30, 467–72.

Segal, Z.V., Williams, J.M.G. and Teasdale, J.D. (2002). *Mindfulness-based cognitive therapy for depression: a new approach to preventing relapse*. Guilford Press, New York.

Seligman, M.E.P. (1971). Phobias and preparedness. *Behavior Therapy*, 2, 307–20.

Seligman, M.E.P. (1975). *Helplessness*. W.H. Freeman & Co., San Francisco.

Seligman, M.E.P. (1988). Competing theories of panic. In: S. Rachman and J. Maser (eds.). *Panic: psychological perspectives*. Lawrence Erlbaum, New Jersey, pp. 321–30.

Seligman, M.E.P. and Csikszentmihalyi, M. (2000). Positive psychology: an introduction. *American Psychologist*, 55, 5–14.

Sell, L. and Robson, P. (1998). Perceptions of college life, emotional well-being and patterns of drug and alcohol use among Oxford undergraduates. *Oxford Review of Education*, 24, 235–43.

Shafran, R., Booth, R. and Rachman, S.J. (1993). The reduction of claustrophobia. II: cognitive analyses. *Behaviour Research and Therapy*, 30, 75–85.

Shafran, R., Cooper, Z. and Fairburn, C.G. (2002) Clinical perfectionism: a cognitive behavioural analysis. *Behaviour Research and Therapy*, 40, 773–91.

Sloan, T. and Telch, M.J. (2002). The effect of safety-seeking behavior and guided threat reappraisal on fear reduction during exposure: an experimental investigation. *Behaviour Research and Therapy*, 40, 235–51.

Storr, A. (1989). *Solitude*. Flamingo, London.

Sue, S., Fujino, D., Hu, L., Takeuchi, D. and Zane, N. (1991). Community mental health services for ethnic minority groups: a test of the cultural responsiveness hypothesis. *Journal of Consulting and Clinical Psychology*, 59, 533–40.

Surawy, C., Hackmann, A., Hawton, K. and Sharpe, M. (1995). Chronic fatigue syndrome: a cognitive approach. *Behaviour Research and Therapy*, 33, 535–44.

Suyemoto, K.L. (1988). The functions of self-mutilation. A review. *Clinical Psychology Review*, 18, 531–54.

Tang, N.K.Y. and Harvey, A.G. (in press). Correcting distorted perception of sleep in insomnia: a novel behavioural experiment? *Behaviour Research and Therapy*.

Teasdale, J.D. (1997). The relationship between cognition and emotion: the mind-in-place in mood disorders. In: D.M. Clark and C.G. Fairburn (eds.). *The science and practice of cognitive behaviour therapy*. Oxford University Press, Oxford, pp. 67–93.

Teasdale, J.D. and Barnard, P.J. (1993). *Affect, cognition and change: re-modelling depressive thought*. Lawrence Erlbaum, Hove.

Teasdale, J.D., Moore, R.G., Hayhurst, H., Pope, M., Williams, S., and Segal, Z. (2002). Metacognitive awareness and prevention of relapse in depression: empirical evidence. *Journal of Consulting and Clinical Psychology*, 70, 275–87.

Thorpe, S.J. and Salkovskis, P.M. (1995) Phobic beliefs: do cognitive factors play a role in specific phobias? *Behaviour Research and Therapy*, 33, 805–16.

Toner, B., Segal, Z.V., Emmott, S.D. and Myran, D. (2000). *Cognitive-behavioural treatment of irritable bowel syndrome*. Guilford Press, New York.

Van Os, J., Gilvarry, C., Bale, R., Van Horn, E., Tattan, T., White, I. *et al.* (1999). A comparison of the utility of dimensional and categorical representations of psychosis. UK700 Group. *Psychological Medicine*, 29, 595–606.

Vanderlinden, J. and Vandereycken, W. (1997). *Trauma, dissociation and impulse dyscontrol in eating disorders*. Brunner Mazel, New York.

Waller, G., Kennerley, H. and Ohanian, V. (2004). Schema-focussed cognitive behaviour therapy with the eating disorders. In: P. du Toit (ed.). *Cognitive schemas and core beliefs in psychological problems: a scientist–practitioner guide*. American Psychiatric Association, Washington DC.

Walsh, B.W. and Rosen, P.M. (1988). *Self-mutilation. Theory, research and treatment*. Guilford Press, New York.

Warwick, H.M.C., Clark, D.M., Cobb, A.M. and Salkovskis, P.M. (1996). A controlled trial of cognitive behavioural treatment of hypochondriasis. *British Journal of Psychiatry*, 169, 189–95.

Warwick, H.M.C. and Salkovskis, P.M. (1989). Hypochondriasis. In: J. Scott, J.M.G. Williams, and A.T. Beck (eds.). *Cognitive therapy in clinical practice*. Croom Helm, London, pp. 78–102.

Watkins, J. (1997). *Living with schizophrenia: a holistic approach to understanding, preventing and recovering from negative symptoms*. Hill of Content, Melbourne.

Wells, A. (1997). *Cognitive therapy of anxiety disorders: a practice manual and conceptual guide*. Wiley, Chichester.

Wells, A. (2000). *Emotional disorders and metacognition*. Wiley, Chichester.

Wells, A. and Clark, D.M. (1997). Social phobia: a cognitive approach. In: G.L. Davey (ed.). *Phobias: a handbook of description, treatment and theory*. Wiley, Chichester.

Wells, A., Clark, D.M., and Ahmad, S. (1998). How do I look with my mind's eye? Perspective-taking in social phobia imagery. *Behaviour Research and Therapy*, 36, 631–4.

Wells, A. and Hackmann, A. (1993). Imagery and core beliefs in health anxiety: content and origins. *Behavioural and Cognitive Psychotherapy*, 21, 265–74.

Wells, A. and Matthews, G. (1994). *Attention and emotion: a clinical perspective*. Lawrence Erlbaum, Hove.

Westling, B.E. and Öst, L.G. (1999). Brief cognitive behaviour therapy of panic disorder. *Scandinavian Journal of Behaviour Therapy*, 28, 49–57.

White, J. (2000). *Cognitive behavioural therapy for chronic medical conditions*. Wiley, Chichester.

White, J.R. and Freeman, A.S. (eds.). (2000). *Cognitive-behavioral group therapy for specific problems and populations*. American Psychological Association, Washington DC.

Whitehouse, A.M. (1994). Applications of cognitive therapy with survivors of head injury. *Journal of Cognitive Psychotherapy*, 8, 141–60.

Wilfley, D.E., Agras, W.S., Telch, C.F. *et al.* (1993). Group cognitive behaviour therapy and group interpersonal psychotherapy for the nonpurging bulimic individual: a controlled comparison. *Journal of Consulting and Clinical Psychology*, 61, 296–305.

Williams, J.M.G., Stiles, W.B. and Shapiro, D. (1999). Cognitive mechanisms in the avoidance of painful and dangerous thoughts: elaborating the assimilation model. *Cognitive therapy and Research*, 23, 285–306.

Williams, J.M.G., Teasdale, J.D., Segal, Z.V. and Soulsby, J. (2000). Mindfulness-based cognitive therapy reduces overgeneral autobiographical memory in formerly depressed patients. *Journal of Abnormal Psychology*, 109, 150–5.

Winters, K. and Neale, J. (1985). Mania and low self-esteem. *Journal of Abnormal Psychology*, 94, 282–90.

Wittchen, H–U., Zhao, S., Kessler, R.C. and Eaton, W.W. (1994). DSM-III-R generalized anxiety disorder in the National Comorbidity Survey. *Archives of General Psychiatry*, 51, 355–64.

Wolff, G. and Serpell, L. (1998). A cognitive model and treatment strategies for anorexia nervosa. In: H. Hoek, J. Treasure, and M. Katzman (eds.). *Neurobiology in the treatment of eating disorders*. Wiley, Chichester.

Yardley, L. and Redfern, M.S. (2001). Psychological factors influencing recovery from balance disorders. *Anxiety Disorders*, 15, 107–19.

Young, J. (1990). *Cognitive therapy for personality disorders: a schema focussed approach*. Professional Resource Exchange, Saratoga Fl.

Young, J., Klosko, J. and Weishaar, M.E. (2003). *Schema therapy: a practitioner's guide*. Guilford Press, New York.

Index